US Navy Airships

A History by Individual Airship

By James R. Shock

This book is dedicated to my wife, Pat, for her patience and understanding

US Navy Airships
(3rd Edition)

By James R. Shock

ISBN 0-9639743-8-6

Published by
Atlantis Productions
P O Box 700
Edgewater Florida 32132

Table of Contents

Foreword

The exploits of our grandfathers in their truculent gasbags may seem like a quaint and distant past that has little bearing on today's world. An enlightened perception of current events would disagree. The need to detect small, stealthy missiles against sea clutter has only become more acute since the last airship delivered to the US Navy last century, the radar picket ship EZ-1A *Vigilant,* flew a typical 35 hour mission with its 40 foot radar antenna. In today's littorals, there are sophisticated predators, weapons that wait... and targets. The submarine's only natural enemy is faster than a nuke boat, undetectable by its sonar and invulnerable to its speedy homing torpedoes. A defensive vehicle removed from the opposing weapon's medium is as priceless an asset now as it was when ZP-14 worked mine hunting in WWII. High mission availability of the WWII mine spotting and ASW airship is overlooked as often as the blimp's *raison d'ˆtre*, victories against *underwater* adversaries, never credited even when using acoustic homing torpedoes. In the last operation where airships were available, six ZPG-2s logged a respectable 1,644 hours in some of the worst Northeast gales and snowstorms ever recorded, yet one crew established today's record of 93 hours on ASW station. A modern dirigible would be equally at home as mothership to semi-autonomous underwater craft hunting mines.

More than 1,000 people owe their lives to airship rescue. The open ocean search capability of the flying carrier ZRS ships could only be duplicated today by basing Unmanned Air Vehicles on a new dirigible, faster than a Coast Guard cutter and cheaper than an airplane, while emulating both. Naturally interoperable with any waterborne or beachhead asset, buoyant craft are naturals for joint operations and are particularly well suited to the challenges of operations other than combat. Navy non-rigids crossed the Atlantic, the Arctic Circle, the pass through the Rockies and the Equator. There is no environment too harsh to monitor fishing grounds or track polluters, no place airships cannot locate the lost, or act as command posts for oil spill or maritime disaster management and recovery.

Twice during the 20th century America has largely ignored, then hastily turned to its Lighter-Than-Air assets. More than a decade has past since the Government's somewhat confused effort to build a military airship. As of this writing the Navy's most recent purchase of a commercial airship ran for only a year.

Mr. James Shock, with his determination to collect every scrap of information, provides for us the true story of their awesome accomplishments. His unwavering effort to chronicle their technology gives us a foundation. May we have the wisdom to utilize his record of recent experience to build a better future.

- Richard G. Van Treuren

Acknowledgements

This research seeks to encompass a history of all US Navy airships including dates, contractor build numbers, Navy Serial Numbers, brief specifications, photographs and notable items on each airship. The work is based on previously published information or data accumulated over the years of collection of records on all airships. This manuscript grew out of an attempt to centralize information from a personal collection of newspaper and magazine articles, journals, manuals, reports and photographs that originated in 1940, as well as contributions from friends with an airship interest. The author had the advantage of growing up in the Northern Ohio area in the period when airships were commonly seen, and when information was frequently available. With the exception of three years of Army service during WWII, the author has been collecting the airship data within. The following persons provided the major assistance, contributed data, reviewed the manuscript and offered suggestions and corrections:

Eric Brothers, The Lighter-Than-Air Society, Akron Ohio; Hepburn Walker, Jr. WWII airshipman and LTA consultant; Donald E. Woodward* of the Association of Balloon and Airship Constructors; Richard G. Van Treuren, Airship Video Historian.

Others that provided information, images, and/or assistance include:

William Althoff, author of *Sky Ships*; George W. Allen, ZPG-3W Command Pilot, Naval Airship Association President; Howard W. Brewster, LTA pilot, NAA; Jeffery Cook, Naval Weapons Center, Warminster, PA; Jarvis Frith, Friends of Cardington Airship Station, Bedford, England; Zenon Hanson*, author of *The Goodyear Airships*; Norman J. Mayer, Consultant, LTA Systems; Dr. John V. Miller, Jr., Director, Archives Services, University of Akron; Richard L. Nye*, LTA pilot, NAA; Dr. Dale Topping*, as longtime editor of the *Bulletin* of the Wingfoot Lighter-Than-Air Society (now *Buoyant Flight* and LTAS); Francis Scales*, NAA; George L. Seibold, WWII LTA pilot; Dr. Richard K. Smith*, author of "An Inventory of US Navy Airships 1916-1961;" Walter Swistak, K-ship pilot, author, *Blimps, Balloons and Bombs*.

2001 Update:
A noted writer stated: "The problems facing historians are gaps in data; new data emerging after sections have been written (even after some pages have been typeset), controversial points; excessive statements that do not meet the criteria for accuracy and inadvertent errors that corrupt the search for historical truth." Included is information that has come to light since publication and includes correction of several areas that were questionable and data that was not available. A great deal of information is in general terms since it could not be identified by specific airship. Personal accounts that could not possibly be substantiated, were only opinions or might prove embarrassing to certain individuals are not included. WWII combat records of the 10th Fleet were declassified in 1996 and have been included where possible. Many former U.S. Navy airshipmen and several others contributed data. The many that made comments and provided information, either directly or indirectly through others, include the publisher and:

L.A. "Beau" Beauregard , S.L. "Si" Beattie, Ted Boyer, Don Block, F.G. Burger, John Brashears, Walter Chimil, Robert T. Connor, Bruce L. Davis, M. Henry Eppes*, John A. Fahey, Robert T. Forand, David A. Frecker, Walter Garyotis, David E. Hayes, James Hughes, John C. Kane*, Charles A. Mills, Lundi Moore*, W. W. Moore, William R. Peeler, Sr.*, James B. Powers, Lou Prost, Albert H. Robbins, John Roda, Lawrence F. Rodrigues, G. M. Roberts, Ford U. Ross, Michael E. Szot*, Donald P. Venton*, William Voda, Hepburn Walker, Jr.*, Warren E. Ward, Bruce Watts, Roy C. Wicker, William E. Wishbow, Jay E. Wright, and Rick Zitarosa.

*deceased

Introduction to US NAVY AIRSHIPS

This study indicates a total of 273 American-built Navy airships (DN-1, B-1 through B-20, C-1 through C-10, D-1 through D-6, E-1, F-1, H-1, J-1, J-3 and J-4, ZMC-2, ZR-1, ZRS-4, ZRS-5, G-1 through G-8, TC-13 and TC-14, K-1 through K-135, L-1 through L-22, M-1 through M-4, fifteen-ZSG-4, eighteen-ZS2G-1, one-ZPG-1, twelve-ZPG-2, five-ZPG-2W and four-ZPG-3W), one German built airship (LZ-126/ZR-3), one Italian-built airship (O-1), seven British-built airships (3-SST, 2-SSZ, 1-North Sea, one rigid R-38/ZR-2), and approximately ten French-built airships for a grand total of 292 airships. This total does not include revised or updated airships of which there were at least seventy-four (forty four ZP2K and 30 ZP3K) and possibly more. The term "Goodyear" in used throughout this research. Goodyear was the prime contractor for most US government airships between 1917 and 1960. The airship design and build groups of the Goodyear Tire and Rubber Company were: Aeronautics Department 1910 to 1923; Goodyear-Zeppelin Corporation 14 December 1923 to 14 February 1941; Goodyear Aircraft Corporation 05 December 1939 to 01 July 1963; Goodyear Aerospace Corporation to 15 March 1987. For over 75 years, Goodyear had been associated with airships, the world's largest airship builder. Most airships had some Goodyear involvement, and when the term “blimp” was used, it was always used with the name Goodyear. The division was sold to Loral Systems Group of New York in 1987 to raise capital to prevent a stock take-over attempt.

The objective of this research was to record as much information as possible on each individual airship. Unfortunately, the items that seem to have been most extensively covered are the mishaps. The positive features such as hours of service, combat experiences, experimental developments, searches, rescues, etc., sadly are not readily available. Actual WWII combat listings in the 10th Fleet records were not declassified until 1996 and are still awaiting extensive research. It was my personal decision to include all available information on each airship, after due consideration of deleting at least some deflations. The work is not intended to be "airship bashing" and reveal all of the problems of airships. The story would not be complete without including these incidents, but they are misleading. Many of the records (particularly the World War II airships) include such words as "wrecked," "destroyed" and "lost" when what was actually meant was "deflated." Loss of gas was the most common occurrence and often due to events not directly related to flight problems, but due to striking hangars, masts, ground handling, etc. These mishaps were readily corrected with new or repaired envelopes that were furnished for such cases. This research indicates a loss of 29 airships (19 confirmed and 10 possible or 17%) from 07 December 1941 through 02 September 1945 and does not include those airships rebuilt and returned to service following an accident. This loss rate is not exceptional for wartime aircraft; for example, of 15,000 P-47 fighter planes built, 5,000, or 31%, were lost in non-combat accidents. The major and minor airship accident rate per flight hour is very close to that of Navy airplanes and the principal causes were similar.

The airships of World War I were designed in a rush for immediate service with no time allotted for proof of concept, development of tactics or facilities. In 1917 there were no suitable airship construction sheds, few experienced or trained airship pilots, a single poorly performing airship (DN-1) and only one hangar (Pensacola). With the letter designations retro-fitted so DN-1 became A-1, the new airship designs were lettered sequentially. The proposed large “G” type was not erected and the letter “I” was passed over to avoid confusion.

Non-rigid airships were neglected between World War I and World War II, particularly in the Navy. The Goodyear Tire and Rubber Company’s commercial fleet of advertising airships was more active, with more flying and development than any of the services. The Army operated many airships, but their mission was never satisfactorily defined. Since funds were limited and support denied, the Army transferred their equipment to the Navy in 1937.

With US entry into World War II, there were only six patrol airships in all, and only four could be considered modern. There were four training airships, and only one airship base, Lakehurst. In 1940, only 92 airship officers were on active duty, 28 of these stationed at Lakehurst with the balance assigned to other non-airship duties. From this nucleus it was necessary to develop mass production of airships, train pilots and crews, develop tactics and provide facilities for the airships and their crews. Reviewing this effort, it can be surmised that most of the losses could rightly be attributed to design, equipment and personnel error.

In the post-World War II years, airship development proceeded at a slow rate due to the competition for funds for the Navy's higher priorities for aircraft carriers, airplanes, missiles, space systems, etc. Further hampering the airships was a total lack of support within the Navy Department.

The officer rank designations used throughout are recommended by the Navy Instruction List and varies from other publications.

Navy and Coast Guard	Army and Marine Corps
ENS - Ensign	2ndLt - Second Lieutenant
LTJG - Lieutenant (Junior Grade)	1stLt - First Lieutenant
LT - Lieutenant	Capt - Captain
LCDR - Lieutenant Commander	Maj - Major
CDR - Commander	LtCol - Lieutenant Colonel
CAPT - Captain	Col - Colonel
COMO - Commodore	BGen - Brigadier General
RADM - Rear Admiral	MGen - Major General
VADM - Vice Admiral	LtGen - Lieutenant General
ADM - Admiral	Gen - General

In this magazine's vision, a fleet of Dirigible, Non-rigid airships were soon to be flying.

Part I: US Navy Pressure Airships Designed For Hydrogen, 1917-1922

The Navy's first complete airship, the DN-1, is maneuvered into its floating Hangar at Pensacola in 1917. U S Navy photo.

Introduction

US Navy interest in airships dates to an early mention in a 1914 *Scientific American* that ran a story "The Navy Wants Dirigibles." The first known announcement of an airship contract for the US Navy was printed in the *New York Times*, 11 March 1915. This announcement was dated 10 March and stated two dirigible balloons were to be purchased. "They will not be as large as Zeppelins, nor will they be of the rigid type," and were to be used for "practice." The specification for this first Navy airship was prepared by LCDR Frank M. McCrary and H.C. Richardson of the Navy Department as Schedule 8058 of 20 April 1915. The specification was very brief and virtually gave the contractor a free hand as most features for an American airship were undeveloped.

The specification stated simply: "A car...to allow of resting on the water, or of moving through same at slow speed; twin screws of swiveling type, secure means of mooring to a mooring mast (though none had then been developed), two motors...and transmission...to assist in rising, descending and maneuvering." Specifications further stated that the carrying capacity was to be for eight men in an enclosed body and a ceiling of 3,000 feet without discharge of ballast. All this was to be accomplished in an airship 175 feet in length.

The DN-1 (Dirigible, Non-Rigid No. 1; A-1)

The announcement in *Aircraft*, August 1915 (reprinted from *Scientific American*) states the contract was awarded to Thomas S. Baldwin in cooperation with the Connecticut Aircraft Company. This same article also described a bow-mooring device and a pyramidal mooring mast anchored in concrete under water supposedly to withstand a 50-mile gale, ambitious to say the least. (Bow mooring masts were not developed in the United States until after World War I.) Contract no. 23681 was awarded to the Connecticut Aircraft Company of New Haven on 01 June 1915 at the extremely reasonable cost of $45,646.25. Two airships were to cost $82,215.12.

Connecticut Aircraft was originally incorporated on 20 December 1913 as the Connecticut Aeroplane Company. Incorporators were E.A. Mulliken of New Haven, Paul Webb of Hamden and Ralph H. Clark of Derby. Principal offices were located at 42 Church Street, New Haven with factory facilities at 134 Haven Street. Four thousand shares of capital stock were issued with a value of $100 each. Sole subscribers were elected officers and directors. The majority holders were Everard Thompson, President, Treasurer E.A. Mulliken, and Samuel C. Morehouse, Secretary. The name was changed to Connecticut Aircraft Company on 30 March 1914. Connecticut was the first in the United States to be exclusively devoted to the manufacture of lighter-than-air craft. The company's first contract was with the Army Signal Corps for military observation balloons of 30,000 cubic feet.

Posing with the DN-1 car are (3rd from left) Herman Widner, a German with balloon experience; (6th from left) Walter Fritsche, assistant pilot; (3rd from right) James Boyle; and (far right) Ed Mullikan Jr., son of the company's treasurer. The Lighter-Than-Air-Society / Eric Brothers

Connecticut Aircraft supposedly also consisted of a German engineer and mechanic, an Austrian test pilot (Hans Otto Stagel), James F. Boyle as Chief Engineer and J.J. Delaunay as production manager. The civilian inspector was Thomas Baldwin and CDR McCrary was the resident Navy inspector. The design was generally based on the German Parseval non-rigid airship. It was evident during the design that the contractor was incompetent, but had entered the contract with enthusiasm and did their best to complete a successful airship. Therefore, the Navy allowed him to continue due, in part, to their own lack of experience.

The control car was built by the Fred Lawley shipyard in Neponset, Mass. The envelope consisted of two plies of cloth with rubber inside, outside, and between the plies. It was constructed by the U.S. Rubber Co. in New Haven. The envelope was erected on a platform in the Portsmouth, New Hampshire, Navy Yard with a submarine as a stable mate. The airship was assembled in the Connecticut State Armory in Hartford, the only structure large enough to house the inflated airship in the area. Difficulties were experienced with weight, the prop-swiveling transmission (which was eventually omitted), a leaking envelope and a poor power plant. Steering and stability problems were referred to the Massachusetts Institute of Technology where Jerome Hunsaker and his assistant Donald Douglas used their wind tunnel and advised both the contractor and the Navy of recommended corrections.

The Navy's first airship, the DN-1, in the Hartford Armory during its 1916 erection.
US Navy / New England Air Museum

The original completion date was set for October 1915, and the *New York Times* announced on 21 September 1915 that the airship was "now practically completed, and will be ready for delivery within a few weeks." The DN-1 was not actually completed until late 1916, air-inflated inside the Hartford Armory and then packed and shipped to Pensacola on 28 November 1916. DN-1 arrived in Pensacola on 14 December 1916 but was not ready for flight until April 1917.

DN-1 was 175 feet in length, 35 feet in diameter, 35 feet in width with a fineness ratio of 5.0 and a volume of 110,000 cubic feet. Static lift was supposed to be 1,604 pounds and maximum speed 35 miles per hour. The control car was boat-shaped and water-tight.

Flight tests were conducted with LCDR McCrary and LT Stanley V. Parker, U.S. Coast Guard,as pilots. One of the original Navy crewmen was Petty Officer James F. Shade[1], later a Goodyear airship pilot. On the day of the first flight, after leaving the floating hangar, the airship settled into the water until Shade was on his toes and up to his chin in the water. The hangar had been the only item to save the airship. It was then returned to the hangar and lightened for the first flight of 20 April 1917. Engines were two *Sturtevant* 140 horsepower motors turning four-blade swiveling propellers, allowing vertical thrust. One engine was removed due to heaviness. The first flight was made by test pilot Stagel with difficulty not only in lack of lift but also in attaining the required speed of 35 miles per hour. The speed was only attained when Stagel flew out to the horizon and pointed the airship downhill. Some maneuvers were made that impressed the audience when he would fly along and then dip to the water and then rise again. These maneuvers were actually to scoop up water to throw on the transmission as the bronze bearing had melted. The next flight was made on the 27th. On 29 April, the DN-1 was damaged by an inexperienced handling party that attempted to drag the control car over the water. The damage out valued the repair cost. Consequently, DN-1 was dismantled and scrapped in the hangar.

DN-1 on the ground at Pensacola in April 1917. The spar to the left appears to be a mooring mast, although the DN-1 is not known to have attempted any bow moorings. However, such moorings were considered in the original 1915 plans. New England Air Museum no.1073

[1] Shade went on to pilot B-type airships.

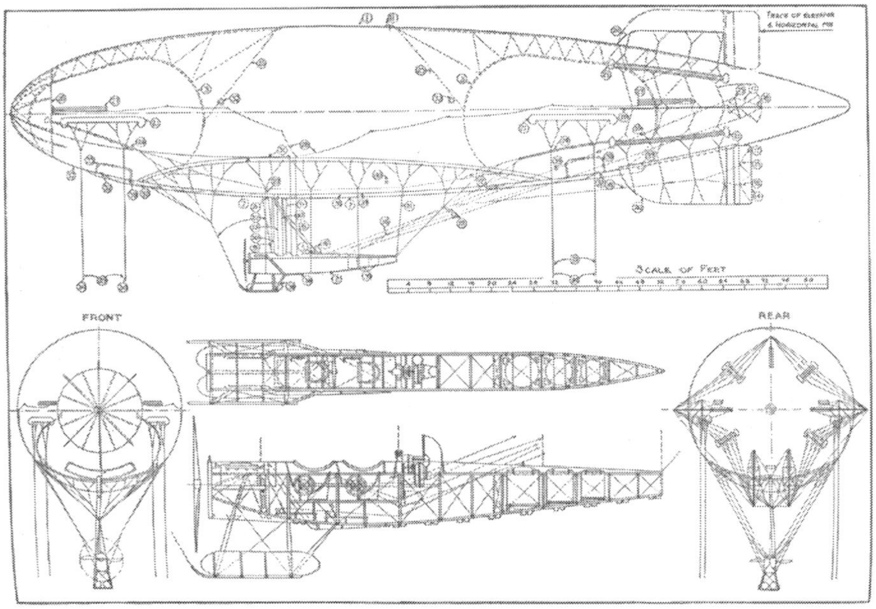

Well publicized, this drawing shows the B-ship's basic concept, but production units had no upper fins and the *Jenny* fuselage was lengthened by one cockpit. Curtiss Museum

The B-type Airships

With the lessons learned from the DN-1, it was determined that the design of non-rigid airships was an art and that there was no point in awarding a contract to an incompetent builder, even though he took full responsibility for the design. It was also learned that a seaplane or balloon pilot was not competent to fly a non-rigid airship without training by an experienced instructor. The Navy Chief Constructor, D. W. Taylor, determined that he would take charge of any future airship development. Jerome C. Hunsaker, Assistant for Aircraft, was directed to prepare a theory of airship design. Hunsaker had previously studied British, French and German non-rigid airships which were summarized in the paper, "The Present Status of Airships in Europe" in June, 1914. He also taught a course in airship design at the Massachusetts Institute of Technology in 1914 and 1915. The United States was generally unaware of progress in Europe since the start of World War I, but there are two explanations as to the origin of the first American production airship. About this time, LT John H. Towers returned from England and reported on the use of non-rigid airships in training and patrol work. Towers had no plans or photographs, but described the airships as a small car, like an airplane fuselage, with seating for two men. From this description, a design was developed for a training airship. This design was altered before completion, as the result of a request from the Chief of Naval Operations on 13 December 1916. The request was for a coastal patrol airship of 12 hours endurance at 35 miles per hour, a crew of three and with the capability of landing and being towed at sea.

Another version of the B-type airship car origin are comments by Stanley Vaughn. Mr. Vaughn and Thomas Baldwin were employed by Glenn Curtiss at the Atlantic Coast Aeronautical Station, Newport News, VA (a subsidiary of the Curtiss Aeroplane and Motor Co. of Buffalo, NY). Drawings of the car design were made on the back of another drawing that was submitted to the Navy and became the basis of the 1917 contract to Curtiss for B-type airship control cars.

The general plan for the B-type was approved in January 1917, with the original plan to order two airships for training purposes. However, on 04 February 1917, the Secretary of the Navy instructed that sixteen B-type airships be ordered for immediate construction. Specifications were sent to five companies: Goodyear, Goodrich, Connecticut Aircraft, Curtiss Aeroplane and Motor Co., and U.S. Rubber Co.

On 19 March 1917, contracts were awarded for 16 B-type airships. Contract No. 29259 was awarded to Goodyear for nine airships, serial numbers A-235 through A-243 (B-1 through B-9). Contract No. 33195 was awarded to Goodrich for two airships, serial numbers A-244 and A-245 (B-10 and B-11). Three awarded to Curtiss were later assumed by Goodrich at cost plus 12½ percentage profit, as Curtiss confined its operations to the construction of 14 control cars, power plants and control surfaces. Contract No. 29262 was to Connecticut Aircraft for two airships, serial numbers A-249 and A-250, B-15 and B-16, whose control cars and surfaces were built by Pigeon Frazer of Boston with engines by Hall-Scott of San Francisco. U.S. Rubber confined their operations to providing envelopes to Connecticut. The "A" serial numbers refer to the control car, and the "E" number was assigned to the envelopes by the Navy. The "B" numbers represent a complete airship.

Curtiss built all of the cars and control surfaces for Goodyear and Goodrich. The cars were basically JN-4 fuselages, originally with an OX-5 engine, lengthened with one cockpit. Mr. Vaughn served as the Curtiss representative for engine assembly and testing at Chicago (White City) and at Wingfoot Lake (Akron).

Goodyear, at their own expense, constructed a complete airship facility at Wingfoot Lake near Akron complete with a hangar, hydrogen generating plant and test facilities. It was classified as Naval Air Station Akron until 1921. Connecticut was the only source with previous experience in erecting a non-rigid airship, however Goodyear was in the best position with experience in balloon and envelope construction and well qualified aeronautical engineers R.H. Upson and R.A.D. Preston. LCDR Frank M. McCrary and LT Lewis H. Maxfield were the first Navy officers trained in balloons by Ralph Upson and Ralph Preston. Thomas A. Baldwin also worked with Goodyear on the erection of their airships. B. F. Goodrich employed early airship pioneer Roy Knabenshue for assistance in erecting their airships. Knabenshue was also the test pilot for the first Goodrich built airship.

The first wartime airship, the B-1, in front of the assembly building at the White City Amusement park in Chicago in May 1917. Note the lower double fin and rudder; later B-type airships had only one lower vertical fin. Goodyear Photo

Navy records dated 01 November 1919, indicate six B-type airships were built at a unit cost of $40,000. Actual contract costs for the 16 airships was $649,250, according to the New Haven (CT) *COURIER* of March 13, 1917. The cost breakdown shown is as follows:
Connecticut Aircraft - two airships at $84,000; Curtiss (contract transferred to Goodrich) - 3 at $122,250; Goodrich - 2 at $93,000 and Goodyear - 9 at $360,000.

The original B-type airships were erected in a building at the White City Amusement Park on the south side of Chicago, Illinois. The building had been leased by Goodrich, as it was the only structure large enough to erect a complete airship in a reasonable vicinity of Akron. Both Goodrich and Goodyear used the building (formerly used for housing exhibition free balloons and "rubber cows") until the airship hangar at Wingfoot Lake was completed when erection was transferred to the Akron area. Although the basic design of the B-type was more or less standard, they varied in dimensions and type of construction according to the manufacturer, for example, some types had no top fin and a double lower fin while others had a small top fin. As experience was gained in both construction and operation, changes were made for improvement.

The Navy established airship facilities at stations located at Chatham, Massachusetts; Montauk and Far Rockaway, Long Island, New York; Cape May, New Jersey; Hampton Roads (Norfolk), Virginia; Pensacola and Key West, Florida; Coco Solo, Panama Canal Zone; and San Diego, California (completed after the 11 November 1918 Armistice).

B-type airship in flight over the Naval Air Station, Chatham, Massachusetts, in 1918.
Kelsey Airviews

B-type Airship General Specifications:

Volume, Original:	77,000 cubic feet (Goodyear produced 12 envelopes [type F] of this volume which included spares).
Revised:	84,000 cubic feet (Goodyear produced 18 envelopes [type FA] of this volume which included spares).
(For 84,000 cubic foot)	
Ballonets:	2, total 19,250 cubic feet
Overall length:	163 feet
Maximum diameter:	31.5 feet
Overall height:	46 feet
Useful lift:	1,840 pounds
Crew:	3
Maximum speed:	47 miles per hour
Cruising speed:	35 miles per hour
Endurance, full speed:	10.9 hours
Endurance, cruising:	26.5 hours
Range, full speed:	512 miles
Range, cruising speed:	927 miles
Ceiling:	8,500 feet
Armament:	1-Lewis machine gun
Engine (1):	Curtiss OX5 100 horsepower on the Goodyear/Goodyear Airships, Hall-Scott 100 horsepower on the Connecticut airships.

The B-type airships are difficult to identify from photographs, as generally they carried no identification until late in the war, however some units carried the "A" serial number on the control car and later units carried the "B" number on the envelope.

Data by Individual Airship:

B-1 - Serial A-235, Goodyear, envelope E-151, erected at White City with the first flight 24 May 1917. Ralph Upson and Herman Kraft were pilots. Two short flights made on 29 May. On the next flight Upson Decided that since performance was satisfactory and, rather than use the small landing field at White City, he would fly directly to Akron and Wingfoot Lake. B-1 departed White City at midnight on 29 May and landed near Medina, Ohio, 10 miles short of Akron, due to an oil shortage, but still a distance record at the time. B-1 remained at Wingfoot Lake for training and was delivered to the Navy 07 August 1917 at Pensacola. A new envelope was shipped 29 December 1917. B-1 was damaged 17 June 1920 due to engine problems, with slight damage to the envelope. It was recommended that the control car be stricken and that the envelope be reused with another control car. B-1 was stricken 14 August 1920 and the envelope (E-151) used with the B-17 airship.

B-2 - Serial A-236, Goodyear, believed completed at White City and held at Wingfoot Lake for training, delivered to the Navy at Key West 22 or 26 January 1918. Apparently also served at Chatham, B-2 established a patrol record in November 1918 by remaining aloft for 32 hours. Crew was ENS T.E. Maythan, pilot, ENS T.B. Null, co-pilot and Chief Carpenter's Mate J.H. "Red" Collier. A similar patrol of 40 hours, 48 minutes was made out of Key West on 24-26 December 1918. Lost at Key West due to engine failure caused by a broken connecting rod on 28 February 1919. Total flying time for B-2 was 333 hours, 29 minutes. Stricken circa February 1919 with the envelope shipped to the Boston Navy Yard on 15 January 1920 and received 04 March 1920.

B-2 is handled at NAS Key West, Florida 26 December 1918
The Lighter-Than-Air Society Collection/University of Akron Archives

<u>B-3</u> - Serial A-237, Goodyear, delivered 22 October 1917. Based at Rockaway 04 December 1917, defective envelope (Goodyear D-11) returned to Akron 09 April 1918. On a flight from Rockaway 10 June 1918, the lower rudder bearing pin carried away because it was improperly braced in the socket. A night emergency landing was made at Naval Base No. 5 at Sayville, Long Island, where repairs were made; B-3 returned to Rockaway 11 June. B-3 conducted many experiments including refueling from ships. Air-sea rescue missions from the submarine chaser SP-58 were conduced with ENS Scott E. Peck as pilot. B-3 may have also practiced a rescue from an N-9 seaplane reportedly near Key West, although records do not indicate B-3 served at Key West. (Photographs show a B-ship in that exercise in which a ladder was lowered and a man climbed off an N-9. see page 40.) Engine problems were encountered on 28 April 1919; B-3 was damaged and repaired at Rockaway. Transferred to Montauk, then to Hampton Roads (Norfolk) 12 December 1919, B-3 was shipped to San Diego, arriving 20 April 1920. Damaged 28 April, B-3 was repaired. Based on dates and airship availability believed to have participated in a search for the fleet tug USS *Conestoga* which was lost somewhere between Mare Island, CA and Samoa in late March 1921. B-3 with three cruisers, 36 destroyers, 2 airplane squadrons and several other ships searched 300,000 square miles in May 1921 with no success. B-3 was damaged again 10 June 1921, but repaired. B-3 was surveyed 07 January 1924 and stricken 03 February 1925.

<u>B-4</u> - Serial A-238, Goodyear, delivered 04 December 1917 and at Hampton Roads (Norfolk) 07 January 1918. Assigned to Cape May, B-4 was damaged 08 August 1918 due to the loss of the rudder post and supporting surface. B-4 was stricken 01 November 1918, its parts used as spares.

<u>B-5</u> - Serial A-239, Goodyear, delivered 11 August 1917, still at Akron 21 September and stricken 31 December 1917. Circumstances are uncertain but believed to have been lost in 1917 due to an engine fire, with the handling party releasing B-5, which then rose until the fire reached the envelope, and its hydrogen.

B-6 - Serial A-240, Goodyear, delivered 03 March 1918 and believed held in Akron for training. Shipped to Rockaway and served at Montauk, B-6 was stricken 07 September 1918.

B-7- Serial A-241, Goodyear, delivered 27 February 1918, first flight at Chatham 22 May 1918. The longest patrol flown was 6 hours, 7 minutes. B-7 lost controls and its rip panel failed to operate after striking power lines along the perimeter of the landing field on 08 June. The lines were later relocated. B-7 was stricken on 16 July 1918; the envelope was used at Chatham for free- and/or kite- balloon(s).

B-ship production did not wait for the Wingfoot Lake hangar doors to be complete. LTAS photo

B-8 - Serial A-242, Goodyear, delivered 25 February 1918, at Rockaway 15 March 1918 and transferred to Hampton Roads 03 November 1918. B-8 also served at Montauk, was shipped to Pensacola 10 November 1920 and arrived 16 November. B-8 was surveyed 29 April 1924 (condition deteriorated) and recommended striking, possibly (but unlikely) shipped to Lakehurst.

B-9 - Serial A-243, Goodyear, envelope E-155, delivered 31 January 1918, at Key West 04 February 1918. On 10 August 1918, the envelope was reported as badly deteriorated due to the effects of moisture and sun and classified as beyond repair on 19 August. A new envelope was recommended and apparently provided. On 21 April 1919, the engine failed due to a broken connecting rod; the envelope was torn in several places. B-9 was stricken 08 July 1919.

B-10 -Serial A-244, Goodrich, envelope E-156, delivered 30 January 1918 or 15 April 1918 (depending on records used). Records state: "control car A-244 was originally on B-10 but when it was stricken it was B-13." Envelope damaged 07 December 1918 at Cape May, it was returned to Goodrich for repair where it was determined repairs were too costly and it was cut up for other usage. In service at Rockaway and Montauk. To add to the confusion, B-10 was at Rockaway 26 May 1920 with records indicating envelope E-156 as unfit and recommended it be replaced. (If E-156 was replaced in March 1919 how could it be on B-10?) B-10 was stricken 18 October 1921.

B-11 - Serial A-245, Goodrich, one record indicates shipped to Pensacola 27 February 1918 and another 08 May 1918. Stricken 15 April 1919.

B-12 -Serial A-246, Goodrich, one record indicates shipped 26 March 1918 and another 06 June 1918. Some records also state B-12 made the first flight at Chatham 06 June, patrolled for 43 days and on 16 July (some reports state 26 July) 1918 was last sighted near Provincetown, MA, then apparently blown out to sea. Three days later B-12 was sighted by a Norwegian steamer and the airship and crew picked up and taken to Halifax, Nova Scotia. Records state B-12 was stricken 08 July 1919.

B-13 - Serial A-247, Goodrich, delivered 11 September 1917. Shipped 10 October to Montauk, arriving 20 October, B-13 was damaged 08 August 1918 when an envelope seam separated. Repaired, B-13 was to be used only at altitude of less than 800 feet and no more than 5 miles out to sea. On removal from the Montauk hangar in a crosswind on 18 August, the handling lines parted and the envelope was damaged. Transferred to Rockaway and to Cape May 05 November 1919, total flying time 450 hours, 22 minutes. B-13 was stricken 30 November 1919.

B-14 - Serial A-248, Goodrich, one record indicates shipped 31 October 1917, another 15 April 1918. Assigned to Montauk where it was determined the control car was weakened by holes improperly drilled during build. In service at Rockaway 24 March 1918 and stricken 16 November 1918.

B-15 - Serial A-249, Connecticut, one record indicates envelope shipped to Pensacola 22 August 1917 and control car 27 September 1917. If so, B-15 was erected at Pensacola, logical since Connecticut did not have an erection building. (Other records state delivery was 11 January 1918.) On 10 June 1918, the envelope was reported as of poor construction and with a faulty air valve. The envelope was apparently replaced, as at Pensacola from 28 January 1919 to February 11 B-15 tested of a method of releasing standard torpedoes. Due to the weight of the torpedo (approximately 1,000 pounds), it was necessary to release an excessive amount of lifting gas to bring it to equilibrium and land. The envelope was apparently again replaced with E-165 from Goodyear on 09 August 1920. B-15 was stricken 05 September 1924.

B-16 - Serial A-250, Connecticut, one record indicates shipped 12 December 1917, another states delivered 15 April 1918. B-16 was assigned to Cape May and stricken 03 July 1918.

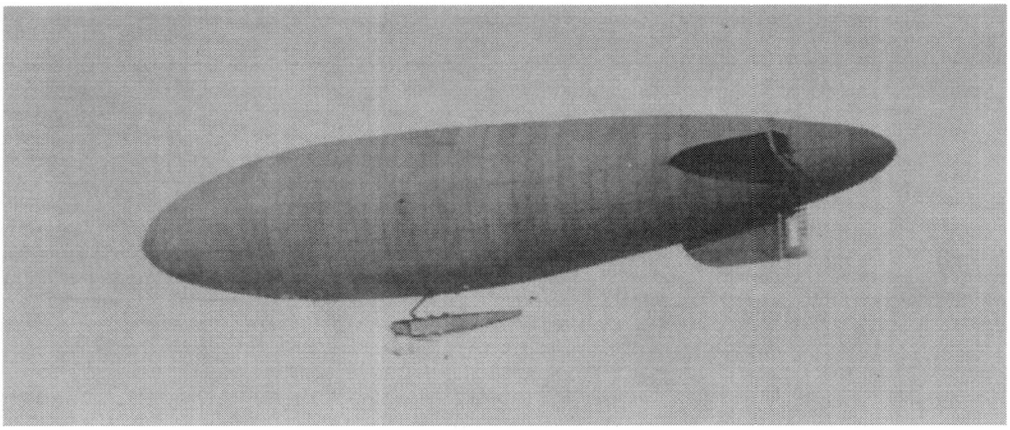

Single- lower vertical fin and rudder B-type airship in flight. LTAS photo

In late 1918/early 1919, Goodyear rebuilt three B-type control cars under Navy contract N-4349: B-17, B-18 and B-19, serial numbers A-5464, A-5465 and A-5467. A complete new B-20 control car, serial A-5257, was apparently contracted prior to B-17 through B-19. Goodyear also was awarded a contract for an unknown airship car A-5466. (This may be the special control car for B-20 but this would not be consistent with the assignment of serial numbers.) B-17 through B-20 were equipped with pusher Curtiss OX5 100 horsepower engines (B-1 through B-16 were all tractor drive engines).

B-17 - Serial A-5464, shipped to Pensacola 25 October 1918 and assembled with envelope E-151 (reused from B-1). This envelope was apparently replaced, as on 05 June 1920, B-17 envelope E-152 was reported in poor condition with high diffusion. The control car was out of line with the recommendation made that the envelope be replaced; the control car was repaired at Pensacola. (This leads to more confusion as on 18 November 1920 it was recommended that envelope E-151 be expended and the control car reused with envelope E-165.) Reports also state B-17 was stricken 01 July 1920 but records show it was back in service again 17 July 1920.

B-18 - Serial A-5465, shipped to Chatham 25 January 1919 and to San Diego 21 October 1919. Arriving 15 December 1919, the control car was in poor condition due to the shipping. With C-6, B-18 was planned for charting of the entire Pacific coast in 1920. On 22 April 1921 the envelope was reported with high diffusion due to continual usage and recommended that it be stored with doping to be scheduled at a later date.

B-19 - Serial A-5467, shipped to Chatham 23 January 1919 (envelope E-149). Due to strong winds the envelope was torn on 13 January 1920; repairs were recommended at Chatham. B-19 was apparently repaired and transferred to Rockaway 08 May 1920. Envelope E-149 was reported as badly deteriorated and unfit for service on 22 June 1920. The envelope was probably replaced as B-19 was not stricken until 18 October 1921.

B-20 - Serial A-5257, special control car 35 feet long, shipped to Montauk 18 September 1918 and to Chatham 28 November 1918. Served at Provincetown, MA. Lost at sea 23 January 1919, stricken 31 March 1919.

B-type airship delivery dates by sequence, source and stricken dates. (Some of the data confusion may be due to "shipping" dates and arrival and acceptance dates.) Hunsaker[2] / NASM[3]

	Sequence#/Serial #/	Delivery Dates	Contractor	Stricken/Lost
1	(B-1) A-235	09 Jul 17[2] / 07 Aug 17[3]	Goodyear	14 Aug 1920
2	(B-5) A-239	11 Aug 17[2]/ 21 Aug 17[3]	Goodyear	31 Dec 1917
3	(B-13) A-247	11 Sep 17[2]/ 10 Oct 17[3]	Goodrich	30 Nov 1919
4	(B-3) A-237	22 Oct 17[2]/ 01 Nov 17[3]	Goodyear	25 Feb 1925
5	(B-4) A-238	04 Dec 17[2]/ 01 Jan 18[3]	Goodyear	01 Nov 1918
6	(B-15) A-249	14 Dec 17[2]/ 27 Sep 17[3]	Connecticut	05 Sep 1924
7	(B-14) A-248	11 Jan 18[2]/ 31 Oct 17[3]	Goodrich	16 Nov 1918
8	(B-2) A-236	22 Jan 18[2]/26 Jan 18[3]	Goodyear	28 Feb 1919
9	(B-9) A-243	31 Jan 18[2]/02 Feb 18[3]	Goodyear	08 Jul 1919
	Sequence#/Serial#	Delivery Dates	Contractor	Stricken/Lost
10	(B-8) A-242	25 Feb 18[2] /15 Mar18[3]	Goodyear	29 Apr 1924
11	(B-7) A-241	27 Feb 18[2]/15 Mar 18[3]	Goodyear	16 Jul 1918
12	(B-6) A-240	03 Mar 18[2]/12 Mar 18[3]	Goodyear	07 Sep 1919
13	(B-10) A-244	15 Apr 18[2]/12 Mar 18[3]	Goodrich	18 Oct 1921
14	(B-16) A-250	15 Apr 18[2]/12 Dec 17[3]	Connecticut	03 Jul 1918
15	(B-11) A-245	08 May 18[2]/27 Feb 18[3]	Goodrich	15 Apr 1919
16	(B-12) A-246	06 Jun 18[2]/26 Mar 18[3]	Goodrich	08 Jul 1919

[2] "The Navy's First Airships," by Jerome C. Hunsaker, U.S. Naval Institute *Proceedings*, August, 1919.

[3] Research at the National Air and Space Museum in 1972 by Zenon Hansen.

The mating of the B-15 control car to its Connecticut Aircraft envelope between piers at Pensacola circa late 1917. The air station's dirigible hangar was no longer on the water. US Navy Photo

World War I Airship Stations and B-type Airship Assignments With Approximate Dates of Operation:

Chatham: B-2 (Nov 1918); B-7 (Mar-Jul 1918); B-12 (Mar 1918-Jul 1919); B-18 (Jan-Oct 1919); B-19 (Jan 1919-May 1920); B-20 (Nov 1918-Mar 1919). Six B-type airships operated, Mar 1918 - May 1920.

Montauk: B-3 (Apr 1919-1920); B-6; B-13 (Oct 1917); B- 14 (Oct 1917 and Jul 1918); B-20 (Sep -Nov 1918). Five B-type airships operated, Oct 1917 to 1920.

Rockaway: B-3 (Dec 1917); B-6 (Dec 1917-Sep 1918); B-8 (Mar 1918); B-10 (Jan 1920-Oct 1921); B-13 (1919); B-14 (Mar 1918); B-19 (May 1920-Oct 1921). Seven B-type airships operated, Dec 1917 to Oct 1921.

Cape May: B-4 (Aug 1918); B-10 (Jan 1918-Jan 1920); B-13 (Nov 1919); B-16 (Dec 1917-Jul 1918). Four B-type airships operated, Jan 1918 to Jan 1920.

Hampton Roads (Norfolk): B-3 (Dec 1917); B-4 (Jan 1918-Aug 1918); B-8 (Nov 1918). Three B-type airships operated, Dec 1917 to Nov 1918.

Pensacola: B-1 (Aug 1917-Aug 1920); B-5; B-8 (Nov 1918-Apr 1924); B-11 (Feb 1918-Apr 1919); B-15 (Sep 1917-Sep 1924); B-17 (Oct 1918- Nov 1919). Six B-type airships operated, Aug 1917 to Sep 1924.

Key West: B-2 (Jan 1918); B-3; B-9 (Feb 1918-Jul 1919). Three B-type airships operated, Jan 1918 to Jul 1919.

Coco Solo: B-types were known to operate there, no details.

San Diego: B-3 (Apr 1920-Jan 1924); B-18 (Dec 1919-Apr 1921). Two B-type airships operated, Dec 1919 to Jan 1924.

The Navy "Table Showing Status of Dirigibles" dated between May and September 1919 (hereinafter "1919 Table") indicates B-4, B-5, B-6, B-7, B-9, B-11, B-12, B-14, B-16 and B-20 were no longer in service. This same table indicates the status of B-type airships as follows: B-1 in service at Pensacola, B-2 deflated 18 July at Key West, B-3 in service at Montauk, B-8 disassembled at Hampton Roads for shipment to Key West, B-10 at Cape May for re-erection, B-13 in service at Rockaway, B-15 at Pensacola for overhaul, B-17 at Pensacola deflated but to be repaired, B-18 in service at Chatham and to be shipped to San Diego and B-19 at Chatham with the envelope deflated due to high gas diffusion. A Memorandum dated 13 January 1920 states six of the original 16 B-type airships had been lost and from the remains three new fuselages were built under Navy order N-4349 (the Goodyear contract for B-17 through B-19). In commission at this time were eight B-type airships, seven of which were to be maintained. B-10 in need of extensive repair was to be deflated when it went out of service. The B-types to remain in service were B-1, B-3, B-8, B-15, B-17, B-18 and B-19.

Envelopes believed to be olive drab in color. Lighter-Than-Air Society photo

Although wartime service was minimal, at least one airship from Chatham was known to have sighted a German U-boat. It notified seaplanes that attempted an attack using tools aboard, as there were no bombs. One B-type airship was in service for fifteen months with its original envelope. Another airship kept a single inflation charge for nine months during which it logged 743 hours of flight time. The airships flew 13,600 hours or approximately 400,000 miles without a fatality. As the B-type was really produced too late in the war to see direct service, they did train pilots for service against the enemy in French airships. Training was also conducted in England using British airships. Records indicate approximately 170 airship pilots were trained during the war. A separate study made of pilots during World War I indicates 168 as a reasonable total with another thirty-two qualified in balloons. There is an interesting story about Jimmy Shade, DN-1 crew veteran, and his Navy service. Shade was flying a B-type airship at Pensacola when, as a result of an argument with his wife, aimed a sand bag for dropping on the roof of his house. His aim must not have been too accurate as he missed his own house and hit a neighboring house. The sand bag went through the roof and ended in the lowest level. Needless to say, Shade was court-martialed and dismissed from the Navy. It is surmised that this is the period when he joined Goodyear (1919). Shade did later return to naval service and, as a Chief Rigger in 1922, was aide to LCDR Joseph P. Norfleet in the National Balloon Race held in Milwaukee, Wisconsin.

C-1 prepares to leave snowy Rockaway New York for sunny Florida. LTAS photo

The C-type Airships

The C-type airship was designed by the Navy to provide increased endurance and with twin engines for greater reliability. Thirty C-type airships were originally planned, however with the Armistice of 11 November 1918 this total was reduced to 15 and finally to 10. Contracts for six airships (C-1, C-3, C-4, C-5, C-7 and C-8) and two spare envelopes were awarded to Goodyear (Contract C-3509) and for four airships (C-2, C-6, C-9 and C-10) and two spare envelopes to Goodrich (Navy contract N-3508). All control cars, each assigned a serial number, were provided by the Burgess Works of the Curtiss Aeroplane and Motor Co. of Marblehead, MA (Navy contract 38700). The envelopes were assigned an "E" number by the Navy with Goodyear using a "D" series for their envelopes.

Data by Individual Airship:

C-1 - Navy serial A-4118, Goodyear envelope D-28 (Navy E-103, replacement Goodyear D-34, Navy E-109) complete 29 August 1918, first flight 30 September, delivered 22 October on a flight from Wingfoot Lake via Washington, DC, arriving at Rockaway 23 October. The flight was commanded by Maj Bernard "Bannie" L. Smith (USMC), with a crew consisting of LT R.A.D. Preston (Goodyear's second aeronautical engineer after Ralph H. Upson), LTJG D.T. Hood, ENS W. L. Hamlen, ENS E.M. Easterly and Goodyear representatives M. Roulette and James Royal. The Aero Club of New York awarded Smith and Hamlen (pilot and co-pilot) their Medal of Merit for this flight. On 12 December C-1 was used to carry an Army JN-4 airplane over Fort Tilden, NY and then launch it in flight, the first American attempt to develop a flying aircraft carrier. The airship was piloted by LT George Crompton and the JN-4 by 1stLt A.W. Redfield. On 12 January 1919 C-1 (LT Stanley V. Parker, USCG, pilot) was flown from Rockaway New York (with fueling stops at Hampton Roads [Norfolk] and Brunswick, Georgia) to Key West Florida, where it participated in submarine torpedo practice near Dry Tortugas. C-1 was apparently accidentally deflated at Key West on 17 May 1919. A replacement envelope (Goodyear D-34, type U, Navy E-109) was shipped to Rockaway. However sources also indicate this same envelope was shipped to the Army Balloon Division at El Paso, Texas 20 April 1920. The "1919 Table" indicates C-1 was at Key West in the process of re-erection with the old envelope shipped to Akron for repairs.

C-1 was erected at Camp Bierne (later Biggs Field), Fort Bliss, Texas in May 1920 and, as a U.S. Army airship, made its first flight 28 September 1920 with 1stLts John W. Shoptaw and Don L. Hutchins, M/Sgt. Chapman and S/Sgt. Barnes as crew. A two hour flight was made 29 September, and on 05 October; C-1 flew over El Paso and the surrounding countryside. Accounts indicate flights were made throughout the balance of 1920. The ultimate fate of C-1 is unknown, however an Army airship status report of 02 December 1920 indicates two C-type airships were on hand. The second C-type airship in the US Army was the C-2.

<u>C-2</u> - Navy serial A-4119, erected with Goodrich envelope (Navy E-134) and control car delivered (incomplete) to Wingfoot Lake 14 September 1918. The completed airship was delivered to the Navy in 1918. No record of service at any of the World War I stations was located and it is possible that C-2 remained at Wingfoot Lake as a training airship. It is known that it was deflated near Hartville, Ohio (south of Wingfoot Lake) on one of the test flights. C-2 was transferred to the Army 14 October 1919 at Wingfoot Lake and delivered to Langley Field, VA. The "1919 Table" indicates C-2 at Akron and to be transferred to Coco Solo, Panama Canal Zone. This completes the history of the Navy C-2.

The original C-2 was replaced by an Army C-2 with an envelope of the same size but with an entirely revised control car and surfaces similar to the later Army TC-type airships. The Army C-2 saw extensive service at Langley Field including development work for future airplane hook-on capabilities, although it was not equipped with a trapeze and no hook-ons were actually made. Flights were also made for the first demonstration of direction of aircraft by radio. Flights were made to Aberdeen, Maryland, Bolling Field, DC and New York City. In addition to Langley Field, C-2 was also based at Aberdeen Proving Ground (Phillips Field) for a period of time. The most spectacular flight of the Army C-2 was the transcontinental flight of 1922. C-2 departed Langley Field 14 September 1922 with refueling stops made at Wingfoot Lake, Scott Field, IL, Brooks Field (San Antonio), TX, Biggs Field (Fort Bliss), TX (local flights were made at all of these locations), Nogales, Ajo and Yuma, Arizona. C-2 arrived at Ross Field (Arcadia), California on 23 September. C-2 made flights to Crissy Field and the Presidio of San Francisco and Rockwell Field (San Diego). The return flight started 10 October from Ross Field with stops at Cochise, Arizona (due to engine trouble) and Biggs Field, Texas. C-2 arrived at Brooks Field, Texas on 10 October. While preparing for 4 local flights to be made 14 October, the wind tore C-2 from the control of the landing party causing it to strike the hangar door framework rupturing the fuel tanks and igniting the airship, the envelope and its hydrogen. Although there were no fatalities, five persons were injured and C-2 totally destroyed.

<u>C-3</u> - Navy serial A-4120, Goodyear envelope (Goodyear D-32, type U, Navy E-104 and Goodrich Navy E-137) completed 15 November 1918, complete airship shipped to Cape May in November 1918. On 07 February 1919, C-3 also demonstrated aerial refueling from surface ships in the vicinity of Cape May. C-3 was also based at Hampton Roads in February 1919. The "1919 Table" indicates C-3 was at Hampton Roads with the control car under overhaul and envelope E-137 enroute from Akron to replace E-104. It was originally intended to use C-3 in the attempt to fly the Atlantic Ocean, later attempted by C-5. C-3 was destroyed in the air near Hampton Roads on 08 July 1921 due to fire caused by a spark from the engine. C-3 was stricken 17 September 1921.

C-4 - Navy serial A-4122, Goodyear envelope (D-29, type U, Navy E-105) complete 15 November 1918, complete airship shipped to Montauk on 22 November 1918. In addition to Montauk C-4 was also based at Rockaway in February 1919 and Cape May in July 1919 and again at Rockaway in February 1920. "1919 Table" indicated it was at Rockaway and deflated due to lack of personnel. C-4 with Goodyear envelope D-68/Navy E- 173 was shipped to San Diego 03 May 1921 arriving in poor condition due to the packing and apparently not inflated. Final disposition is unknown. (Some sources also report the Navy C-4 was turned over to the Army, but this is not correct.)

C-5 on the ground, possibly in Newfoundland in preparation for the abortive attempt to fly the Atlantic Ocean in 1919. US Navy Photo

C-5 - Navy serial A-4126, Goodyear envelope (D-30, type U, Navy E-106) completed on 14 February 1919, complete airship shipped to Cape May in May 1919. C-5 is listed as shipped to Chatham 24 October 1919. In addition to Cape May, C-5 also served at Montauk, the starting point of the attempt to cross the Atlantic Ocean in 1919. C-5 departed Montauk 14 May and flew to St. Johns, Newfoundland where the cruiser USS *Chicago* was positioned to assist with officers and men for a handling party. The C-5 crew included LCDR E. M. Coil (commanding), LTs Scott E. Peck and J. B. Anderson and LTJG E. O. Campbell (pilots), ENS E. M. Esterly (radio), Chief Machinists Mates G. H. Blackburn and T. L. Mooreman engineers). C-5 arrived at St. Johns on 15 May after a flight of 1,115 miles (some reports state 1,050 and 1,200 nautical miles) in 25 hours, 40 minutes. The plan was to fly from St. Johns to the Azores, approximately the same distance as Montauk to St. Johns. It was planned to burn hydrogen in the engines to increase range and compensate for the loss of fuel weight without wasting the hydrogen's energy. C-5 was held by a party of approximately 100 men (there were no mooring masts at this time) at St. Johns when sudden gales wrenched C-5 from the hands of the handling party. The crew was aboard the *Chicago* when the gales were reported and rushed ashore in an attempt to take-off to save the airship, however this seemed impossible and an attempt was made to pull the envelope rip panel to release the hydrogen. This failed when the rip panel release jammed and then snapped. Another attempt was made to use a knife to release the lifting gas, but the handling crew reported they could no longer hold the airship. The crew jumped from the control car and C-5 disappeared over the Atlantic.

Several inconsistent reports on the ultimate fate of C-5 appeared in newspaper accounts at the time. The first report stated C-5 was sighted by a British ship and changed to state the sighting was an iceberg. The final report was made by the British warship *Nipigon* and stated they sighted the C-5 1,000 feet in the air, three miles from the ship and then settling to the surface. After waiting 4 hours for an American destroyer, the British ship proceeded on its way. C-5 was never located and the *Chicago* started its home trip on 17 May. C-5 was officially stricken 20 August 1919.

C-6 - Navy serial A-4125, Goodrich envelope (Navy E-133) and Goodyear envelope D-36/Navy E-111, complete airship shipped to Montauk 04 February 1919. Erection was started but not completed due to lack of personnel and the station being closed. Shipped to San Diego 21 November 1919 and received 06 December 1919, the first flight under Goodyear envelope D-36/Navy E-111 was on 01 March 1920. It was planned to use the C-6 in the charting of the entire pacific coast with the B-18. C-6 was lost 30 September 1920 at Laurel Canyon enroute to San Pedro for fleet maneuvers and stricken 30 December 1920.

C-7 shortly after take-off at NAS Hampton Roads (Norfolk), Virginia, December 1921, the first flight of a helium-inflated airship. Note the oversized counter balanced rudder. U S Navy/ Martin R. Copp

C-7 - Navy serial A-4127, Goodyear envelope (D-35, type D, Navy E-110) complete 21 November 1919. Shipped to Pensacola 29 November 1919 and received 20 January 1920, C-7 was not immediately erected. Envelope Goodyear D-35/Navy E-110 was damaged 29 July 1920 by striking the hangar doors and replaced with a new envelope (Goodyear D-31/Navy E-107). C-7 was reassigned to Hampton Roads with Goodyear envelope D-72, type UA, and made the first flight of a helium inflated airship on 01 December 1921. Crew on this flight consisted of LCDRs R.F. Wood and Zachary Lansdowne, and LT Charles E. Bauch. As a demonstration, C-7 was then flown to Washington and Anacostia, 05 December with LCDR Lansdowne as pilot. Approximately 15 helium inflated flights were made at Hampton Roads. C-7 was the only airship at Hampton Roads at this time. Discrepancies exist as the final deflation of C-7 with some sources stating March 1922 and others March 1924. It is believed that the 1922 date is correct.

C-8 - Navy serial A-4123, Goodyear envelope (D-33, type U, Navy E-108) complete 09 April 1919, complete airship shipped to Cape May 03 June. One report states that on 03 June LT R.R. "Rip" Paunack was awarded the Distinguished Flying Cross when he saved the hydrogen inflated C-8 and 6 crewmen by straddling a support beam and pulling himself away about 10 feet from the control car with nothing below him but space, to extinguish a blazing carburetor. On 01 July 1919, C-8 departed Cape May on a training flight with LT R. J. Learned (commanding), CDR R. D. Weyerbacher (navigator), ENS O. W. Tyndall (co-pilot), Warrant Machinist B. F. Sherman (chief engineer), Machinists Mate 1st Class V. D. Keller (engineer), Electricians Mate 1st Class F. C. Lynch (radio) and passengers CDR R. D. Quiqley and LTJG A. R. Tilburne. The forward part of the vertical fin collapsed in bumpy weather. It was decided a landing was necessary before greater damage might occur. C-8 was landed in the vicinity of Camp Holabird, Maryland and a ground crew assembled from the local troops. C-8 was moored with a cable and repaired as much as possible with the intention of returning to flight and proceeding to Cape May. Through some unknown cause it was believed the hydrogen was ignited and C-8 destroyed by fire. C-8 was officially stricken 20 August 1919.

C-9 - Navy serial A-4124, Goodrich envelope (Navy E-132, "1919 Table"), and received at Wingfoot Lake 23 October 1919, Shipped to Pensacola in 1919 but not erected; shipped to Coco Solo 01 March 1920. Transferred to Hampton Roads 01 March 1922. C-9's ultimate fate is unknown.

C-10 - Navy serial A-4121, Goodrich envelope, Navy E-135, first flight 10 May 1919. Damaged, C-10 was repaired and shipped to Chatham, arriving 14 November 1919 but was not erected. Shipped to Rockaway 08 May 1920, envelope E-135 was damaged when the fabric separated. Repaired (some data states with envelope E-132 which disagrees with "1919 Table"), C-10 was damaged again while covering the America's Cup Race at Jamaica Bay 21 July 1920 (LTs A.W. Evans and L. A. Koor, pilots). C-10 was destroyed 31 August 1921 in the hangar fire at Rockaway (which also destroyed D-6 and H-1) and was stricken 18 October 1921.

C-14 and C-52: One other airship designated as C-14 and another designated C-52 served with the Army. They were not Navy C-types. They were very different in design, helium inflated and resembled the later Army TC-type airships. The C-14 airship was assembled at Langley Field in September 1922.

C- type Airship General specifications:

Volume: Original - 172,000 cubic feet (Goodyear type U of which a total of 13 were fabricated that included spares and not necessarily for the Navy C-type). Revised - 181,000 cubic feet (Goodyear type UA of which a total of 7 were fabricated that included spares and not necessarily for the Navy C-type).

Ballonets (2):	Maximum volume 55,250 cubic feet
Overall length:	196 feet
Maximum diameter:	42 feet
Overall height:	54 feet
Useful lift:	4,050 pounds
Crew:	4
Maximum speed:	60 miles per hour
Cruising speed:	40 miles per hour
Endurance, full speed:	14.8 hours
Endurance, cruising speed:	31.2 hours
Range at full speed:	890 miles
Range at cruising speed:	1,250 miles
Ceiling:	8,600 feet
Armament:	One Lewis machinegun and four 270 pound bombs
Engines (2):	Hispano-Suiza, 150 horsepower, C-1 thru C-4, C-6 and C-8 thru C-10 Union, 125 horsepower, C-5 and C-7.

C-type airship probable delivery (or shipping) dates or known first flight date. No explanation is offered for the "C" number and serial number sequencing system.

Shipping Date	Sequence Number	Manufacturer
14 Sep 1918	C2 (A4119)	Goodrich
30 Sep 1918	C1 (A4118)	Goodyear (delivered on1^{st} flight)
19 Nov 1918	C3 (A4120)	Goodyear
22 Nov 1918	C4 (A4122)	Goodyear
04 Feb 1919	C6 (A4125)	Goodrich
08 May 1919	C5 (A4126)	Goodyear (1st flight)
10 May 1919	C10 (A4121)	Goodrich
03 Jun 1919	C8 (A4123)	Goodyear
23 Oct 1919	C9 (A4124)	Goodrich
29 Nov 1919	C7 (A4127)	Goodyear

The Navy records dated 01 November 1919, indicate four C-type built and three under contract. Unit cost is shown as $60,000.

(Above, left) C-type airship car, possibly the C-1. Note "finger" patches of the external suspension (above, right). US Navy photos.

World War I Air Stations and C-type Airship Assignment With Approximate Dates of Operation

Chatham: C-10 (Nov 1919)
Montauk : C-4 (Feb 1919); C-5 (May-Aug 1919); C-6 (Feb 1919)
Rockaway: C-1 (Oct -Jan 1919); C-4 (Feb-Jul 1919 and Jan-Feb 1920); C-10 (May 1919-Oct 1921)
Cape May: C-3 (Nov 1918-Feb 1919); C-4 (Jul 1919); C-5 (1919); C-8 (Jun-Aug 1919)
Hampton Roads: C-3 (Feb 1919-Sep 1921); C-7 (1921-1922); C-9 (Mar 1922)
Pensacola: C-7 (Jan 1919-Jul 1920); C-9 (Oct -Dec 1919)
Key West: C-1 (Jan 1919-Apr 1920)
Coco Solo: C-9 (Dec 1919- Mar 1920)
San Diego: C-4 (May 1921); C-6 (Dec 1919-Dec 1920)

The D-Type Airships

The D-type airship was designed to correct several complaints with the successful C-type airship. The D-type airships were authorized 16 July 1918 with an original order for twenty. Only five service type airships were built with Goodyear to originally provide the envelopes for D-1, D-2 and D-4 (contract no. 3509, 1919) and Goodrich the envelopes for D-3 and D-5 (contract 35-8, 1919). Control cars were provided by the Naval Aircraft Factory at Philadelphia and shipped to Wingfoot Lake where they were mated to the Goodyear and Goodrich envelopes. In addition to control cars, the Naval Aircraft Factory at Philadelphia provided D-type surfaces retro-fitted to C-type airships at Cape May in 1919.

A rare view of D-1 on the ground at Wingfoot Lake (Akron), Ohio, June 1920. D-1 was lost in the Wingfoot Lake hangar fire of 19 July 1920. Goodyear / A. O'Neil / R. Wolcott /D. R. Smith

Improvements over the C-type airship included a redesigned control car. The fuel tanks were moved from the car and mounted on the envelope along the equator to provide greater crew space. The engines were moved from the sides to the rear of the car to reduce noise and propeller blast. The Navy 01 November 1919 records indicate five D-types were under contract at a unit cost of $60,000. A sixth D-type was built, but with an entirely different control car than D-2 through D-5. D-6 was designed to provide an enclosed, boat-like car (similar to the later J-type airships) and with the fuel tanks located inside. D-1 through D-5 never actually served with the Navy and were transferred to the Army. (The D-1 was destroyed by fire at Wingfoot Lake 19 July 1920 prior to the Army acceptance.) D-6 was primarily experimental and was destroyed by fire at Rockaway 31 August 1921. In an attempt to reconcile the Navy serial numbers and the complete airship numbers, the system was revised to reflect the sequence of construction rather than the contract date. Goodyear actually built the envelopes for D-1, D-2, D-3 and D-6 and Goodrich D-4 and D-5. This change is reflected in "Navy Procurement Charts for November 1, 1920." Unfortunately, the original numbers and envelope sources remained shown in published data such as the "1919 Table." The Navy 01 November 1919 records indicate five D-type were under contract at a unit cost of $60,000. Records also indicate D-2, D-3, D-4 and D-5 were transferred to the Army at a total cost of $264,000.

In addition to the transfer of the C and D-type airships to the Army, the Navy also transferred the French-built airships ZDUS-1 (Army RN-1 that saw extensive service) and the Astra-Torres T-1 (never erected) and three British-built SS Zero-type non-rigids.

Data by individual airship:

D-1 - Navy serial A-4450, Goodyear envelope D-38, type UA, 180,000 cubic feet (Navy E-112) completed 04 May 1919, control car received 21 November 1919, first flight 13 July 1920. Destroyed that day by fire in the Wingfoot Lake hangar that burned the Goodyear Pony Blimp envelope no. D-58 and a free balloon. D-1 was stricken 30 July 1920.

D-2 - Navy serial A-4451 (also recorded as S-1021), Goodyear envelope D-40, type UA (Navy E-114) completed 20 September 1920, transferred to the Army and flown to Langley Field, Virginia, via Washington, DC on 31 October 1920. The delivery flight was commanded by LT Charles E. Bauch with LTJG Arthur T. Sewell (later a Goodyear airship fleet and WWII pilot), Chief Machinists Mate Robert Farris, Chief Quartermaster James F. Shade ("the Pensacola B-ship bomber") and 1stLt George W. McEntire of the Army Air Service. The Army D-2 was based at Langley Field and participated as an observation aircraft during the so-called BGen "Billy" Mitchell bombing tests in 1921. On return to Langley Field (1stLt Orvil A. Anderson, pilot) 21 July 1921, one of the engines failed while 30 miles out to sea. D-2 reached shore with damage to both envelope and control car, however there were no injuries. Reports indicate D-2 was not rebuilt. (See D-5 as D-2-2.)

D-3, after transfer to the Army, was used in airplane hook-on tests. US Army photo.

D-3 - Navy serial A-4453, Goodyear (originally to be Goodrich) envelope D-39 (Navy E-113) completed 21 March 1921. Test flown at Wingfoot Lake, transferred to the Army and shipped to Langley Field where it was re-erected as part of training by Army Airship School (10th Airship Company) personnel. Used for experimental program with bow mooring masts then being developed by the Army. D-3 participated in the “Mitchell” bombing tests in 1921 as an observation aircraft. D-3 was transferred to the 18th Airship Company at Aberdeen Proving

Ground, Maryland where on 10 November 1922 it flew to New York City. Landing at Mitchell Field for refueling, D-3 proceeded to Hartford, Connecticut for refueling and then to the U.S. Military Academy at West Point, New York. D-3 returned non-stop to Aberdeen landing on 11 November. Maj Oscar Westover commanded the flight and Capt William E. Kepner was operations officer. D-3 was badly damaged on being removed from the Aberdeen hangar 19 January 1923 and was rebuilt at Langley Field making its first flight after rebuild 06 August 1923. D-3 was used for the investigation of airplane hook-ons with a trapeze attached for experiments with an Army DH-4 airplane. On 18 September 1923, 1stLt Rex M. Stoner attempted to make contact using a Sperry "Messenger" airplane but was unable to do so due to insufficient speed of the airship. New engines were installed and a second series of tests conducted over Aberdeen. The hook-on tests consisted of keeping a specially installed contact rod fastened with elastic at the lower end so that it would bend with pressure from the trapeze. No actual attempt was to made to hook-on the airplane. D-3 was probably deleted in early 1924 when the Army TC-type airships were placed in service.

D-4 - Navy serial A-4452, Goodrich (originally to be Goodyear) envelope Navy E-139, completed approximately October 1920. D-4 was based at Langley Field where it also participated in the "Mitchell" bombing tests as an observation platform, and in mooring mast experiments. Transferred to Scott Field, Illinois, D-4 is known to have been deflated in 1922 while attempting to moor to a mast. Possibly deleted after this incident.

D-5 - Navy serial A-4454, Goodrich envelope (probably Navy E-138), assembled airship completed approximately late 1920 with shipment to Richmond, Virginia, and eventually Fort Omaha, Nebraska, the headquarters of the Army Balloon and Airship Division. No record was located of the D-5 being assembled or flying at Fort Omaha and it is assumed it was stored until transfer to Scott Field in late 1921/early 1922. There also is no record of the Army operating an airship designated as D-5, however a second D-2 airship was operated and it is believed this airship replaced the original D-2 lost 21 July 1921 on return from the "Mitchell" bombing tests. For reference, this researcher has designated this airship as D-2-2.

Apparently the D-2-2 was stored at Scott Field until late 1922 and then erected by the airship class of the Balloon and Airship School. With the Union engines replaced by two Wright "V" type engines developing 180 horsepower, D-2-2's first flight was made 06 February 1923. Radio communications were established with Scott Field; pilots on this flight were 1stLts H. H. Holland (command), Arthur Thomas (direction) and D. L. Hutchins (altitude). A second flight of 3.5 hours was made on 08 February with 1stLts Holland (command), Thomas (direction) and Ira Koenig (altitude). On this flight radio conversations were held with a St. Louis radio station, a "first" at that time. As a training airship at Scott Field, D-2-2 suffered a punctured envelope that collapsed the tail and was possibly deleted at this time.

D-6 - Navy serial A-5972, Goodyear envelope D-42 (type UA/ Navy E-116) completed 04 April 1921. The control surfaces and special project control car (known as the D-1 Enclosed Cabin Dirigible Car) were built by the Naval Aircraft Factory at Philadelphia with LTJG Leroy Grumman as project engineer. When Grumman left the Navy for Loening Aircraft (later Grumman Aircraft) he was replaced with LT Ralph S. Barnaby. The control car resembled an old streetcar on a lifeboat hull. With steel tube structures for the two engines, D-6 was similar to the later J-type airships. The control car was shipped to Rockaway and installed with the envelope from Goodyear. D-6 made one test flight, the only D-type to actually see Naval service. D-6 was destroyed in the Rockaway hangar fire of 31 August 1921 with C-10 and H-1. D-6 was stricken 18 October 1921.

D-type Airship General specifications:

Volume:	190,000 cubic feet (C-type with an additional 6 foot panel)
Ballonets (2):	Maximum volume 55, 250 cubic feet
Overall length:	198 feet
Maximum diameter:	42 feet
Overall height:	58 feet
Useful lift:	4,340 pounds
Crew:	4
Maximum speed:	58 miles per hour
Cruising speed:	40 miles per hour
Endurance, full speed:	17 hours
Endurance, cruising speed:	37 hours
Range at full speed:	985 miles
Range at cruising speed:	1,480 miles
Ceiling:	8,800 feet
Armament:	One Lewis machine gun and four 270 pound bombs
Engines (2):	Union 125 horsepower (generally)

The D-1 airship car. Note forward machine gun mount. Goodyear photos

Estimated delivery dates or known first flight	Serial Number	Manufacturer
13 Jul 1920	D-1 (A-4450)	Goodyear
Oct 1920	D-2 (A-4451)	Goodyear
Oct 1920	D-4 (A-4452)	Goodrich
Late 1920	D-5 (A-4454	Goodrich
Mar 1921	D-3 (A-4453)	Goodyear
Aug 1921	D-6 (A-5972)	Goodyear

The E-1 Airship

Apparently, Goodyear had performed work on a proposed commercial airship for several years prior to World War I. The airship supposedly was to be used for a trans-Atlantic flight, probably by Walter Wellman or Melvin Vaniman. Three single engine cars had been designed or possibly constructed, but the envelope was evidently not, due to the start of World War I in Europe in 1914.[4] Goodyear designed an envelope for each of the cars and offered them to the government in a speculative manner. The Navy accepted two designs (E-1 and F-1) and the Army one design (A-4). These airships were of the same envelope volume (95,000 cubic feet) as the later Goodyear Pony Blimps.

E-1 at the Airship School, Naval Air Station, Pensacola, 1919. US Navy/Goodyear Photo

E-1 Airship General Specifications:

Volume:	95,000 cubic feet
Ballonets (2):	16,500 cubic feet (maximum)
Overall length:	162 feet
Maximum diameter:	33 feet
Overall height:	49.5 feet
Useful lift:	2,050 pounds
Crew:	3
Maximum speed:	56 miles per hour
Cruising speed:	35 miles per hour
Endurance, full speed:	6.8 hours
Endurance, cruising speed:	19.2 hours
Range, full speed:	380 miles
Range, cruising speed:	602 miles
Ceiling:	8,000 feet
Armament:	None
Engine (pusher):	probably Thomas Morse, 145 horsepower, V-8, 4-bl. prop

---

[4] The account of the three engine cars for a Goodyear commercial airship prior to World War I is from AN INVENTORY OF U.S. NAVY AIRSHIPS, 1916-1961, by Richard K. Smith. This information was not located in any other record. Goodyear assembly drawings are dated 1918; perhaps their design is 1914.

E-1, Navy serial number A-4109 (also A-249) was procured on contract no. 38701 dated 05 June 1918. Goodyear order no. W.O. 1972 with envelope D-23 (type FB/Navy E-102) delivered to Wingfoot Lake 19 September 1918 with control car number C-1 was the first complete control car built by Goodyear. The first flight was probably in October 1918, with 33 flight hours amassed in the vicinity of Akron prior to shipment to Pensacola 16 December 1918. E-1 was erected by the Airship School at Pensacola and commissioned 08 January 1919 as a training airship, along with B-15. Goodyear also provided a spare envelope (D-168, type FB, Goodyear order 0-7160) under Navy contract 6205 which was shipped to Pensacola 08 December 1920. The Navy records of 01 November 1919 indicate the cost of E-1 was $55,000.

E-1 was apparently damaged 19 February 1919 and returned to service 04 March. On 20 March (some reports state 22 March), the counter-balanced rudder carried away during an instruction flight while three miles from the Pensacola landing area. E-1, then piloted by a student, was relieved by ENS Edward Mulliken, the instructor. With careful maneuvering and good judgment, E-1 was landed safely. The rudder was replaced with a type FA non-counter-balanced rudder and stabilizer, then test flown 21 March. E-1 was reported handling as well, if not better, than with the original rudder. E-1 was deflated 26 March due to excessive loss of gas and stretching of the envelope seams, repaired and then damaged while attempting to enter the hangar on 08 May 1920. Repaired once again, a forward rip panel blew open 20 May with E-1 settling on shore near Perdido Bay (west of Pensacola). Goodyear shipped a new envelope (D-55, type FB, Navy E-168) to Pensacola on 08 December 1920. E-1 was in service only at Pensacola, placed in storage in 1924 and removed from inventory 05 September 1924.

(Top) E-1 car; Goodyear Tire & Rubber Co. Colection/University of Akron Archives
(Bottom) F-1 car. Lockheed Martin Collection/University of Akron Archives

The F-1 Airship near Naval Air Station Norfolk, 1919 **US Navy / M. R. Copp**

The F-1 Airship

F-1, Navy serial A-4348, was the second airship to utilize a control car apparently built (or designed) by Goodyear prior to World War I. F-1 was procured on contract no. 39918 dated 17 July 1918, Goodyear order W.O. 2996, with envelope D-37 (type FB)/Navy E-101 and control car C-2. F-1 was classified by the Navy as "Experimental Engine Testing Dirigible." F-1's first flight made at Wingfoot Lake 11 February 1919 and it was flown to Hampton Roads on the same date. The 01 November 1919 records state a unit cost of $50,000. Problems were encountered on the delivery flight near Catlett, Virginia, when the envelope was ripped and deflated. F-1 was repaired and was back in service 28 April 1919. Goodyear also provided spare envelope D-54/Navy E-167 on Navy contract 6205 and shipped to Hampton Roads 21 January 1921. F-1 served only at Hampton Roads and was removed from inventory 09 November 1923.

F-1 Airship General Specifications:

Volume:	95,000 cubic feet
Ballonets (2):	16,500 cubic feet, maximum
Overall length:	162 feet
Maximum diameter:	33.5 feet
Overall height:	49.5 feet
Useful lift:	2,300 pounds
Crew:	3
Maximum speed:	52 miles per hour
Cruising speed:	34.2 miles per hour
Endurance, full speed:	17.5 hours
Endurance, cruising speed:	34.2 hours
Range at full speed:	910 miles
Range at cruising speed:	1,225 miles
Ceiling:	8,000 feet
Armament:	none
Engine*	probably Union 6 cylinder, 2 blade prop

*Conrary to photos, one record reads "tractor: Union, 8 cylinder, 125 horsepower." It is possible the Army A-4 and/or the two Navy ships tried a Curtiss "OX" engine or 90 or 100 hp, records disagree.

(The proposed very large G-Type Airship was never built, see G-1.)

The H-1 Airship

H-1 in front of the Naval Air Station, Rockaway, Long Island, New York, July 1921.
Naval Historical Center (NH) 90098

The H-type airship was originally planned in the 1919 period as a twin-engine patrol airship of approximately 80,000 cubic feet volume. It was suggested by CDR Lewis H. Maxfield that a small airship type could double as a kite balloon, be towed by a cable and have the ability to maneuver on its own once the towing cable was released. Both the Army and Navy had used kite balloons during World War I, the Army with so much success for observation and artillery direction that they continued to use forms of the kite balloon until 1942. The Navy's use of the kite balloon was primarily for training and coastal observation and mostly unsuccessful attempts at towing balloons from ships. It was based on this thought that the original H-type patrol airship was discontinued and a "Towing Airship" designed. The new H-type design resembled the Goodyear Pony Blimps of 1919 with a volume of 35,300 cubic feet but with a control car adapted to Navy requirements.

Goodyear was awarded Navy contract no. 51214 (Goodyear order R-4685) on 30 June 1920 for the "Towing Airship," Navy serial no. 5973. Goodyear envelope D-64 (type AB, 43,030 cubic feet)/Navy E-169 was completed 04 April 1921 along with single engine control car C-10. It is assumed H-1 was test flown at Wingfoot Lake in April and then delivered by rail to Rockaway on 03 May 1921. By 02 August 1921 six trial flights had been made and on 05 August H-1 was scheduled for speed trial flights. On this flight, the single engine developed a problem. H-1 settled hard on the surface and the crew was thrown out. H-1, now 400 pounds lighter, leaped back into the air and flew off minus the crew. It came to rest on farmland near Scarsdale, New York where a thoughtful farmer tied it to a tree *using the release cord of the rip panel*. During the night H-1 deflated. On 31 August 1921, what was left of the H-1 was destroyed in the Rockaway hangar fire, along with D-6 and C-10.

Control car Goodyear serial number C-10 nears completion, March 1921. Hepburn Walker, Jr.

Goodyear was awarded a supplemental contract (O 90088) dated 30 June 1921 for a second H-type that was requested that the Navy provide for the Army. Goodyear provided envelope D-74 (type AB, 43,030 cubic feet, Goodyear order S-6148) and control car C-17. This H-type was slightly different in design and was designated by the Army as A-121, later revised to OB-1. A-121 (OB-1) was shipped to the Army Air Service at Fairfield Intermediate Depot (Wilbur Wright Field), Ohio on 25 July 1922. Cost of the OB-1 was $45,000. The control car of the OB-1 varied from the Navy design and was fitted with the Vickers mooring gear and a small castering wheel. OB-1 was originally inflated with hydrogen but replaced by helium in August 1923. OB-1 served at Wright Field, primarily for engineering tests, and at Scott Field, Illinois. OB-1 was deflated 06 October 1923 and not re-erected, as the Army TA-type airship was being completed for one-man airship training.

H-1 General specifications:

Volume:	43,030 cubic feet
Ballonet (1):	8,600 cubic feet (approximately)
Overall length:	94.8 feet
Maximum diameter:	32.7 feet
Overall height:	30.8 feet
Useful lift:	1,146 pounds
Crew:	2
Maximum speed:	49.5 miles per hour
Endurance, full speed:	7 hours
Range at full speed:	346 miles
Ceiling:	6,000 feet
Engine:	Lawrance L-4, 60 horsepower at 1,500 rpm, 1-two blade propeller

The J-type Airships

The design of the J-type airship was prepared in March 1919; the result of a request to provide a twin-engine coastal patrol airship, similar to the C and D-type, approximately the same size, but with a simple boat-like control car that could land on water. (This request may have been the basis for the "D-1 Enclosed Cabin Dirigible" for the D-6.) The design of the J-type was a joint venture between the Navy Bureau of Aeronautics and Goodyear. The envelope was designed to have only one ballonet, to reduce weight. This was based on the H-1 and reports from pilots that served with WWI French Zodiac non-rigid airships of their satisfactory performance during the First World War. In 1921, Contract no. 54160 was awarded to Goodyear to produce two J-type airships. Based on field experience with the single ballonet J-1, the second J-type, serial A-6112, was held at the Naval Aircraft Factory in Philadelphia, Pennsylvania, and the control car used with the J-4.

Data by individual airship:

J-1 - Navy serial A-6111, Goodyear envelope D-73 (type J, 175,000 cubic feet and Goodyear order S-6167) / Navy E-177 and control car C-16. J-1 was test flown 31 August 1922 at Wingfoot Lake by ENS Charles Bauch. Shipped to Hampton Roads, it made the first flight 04 January 1923 and was accepted on 06 February. J-1 operated at Hampton Roads until airship activity ceased there in the spring of 1924. J-1 was shipped to Lakehurst and erected in Hangar No. One on 02 May 1924. On 10 May 1924, J-1 was placed in service, the only non-rigid then in Navy service. Although J-1 was difficult to handle due to the single ballonet, it was used for training crews to man future rigid airships. The first New Jersey flight was made 16 May 1924, with LT C.H. Havill commanding. Both LCDR Zachary Lansdowne and LT Charles E. Rosendahl made training flights in J-1. During the last two weeks of May, at least five flights were made in the area of Lakehurst to advertise the air circus held at the air station on the weekend of 30 May. J-1 participated in the air circus, with flights offered to lucky contest winners. J-1 was retired in August 1924 to conserve helium that was costly, always in short supply and required for the rigid airships.

J-1 car.   Curtiss Museum photo.

J-2 - Planned as Navy serial A-6112, a true J-2 airship did not exist. Goodyear records indicate a control car (C-18, Goodyear order S-6146) was shipped to Philadelphia 05 April 1923 for a J-type. It is assumed that, with the cancellation of the second J-type envelope due to its unsatisfactory performance with a single ballonet, and the change from hydrogen to helium, the control car was completed by Goodyear and then shipped to the Naval Aircraft Factory for storage. It seems to have been used for the J-4. Most sources indicate the next control car for the Navy was the TC-type acquired for the J-3.

J-3 at Lakehurst, 1932. Hepburn Walker, Jr. collection.

J-3 - (serial A-7382) has been stated by some sources as originally the Army TC-1. This is incorrect, as the TC-1 was destroyed by fire at Wright Field, Ohio on 06 June 1923. The Navy had requested TC-type envelopes from the Army and two TC-types were provided. One from Aberdeen was sent to the builder, Airships, Inc. but proved too worn. Another was sent from Langley Field. The Navy requested a new envelope from a current Army contract with Goodyear, which was to be modified for the J-3. Goodyear records indicate envelope D-97, government order no. E-193, as sold to the Navy by the Army and shipped to Lakehurst 11 August 1926. An Army TC-type control car from Aberdeen was provided to the Navy by the Army. The actual serial number, date of manufacture, etc. for this Army control car is unknown.

In late 1926, instruments were stripped from the J-1 for use in the J-3 control car. The first flight of J-3 was 12 October 1926, entering service late that year. J-3 and J-4, along with the USS *Los Angeles* and the Army TC-5 and TC-10-254, participated in the fly-over for the Herbert Hoover inauguration on 04 March 1929. J-3 served at Lakehurst her entire career as a training airship. On April 4, 1933 when reports of the loss of the USS *Akron* and the reported sighting of survivors reached Lakehurst, LCDR Jesse L. Kenworthy, acting commanding officer at Lakehurst, ordered the J-3 readied by LT John M. Thornton, in charge of non-rigid operations. J-3 was launched for flight after the storm winds had decreased. J-3 was commanded by LCDR David Cummins, with LTJG William A. Cockell, and Thornton; Chief Pasquale Bettio (of O-1 fame), Machinists Mates Walter Myers and Kensel Sprague and Chief Radioman Harley Manley were aboard. J-3 searched fifteen miles out to sea when an engine mount broke. J-3 landed on the shore near Beach Haven, New Jersey. A controlled landing was made impossible by winds, but after attempting to rip the envelope, J-3 was blown out over the ocean were it deflated. LCDR Cummins and Chief Bettio died due to sustained injuries, and were taken aboard the Coast Guard flying boat Sirius. The others were rescued by a New York City Police amphibian, which flew to shore carrying several men on its pontoons.

J-4 - J-4 used the original J-2 control car (serial A-6112, Goodyear no. C-18) that had been stored at Philadelphia since April 1923. J-4 was erected at Lakehurst with spare envelope E-197 and test flown in November 1927. J-4 (as stated for the J-3) participated in the fly-over for the Hoover inauguration 04 March 1929. J-4 visited the mooring mast under construction on top of the Empire State building (left). J-4 served at Lakehurst as a training airship until 1933 when it was transferred to Naval Air Station, Sunnyvale (later Moffett Field), California. The first flight of an airship at Sunnyvale was by the J-4 on 29 June 1933. The car was "housed over," given a windowed enclosure, by civilian workers at Moffett. After the loss of the USS *Macon*, the US Army took over Moffett Field, but reports of the J-4 as an Army airship at Moffett Field are incorrect. J-4 was returned to Lakehurst via rail on 10 May 1935, arriving 22 May. J-4 experimented with a light blue painted envelope for camouflage. J-4 was used to test a seawater ballast pickup system. J-4 also demonstrated a sea-anchored rope ladder and a stretcher rescue pickup. The airship alighted on the water and took aboard a "mail" bag. J-4 remained at Lakehurst and was used, despite its age, in the early World War II "neutrality" patrols in the vicinity of New York harbor. The obsolete J-4 was retired once the more modern patrol airships were on order, used for mooring out tests, then stricken 30 March 1940. The J-type airship served, in one form or another, from 1922 to 1940.

J-4 at Lakehurst. Tupper photo from the collection of Hepburn Walker, Jr.

General Specifications:	J-1	J-3/TC-1/J-4
Volume (cubic feet):	174,800	210,600 Ballonet (cubic feet):
	1 - 53,450	2 - 56,500
Overall length:	168 feet	196 feet
Maximum diameter:	45 feet	44.5 feet
Overall height:	58 feet	58 feet
Useful lift:	4,488 pounds	4,600 pounds
Crew:	4 or 5	5 or 6
Maximum speed:	52 knots	52 knots
Cruising speed:	35 knots	40 knots
Endurance, full speed:	30.8 hours	52 hours
Range at full speed:	1,848 miles	780 miles
Range at cruising speed:	?	840 miles
Ceiling:	?	8,000 feet
Engines (2):	Union, 130 horsepower at 1,400 rpm	

Detail of "housed over" car; J-4 could land on water. US Navy Photo

Airship Rescues: It should be noted that several rescue demonstrations were staged using these early hydrogen-filled airships. In addition to the B-ship rescue seen here, motion picture cameras captured a similar C-ship rescue simulation in Florida. The helium filled J-4 made a rather elaborate rescue demonstration for the newsreel cameras. With a water bag acting as anchor, Anton Heinen climbed off a boat and up a ladder to the J-4 car. Later a simulated stretcher patient in a raft was hauled up into the airship. Sadly, these lessons were forgotten and would have to be re-learned during World War Two. Publisher's collection.

Part II: Italian, British and French Airships of the US Navy, 1917-1922

Introduction

US Navy airship personnel trained in England, France and Italy during World War I, and airships were procured from each of these countries. All such airships were non-rigid except for the Italian O-1 and the later British rigid airship R-38 or Navy ZR-2. Information on the airships in this section was the most difficult to locate and may be questionable, as many details are lacking or not fully understandable. No American-built airships operated in Europe during World War I. During that war, the U.S. Navy established airship and kite balloon stations in Canada, Great Britain and France. The base in Canada was an observation or kite balloon station at Halifax, Nova Scotia. Bases in Great Britain at that time included a kite balloon station at Berehaven (Castletownbere), Ireland. Although operational in May 1918, the personnel were soon transferred to Brest, France. The station was re-established at Queenstown (Cobh), Ireland, in October 1918, and disestablished in February 1919. Although these were the only Naval Air Stations in Britain, US Navy, and later US Army, airship personnel trained at the Royal Naval Air Service/Royal Air Force stations at Cranwell and Howden, England, with kite balloon training at Roehampton.

In France, six bases were established as Naval Air Stations. Three stations, Brest, La Trinite and La Pallice, were for kite balloons. The kite balloon station at Brest was active throughout the war. Navy personnel arrived in November 1917 to establish the kite balloon and seaplane base at Brest. One balloon hangar is believed constructed by the U.S. Army Engineers. The kite balloon stations at La Trinte (operational 01 October 1918 and disestablished 05 February 1919) and La Pallice (never operational) saw very little service. Three stations, Paimboeuf, Guipavas and Gujan, were airship. Only Paimboeuf was active during the war as a U.S. Naval Air Station; Paimboeuf was the most active airship base in France. U.S. Navy crews trained in French airships beginning 30 November 1917. The first American patrols were made as early as 24 February 1918, prior to the 01 March 1918 commissioning of Paimboeuf as a U.S. Naval Air Station. Construction of the airship station at Guipavas was started 11 March 1918 and it became operational 11 November 1918. Gujan was established as an air station 03 February 1918; construction started 20 February, but it was never operational. An additional airship station was planned at Rochefort in France. It was never developed by the U.S. Navy, but was used by French naval airships.

Airship personnel (Army and Navy) also served in Italy at Ciampiano, near Rome, the major Italian Naval airship base. The U.S. Navy acquired one Italian airship, the O-1.

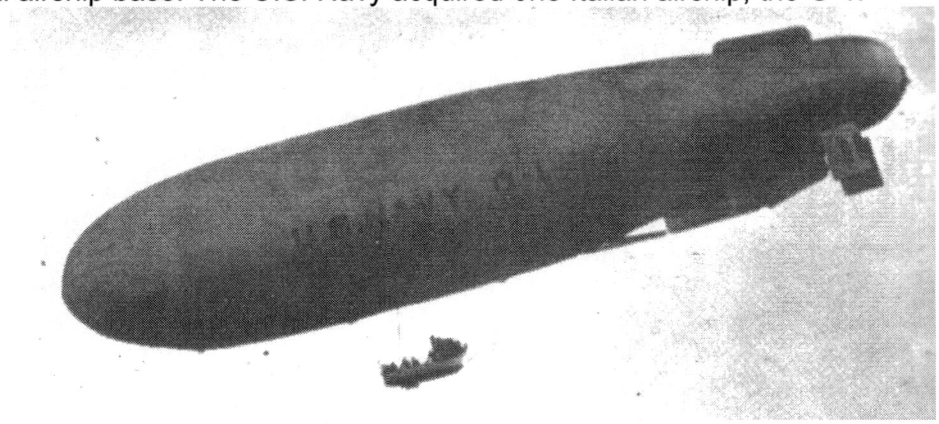

The US Navy O-1 in flight near NAS Norfolk, July 1921. NARHR. 229.7.21-1800.97/8

The Italian-built Semi-Rigid O-1. Hepburn Walker, Jr. Collection.

The O-1 Airship

The O-1 was the only semi-rigid airship to ever to serve with the Navy, and is the least known or photographed Navy airship. (Semi-rigid airships operated by the Army were the Italian-built *Roma* in 1921/1922 and the Goodyear RS-1 1926/1928). O-1 was built by Stabilmento Construzioni Dirigible de Aerstat (SCDA, more commonly known as S.C.A., Factory for Aeronautical Constructions) and was authorized for purchase by the Navy 17 January 1919. The O-1, serial no. 5587, was typical of the early Italian design, with a rigid keel that ran the length of the envelope. O-1 had a control car suspended a considerable distance from the envelope, and used box kite shaped tail surfaces. The O-1 envelope had five gas compartments, each with a ballonet. The control car was boat-shaped and open, with two engines on outriggers at the stern. The first flight was made at Ciampiano, Italy 27 March 1919. O-1 was shipped from Genoa, Italy, to Philadelphia, Pennsylvania, leaving 24 May 1919 and arriving 17 June. Sent to Akron for review, O-1 was then shipped to Cape May for erection under the direction of LT Raffe Emerson who had trained in Italy and qualified as Italian Dirigible Pilot No. 122. Assisting Emerson were Harry H. O'Claire of the Navy, two Italian Navy Officers (a LT and a Warrant Officer) who had accompanied the airship from Italy, and Italian-speaking U.S. Navy airshipmen. The 01 November 1919 Navy records indicate the unit cost for O-1 was $50,000. The first flight in the United States was 16 September 1919 at Cape May.

In the days before extreme sensitivity on the part of everyone, O-1 was referred to as the "Wop Ship." A flight from Cape May on 31 December 1919, with O'Claire and LTs Smith Bradford and Charles Bauch as crew, encountered thick fog and stiff head winds. O-1 was over Wilmington, DE when low fuel caused a return to Cape May. On approach for landing both engines failed. O-1 was free ballooned to an area near Pennsville, New Jersey, where gas was valved and a landing made in a peach orchard. Bauch and O'Claire swung out from the control car and caught the long handling lines. When low enough, the lines were secured to trees while LT Bradford valved the hydrogen gas. The landing was made about 01:00 on New Year's morning in bitter cold and snow. To keep warm, alcohol anti-freeze was mixed with coffee by the crew. LT Bradford scouted around and located a farmhouse. Making sure O-1 was secure, the crew went to the farmhouse and notified the commanding officer at Cape May and the local sheriff of the condition. O-1 was soon surrounded by spectators, who were requested to handle all lines (after some instruction). O-1 was moved into the open with the intention of returning to Cape May, however the request for fuel and hydrogen from Cape May was refused. LTs Bauch and

Bradford were ordered to return with O'Claire to deflate O-1. O'Claire utilized the inexperienced spectators to assist him and with great difficulty pulled the rip panels, completely deflated the bag. They removed the engines for return. A work party from Cape May arrived and instead of the railroad providing a flat car, a boxcar was sent. O'Claire was ordered to load O-1 in the boxcar, which made it necessary to break some of the keel girders. O-1 was shipped to the Camden, New Jersey Navy Dump for storage. Chief Bettio,[5] who assisted in the erection and spoke Italian, requested permission to repair and re-erect O-1. Permission was granted and O-1 was erected at Cape May. In June 1921, LT Ralph S. Barnaby, while on duty at the Naval Aircraft Factory as a project engineer, was ordered to temporary additional duty at Hampton Roads to carry out test flights on anti-aircraft target gliders he had designed and built. A mount and release mechanism was installed under the control car of O-1. During 06 to 09 July 1921 the gliders were taken aloft to approximately 3,000 feet over lower Chesapeake Bay and released. Pilots on these tests included LTs Erdman, McCallman and Johnson. Actual date of final deflation of O-1 is unknown, however it was probably late 1921 or early 1922.

O-1 Airship General Specifications:

Volume:	127,000 cubic feet
Overall length:	177.8 feet
Maximum diameter:	35.4 feet
Maximum speed:	56.6 miles per hour
Empty weight:	5,850 pounds
Gross lift:	9,120 pounds
Useful lift	3,290 pounds
Keel:	Articulated steel
Engines (2):	Colombo, 125 horsepower

The British Airships

(For R.38 / ZR-2, see pages 55-56.) In Great Britain, U.S. Navy crews served with British crews in training and on patrol. Near the conclusion of the war, the Navy apparently purchased three SST (Sea Scout, Twin), two SSZ (Sea Scout, Zero) and one NS (North Sea) type airships. No record of Navy service apparently exists on the three SST airships; although they are known to have been transferred, they may not have seen service with the Navy. They did serve with the Army, and may have been immediately transferred, explaining why no Navy records appear to have been maintained. The three SST-type airships transferred to the Navy were SST-9, SST-11 and SST-12. Completed by the British in October 1918, they were transferred in June 1919. In British service, SST-9 had flown 98 hours; SST-11, 38 hours and SST- 12, 39 hours. No Navy serial numbers were authorized, although purchased by the Navy as the only service operating airships at the time.

The Army trained airship personnel in England near the end of 1918; however, all airships were under Royal Air Force or US Navy control. The Navy acquired all ships, and after arrival in the United States, they were transferred to the Army in the 1919/1920 time frame. (This was the period that the Army trained in non-rigid airships and the Navy began concentrating on the rigid airship.) The only specific reference to a British SST identification is an "SST-3", which was probably a U.S. Navy designation for the third airship (SST-12). The SSZ airships were confused in Navy records and recorded as O-SS type airships. There were a total of 13 SST-types erected by the British during World War I. An additional 100 were under construction or on order when the Armistice was signed.

---

[5] Bettio would be lost in the attempt to rescue USS *Akron* survivors, see J-3.

SST Airships - In general, the SST-type airships were modified original World War I British non-rigid designated SS. The SST had a length of approximately 166 feet, a diameter of 35 feet and was powered by two Sunbeam 100 horsepower or two Rolls-Royce 75 horsepower pusher engines mounted at the stern of the control car. Envelope volume varied from 96,000 to 100,900 cubic feet. Top speed was about 60 mph.

In Army service, the SST-type airships were probably erected at Langley Field, VA. One airship assigned to the 8th Balloon Company of the First Surveillance Group based at Fort Bliss (Camp Owen Bierne / Biggs Field, El Paso), Texas, was for patrol of the Mexican border. One at Brooks Field (San Antonio), Texas, was for training. The three airships served at Langley Field, Biggs Field, Brooks Field and Scott Field, Illinois, and were in service until late 1923 or early 1924. New envelopes were provided by Goodyear in August of 1921 and identified as SST (Mullion) type (96,000 cubic feet, D-65, D-66 and D-67). The Mullion refers to the British airship station where they were originally designed and erected.

SSZ Airships - The two SSZ-type airships acquired from Britain were the SSZ-23, completed in January 1918, and SSZ-24, completed in November 1917. SSZ-23 was transferred to the U.S. Navy on 14 August 1918 (with 336 flight hours) and SSZ-24 in November 1918 (with unknown flight hours). Navy records indicate serial numbers A-1029 and A-1030 were assigned to these airships; A-1029 was later cancelled. SSZ-23 was originally assigned serial number A-1030 and SSZ-24 was assigned A-1029.

Specifications for the SSZ-type airship were similar to the general SS-type. It was about 143 feet in length, 27.75 feet in diameter, with a streamlined boat-shaped control car. Manned by a crew of three, they were powered by a single Rolls-Royce 75 horsepower pusher engine. The SSZ was the most numerous single type erected by the British during World War I. Seventy-seven were constructed by Armistice time, when fifteen were canceled. Fifty-three SSZ-types were in service in November 1918. In addition to the SSZ-23 and SSZ-24 transferred to the US, SSZ-21 and SSZ-22 were transferred to France. The 01 Nov 1919 Navy records indicate a cost of $55,000 for the SSZ-type.

SSZ-23 - based at East Fortune (Scotland), Cranwell, Howden, and the mooring-out station was at Lowthorpe (England). It was used for training US Navy crews and for patrol. It once made a non-stop flight of 26 hours. SSZ-23 had been sent to France for US Navy crew training. On 02 August 1918 it was approved for a training assignment to the Naval Air Station, Cape May, New Jesery. It was returned to Howden on 16 August 1918, SSZ-23 was in the process of having a new control car mated to the envelope in preparation for shipment to the United States. A fire occurred in the hangar when a technician switched on radio equipment and ignited the gasoline being used to clean the car. Airships lost in the fire were SSZ-23, SSZ-38, SSZ-54 and the rigid airship R.27.

Probably due to the lack of serial numbers, confusion exists for these airships. The three SST-types apparently never served as Navy airships. There was a change in serial numbers of the two SSZ airships, with a record of only one in service.

Information from the National Archives and the files of the Bureau of Construction and Repair states: "On 22 November 1917, designating numbers A-1029 were assigned to the British dirigible SSZ-24, and A-1030, to the second purchased British dirigible SSZ-23. Dirigible A-1029 arrived at the New York Navy Yard about 01 March 1918, and then was shipped to Akron about 15 March for tests by the Goodyear company. Subsequently, A-1029 arrived at Hampton Roads, Va., during June 1918, the dirigible having been shipped from Baltimore. SSZ-23, which was A-1030, had been sent to France for the purpose of training Navy pilots. On 02 August 1918, the Navy approved the consignment of this dirigible to Cape May, New Jersey, but the exact date of its arrival is not known. The Navy's Memorandum of 24 December 1919 states that on 05 February 'All parts for dirigible A-1029 were shipped to Cape May on same date for use in erection of dirigible SSZ-23.' A bottom note on the memorandum states: 'It is evident that the SSZ-23 Dirigible is really A-1030, which has been given the designating number A-5563'". Another interpretation of the British SSZ-23 and SSZ-24 is that SSZ-24 was cannibalized for spare parts and used in the erection of SSZ-23 at Cape May. This could possibly answer the question of canceled serial number A-1029.

<u>SSZ-24</u> - (Navy serial A-1029) acquired by the Navy 22 November 1917, received at the New York Navy yard in March 1918, then shipped to Akron for Navy/Goodyear tests about 15 March 1918, first flight 6 April 1918. Deflated and damaged in handling, repaired and test flown 8 May 18, "awaiting orders" on 25 May. Shipped to Naval Air Station, Hampton Roads (Norfolk), Virginia, there appears to be no record that SSZ-24 was flown at Hampton Roads. There is a report that an O-SS (SSZ) was destroyed by fire at Hampton Roads in the summer of 1918. It is therefore reasonable that this was the SSZ-24. This explains why no flights appear in the record and the serial number A-1029 canceled. There are no records of any flights of SSZ-24 in England; there is some question that it may have been sent to France. This appears unlikely as it was acquired on 22 November 1917 and arrived in New York on 15 March 1918. Considering the time involved in packing, shipping, arranging for transportation during wartime, etc., a period of less than three months is highly conceivable.

<u>SSZ-23(2)</u> - Original Navy serial A-1030 (later A-5563) was completed in January 1918 (after SSZ-24). It is shown in British logs as "USA" and SSZ-23 in March 1918. Previous to this time, it was based at Cranwell for training, then assigned to patrol activities from Howden until 18 May, and then to the mooring-out station at Lowthorpe. Patrol flights from Howden included eight in March, seven in April and nine in May. Significant flights that occurred from Howden included the sighting of a sinking British submarine on 05 April. SSZ-23 intercepted a destroyer, which rescued the survivors. (This may have been the event that prompted the award of the British Distinguished Flying Cross[6] to ENS Phillip Barnes by King George V. Barnes also achieved an endurance record flight of 30 hours, 18 minutes in 1918.) At Lowthorpe, ten flights were made in May, seven in June, five in July and two in August. On 14 August SSZ-23 was returned to Howden where it was in the rebuilding process when the fire of 16 August occurred.[7]

<u>SSZ-23</u> Acquired on the same date of 22 November 1917, its exact date of arrival in the US is unknown. It is known to have been at Cape May for erection on 05 February 1919 and was in

---

[6] ENS N.J. Learned was also awarded the British Distinguished Flying Cross by King George V for attacking a U-Boat. At the time, Learned was apparently in command of the British SSZ-29 based at Capel near Folkestone, England.

[7] Wingfoot Lighter-Than-Air Society BULLETIN, Vol. 16, No. 7, page 8, May 1969; statements by Zenon Hansen on the serial numbers for the SSZ airships.

service there in April 1919. By 18 June 1920, the envelope was declared unfit for further use and SSZ-23 was stricken. Some records refer to the airship as Z-2 with Navy envelope E-53. North Sea Airships - The NS-type airship was the largest non-rigid erected by the British, with a volume of 360,000 cubic feet for the tri-lobe Astra-Torres type envelope. Its length was 262 feet, the maximum diameter was 56.75 feet, and it was 69.25 feet in height. Two Rolls-Royce 250 horsepower engines powered separate engine cars. The forward control car was 35 feet in length and 6 feet in height. It was totally enclosed for a crew of ten and had sleeping accommodations for four. The control car was connected to the engine cars by a wooden gangway supported by cables from the envelope. The designed endurance was 21 hours at 57.5 mph. NS-11 set a record of 101 hours in the air, covering 4,000 non-stop miles in 1919. A total of seven North Sea types were constructed; one was canceled. There were six of the type in service in November 1918. U.S. Navy records of 01 November 1919 indicate only one NS-type was acquired, at a cost of $100,000. Both U.S. Navy and U.S. Army officers were trained in the North Sea airships in 1919. Training was conducted in the NS-7, NS-8 and NS-11 at Howden, England as well as Longside and East Fortune, Scotland.

Navy records indicate the one North Sea type airship was assigned serial number A-5580. Records indicate that the airship was the NS-1; this is in error, as the actual airship transferred was the NS-14. It made its first flight 02 February 1917 at Kingsnorth, England. NS-14 also was in service at Pulham. It was dismantled 22 February 1918 after accumulating 206 hours of flight time. NS-14 was sold to the Navy and transferred 8 November 1918. It was shipped to Wingfoot Lake 22 April 1919, arriving 17 May. NS-14 was then shipped to Hampton Roads (Norfolk, Virginia) on 13 December 1919 and received 30 January 1920. No records could be located of flights in the United States.

Research of British non-rigid airships during World War I indicates that approximately 214 various types were erected, 26 were rebuilt and 27 were transferred to Allies (France, Italy, Russia and the United States). 103 airships were in service 01 November 1918. An interesting facet on the British airships includes the surplus balloons, airships, gas plants and hangars allotted to Canada. By February 1920, only 12 airships, 6 kite balloons, silical generating plants and hangars were available, but selection had to be made at once to save them from disposal. The Canadian Air Board accepted all available Coastal Star, SST, SSZ, kite balloons and hangars. In February 1921, four SS with 100% spares and three SST with 80% spares were received at Camp Borden, Ontario (northeast of Toronto). Many of the envelopes were received in poor condition due to the packing method and shipping. No satisfactory area was available to dry the wet envelopes for inflation. Airships were offered, at no charge, to lumber companies. After a study of operating costs, the Keewatin Lumber Company in northwestern Ontario agreed to the use of airships for timber cruising and forest inventory. Hangars were to be erected at Fort Francis and Kenora. One airship was rigged; the need for skilled men for rigging, envelope repair and engine overhaul held up any actual flying. Before proper arrangements could be made, the time had passed for the airships to demonstrate their capability.

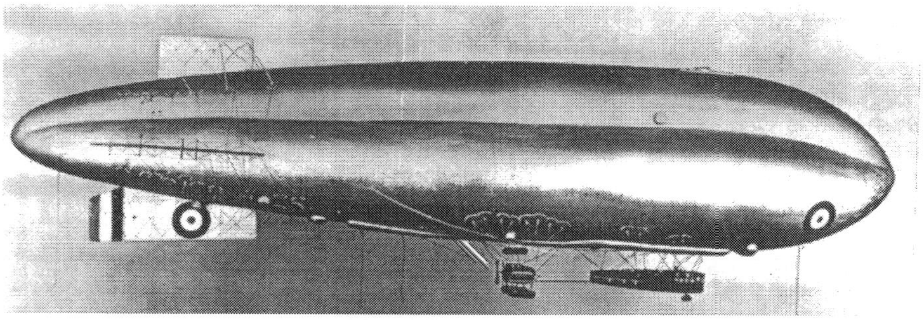

Artist's concept of NS airship. Author's collection.

The French Airships

Information on the French-built airships in US Navy service is sketchier than that for the British-built airships, so accuracy of the following is not guaranteed. In addition to the airship type designations (AT for Astra-Torres, Z for Zodiac and CM for Chalais Meudon), most of those assigned to Paimboeuf were also given a "P" number (which is shown in parentheses). Apparently, the French airships flown in France and then transferred, assigned or ordered were the following: AT-1(P-1), AT-13 (P-4), AT-17, AT-18, T-2 (*Capitaine Caussin*), CM-5, CM-6, VZ-3 (P-2 was in US service but returned to the French prior to the armistice), VZ-7 (P-3), VZ-13 (P-5) (there is some confusion on the VZ-type as there are also references to a VZ-8, ZDUS-1, ZDUS-2 and ZDUS-3. This totals thirteen airships of French design. Six of these were actually received in the United States by the Navy, and assigned serial numbers. The CM-5 was sold to Goodyear for proposed passenger and mail flights between Akron and Detroit. Records indicate that the majority of the airships shipped from France were received in poor condition. This was probably due to inadequate packing and shipping. The effects of salt water on components (rubberized cotton envelopes, varnished wood in control cars, untreated metal parts not corrosion resistant, etc.) were not checked as the airships remained in their packing crates for long periods of time.

AT-1 - Transferred to Paimboeuf on 30 January 1918. Assigned to US Navy 01 March 1918, the date when Paimboeuf was designated a U.S. Naval Air Station. AT-1 made its first flight under American control on 03 March. On 27 April 1918, commanded by LT F. P. Culbert, with a crew that included ENSs M. P. Delano, A. D. Brewer and T. E. McCracken, AT-1 completed a 25 hour, 43 minute flight out of Paimboeuf during which they escorted three convoys through a mined zone. This was the longest flight then on record. The crew was officially commended by the French Minister of Marine. On 17 August 1918, Assistant Secretary of the Navy Franklin D. Roosevelt, on a tour of overseas facilities, was a passenger on AT-1. It was deflated for shipment to the U.S. on 10 September 1918. Assigned serial number 5472 and stored at the Naval Aircraft Factory at Philadelphia, AT-1 was recommended for striking 08 May 1920 and stricken on 17 July 1920. Flights in the US, if any, are unrecorded.

AT-1 had the standard tri-lobe Astra-Torres type envelope with a volume of approximately 212,000 cubic feet. It was 223 feet in length, had a 47.4-foot maximum diameter and was 64 feet in height. AT-1 had two engines.

AT-13 (P4) - Flown from Paris to Paimboeuf on 30 August 1918. On 01 October, AT-13 flew patrol for one convoy, then changed course to patrol for another convoy. Two shots were fired at a rock for target practice from the onboard 47 mm cannon. On the second shot the firing spring broke, putting the gun out of action. At about 2:30 PM the new convoy was met and AT-13 circled overhead. With two storms approaching, AT-13 took a heading to pass between the two convoys when a suspicious object was sighted and investigated. While a mile away, it was made out to be a submarine which opened fire on the AT-13. Thirteen shells were fired from the submarine, but with the 47mm cannon out of action, fire from the AT-13 could not be returned. The submarine was pursued and a position taken for a bombing run, but the wind proved too strong to overtake the submarine. The convoy was notified of the submarine in the area, and AT-13 continued the chase until the sub escaped due to the darkness. It is possible the submarine was actually British. (On 15 March a French airship had sunk the British submarine D-3 due to a recognition-signal error.) 200 hours and 30 minutes were flown by AT-13 to October 1918. On 13 December, AT-13 (with *Capitaine Caussin*) flew as an escort for President Wilson aboard the USS *George Washington* from England to Brest.

One personal account regarding AT-13 that came to attention was that a spare firing spring for the 47mm cannon was available but was dropped overboard in the excitement. Not all of those aboard believed there was a submarine in the area as visibility was poor and a strong tide was striking rocks and shoals. Some thought that the waves and spray breaking over a rock may have been mistaken for gunfire and, as the rock became covered with water, it would appear the submarine had submerged. It is reported that further investigation of German records showed that no U-boat reported such an encounter. The only U-boat that did not report on 1 October 1918, and could possibly have been in the area, was commanded by an experienced captain that would not have likely been in a rocks and shoals area attempting to repel an airship. Eighty some years after the incident, this statement seems more realistic.

AT-13 (above) was deflated at Paimboeuf on 16 December 1918 and shipped to the U.S. on 26 January 1919. Although it served as a US Navy airship, it was never assigned a serial number. It was stored at the Hampton Virgina Supply Station, shown as "scheduled for sale" and stricken 22 October 1920. The AT-13 was approximately 293,000 cubic feet in volume.[8]

AT-17 - This was a sister ship to AT-18 and was still it the factory at Armistice time, with delivery promised for December. It was apparently completed, transferred to the Navy and shipped to the United States. Moved to Wingfoot Lake, it was transferred to the Army at Langley Field 22 October 1919. There is no record of a Navy serial number or service with the Army.

AT-18 - This airship was still at the factory at the Armistice, with delivery promised for 01 January 1919. Apparently cancelled by the US Navy, it May have served with the French Navy with a new envelope and engines as the *Escourteur* E-5 (or E-6) until 1936. The 01 November 1919 Navy records indicate only one AT-type in inventory, at a unit cost of $80,000.

T-2 (*Capitaine Caussin*) - was flown from Paris to Paimboeuf on 18 April 1918. A twin-engine airship of approximately 335,000 cubic feet volume, it was used for training US Navy crews at Paimboeuf and Guipavas. On 25 April, after losing pressure due to a stuck hydrogen valve, T-2

[8] Wingfoot LTAS BULLETIN, Vol.12, No. 7, page 6, May, 1965 (AT-18) - Comments by Don Woodward agreement with R.K. Smith (12/3/7) on AT-1, AT-13 and the three Zodiac airships.

struck the water and two men were thrown into the sea. CDR Lewis Maxfield swam to the rescue of the two men, and T-2 drifted ashore. Maxfield was recommended for a gold life-saving medal. T-2 was repaired and reinflated 26 July. It was not officially turned over to the Navy until 23 November 1919. With AT-13, it flew as an escort for President Wilson aboard the USS *George Washington* from England to Brest on 13 December 1918. It was deflated at Guipavas on 14 December 1918, shipped to the US on 13 January 1919 and was in storage at Hampton Roads in mid-1919. There is no record of a Navy serial number or flights in the US.[9]

CM-5 - was a twin-engine airship of approximately 320,550 cubic feet. CM-5 was 262.5 feet in length, 45.7 feet maximum diameter, and had a control car 52.5 feet length. CM-5 was powered by two 230 horsepower Salmson radial engines. At the factory at the time of the Armistice, it was promised for January 1919. This airship was apparently accepted by the Navy. The components were scheduled to arrive in New York from France in May 1919. Sold to Goodyear in 1920, they planned on using the airship for daily eight hour round trips between Akron and Detroit. Service was scheduled to start September 1920. Due to economics, CM-5 was never erected. A power car of CM-5 was stored at Wingfoot Lake until donated to the Connecticut Aeronautical Historical Association at Windsor Locks, Connecticut (now the New England Air Museum) in August 1980. There is no record of a Navy serial number or flights in the US. [10]

CM-6 - Sister ship of CM-5, at the factory at the time of the Armistice with delivery promised for February 1919. Apparently canceled, there is no record of flights or Navy serial number.

VZ -7 (P-3) Delivered to Paimboeuf on 08 June 1918, Vedette Zodiac-7 was twin-engined, with a volume of approximately 99,000 cubic feet. It made seventeen flights totaling 164 hours, 55 minutes to 18 August. It flew seventy-one additional hours by 18 September. Assigned serial number 5592, it was shipped to the Naval Operating Base at Norfolk early in 1919, then to Coco Solo, Panama, on 24 July 1919. Reported in poor condition 27 August at Coco Solo, it was stricken 30 October 1919.[11]

VZ-13 (P-5) - Some sources identify this airship as VZ-2, which May be a designation applied to the airship by the Navy as the second VZ-type received (VZ-8 is shown as VZ-1). Delivered to Paimboeuf 25 October 1918, it flew every day until 05 November when it was deflated for shipment to the US. Shipped to Norfolk (with VZ-7) early in 1919, it was assigned serial number 5593. Then shipped to Coco Solo, it was regarded in poor condition and stricken about October 1919.

VZ-3 (P-2) was transferred to the U.S. Navy at Paimboeuf on 20 March 1918; however, it was transferred back to the French on 26 September 1918.

---

[9] Wingfoot LTAS BULLETIN, Vol.12, No.3, page 7, January, 1963, "An Inventory of Navy Pressure Airships, 1916-1941", by Richard K. Smith. In several instances T-2 and *Capitaine Caussin* were considered two airships, when in fact they were the same airship. Wingfoot LTAS BULLETIN, Vol 12, No. 7, Pg.6 May 1965 (T-2) - Comments by Lord Ventry, statements on ZDUS-1, CM-5 control car, T-2 and *Capitaine Caussin* were the same airship. VZ-3 also appears as a change from the original AN INVENTORY OF U.S. NAVY PRESSURE AIRSHIPS by the same author. There is also some confusion regarding the designation of VZ-7 as VZ-8.

[10] CM-5, THE GOODYEAR AIRSHIP, by Zenon Hanson. Following the Armistice, there were rumors that Assistant Secretary of the Navy, F.D. Roosevelt, allegedly made a statement after the sale similar to "Thank God, we got rid of another one," or words to that effect. Hearsay only, but sounds reasonable to this author.

[11] There is some confusion on this airship. Some records indicate it was VZ-8; it May have been designated VZ-1 by the Navy after its transfer to the US.

The French Zodiac ZD-1 / ARMY ZDUS-1/RN-1 transferred to the Army and shown in flight at Langley field, 15 April 1920. USAF 5525-AS

ZDUS-1 (also designated ZD-1 and RN-1) - This Zodiac airship (along with ZDUS-2 and ZDUS-3) was ordered 05 June 1918. ZDUS-1 made its first flight at St. Cyr, France, in the spring of 1919. It was shipped to the United States sometime in 1919. A Navy serial number was not assigned; apparently, no Navy flights were made by this airship. Transferred to the US Army 14 October 1919 at a cost of $100,000, ZDUS-1 was erected at Langley Field, Virginia. RN-1 was the final Army designation for this airship, which served at Langley Field, as well as Scott Field, Illinois. At Langley Field on 11 September 1920, RN-1, with the Army A-4 and (former Navy) C-2, flew in formation to demonstrate the first direction of aircraft by radio. As an Army airship, it made many "cross-country" flights in the vicinity of Langley Field. These included flights to Richmond, Virgina on 29 September 1920 and a flight of 159 miles to Washington, D.C. on 12 October. RN-1 also participated in the Mitchell bombing tests in 1921 as an observer platform. A flight to sea as part of an aerial salute was made to greet President Harding on his return from France aboard the *Pastores* in 1921.

RN-1 was rebuilt at Scott Field in 1923 with new control surfaces. A new envelope increased the volume from 326,500 to 340,000 cubic feet. The two 250 horsepower Renault pusher engines were replaced by American Liberty engines during the rebuild. In November 1923, the Army made a study for an RN-1 flight to Panama, but it never took place. RN-1 was placed in storage at Scott Field in 1924. RN-1 was the largest non-rigid airship by volume in US service after World War I and up until the 349,000 cubic foot TC-13 of 1933. Its length was 264 feet; it had an envelope diameter of 49.5 feet and a height of 65.7 feet. (It exceeded the later TC-13 in length, but not in diameter and height.) The French had equipped the large, eight-man control car with a 75 mm gun firing a 13-pound shell; however, it was not remounted in the US.

ZDUS-2 (ZD-2) - This airship was a sister ship to the ZDUS-1 and was apparently completed in February 1919 and shipped to the United States. No other details are known, except that it was in storage at the Fleet Supply Base at Norfolk sometime in 1919.

ZDUS-3 (ZD-3) - Also a sister ship to the ZDUS-1; believed completed in March 1919 but later canceled.

There are Army references to ZD-1 through ZD-5, however, ZD-1 through ZD-3 shown as ZDUS-1 through ZDUS-3, is incorrect. ZD-1 through ZD-3 (and ZD-4 and a ZD-5) were ordered for a French Navy program in October, 1916, with service planned for late 1917 or early 1918. These airships had no connection with ZDUS-1 through ZDUS-3 which were ordered by the US Navy. All of the ZD-types were built by Zodiac and were approximately the same design.

Summary of French airships flown, assigned or transferred to the Navy (Based on best available information):

Total airships ordered, transferred or assigned	13
(AT-1, AT-13, AT-17, AT-18, T-2, CM-5, CM-6, VZ-3, VZ-7, VZ-13, ZDUS-1, ZDUS-2 and ZDUS-3.)	
Confirmed shipment to the United States	8
(AT-1, AT-13, AT-17, CM-5, VZ-7, VZ-13, ZDUS-1 and ZDUS-2.)	
Returned to France prior to the Armistice	1
(VZ-3)	
Believed cancelled	3
(AT-18, CM-6, ZDUS-3.)	
Actually transferred and assigned serial numbers	3
(AT-1 [5472], VZ-7 [5592] and VZ-13 [5593].)	
Transferred from the Navy	4
(To the Army AT-17, ZDUS-1, ZDUS-2; To Goodyear CM-5.)	
Known to have been flown in the United States	1
(ZDUS-1 / RN-1)	

The British North Sea type airship set a flight endurance record for non-rigids. Walter Swistak.

Part III: Rigid and Metalclad Airships

The "spotlighted" USS *Akron* (ZRS-4) emerges from NAS Lakehurst hangar number one while USS *Los Angeles* (ZR-3) remains docked. Tupper photo from the collection of Hepburn Walker, Jr.

Introduction

The original proposal for a U.S. Navy rigid airship was made in 1913. This proposal was based on a French report of a German Army Zeppelin (Z IV) that made a forced landing in France in April, 1913. The landing allowed the French to examine and record information which was made available to the U.S. The Navy General Board determined an airship had value for the fleet and steps were taken in 1916 to obtain an airship to be built by the Vickers group in England. Britain, then involved in World War I, had no choice but to deny the request. In 1917, lacking experience in the design of a rigid airship, the Joint Army-Navy Board created an American design organization supported by both Army and Navy funds. This organization became the responsibility of the Navy Department. A design designated DR-1, based on the German Schutte-Lanz wooden rigid airships, was reviewed in December 1917. Although there were many American innovations in the design, no more than a test section was constructed in a shipyard. It was not until July, 1919, that funds were approved for the construction of a hangar (Lakehurst, New Jersey) for two large airships, and the purchase of one rigid airship in England (ZR-2) and the construction of one (ZR-1) in the United States.

Numerous articles and books[12] have been written on the rigid airships as well as the unique ZMC-2. No attempt is made to reproduce all the information available in these many sources. Since the metalclad airship was unique in the Navy, its classification as a rigid is controversial. The ZMC-2 is known to have flown on at least two occasions at twenty knots without ballonet air pressure. These flights would indicate that it was a "rigid" airship, at least at low speeds. Discussions continue as to class the ZMC-2 as a "rigid" (it had internal rings) or as a "non-rigid" (the form was maintained by gas and air pressure).

[12] There are many sources on these airships. The most complete with greater detail (and used as a reference) are:
Douglas H. Robinson and Charles L. Keller, "Up Ship": U.S. Navy Rigid Airships 1919-1935, Annapolis: Naval Institute Press, 1982.
Richard K. Smith, "The Airships *Akron* and *Macon*: Flying Aircraft Carriers of the U.S. Navy," Annapolis: U.S. Naval Institute, 1965.

The ZR-1, USS *Shenandoah*

The ZR-1 was an American design that, lacking actual experience, was based on foreign practice. Patterned on plans made available to the Allied powers following the French capture of the German Zeppelin L49 in October 1917, it was influenced by an investigation of post-World War I Zeppelins and observation of British construction methods. The Aluminum Company of America was tasked to reverse engineer "airship metal" only from samples of L49 and patent information. Packard manufactured the first engines. It was determined, in 1919, that the structure would be fabricated at the Naval Aircraft Factory in Philadelphia, with final assembly at a new hangar to be erected at Lakehurst, New Jersey. The design was started in September 1919, and after several alternate proposals, assembly was started at Lakehurst in April 1922. CDR Ralph Weyerbacher, USN Bureau of Construction & Repair, was superintendent of construction. ZR-1 was completed 20 August 20 1923. She was christened by the wife of Secretary of the Navy Edwin H. Denby, its name said to mean "Daughter of the Stars." ZR-1 made its first flight 04 September 1923 and was commissioned on 10 October. The cost of ZR-1 was $1,500,000.

The first American built rigid airship was experimental. ZR-1 provided training and operating experience for those involved in a new and unfamiliar field. Her design dated to hydrogen inflation, but she was always inflated with helium; she was the first rigid airship to learn the restrictions imposed by helium lifting gas. Her first commanding officer was CDR Frank McCrary, though actual flight commands were given by the hired "airship test pilot" ex-Zeppelin commander Anton Heinen. ZR-1 operated from Lakehurst and was flown primarily along the East coast, although within five weeks it visited the National Air Races at St. Louis. One incident that attracted wide attention happened on 16 January 1924 when winds that reached over 70 miles-per-hour blew the ship from the tower mast at Lakehurst. The mooring fitting was torn from the bow, leaving a gaping hole, deflating the two forward cells. The upper fin was also heavily damaged. With skillful handling by the partial crew under Heinen aboard at the time, ZR-1 rode out the storm making a circuitous route to be landed at Lakehurst. She was repaired with a strengthened bow. McCrary was relieved by LCDR Zachary Landsdowne, who flew combat missions in European airships and flew on British rigids.

The Lakehurst Engineering Department fitted various experimental engine exhaust water recovery radiator configurations to help eliminate the need to vent precious helium gas after burning off gasoline weight. ZR-1 provided a platform for parachute jumpers from the Lakehurst-based rigger's school. In August 1924, ZR-1 became the first airship to moor to a mast aboard a ship at sea, the oiler converted to airship tender, USS *Patoka* (AO-9/AV-6). The most famous flight of the ZR-1 was a "rim flight" trans-continental trip that started on 06 October 1924, from Lakehurst with stops at temporary high-mast mooring facilities at Fort Worth, Texas, San Diego (North Island), California, and Camp Lewis (Tacoma), Washington. ZR-1 returned to Lakehurst on 25 October demonstrating the ability to operate from her main base and established a record longest journey made by an airship. On return, the ZR-1 helium was transferred to the USS *Los Angeles,* and ZR-1 was suspended and shored up for extensive overhaul.

The sixth engine was removed from the forward car. Radio equipment and a two-burner galley were installed in place of the engine. To prevent helium leakage in excess of allotment, covers were fabricated to seal a number of the helium cell emergency valves. It was not until June 1925 that ZR-1 was re-inflated with the limited amount of helium then available. Flights along the east coast and maneuvers with the fleet were conducted, including scout operations with the battleship USS *Texas*. Additional moorings to the *Patoka* were conducted through July and August 1925. On 02 September 1925, ZR-1 departed on a flight that was to include the mid-west and cover almost 1,330 miles culminating in a mooring to the new tower mast erected by Henry Ford at Dearborn, Michigan. In the early morning of 03 September, ZR-1 entered a storm over southern Ohio, whose violent updrafts carried the airship beyond pressure height, expanding her gas cells, followed by structural failure. The bow section was free-ballooned to safety near Sharon, but the control car and two engine cars broke free, carrying their occupants to their deaths. The mid and stern sections settled near Ava, Ohio. Of the forty-three aboard, fourteen men died and twenty-nine survived. Those lost were:
LCDR Zackery Lansdowne; LCDR Lewis Hancock, Jr.; LT John B. Lawrence; LT A. Reginald Hougton; LTJG E. W. Sheppard; Riggers CPO Everett P. Allen; James W. Cullinan; Pilot 1/c Ralph T. Joffray; Machinists CPO Charles H. Broom; 1/c Celestine P. Mazzuco; 1/c James A Moore; 1/c Bart B. O'Sullivan; 1/c William H. Spratley; and Chief Radioman George Schnitzer.

ZR-1 was formally stricken on 05 September 1925. During its life, ZR-1 had made fifty-nine flights for a total of 740 flying hours.

Basic characteristics of ZR-1 (after May 22, 1924):

Hull air displacement:	2,289,861 cubic feet
Gas cell (20) volume:	2,115,174 cu. ft.
Length:	682 feet
Maximum diameter:	78 feet, 9 inches
Speed/endurance:	51 knots, 2,250 miles, 50 hours; 54 total, 40 flight
Total Weight:	41 tons

Control car of the ZR-1. Design closely resembles the German Zeppelin L49, captured intact by the French in World War I. Later this engine was removed and radio equipment installed.
US Navy photo.

R.38 aloft showing US Navy markings. US Navy photo.

The ZR-2 (British-built R.38)

The Navy's first rigid airship proposal made in 1913 gained greater interest as the result of Zeppelin achievements during World War I. The British rigids were completed too late in the war to have a major effect, since the war was over in November 1918. Since a Zeppelin was unavailable to the US, the choice was obviously limited to a British airship. The purchase of a ship abroad was authorized In July 1919.

R.38 was designed in August/September, 1918, ordered in September, and was built by Short Brothers (Royal Airship Works in 1920) at Cardington, Bedfordshire. Construction was started in February 1919, and the sale to the United States was approved 09 October 1919. The U.S. agreement for purchase was on 23 October. R.38 was completed on 07 June 1921, and made its first flight at Cardington on 23 June. Although it was never christened or commissioned, it was decorated with American markings and American crews were trained aboard to fly it to the U.S. Later based at the British airship base at Howden, Yorkshire, it made its fourth and last flight on 23 August.

During tests of high-speed turning, the ZR-2 structure failed and she broke into two pieces. The forward section fell into the River Humber; fire and smoke appeared as gasoline spread on the water. This was followed by two explosions. (The official accident report held gasoline fire on the water as the major cause of lives lost, and led to the adoption of diesel fuel for later British rigid airships.) The broken stern did not catch fire and settled on a sand bar in shallow water.

There were forty-nine men aboard (thirty-two British and seventeen American) but only five survivors. Of the survivors, four were British and one American (Rigger Norman Walker). The British lost many experienced airshipmen, but they still had a cadre of others. The US Navy loss was not only tragic but also devastating to the program, having claimed the most trained and qualified rigid airshipmen.

A plaque hanging in the Royal Aeronautical Society lists the following names:

(British Officers and other ranks) Air Commodore E M Maitland; Flight Lieutenants – I C Little, R S Montague, J E M Pritchard, G M Thomas; Flying Officers – T F Matthewson, V H Wicks; Flight Sergeants – W H Greener, S J Heath, A T Martin, J Rye, F Smith, H Thompson; Sergeants – F E Burton, J W A Mason; Leading Aircraftsman – G S Anger, W Oliver, J N Wilson; Aircraftsman 1st Class – C W Donald, J C Drew, C W Penson, E E Steere; Aircraftsman 2nd class – R Parker, R Withington; Civilians – C I R Campbell, F Warren, C W Duffield, J R Pannell.

(American Officers and other ranks) Cmdr L H Maxfield; Lieutenant Commanders – V. N. Beig, E. W. Coll; Lieutenants – M. H. Esterley, H. H. Hoyt, C. G. Little; Chief Machinists Mates – R. M. Coons, L. E. Crowl, J. T. Hancock, W. Julius, A. L. Loftin, W. J. Steele, G. Welch; Chief Riggers – C. I. Aller, M. Lay, A. D. Pettit.

ZR-2 made only four flights totaling 57.35 hours. Contract cost to the U.S. was $1,920,000 plus spare parts. The contract had stipulated one-quarter of the final payment would be due on acceptance, which did not occur. The ZR-2 experience eventually cost the Navy $982,000, which included crew training.

Basic characteristics, R.38/ZR-2:

Hull air displacement:	2,960,000
Gas cell volume	2,724,000
Length:	699 feet
Total height:	92 ft.
Maximum diameter:	85 ft. 6 in.
Maximum /normal speed: mph	71 / 67
Cruising speed/endurance: miles	45 mph / 9470
Crew (flight):	30
Static ceiling:	21,900 ft.

The ZR-2 control car (above) was small in relation to the other rigid airships. Under construction at Cardington, 1920, (below) shows the R.37 framework to the right of the nearly complete R.38. Author's collection.

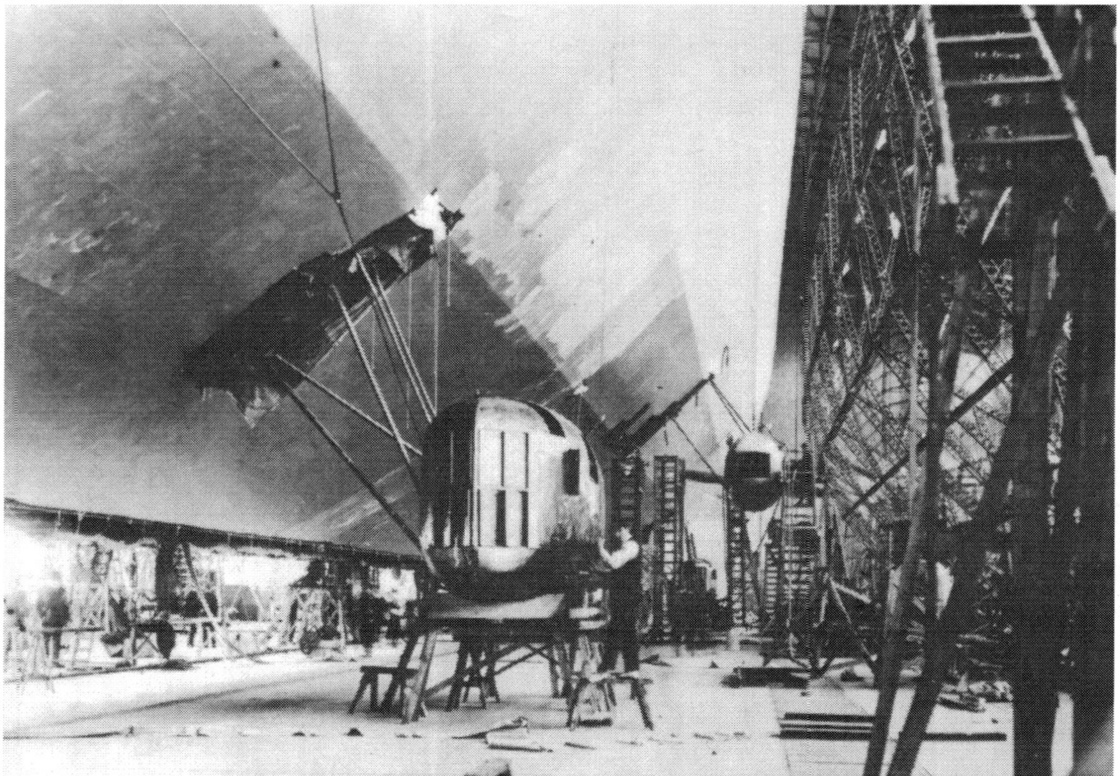

The ZR-3, USS *Los Angeles*

The ZR-3 was designed and built by the Zeppelin Company in Friedrichshafen, Germany, as build number LZ-126. The interest in obtaining a rigid airship for the Navy was expressed in 1919, but due to the destruction of seven surviving German naval Zeppelins (two were originally designated for the US) in June1919, efforts were fruitless. The refusal of the US Senate to ratify the Versailles Treaty, also signed in June 1919, and the fact that the US did not sign a peace agreement with Germany until October, 1921, further complicated matters.

ZR-3 returns from a local flight for the Siamiese Royal party. Hepburn Walker, Jr.

The U.S. Army Air Service made the first overtures to acquire a Zeppelin as the Great War ended. It had been established in July 1918, that the Navy would be responsible for rigid airships and the Army for semi- and non-rigids. The Army's efforts were halted, and they turned their attention to acquire a semi-rigid in Italy. To obtain a Zeppelin it was necessary to overcome certain provisions of the Versailles Treaty. Also to overcome were the Inter-Allied Aeronautical Commission of Control, and the British and French that desired to build rigid airships but did not have the proven design, building or operating experience of the Germans. The loss of the British-built R.38 (ZR-2) in August 1921, was instrumental in swaying approval of the British. To satisfy requirements of the Versailles Treaty, specifically that Germany was not permitted to build any "war materials," the LZ-126 was to be "non-military" with a mission limited to "civil" purposes. A contract for the LZ-126 was signed in June 1922. Design and construction was hampered by the reluctance of some in the Zeppelin organization to share design details with the Americans. This was overcome when the Zeppelin Company was reminded that it was the US Navy's desire for a rigid airship that saved the company from the destruction of their facilities at Friedrichshafen, which had been one of the intentions of the Versailles Treaty. With this is mind, Zeppelin management expended every effort to make LZ-126 the best rigid ever built to that time, while providing prestige and confidence to the German people. They were very successful on all counts.

Construction of LZ-126 was started in June, 1922. Engine design and procurement were not finalized until August, 1924, and the first flight was made 27 August 1924. Five flights were made over Germany and Switzerland, the last flight lasting almost thirty-four hours with seventy-one persons aboard. Although often referred to as a "reparations airship," it was considered "compensation" for the two Zeppelins intended for the U.S. but destroyed in June 1919. Cost to the German government was $713,332 and to the U.S. government, $150,000 including three months training for American crews at Lakehurst, as well as spare engines. LZ-126 departed Friedrichshafen for the crossing to the U.S. on 12 October 1924. The crew was twenty-seven with three U.S. Navy and one Army Air Service observers aboard. On October 15, LZ-126 landed at Lakehurst and entered the hangar to become the ZR-3.

With the ZR-3 safely in the hangar at Lakehurst, the airship was shored up from below and suspended from the hangar roof. Hydrogen was vented from the gas cells, but there was a problem. The ZR-1 was returning from the trans-continental flight and there was not enough helium available for ZR-3. Helium was transferred when ZR-1 returned and the first American flight was made on 25 October 1924, when she flew to Washington, D.C., to be christened (by the wife of President Calvin Coolidge) USS *Los Angeles*.

From christening onward, many refinements were made; she began a long career of training and experimental flights. She practiced mooring to the tower mast at Lakehurst and on 15 January 1925, made the first of many moorings to the mast aboard the surface ship USS *Patoka*. She made many flights along the Atlantic seaboard and to the Caribbean and Panama and portions of the mid-west states as far west as Minneapolis, Minnesota. In June, 1925, the helium in the gas cells was transferred back to the ZR-1 for what proved to be ZR-1's last flight.

ZR-3 resumed flights in April, 1926, under the command of CDR George Steele, then LCDR Charles E. Rosendahl. Many at-the-time exceptional flights were made for calibrating radio stations as well as publicity flights to foster interest in rigid airships. On the ground, she was used in the development of the low stub mooring mast and new handling equipment. On 15 October 1926, she moored to the tower mast erected by Henry Ford at Dearborn, Michigan.

One event of particular interest occurred 25 August 1927. Moored to the tower mast at Lakehurst with only a watch crew on duty, a sudden sea breeze lifted the stern and before corrective action could be taken, ZR-3 did a "nose-stand" at the mast. A complete revolution was made from the original position to a directly opposite position. Damage was minimal, but photographs of the incident did not appear in the U.S. until after World War II. The experience led to rapid development of the low or stub mast and improved ground handling.

USS *Los Angeles* (ZR-3) showing experimental water recovery apparatus. Tupper photo from the collection of Hepburn Walker, Jr.

On 27 January 1928, ZR-3 landed aboard the aircraft carrier USS *Saratoga* at sea. In 1929, ZR-3 began experimenting with launching and retrieving airplanes while in flight. (This system had first been proposed for the ZR-1 in 1925.) A "trapeze" was installed on the ZR-3 in December 1928. Refinements to the trapeze and trim of the ZR-3 were carried out in the hangar at Lakehurst and on 03 July 1929, the first test flights were made, but were unsuccessful due to malfunction of the trapeze release. On 20 August, the first hook-on to the trapeze was made. The hook-on and release were demonstrated to Navy officials and at the National Air Races held in Cleveland, Ohio, in August-September, 1929. In May and July of 1930 a glider was released for solo flight. The last long flight of the ZR-3 was in February, 1931, when it participated in maneuvers in the Caribbean and Panama. It was away from Lakehurst for twenty- seven days and traveled a total of 14,500 miles during 272 flying hours.

On 02 November 1931, ZR-3 overflew Washington, D.C. with the ZRS-4, the only time two Navy rigid airships appeared together in flight. Training flights, particularly for the crews to be assigned to the new ZRS-4 and ZRS-5, continued until the last flight on 24-25 June 1932. She was officially decommissioned 30 June 1932, but was to remain in readiness on thirty-days notice. In mid-December, 1934, inflated with helium and with fuel and ballast, she was undocked for testing of mooring equipment. Mooring tests continued until it was finally docked on 18 November 1937. Although attempts were made for recommissioning, it was stricken from records on 24 October 24 1939. In September, the scrapping operation started and by January 1940, the disassembled duralumin framing had been sold for scrap. ZR-3 had made 331 flights totaling 4,181 hours.

ZR-3 basic characteristics:

Hull air displacement:	2,764,461 cubic feet
Gas cell volume:	2,559,110 cubic feet
Length:	658.3 feet
Height:	104.5
Maximum diameter:	90.7
Total horsepower:	2000 (five Maybach engines)
Full speed / Endurance:	65 knots / 2,825 miles, 43 hours
Cruising speed / Endurance:	48 knots 5,770 miles, 119 hours
Crew:	54 total, 40 flight

Hook-on airplanes used on USS *Los Angeles* (ZR-3)

Vought UO-1, Standard fleet observation plane, powered by Wright E-3 180 hp radial. BuAer Ser. 6615 was modified with a "skyhook" by the Naval Aircraft Factory in the fall of 1928. Top speed was some 120 mph. NARA photo (left)

Consolidated N2Y-1: While six N2Y-1s (BuAer Ser. 8600- 8605) were procured from Fleet Aircraft Corporation in March of 1930, images show only four photographed at one time with "skyhooks" at Lakehurst. Powerplant was a Kinner K-5 115 h.p. radial for a top speed of 108 mph. Publisher's collection (right). The Curtiss XF9C-1 was tested on the ZR-3 trapeze and a Prüfling glider was dropped from the airship on two occasions.

The Metalclad ZMC-2

The ZMC-2 was the brainchild of Ralph H. Upson, former chief aeronautical engineer for Goodyear, free balloonist and airship pilot. Associated with airships since 1911, he was convinced that aluminum was the most practical material for an air vehicle and left Goodyear. In 1923 or '24, Upson teamed up with Carl B. Fritsche and convinced him of the practicality of an all-metal airship. Fritsche was a visionary and a gifted salesman with the ability to attract the major engineering and financial community in Detroit to form the Aircraft Development Corporation (later the Metalclad Airship Corp.) of the Detroit Aircraft Corporation. Active in the corporation were Fritsche as president and Walker C. Morrow, Edwin J. Hill, Upson, Arthur G. Schlosser and Vladimir Pavlecka. Principal engineers in addition to Upson were Pavlecka, W.A. Klikoff and Sven Rasmussen, a group with a truly international background, American, Czech, Russian and Danish.

Several all-metal airships had been constructed worldwide since 1897, but the design and construction of the ZMC-2 was unique. It was the only successful metalclad airship anywhere. (One other American metalclad airship, the *City of Glendale* was erected by the Slate Aircraft Corporation of Glendale, California. An overlooked tied-off valve caused a seam to burst, and repair was judged too difficult. It only floated, it never actually flew under power.)

An MC-0.8 [80,000 cubic feet] was proposed in 1924 for the Army. Erection would have been in the Army hangar at Scott Field. It has been reported that a "ZMC-1" was partially completed but that exposure tests revealed corrosion and embrittlement of the duraluminum plating. "Alclad" aluminum, a creation of the Aluminum Company of America following the loss of the ZR-1, was used for future construction. (This new metal was a duraluminum sandwich; the center section was duraluminum, coated on each side with pure aluminum. However, it was heavier than the originally planned material.) Congressmen from Michigan finally pushed through a measure to fund a single prototype for the Navy, which had shown no interest in the design. Contract no. 446 was awarded for construction on 06 October 1928. Specialists were attracted to the organization to engage in the actual construction included Edwin J. Hill, from the Naval Aircraft Factory, who invented a skin-riveting machine used to assemble 0.008 and 0.0095 inch thick aluminum sheets. This was a revolutionary development used for the hull construction, and later in the production of airplanes. To prove design theories, a full size section, 29 feet in height, 34 feet in diameter and weighing 400 pounds, was tested to destruction. Gas retention was also tested, proving the theoretical gas tightness was confirmed beyond expectations. Tests were made on reducing pressure on the hull to determine the effect on the structure. Many folds were created and it appeared the metal was permanently distorted, however when pressure was raised the test section returned to its original shape and it was impossible to find where the buckles had occurred.

The airship (serial 8282) was erected in a hangar constructed at Grosse Ile, south of Detroit, Michigan. The first rivet was driven in the bow section 07 March 1928. The hull sections were built in vertical position on the floor of the hangar, and the two halves joined together in February 1929. The control car was completed and engines installed in June; the control car was attached to the hull in July, and helium inflation completed in August. As an example of the methods used by defense contractors and the early air pioneers in the 1930's period, ZMC-1 and ZMC-2 cost a total of $750,000. The Aircraft Development Corp. had agreed to equally split with the Navy on the expense of the project and, if the cost exceeded $300,000, to bear the additional cost. Consequently, Aircraft Development lost $450,000 on the project. (This does not include the cost of the hangar that was erected at Grosse Ile.)

Ralph Upson (composite photo from a decade earlier when still at Wingfoot Lake); Art J. Schlosser; Edward J. Hill; Captain William Kepner, USA, pilot; MSergeant Joe Bishop, crewman; Carl Fritsche. Courtsey Robert Slate.

The first flight was on the afternoon of 19 August 1929. Army Air Corps Capt William J. Kepner and MSgt Joseph Bishop (both on temporary leave) were pilot and engineer, and Carl Fritsche was aboard. The flight of 49 minutes, 55 seconds was held in the presence of the Navy Survey Board, consisting of CDR Garland Fulton, LCDR William K. Harrill, LTs Charles E. Bauch, George V. Whittle, C.V.S. Knox and H.J. Dugan. Dugan had been resident inspector at Grosse Ile and was to fly the airship. LT Bauch, a more experienced pilot, was also made available for flying. ZMC-2 made several local flights, including a 30-hour acceptance flight, and on 25 August was flown to Cleveland for appearance at the National Air Races. On 11 September, ZMC-2 departed Grosse Ile for Lakehurst with Kepner, Bishop and Dugan aboard. Landing was on 12 September after the 600 mile, non-stop flight. Capt Kepner remained with ZMC-2 at Lakehurst for 5 days to check the airship for gas loss. Several holes were discovered in the hull, results of “friendly fire” from some boys. On Kepner's departure, LT Dugan assumed command.

On 16 September 1929, flights were made over New York City. High speed trials were conducted. All necessary tests were completed by 25 September. Each test was successful on its first attempt, with a safe margin over contract requirements. The airship made many flights in the Lakehurst area, joining K-1 for the New York Fleet Review in May 1931. Nine hour flights were common and for a time the ZMC-2 operated from the Army airship base at Langley Field. Pilots found ZMC-2 more difficult to control due to its short length; problematic was the difference in temperature in the hull near the ground and that encountered at normal operating altitude. ZMC-2 also operated from the reconstructed hangar at Cape May, New Jersey.

The first inspection deflation in 3 years was made in the latter part of 1932. The plating and sealant was found in good shape and it was reinflated and returned to service. Although ZMC-2 was in service until 1941, it was only occasionally operated, since the Navy really did not want the airship. For example, the last overhaul was in December 1938 and it was flown only 5 hours to 25 April 1941. ZMC-2 was flown each year on her anniversary date of 19 August. ZMC-2 was always handled manually, since it was never equipped with mooring fixtures.

Predisposed to find it unfit, a report caused ZMC-2 to finally be retired in the summer of 1941. The airship was hastily disassembled, the sailor crew dressed in Sunday whites. The control car relocated to the Lakehurst non-rigid hangar (No. 4) where it was suspended from the overhead structure and used for training mechanics. ZMC-2 had been in service for 12 years, a truly remarkable record for an experimental airship.

ZMC-2 General Specifications:

Volume (cubic feet):	202,200
Ballonets (2) (cubic feet):	50,600
	(25% of total volume; front 22,600, rear 28,000)
Fineness ratio:	2.83 (length/diameter)
Overall length (feet):	149.5
Maximum diameter:	52.7
Overall height	64.5
Useful lift (pounds):	2,700
Crew:	3
Maximum speed (miles per hour):	62-70 (440 horsepower)
Cruising speed (mph):	50-52 (220 horsepower)
Endurance, cruising speed:	11 hours
Maximum range (still air):	1,000 miles
Range at cruising speed:	680 miles
Ceiling (feet):	9,000
Engines (2):	Wright J-5,220 horsepower,
Propellers (2):	9 feet, 2 inches, all metal
Aluminum hull thickness:	0.0095 inches
Fins (8, all metal):	440 square feet
Control car:	
Length (feet):	24
Width (feet):	6.5

Aircraft Development did additional airship related work, including the tower type mooring masts at Ford Airport, Dearborn, MI and at Scott Field, IL. They also built some all-metal control cars for the Army and some airplane control surfaces. Metalclad airships were in the design phase at Aircraft Development until at least 1931 when the Army investigated the design of a large rigid airship (3,500,000 cubic feet) for carrying airplanes. Some reports indicate $200,000 was proposed by Congress for preliminary construction, however this did actually not occur.

G-Z design concept dated 1927 shows key design features changed in 1928, '29, and '30.

The Zeppelin Rigid Scout (ZRS) Program

A large rigid airship for scouting and carrying airplanes for the Navy was proposed in March, 1924. The limiting factor for a large rigid was the inside length (804 feet) and door height (172 feet) of the hangar at Lakehurst. The Goodyear-Zeppelin Corporation of Akron, Ohio had been formed in 1923 with Dr. Karl Arnstein and twelve engineers from the Zeppelin Company that arrived in 1924. Following the in-flight breakup of the ZR-1, in 1926 Congress authorized the construction of two larger rigid airships and an operating base on the west coast (Naval Air Station, Sunnyvale-Mountain View, Moffett Field). The original bids were to be received by May 16, 1927, but various designs were proposed and competitive bids were required. No other bidders other than Goodyear had the expertise to design and build a rigid airship of the type proposed. The design of the ZRS evolved through the period LZ-127 *Graf Zeppelin* brought the idea of fuel gas to fruition; such a plan was considered following experiments with the non-rigid K-1. Of the three G-Z proposals submitted to fulfill the Navy's Design No. 60 competition, the three-keel, deep main ring design won out. A contract between the Navy and Goodyear-Zeppelin was signed on October 6, 1928, and a modern hangar for erection was started at Akron in May, 1929. The hangar was mostly complete in November, and ZRS ring assembly began.

ZRS-4 and ZRS-5 were basically the same in overall appearance. Modifications and refinements to ZRS-5 included streamlining of the engine outriggers; moving engine water radiators along the hull under scoops; and adding covers for the top hull vents. On *Macon*, three-bladed steel propellers replaced two bladed wooden props during builder's trials, which increased top speed. Structural and fitting refinements resulted in increased useful lift. There were numerous other refinements; gas cell valves were decreased from four to three per cell; the hangar bay was capable of holding five airplanes, while ZRS-4 had been awaiting modification to hinge two girders to allow more than three planes to be carried.

Signing the ZRS contract found many principals together (from l, sitting) Paul W. Litchfield, President of G-Z; SecNav Curtiss Wilbur; (Standing, from left) W.C. Young, Dr. Karl Arnstein, chief G-Z designer; Jerome C. Hunsacker, G-Z; Edward P. Warner, Fred Wahl, L.H. Baker, CDR Garlon Fulton, USN, M. A. Kraus.
(inset) G-Z Vice President & ZRS business manager Fred M. Harphan.

Main ring 170 was the forward terminus of the keel walkways, connecting to the forward centerline passageway. Topside of the bridge and to starboard were officer's bunkrooms. To port were, forward to aft, Captain's office (right), aerologist's office (center, note speaking tube) and the radio shack (left). US Navy, Moffett Field photos via Hepburn Walker, Jr. and Ed Fielding.

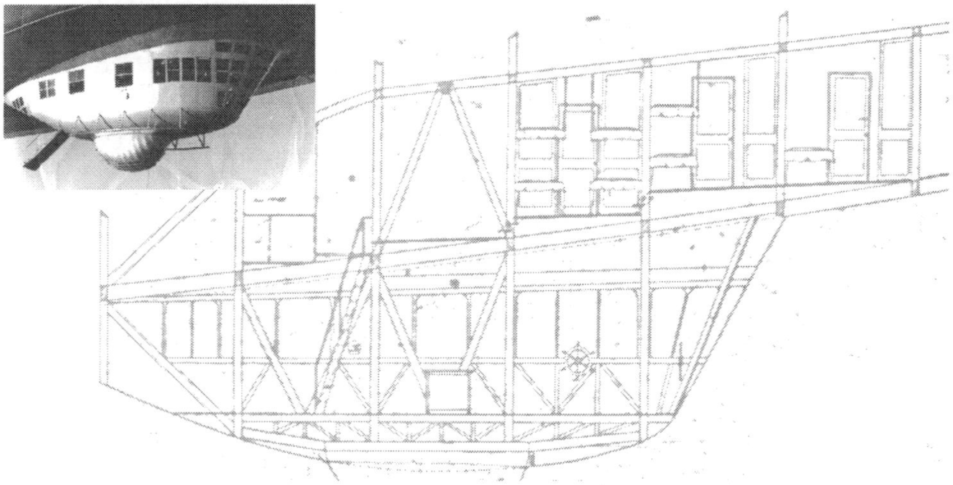

Main ring 170 also connected to the control car's ladder (above right, looking forward). Next section forward contained the navigator's charts and table. Most forward, the bridge, was separated by a sliding door. Looking aft from the bridge's center rudder wheel, to starboard (below left) are the multi-levered engine annuciators, 1-2, 3-4, 5-6, and 7-8, featuring not only speed and thrust direction but commands to cut in or out the power-robbing water recovery condensers. On the aft bulkhead are the phone (left) and the individual gas valve controls (right) below a diagram of the ship's cells. All cells could be vented at once using the wheel. To port is the altitude pilot's station, with the elevator wheel. Seen are the altimeter, inclinometer, vertimeter, superheat meter, and other instruments. At his upper right is the weight control chalkboard, for logging the fuel, water, airplanes and other loads in each main bay. Regular ballast dumping toggles, emergency ballast (later, fuel on ZRS-5) and fuel dumping toggles are below the board. US Naval Institute, Moffett Field photos; National Archives Cartographic Division.

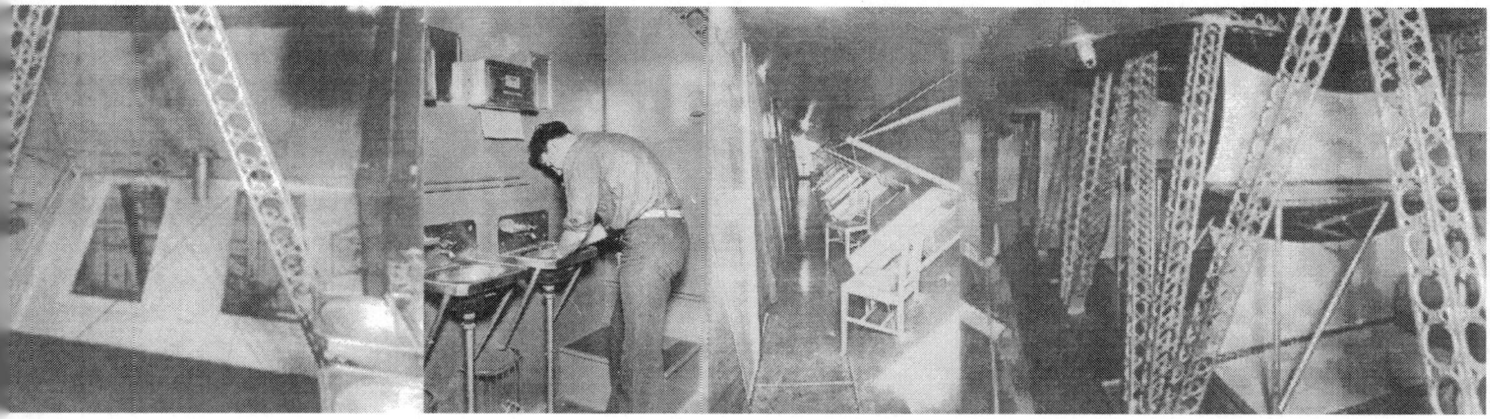

Below bay / cell VII, outboard of the airplane hangar, were the crew compartments. On port (far right, looking forward toward man ring 147.5) are enlisted and CPO bunks; looking aft and outboard, permanent chairs mounted by the windows. Aft toward main ring 125 was the enlisted head, looking inboard the passageway across the hangar to the chow hall, and (far left) the outboard view with its windows; toilets on aft bulkhead. USN Institute and Moffett Field photos.

Hangar bay (left, ZRS-4 after trapeze improvements) featured an X-shaped monorail airplane handling system. The fork seen at top was positioned over the propguard and a pin inserted; hook released, weight transferred, the plane was winched to one of four outboard positions. Aft was the spy basket, which could be lowered through the flip-up doors without unbolting the main sliding hangar door. US Navy photo. Outboard starboard at 147.5 were the officer's head, bunkroom and wardroom. Next aft was CPO's dining area, (below right) also doubling as a battle dressing area. Next aft was the enlisted dining room with its coffeepot pass-through to the galley, which featured a propane-powered stove. Last aft was the twin-dynamo generator room (extreme left).

The ZRS-4 USS *Akron* (above, left, Bay VII windows visible) is distinguishable from its sister ZRS-5 USS *Macon* (right) via the engine accessories. Engine water-cooling radiators were pylon mounted on *Akron*, but placed on the hull under a scoop on *Macon*. Following trials, *Macon* featured three blade steel propellers with streamlined housings. Photos courtesy Roy Gibbens

Basic characteristics, ZRS-4 and -5

Hull air displacement:	7,401,260 cubic feet
Gas cell (12) displacement:	6,850,000 cu ft
Length:	785 feet
Height:	146.5 ft
Maximum diameter:	132.9 ft
Engines:	8 Maybach VL-2, total 4480 horsepower;
Maximum Fuel Capacity:	126,000 lbs.
Useful lift:	152,644 pounds (ZRS-4), 160,644 (ZRS-5)
Full speed:	69.5 knots (ZRS-4), 75.6 (ZRS-5)
Standard speed:	65.0
Endurance:	4,855 nautical miles, 75 hours
Cruising speed:	55 knots
Endurance:	5,940 nautical miles, 108 hours
Crew:	Full, 91; flight, 60
Airplane hangar capacity:	3 (ZRS-4 awaiting mod) 5 (ZRS-5)
Airplane pilots / mechanics	5 / 4

The keels were passageways for the keel watch (far right) to walk his beat and report by telephone; voice tubes (above phone) ran as far aft as engines 1 & 2. Each of the eight Maybachs were housed in fireproof rooms whose doors opened into the keel. Goodyear and US Navy photos, via Ed Fielding, Hepburn Walker, Jr.

Main ring 35 was the terminus of the keel walkway. To proceed further aft a walkway inside the lower vertical fin (far right) was used. A ladder lead to the line-handling platform (center) and finally to the emergency control station, a fully equipped miniature bridge (left). Note egress door in the deck. US Navy photos.

Late in the airship's lives, water recovery condensers were a visible difference. *Akron* (above, at Lakehurst) had adopted the smaller Lakehurst Mk 4 units on all but engine #5 by March of 1933. *Macon* (below, at Opa-Locka) had deleted condensers #3 and #4, with intentions of removing both drive trains. Hepburn Walker Jr. and Roy Gibbens photos.

The USS *Akron* (ZRS-4) at Opa-Locka, Florida, in 1933. Original G-Z water recovery condensers on her starboard side have been replaced with the Mk 4 units. Many hatches are open to cope with the Florida heat. NARA photo.

The ZRS-4, USS *Akron*

Construction of ZRS-4 was officially started in November, 1929, with the golden rivet squeezed by RADM William Moffett as the ZR-3 flew overhead. The first complete bay, five, was erected on stands and equipped with helium cell V for a full cell pressure test. During the *Graf Zeppelin's* around the world flight in summer 1929, his lower vertical fin and rudder were damaged during a hazardous takeoff. Said to be as a result, Navy officers pushed for Design change number 2 of 1930, radically altering the fin shape and moving the control car aft so the tail would be visible from the bridge. On August 5, 1931, ZRS-4 was christened "USS *Akron*" by Lou Henry Hoover, wife of President Herbert Hoover.

The first flight was made on September 25, 1931. Ten trial flights of 124 hours were conducted from Akron. On October 21-22, ZRS-4 was delivered to Lakehurst and commissioned on October 27, LDCR Charles Rosendahl, Captain. She made a flight over New York City and joined with the ZR-3 over Washington on November 2, 1931, the only time in history two helium-filled rigid airships would be aloft at once. *Akron* participated in fleet maneuvers in January, 1932, but without airplanes; the exercise was not a great success for the airship. Due to problems in the design and building of a trapeze to fit ZRS-4, elements of the ZR-3 trapeze were cannibalized. Use of the sub-cloud observation car or "spy basket" was terminated when it was proved aerodynamically unstable. *Akron's* lower vertical fin was badly damaged during a ground-handling incident, and a G-Z team arrived from Akron to conduct repairs. On May 8, she began a flight to the west coast. Moorings were made at Camp Kearny (near San Diego), California and a temporary stub mast at Sunnyvale-Mountain View (its hangar was then under construction). She was flown as far north as Washington State. *Akron* was away from Lakehurst for thirty-eight days. The last few of the six F9C-2 planes were not received until September and the updated prototype was not delivered until January, 1933; four were designated for the ZRS-5.

The NASL Engineering department developed the Mark IV water recovery condenser system. Beginning with engine seven in July of 1932, these lighter and more efficient units gradually replaced the original G-Z units. (Above, as she appeared over the Miami Air Races in 1933, all but #6 changed over.) Two-bladed Hamilton-Standard steel propellers replaced wooden props.

Flights were made to Florida, over Cuba and over Panama in March, 1933. One of the final flights in March took her west as far as Lakes Erie and Ontario and lasted seventy-two hours before landing at Lakehurst. On April 3, 1933, ZRS-4 started on what was supposed to be a routine training and radio calibration flight. Departing Lakehurst for a two or three day cruise along the New England coast to calibrate radio direction finding stations, seventy-six men were aboard, including RADM William A. Moffett, Chief of the Bureau of Aeronautics. A unpredicted severe storm was encountered. The lower fin struck the sea early on the morning of April 4 off Little Egg Inlet, near the New Jersey coast. Since there were no life jackets and apparently only one raft, most of the 73 victims drowned in the chilly Atlantic. With only three survivors, the exact cause was difficult to determine and several possibilities were presented. (Discussions continue to this date.) The flight manifest (courtesy Eugene "Pete" Calande, engineman, reads:

OFFICERS. Comdr. Frank C. McCord, Commanding; Lieut-Comdr. Herbert Wiley (surv.); Lieut-Comdr. Harold E. MacLellan; Lieutenant George C. Calnan (CC); Lieutenant Herbert M. Wescoat; Lieutenant Richard F. Cross, Jr.; LTJGHammond J. Dugan; LTJG Charles F. Miller, Lieutenant (jg) Morgan Redfield; Lieutenant (jg) Wilfred Bushnell; Lieutenant (jg) Cyrus T. Clendening; Chief Machinist George C. Walsh.
OFFICER PASSENGERS. Rear Admiral William A. Moffett; Comdr. Fred T. Berry; Lieutenant Joseph H. Severyns, Comdr. Harry B. Cecil; Lieutenant (jg) Robert E. Sayre; Lieutenant (jg) Charles H. Calloway; Colonel A. F. Masury, U S Army Reserve.
CREW Anderson, Victor C. L. AMM3c; Angeles, Maximo Matt1c; Arthur, Wellington K. ACMM; Austin, Wilton G. BM2; Ballard, Henry A. BM2c; Barnhart, Bennie, Cox.; Baughman, Harold R. F3c; Boelsen, Peter AMM2c; Boswell, Henry L. CBM; Carlson, Arthur E. CBM; Carr, Stewart S. CEM; Cooper, Fred AMM2c; Copeland, Robert W. CRM; Cridlin, Stanley L. AMM3c; Deal, Richard E. (surv.) BM2; Dean, Carl C. CBM; Duncan, Lester G. F3c; Engler, Ralph F., Cox; Erwin, Moody E. (surv.) AM2c; Eschette, Horace P. SC1; Fahey, Lawrence E. AMM2; Fennessy, Edward ACOM; Fink, Elmer E. CTM; Graves, Hilbert N. AMM3c; Hill, William T. PhM1c; Hoover, Paul S. SC3c; Hulting, Lewis O., Cox.; Jandick, Paul A. CBMM; Johnson, Rufus B. BM2c; Latham, W. R., CBM; Lamkin, H. R. Seaman 1/c; Liles, Leon D., CAerog; Lipke, Donald H. Amm2c; Magnuson, Fridolf R. AMM3c; McLellan, Benjamin C. AMM2c; Morlen, Herschel L. RMC; Oronez, M. Matt 1/c;Quernheim, A.C., ACMM; Rader, Leonard G., Cox; Russell, William A. ACCM; Rutan, Lucius W. ACMM; Rytell, John J. AMM1c; Shauger, Paul R. AMM3c; Shevlowitz, Joseph ACMM; Slayton, Douglas C. RM3c; Starr, Fred W. Sea1c; Stine, Ralph C. QM1c; Swidersky, Toney F., Cox; Thigpen, Benjamin J. Jr. AMM3c; Tomes, Gerald L. F3c; Ulrich, Oliver E. BM2c; Walck, Lewis T. AMM2c; Weeks, John L. Sea2c; Wind, Nobart AMM3c; Zanetti, Joseph Amm3c; Zimkus, Joseph J. BM1c.
STATION ENLISTED MEN Hackett, Earl P. CAerog.

ZRS-4 was formally stricken on April 30, 1933, after seventy-four flights of 1,696 hours. Cost of ZRS-4 was $5,375,000.

The Hook-on Airplanes used by the USS *Akron* (ZRS-4)

Improvements made to the Consolidated N2Y-1 (left, on ZRS-5) included deletion of trainer yellow color, in favor of a silver paint color; reworked hook-on mechanism and a hatch combing allowing outsized cargo to be carried inside the fuselage. These simple airplanes, lacking radios and with lackluster performance, served as the airship's personnel transport and cargo-on-board delivery. Moffett Field photo

<u>Curtiss XF9C-1</u>, (Right) BuAer Ser. 8731: delivered March 1931 was evaluated as "too hot" for carrier use. It wound up at Lakehurst for airship consideration. It had a 421 h.p. Wright R-975 C engine. NAF equipped it with a "skyhook" and 27 OCT 31 tests on ZR-3 were successful. US Navy photo. Curtiss built an improved model, eventually designated XF9C-2 but, procured after the production units, thereby assigned Bu Aer Ser# 9264 and arriving at Lakehurst last, in January of 1933.

<u>F9C-2 *Sparrowhawk*</u>: Six production F9C-2 aircraft, Bu Aer Ser. 9056 through 9061, were delivered to Lakehurst by the end of September, 1932. Powered by the Wright 438 h.p. R-97-E3, in a dive the airplane could supposedly reach 295 mph. Dubbed *Sparrowhawk*, the aircraft each had its own color coded accents, including the belly band with airship's name, wheel pants, and cowling. All planes eventually featured the "man on the flying trapeze" insignia. All were operated from their airships without serious incident. Courtesy Eric Brothers

USS *Macon* (ZRS-5) operating in California. US Navy photo courtesy NAS Miramar PAO.

The ZRS-5, USS *Macon*

As part of the original $8,000,000 contract to Goodyear-Zeppelin for two rigid airships, ZRS-5 sub-assemblies were started in May 1931. On July, 4, 1932, a delegation from Macon, Georgia, attended a ceremony at Akron when the bow structure was hoisted in position on the completed framework. On March 11, 1933, it was christened by Jeanette Beverly Moffett, wife of RADM Moffett who was to lose his life aboard the ZRS-4 less than a month later. The first flight was made on April 21, 1933, with 105 persons aboard. Three test flights were made from Akron. ZRS-5 was commissioned on June 23, CDR Alger Dressel, Captain. ZRS-5 remained at Lakehurst for crew training and extensive practice in the launching and retrieving by the four airplane pilots assigned. On October 12, she departed Lakehurst for her new home station at Sunnyvale-Mountain View, California.

Landing at Sunnyvale on October 15, USS *Macon* became a major attraction in the San Francisco Bay area. Her career was followed with enthusiasm by locals as well as the senior naval command which was to determine her military value with the US Fleet, then on the west coast. The first exercise with the fleet was November 15-16, 1933. Two of the trapeze airplanes were used with minor success in locating the fleet. Results on the next exercises, January 3-5, 1934, were much better, although ZRS-5 was "shot-down" twice from fleet anti-aircraft fire and carrier fighter planes. The next fleet exercise was on February 20-21, in bad weather, and ZRS-5 was again "shot-down." On April 10, another technical mission was conducted with the fleet with similar results. Admittedly, the ZRS-5 scouting planes were not used to the best advantage and not in the best weather. The impression with the fleet was not the "rousing success" expected, although two good reports were made by the fleet commander with the results inconclusive. The 1934 exercises led to the development of a highly successful search system with the trapeze planes.

On April 20, 1934, ZRS-5 departed Sunnyvale for maneuvers in the Caribbean and using the auxiliary mooring facility at Opa-Locka, Florida. The flight was made in 54.5 hours at relatively low altitude, through mountain ranges and sometimes violent winds. Damage was incurred to the girders in the area of the horizontal fin. Temporary repairs were made with onboard shoring materials in flight and, on April 22, it moored to the Opa-Locka mast. Since wind tunnel tests had shown a weakness in the tail design, G-Z had been constructing a fix. Available parts allowed some repairs to be made at Opa-Locka over a nine-day period. It was determined that the main frame structure near the four fins required permanent repair to correct the problem. However, this was not considered urgent and was to be accomplished as the opportunity became available. ZRS-5 participated in fleet exercises until it departed for Sunnyvale on May 16, arriving on May 18.

Evaluation of the airship's performance recommended removal of two drive trains, and this began by removing water recovery radiator condensers #3 and #4. In July 1934, under a new commanding officer, LCDR Herbert V. Wiley, the ZRS-5 began a series of innovative developments and improvements of the hook-on airplane system of search. In addition to extending the range and speed of the airplanes by removing the fixed landing gear, a radio homing device was developed allowing greater search distances. Use of the revised sub-cloud observation car or "spy basket" was demonstrated. Experiments were also conducted with a pilot rescue sling, a modified life raft on a long cable. A seawater ballast water pickup device was also evaluated.

On July 18, 1934, ZRS-5 departed Sunnyvale on a scouting mission that was to cause some controversy in the Navy high command. 1,500 miles from land and over the Pacific, its trapeze planes located the heavy cruisers USS *Houston* and USS *New Orleans,* which were en route from Panama to Hawaii. Newspapers, magazines and souvenir letters were dropped for President Roosevelt then aboard the *Houston*. The President issued a "well done" message, but fleet commanders were displeased for not being informed of the plan and issued a censure at what they consider "misapplied initiative". The same procedure was successfully repeated in searching for liners and freighters between Hawaii and San Francisco without publicity. Between the "Presidential mission" and November 1934, fourteen flights, for a total 404 hours, were made perfecting the use of the hook-on planes.

Operating from the Camp Kearny stub mast, an exercise with the fleet was held on November 7, 1934. ZRS-5 was complimented on excellent scouting and radio reports by the airship's planes. Reinforcement parts for the fins were received from Goodyear-Zeppelin and between November 10 and February 10, 1935, the G-Z team and sailors installed them, as time permitted, on the lower and horizontal fins. The more time consuming reinforcement of the top fin was postponed until an overhaul period in March when cells 0 and I could be deflated.

On December 6-7, a tactical exercise was conducted. ZRS-5 was the first to locate two catapult airplanes from the USS *Cincinnati* that had exhausted their fuel and were down at sea. Training and further development of the airplane scouting system continued in January and February, 1935. Night operations with the trapeze planes became routine at the time carrier planes were required to be aboard before dark. Smoother nighttime air was said to ease the operation as both vehicles moved in the same medium. Refinements to the airships' ground handling system pioneered at Lakehurst found all evolutions at Moffett executed without a mishap or damage to the airship. Preparations for deployment to Ewa, Hawaii's mast circle site were underway. Two additional outside aircraft "perches" for two more main rings were made and were to be added.

On February 11, 1935, ZRS-5 departed Sunnyvale to search for the fleet in transit from San Diego to San Francisco. The fleet was located with ZRS-5 remaining undetected. On February 12, it was released from the exercise and headed for Sunnyvale. The weather deteriorated with fog, rain and low visibility. In late afternoon, off Point Sur, ZRS-5 may have been struck by an exceptionally severe gust of wind, the un-modified upper fin was torn from the stern and two gas cells in the area of the tail were punctured. The lack of a emergency plan and missteps by various crewmembers resulted in her climbing above pressure height and losing an intolerable amount of helium. *Macon* settled stern first into the sea. Only two persons of the eighty- three aboard were lost. Chief Radioman Daley had lost his glasses and jumped from too great a height; steward Florentino Equiba, afraid to swim, was last seen climbing on the structure. The outer covering caught fire, following control cabin flares igniting gasoline on the water. ZRS-5 was formally stricken from the record on February 26, 1935. It had made fifty-four flights of 1,798 hours. Cost was $2,450,000.

The Hook-on Airplanes used by the USS *Macon* (ZRS-5)

F9C-2 Sparrowhawks: **Following the loss of ZRS-4, hook-on airplanes were reassigned. The largely metal F9C-2s could have their arresting hooks re-attached, and in one *Macon* mission actually operated on the USS *Lexington* (left). Tailhook Photo Service.**

N2Y-1s: (above, right) Shades of *Star Trek's* transporter device, a pilot ferries a passenger to the surface via N2Y-1 from USS *Macon*. Moffett Field photo.

After USS *Macon's* transfer to the West Coast the insignia patches were removed and the tails painted black for ComAirBat uniformity. Once aboard the airship, the F9C-2's landing gear was removed in favor of a longer-ranging fuel tank. The aircraft were eventually fitted with homing gear to show the position of the "mother ship" at all times, allowing free flight of some 200 miles distant without wheels. Moffett Field photo (left)

Waco XJW-1: Related to the popular UPF model line, Waco literature designated this aircraft F-2. Two units were procured and assigned BuAer numbers 9521 and 9522. Weight, 2355 pounds; wingspan 29'6"; length 20'8"; powerplant Continental R-670-98; top speed 128 mph. Replacing the very basic N2Y-1s, the Waco also featured removable hatch combing to accommodate outsized cargo, such as a stretcher. A practice medevac is seen on the right. Moffett Field photo

Epilogue to the US Navy Rigid Airships

The loss of the ZRS-5 was the end of rigid airships operated by the US Navy. Allison VG-1710 engines were under development in 1935 as replacement for the German Maybachs in the ZRS-5. Although not fully developed as an airship engine, the V-1710, with modifications, was used for Army Air Forces fighter planes of World War II, the most notable being the Lockheed P-38. *Macon's* loss did not end the desire by many who still believed in the potential and future of the rigid airship. During 1936-1937, a series of design studies were made of larger ships that would carry nine dive-bombers. This was the designated type ZRCV (CV for aircraft carrier) and was proposed with a volume of 9,550,000 cubic, a length of over 897 feet and a maximum diameter of almost 148 feet. It was to be powered by eight of the 750 horsepower V-171C engines that were under development by Allison in 1935. The engines would not have been located inside the hull, as in the ZRS-4 and ZRS-5, but paired in four outside power cars driving four-bladed propellers. In 1937, the Navy General Board made the decision that a ZRCV would be necessary to properly evaluate a rigid airship, but felt that it should not be built at the time.

The Durand Committee, consisting of distinguished scientists, had been formed following the loss of the ZRS-5. They submitted a report in 1937 that recommended continuation of a rigid airship program with a "large airship built not as an adjunct to the fleet, but rather a flying laboratory or flying training ship". Based on the Durand Committee report, a five-year program for 1937-1941 was proposed by the Navy Bureau of Aeronautics. Exclusive of non-rigid airships, it included a training airship to replace the ZR-3, two ZRS-types and an experimental metalclad with a volume of 1,500,000 cubic feet. The total of $16,750,000 was considered unjustifiable for experimental ships and went no further.

Designers of the metalclad airship would later have ALCOA's much stronger 24S-T available as a building material. Nearly half again as strong as the ZMC-2's 17S-T, the new aluminum could be spot-welded, making even the remarkable automated riveting machine obsolete. Carl B. Fritsche's 1938 query article "Why Has The Airship Made Greater Progress?" pointed out the airplane had made improvements in its speed, range and performance due to better aerodynamics and better propulsion. He concluded the transition to all-metal airplanes was a logical path for airships as well: "The abandonment of fabrics in construction, utilizing the most modern alloys available... In fact, a fabric covered airship cannot be built strong enough to fly at 150 miles per hour and still carry a decent payload." In view of the ZMC-2's long service, excellent record and the fact tests proved the metalclad would not have caught fire even if filled with hydrogen, one can certainly bemoan the Navy's shunning the metalclad airship. The legacy that remains of Aircraft Development and the ZMC-2 was C.P. Burgess's designation as the metalclad as the "ultimate airship".

In the spring of 1938, a training rigid was authorized, the ZRN with a volume of 3,000,000 cubic feet and provisions for two trapeze planes. By Presidential order the training ship was to be limited to 325 feet in length. With initial funds provided, the design was revised and bids solicited in the fall of 1938. Metalclad Airship of Detroit and Goodyear-Zeppelin submitted proposals. The Metalclad bid was high and Goodyear-Zeppelin, as the low bidder, was awarded a contract. To be practical, and be aerodynamically sound, the volume of a "classic" rigid could only be 1,000,000 cubic feet and it could not carry even one trapeze airplane. Goodyear had submitted (under protest) two alternate designs for the 325 foot long proposal, an airship of 3,000,000 cubic feet volume and capable of carrying three trapeze airplanes (as originally specified by the Navy) and a four-engine non-rigid of 800,700 cubic feet volume.[13]

[13] The ZPG-2, 2W and 3W airships built 1953-1959, exceeded 1,000,000 cubic feet volume.

The non-rigid design was submitted to show it could provide approximately the same performance for about half of the cost. Although Goodyear-Zeppelin was low bidder, the Metalclad design was deemed, by Navy designers, as most desirable considering the 325-foot length and neglecting cost. Metalclad Aircraft proposed a joint venture to fulfill the contract, but Goodyear-Zeppelin rejected the idea. Efforts continued by the Navy Bureau of Aeronautics for the larger ZRN into 1940, but when the entire situation became confusing to Congress, the appropriations were removed in June.

In 1944, with completion of the contracts for the World War II non-rigid airships, Goodyear Aircraft (the successor to Goodyear-Zeppelin) proposed using the unexpired portion of the authorization for a rigid airship. It was estimated that if a contract was finalized by January 1, 1945, the 3,000,000 cubic foot ZRN training airship could be delivered by October, 1946, and a 10,000,000 cubic foot cargo ship (with variations as an aircraft carrier and hospital ship) could be completed by April, 1947. The Navy General Board recommended approval for funding the ZRN and two cargo ships, but no action was taken. This was the final effort by the Navy to obtain a rigid airship. The Navy postwar policy statement of January 23, 1947, made no mention of rigid airships. This marked the end of rigid airships for the U.S. Navy.

The conduct of the Pacific air war would have been somewhat different had the ZRCV, as depicted here by artist Cortney Skinner, been available in 1942. Navy Officers Richard Barkley and Frank Buckley self-published a book pointing out its advantages to the Navy. Built quickly and cheaply away from labor-short coastal areas; invulnerable to torpedoes, mines and sandbars; similar number of airplanes on target for lesser cost than a CVE, far fewer lives at risk, lost ship replaced in six weeks, etc. etc. The novel "ZRS" by Rowan Partridge offers one interpretation of how the flying aircraft carrier would have been used, had the Navy "brass" or the US Congress been listening to proponents in 1938.

Part IV: Pressure Airships Designed for Helium, 1929-1942

The K-1 Airship

The K-1 was produced in an attempt by the Navy to have a more modern airship than the J-types then at Lakehurst, which had originally been designed for hydrogen. The first airship for either the Army or Navy with an internal suspended control car, K-1 was a unique airship testbed. The 1929 Navy design No. 88 featured not only air ballonets, but also a special 51,700 cubic foot ballonet for carrying gaseous fuel, as proven successful by the *Graf Zeppelin*.

As airships needed special authorization from Congress for purchase (which was not likely), a "universal" control car that could also be used with the J-type airship was ordered from Navy maintenance funds. In order to avoid criticism for by-passing Congress, the control car was ordered through the Naval Aircraft Factory; the envelope, for "fuel gas experiments," from Goodyear. This method of procurement gave the impression that a new airship was not being procured. Navy records do not indicate a serial number for K-1.

Goodyear envelope D-129 (type K, 320,000 cubic feet) and control surfaces F-96 (Army TC-type) were ordered on Navy contract no. 17654 (Goodyear order G -1132) and shipped to Lakehurst in May 1930. The control car (referred to as type J/K), envelope and control surfaces were assembled at Lakehurst in the fall of 1931 with the maiden flight on 03 October, the first government airship with the control car suspended internally and flush to the envelope. Without large gasoline tanks, the control car featured bunks for the relief crew and a galley. The first Navy airship with a taxi wheel, the helium-filled K-1 pioneered mechanical ground handling equipment for non-rigids. K-1 was initially equipped for a spy basket (from the Army TC-13).

The fuel gas arrangement proved highly satisfactory. About the same weight as air, it contributed to an increase in range and endurance through easier maintenance of static equilibrium during long flights.

A serious drawback was that the lifting gas could become contaminated by both air and fuel gas, and at the time, there was no way to purify the helium. This meant the helium had to be vented to the air, an expensive method when funds for helium were dear, and the allotment was needed for the rigid airships. K-1 was not popular with crews, and it was said to be uncomfortable. While based at Cape May, the airship was damaged, and then shipped to Goodyear at Akron for repair, arriving 31 January 1932. K-1 was repaired and equipped with more powerful engines under Navy contract no. 30769. K-1 was given a test flight at Wingfoot Lake, and then flown to Lakehurst on 09/10 August 1933. Once the J-4 was transferred to Sunnyvale, K-1 and the ZMC-2 were the only flying airships at Lakehurst, a condition that lasted until 1937. K-1 incurred another accident and was returned to Akron arriving 25 May 1935. The envelope sustained a tear 25 feet in length and a new envelope (Goodyear D-148, type 320,000 IC, order G -1573) was ordered on Navy contract no. 43205. Erection was completed at Wingfoot Lake 27 January 1937. The last flight was made in September 1940. Then K-1 was used for mooring out experiments, including snow removal at Lakehurst. It was stricken 31 October 1941. (Several accounts state incorrectly that the K-1 was the prototype for the WW II K-type patrol airships. This was actually the K-2.)

K-1 Airship General specifications:

Volume (cubic feet):	319,900
Ballonets (2, cubic feet):	104,400 (maximum)
Fuel gas ballonet (1, cubic feet):	51,700
Overall length (feet):	219.2
Maximum diameter:	53.9
Overall height:	70
Useful lift (pounds):	7,684 (includes 3,929 pounds of fuel gas weighing 0.076 pounds per cubic foot, total fuel 5,150 lbs.)
Maximum speed:	55 knots
Cruising speed:	40 knots
Range at full speed:	940 miles
Range at cruising speed:	1,640 miles
Engines (2):	Wright R-975-20, 300 horsepower at 1,800 rpm

The G-1 Airship

The original Navy G-type was planned in 1919 following the C- and D-type airships. This G-type of 360,000 cubic feet volume was to be a high endurance patrol type, with an enclosed control car and sleeping accommodations for the crew. It was to carry no less than a 3-inch gun. The concept increased in size to 400,000 cubic feet, but by the 1919 contract time, it was decided this was too large; non-rigid airships should not exceed 200,000 cubic feet. The next major airship should be a 2,000,000 cubic foot rigid; the original G-type design was then cancelled.

The 10 passenger *Defender* (Goodyear type GZ-6) was erected at Wingfoot Lake on Goodyear order EPP-35-'29 with envelope D-124 (178,000 cubic feet, type ZPA), control surfaces F-92 and control car C-44. The first flight was made at Wingfoot Lake on 20 August 1929. On 30 August *Defender* was christened with a bottle of liquid air at the 1929 Cleveland National Air Races by Amelia Earhart. The largest of the commercial Goodyear advertising fleet, *Defender* (NC-12A) was the fleet's flagship. *Defender* made aerial tours throughout the States with WWI blimp pilot Jack Boettner, later a WWII LTA officer. The G-1 was originally equipped with Warner SS-50, 145 horsepower engines and wooden propellers (same as the original L-ships). The airship experimented with diesel engines in 1931-1932, likely the Packard radials. It was placed in storage 25 September 1934.

Defender was procured by the Navy on contract no. 44308 dated 23 September 1935 as serial No. 9999. *Defender* was fitted with a new envelope (Goodyear D-145, 183,000 cubic feet, type ZPA) and delivered to Lakehurst 05 October 1935. Designated G-1, it was used for utility and training purposes with its wood trim interior appointments intact. G-1 was the most modern airship in the Navy; it was exceeded in size only by the K-1. G-1 was flown to Philadelphia 01 June 1940 (with K-2) for the launching of the USS *Washington*, the first of a new battleship class. (Additional larger G-type airships were constructed during World War II. These airships were G-2 through G-8; G-8 remained in service until 1952.)

G-1 conducted a secret wartime mission on 08 June 1942 with five scientists aboard along with the crew. G-1 and L-2 were conducting nighttime visual and photographic observation of experimental underwater flares. Maneuvers were being held with Coast Guard Cutter no. 4344, and the L-2 attempted to communicate with the cutter by flashing light. The cutter's light failed and contact was not made. L-2 then attempted to contact G-1 by flashing the control car sidelights, but this was also unsuccessful. Apparently no contact was ever made between the airships on the dark night.

Tragic collision of the G-1 and L-2 as depicted by James Simpson.

G-1 was flying without lights and L-2 was flying with red and green running lights and a white undercar light. As L-2 was still trying to communicate with the cutter, G-1 passed in front of it and was struck by the bow of L-2 just forward of the control car. Despite evasive action by the pilot of L-2, both airship envelopes were ripped and tangled together with both settling into the ocean near the cutter. The control cars sank immediately but were buoyed up by the gas remaining in the envelopes. There was a muffled explosion accompanied by a flash of light from under the wreckage immediately after the control cars sank. Twelve lives were lost; the only survivor was ENS Howard S. Fahey of the L-2.

G-1 Crew: LT Frank A. Trotter (former Goodyear airship pilot), ENS Clarence C. Ross, ENS Kenneth G. Lee, Ole V. Roos, Aviation Chief Machinists Mate, William H. Herdon, Jr., Boatswains Mate First Class, Dr. Frank C. Gilbert, New London, CT, Dr. Charles R. Hoover, Middletown, CT, Dr. Lorenz S. Moyer, Minneapolis, MN.

L-2 Crew: LCDR Clinton S. Rounds, Raymond C. Poteet, Aviation Chief Machinists Mate, Dr. Arthur B. Wyse, San Diego, CA, Israel H. Tilles, San Diego, CA.

G-1 Airship General Specifications:

Volume (cubic feet):	183,000
Ballonets (2, cubic feet):	39,200 (maximum)
Overall length (feet):	186.67
Maximum diameter:	42.8
Overall height:	62.0
Useful lift (pounds):	4,115
Crew:	2 or 3, 7 or 8 passengers
Maximum speed:	56.5 knots
Cruising speed:	47.8 knots
Endurance at full speed:	10.6 hours
Endurance at cruising speed:	16.7 hours
Engines (2):	R-670-2, 210 horsepower at 2,100 rpm; 2 adjustable pitch single blade propellers, 9 feet, 3 inch arc

The TC-13 and TC-14 Airships

In the period between 1919 and 1937, the US Army operated more airships than any other group in the world. These were all non-rigid except for the semi-rigids *Roma* (built in Italy) and the Goodyear-built RS-1. The giant rigid airships received the publicity and were of greater interest to the general public. Consequently, the Army airships received only minimum recognition. Like the Navy, Army airship service had the same appropriation problems; funding was never large in comparison to other military and naval budgets. During this period, and including the SC-1 of 1908, the Army operated approximately 60 airships and/or motorized observation balloons. (The latter were really airships that could operate as an airship or as a tethered observation or kite balloon.) Of this total, six were former Navy airships (C-1, C-2, D-2, D-3, D-4 and D-5) and four (3 British SST-types and the French RN-1) were airships originally acquired by the Navy. The Army tried unsuccessfully over the years, up to 1936, to acquire a rigid airship, but this never was approved. Of the 60 airships, no more than approximately five or six were operated at any one time.

TC-13 (USA) in flight. US Army photo.

<u>TC-13</u> (US Army) - TC-13 was built completely by Goodyear and erected at Wingfoot Lake on Army Air Corps order no. W-535-AC-5055 with envelope D-138 (350,000 cubic feet, type TC improved, Goodyear order G-1310) and control car C-48. Although rarely used, the official designation was TC-13-325. A separate contract was issued for erection, originally to be complete by 21 September 1932. The TC-13 envelope was similar to the Navy K-1 with three parallel panels (13.08 feet) inserted to obtain the necessary volume (349,000 cubic feet vs. 320,000 cubic feet of the K-1). Helium shortages, weather, the depression bank holiday and expenses for the Army personnel (at one time they paid their own expenses) delayed erection. The first flight was not made until 27 April 1933. TC-13 was designed for short-range reconnaissance and coastal patrol in conjunction with fortified harbors. The control car was 40 feet in length and divided into five compartments. The car originally had a pontoon at the front (for water landing) and a taxi wheel at the rear (for heavy take-offs). The pontoon proved effective only in calm sea and was later removed and replaced with a front caster wheel. The

envelope had a five-fin empennage to provide ground clearance during heavy take-offs. Other features included were special mufflers for the engines for quiet operation, a sub-cloud observation car opening, and armament of machine guns and bombs. Total cost, including engineering, the observation car, spare parts and erection was $159,350, with only a 2% increase on the control car and 3% on the envelope. (An interesting comparison to modern day contract over-runs!)

The first flight of 27 April 1933 was made with Maj William E. Kepner as test pilot. 110 hours, 55 minutes were flown before it was turned over to the Army at Langley Field for further test flights by 1stLt Orvil A. Anderson. TC-13 was highly successful and was used for a variety of tests including sea anchorage and use of the sub-cloud observation car. Air speed tests reached 78 miles per hour (indicated), and an altitude of 9,800 feet was reached.

Following completion of all test phases, TC-13 was assigned to the 19th Airship Company at Langley Field, with Lt James Shively as pilot. Many flights were made in the Langley Field area. One flight to Miami included Air Corps maneuvers and tests made with expeditionary mooring masts. Flights were also made to Scott Field, Illinois and Lakehurst. Following the loss of the USS *Macon* in February 1935, the Army assumed control of the former Naval Air Station, Sunnyvale, California (Moffett Field). On 24 October 1935 TC-13 departed Langley Field and was flown to the new station with stops at Maxwell Field, Alabama and Brooks Field, Texas. Many flights were made in the California area, and a flight was proposed to Luke Field, Hawaii in early 1937. Flights were made in the San Francisco area with the last Army flight made on 02 June 1937. While in Army service (April 1933 through June 1937) approximately 3,400 hours were flown with the longest flight over 76 hours and 1,345 miles. (See TC-13 USN)

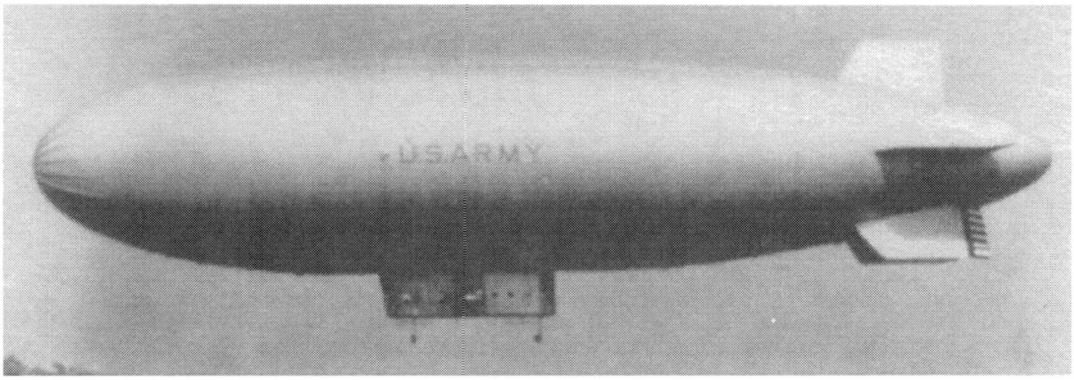

TC-14 - (US Army technically TC-14-351, above) was the last Army airship (with the exception of motorized observation balloons) to be delivered. The TC-14 control car was provided by Mercury Aircraft (formerly Aerial Services Corporation) of Hammondsport, NY and the envelope by Goodyear (D-146, 357,000 cubic feet, order no. G-1510) on Air Corps contract W-535-7047. TC-14 was designed primarily for training, scouting and observation. An interesting feature of TC-14 was that it originally had three engines. Two Pratt and Whitney YR-985's of 305 horsepower each were on outriggers. A small Martin 333, 120 horsepower pusher engine at the rear of the control car was for low speed silent operation. The control car was equipped with front and rear caster wheels and had belly-mooring capabilities. The empennage was the five fin surfaces as on the TC-13. The control car was shipped to Scott Field 24 August 1934 and the envelope shipped 15 May 1935. Erection was at Scott Field by Army personnel and was completed in the fall of 1935. TC-14 was assigned to the 9th Airship Squadron at Scott Field for its entire career where it engaged in research and development projects. Tested items were automatic pilot for rudder control (successful) and an observation platform on the top of the envelope (not successful). TC-14 was equipped for sea anchorage gear, which was never installed, and for the sub-cloud observation car, which was never used and removed in 1938.

Due to its assignment, TC-14 saw less actual flying time than TC-13 that was assigned to the tactical 19th Airship Squadron at Langley Field. Cost of the TC-14 was $99,188.20; ($39,250, control car, $59,938.20, envelope), plus engineering, government furnished items (engines, radio, etc.) and erection by the Army at Scott Field. (See USN TC-14)

The US Army was flying only the TC-11, TC-13 and TC-14 by March of 1937. The Army terminated their airship operations on 30 June 1937. Two small airships (TE-3-301 and TE-3-321) that were reclassified as motorized observation balloons, and several others of the latest motorized observation balloons were retained. (The Army continued to operate observation balloons until February 1942.) Their remaining equipment was offered to the Navy, which on 19 July 1937 agreed to accept this equipment, even though the majority was obsolete. It included mooring masts, engines, spare parts, two TC-11 envelopes (1928 and 1932), and three TC-10 envelopes of 1931 and 1932 vintage. The designed-for-helium, suspended car TC-10 airships (3 each, 1924 and 1925 vintage), one TC-11-271 control car (1927) were shipped. The more modern airships TC-13 (1932) and TC-14 (1935) were the only airships re-erected and flown by the Navy. The original value of this equipment to the Army was $392,000 and was finally evaluated at $39,000.

TC-14 mechanic's station, with navigator's table visible forward. Curtiss Museum photo.

The Army equipment was actually transferred in January 1938. Maj Clarence Lober and Capt Gerald Johnston were assigned to Lakehurst to assist in assembly of the TC-14. In 1943 the balance of the Army airship equipment (the two TE-3 airships, never flown after 1937) and the motorized observation balloons were also transferred to the Navy but not used in service.

US Navy TC-13 at Watsonwille, California, serving with ZP-32 in 1942. The old belly mooring point was utilized by cutting down a standard type II mast. Charles Mills photo via Don Woodward.

<u>TC-13 (USN)</u> was not inflated by the Navy until early 1940, after Goodyear provided a new envelope (D-154, type 357 M, TC-13) on contract NOS-61433, shipped to Lakehurst 26 May 1939. In this same time frame the sub-cloud observation car hatch was also removed. In September 1940, TC-13 made a 37-hour flight to Bar Harbor, Maine to calibrate a radio compass with a landing planned at Newport, Rhode Island but, due to strong winds, was landed

at Portland, Maine and then returned to Lakehurst. TC-13 was continually up-graded with wheels added, envelope increased in volume, engines improved, etc. TC-13 was one of only six airships available for long-range patrol at our entry into World War II (the other airships were TC-14, K-2, K-3, K-4 and K-5). On 12 January 1942, following the Pearl Harbor attack, TC-13 (and TC-14) were shipped by rail to Moffett Field, arriving 24 January. They became the first patrol airships assigned to the first west coast airship patrol squadron (ZP-32), placed in service 08 February. TC-13 was assigned to escort fleet elements I March 1942, often with former Goodyear pilot John Rieker as command pilot. The crew once mistook an unannounced US submarine *Gato* (SS-212) periscope for enemy sub as sub practiced lining up for torpedo run on US Navy battleship USS *Pennsylvania*. TC-13 attacked with four depth bombs and the battleship retreated before a destroyer signaled sub was "friendly." *Gato* surfaced, then returned to Mare Island for repairs to damaged diving planes and knocked out instruments. The official investigation cleared Rieker, agreeing the airship crew acted alertly and skillfully, in light of the earlier Japanese sub action off California. There were no injuries, and the sub was repaired in dry dock. Rarely publicized, the unfortunate incident proved that even without sensors the airship was capable of inflicting damage on a submarine (see K-6). While a member of ZP-32, TC-13 flew 153 squadron missions for a total of 1,514.3 hours. Total service (Army and Navy) for TC-13 was over 5,000 hours. On 05 November 1942, TC-13 was relegated to training service. Recommended for striking 22 February 1943, it was stricken 31 March and dismantled 07 June.

US Navy TC-14 in flight near Lakehurst. US Navy photo.

TC-14 (USN) was re-erected in 1938 at Lakehurst. TC-14 served at Lakehurst until shipped to Moffett Field (with TC-13 and arriving 24 January 1942) to join the ZP-32. The first flight at Moffett Field was made 01 February and the first squadron flight on 09 February 1942, with LT W. W. Boyd, pilot. The first mission of TC-14 was a patrol with the Pacific fleet. TC-14 searched for the Japanese submarine I-17 that shelled the Bankline Oil Refinery near Santa Barbara, California 23-24 February 1942. Nothing was located but it was able to provide escort for two tankers in the area. On 16 November 1942, TC-14 was relegated to training duties. It served until the summer of 1943 when it was deflated and stored. After deflation, TC-14 was shipped to Lakehurst, re-erected without engines and used as a dummy airship for mooring-out tests. It was deflated at the mast in the summer of 1944 and the control car was scrapped. With ZP-32, 201 squadron flights for a total of 1,543 hours were made.

General specifications, Army TC-13 and TC-14 and approximate 1942 Navy configuration:

	TC-13	TC-14	Navy, 1942
Volume (cubic feet)	349,600	357,000	357,000
Overall length (feet)	232.25	235.52	235.5
Maximum diameter	53.9	53.9	53.9
Overall height	68.0	70.0	70.0
Useful lift (pounds)	9,320	9,514	8,500
Maximum speed (miles per hour)	62.2*	59.5	≈65
Cruising speed	50	50	50
Endurance, full speed (hours)	24+	≈24	≈30
Endurance, max cruising speed	30+	≈30	48
Ceiling (feet approx.)	9,000Δ	9,000	≈9,000
Crew:	8 to 10	8 to 10	8 to 10
Engines (2):	R-1340-2	R-985-40	R-1340,400 hp
	375 hp @	335 hp @	
	1850 rpm	2100 rpm	
Propellers	3 blade	3 blade	3 blade
Arc	12.5 feet	10.5 feet, plus one Martin 333,120 hp	

* Attained 78 miles per hour (indicated) on one occasion.
+ 60 hours at slow speed (35 miles per hour), 30 hours (51 mph) and 24 hours (57 mph). Actually flown for 76 hours on one occasion.
Δ Attained 9,800 feet on one occasion.

TC-14 spent her final days masted at Lakehurst without engines, testing envelope waxes for snow resistance. US Navy photo.

Purchased "off the shelf" from Goodyear, the *Ranger* became L-2. Note belly mooring in use with crew vehicle. Goodyear photo.

The L-1, L-2 and L-3 Airships

As the need for more modern training airships became apparent with the uncertainty of conditions in Europe, Navy contract no. 56352 dated 11 August 1937 was awarded to Goodyear for the construction of the L-1. (This contract also included the first modern patrol airship, the K-2.) The L-type was the standard Goodyear commercial airship. The Navy version was considered a primary training airship, with the G-type designated the advanced trainer. With L-2 and L-3 in 1941, there were a total of 22 L- types eventually in service. These included five commandeered Goodyear commercial airships.

L-1 - Navy contract 56352, serial no. 1210, Goodyear envelope D-152 (type 123,000 cubic feet) and completed in 01 March 1938, control surfaces F-103 and control car C-50 delivered to Lakehurst in April. The cost for L-1 was approximately $65,200. L-1 was a testbed for various ideas; she attempted at-sea refueling from an oiler. The L-1, like the J-4, also experimented with a blue-gray painted envelope, but was restored to the silver finish. Actually used for patrol early in WWII, L-1 served at Lakehurst as a primary training airship. Following WWII, L-1 was equipped with a single float and water landings were tested on Wingfoot Lake. This test was followed by a more advanced twin pontoon gear with which operations were performed on Lake Erie. A small wobble pump was employed to take on water ballast. Returned to Lakehurst 08 January 1947, by LT D.F. Patzig, pilot. It was sold to Douglas Leigh Sky Advertising in 1952. Final disposition unknown but several sources indicate L-1 collided with G-1 on 08 June 1942; this is incorrect. L-2 was in that accident.

L-2 - L-2 was the original Goodyear type G –17, christened *Ranger* NC-10A with envelope D-158 (type T, 123,000 cubic feet) and control car C-58. The first flight of *Ranger* was 13 August 1940. With the award of Navy contract no. 78121 (which also included L-3, K-3, K-4, K-5 and K-6) dated 25 September (some records state October) 1940, *Ranger* became Navy serial no. 7029 with new envelope D-161 (type T, 123,000 cubic feet) L-2 was delivered to Lakehurst via

Washington, DC, on 01 February 1941 by Goodyear's pilot Karl Fickes. L-2 apparently attained a record speed of 78 knots between Akron and Washington. L-2 was deflated while making a practice take-off at Lakehurst, striking some trees on the southern edge of the air station and settling gently to the ground. Newsreel cameras recorded the aftermath. Pilot in charge was LT Henry F.Burgeind. L-2 was repaired and returned to service. On 08 June 1942, it collided with G-1 and was lost. (See G-1)

L-3 - Navy contract 78121, serial no. 7030, Goodyear envelope D-167 (type T, 123,000 cubic feet) and control car C-63 and flown to Lakehurst 09 June 1941. Believed based on the east coast during the war. This is no record of service at Moffett Field, yet a NARA film lists one film as "A Navy blimp, L-3, is taken from its hangar and unmoored at Fort Lewis, Washington."

L-1 through L-3 Airships General Specifications:

Volume (cubic feet):	123,000
Ballonets (2, cubic feet, each):	29,400 maximum
Overall length (feet):	147.5
Maximum diameter:	39.8
Overall height:	54.0
Useful lift (pounds):	2,540
Maximum speed (knots):	53
Cruising speed:	40
Endurance at maximum speed (hours):	5.6
Endurance at cruising speed:	11.9
Armament:	None, training only
Engines (2):	Warner "Super Scarab" R-500-2, 145 horsepower, 2,050 rpm, direct drive, no gearing, flat pitch propellers, arc of 8.0 feet

The K-2 on rollout day, the only K-type assembled in the Airdock. Goodyear photo.

The K-2 Airship

The K-2 was the largest patrol airship to be designed and flown by the Navy since the D-type of 1919. K-2 was the prototype of the 133 K-types built for service during World War II. A 1935 Navy design memo specified the next experimental airship, obviously numbered K-2, should have a fuel bladder with superior performance to that in the K-1, but this was deleted by 1937. Navy serial 1211, Goodyear envelope D-153 (type K-2, 404,000 cubic feet), control surfaces F-104 and control car C- 51 procured on contract no. 56352 (which also included the L- 1). K-2 cost about $163,000. K-2 was erected in the Goodyear-Zeppelin Airdock, the first airship to be erected in that hangar since the USS *Macon* in 1933. The first flight was made at the Akron Municipal Airport (now Fulton Field) on 06 December 1938, and K-2 was delivered to Lakehurst on 16 December. LCDR Emmett Sullivan was officer-in-charge of flight tests and test pilot during the acceptance flights. The envelope was damaged when K-2 was deflated in trees at Lakehurst in May 1939 due to improper ballonet trim. Repaired by Goodyear, K-2 returned to Lakehurst 21 November 1939 and was re-erected by the Overhaul and Repair Department.

On 01 June 1940, K-2 was flown to Philadelphia for the launching of the USS *Washington*, a new battleship class. K-2 was the workhorse in developing procedures and flying prototype equipment for wartime use. K-2 performed a multitude of assignments including use as a platform for parachute rigger school jumpers. K-2 participated in the "neutrality" patrols in 1939-1940 and observation of torpedo practice with Submarine Squadron 2 at New London, CT. K-2 performed experimental towing of water recovery bags, ran development of bombing equipment and practice bombing in 1941, and carried the prototype of LORAN (long range navigation) in June, 1942. Among many test assignments, K-2 was also used to measure light levels off the Atlantic coast to develop more effective blackout procedures. Among many innovations, K-2 was equipped with hydraulic landing gear designed by the Cleveland Pneumatic Tool Company, though this was not built into production versions. K-2 was retro-fitted with a machine gun turret in 1942. K-2 remained at Lakehurst throughout World War II. The date of final deflation is unknown.

K-2's modified car, 1943

General specifications:	
Volume (cubic feet, original):	404,000
Ballonets (2, max original):	100,000
Overall length (feet):	248.5
Maximum diameter	57.85
Overall width:	62.52
Static lift (pounds):	9,400
Dynamic lift:	2,000
Service load:	4,600
Speed, maximum (knots):	65
Speed, cruising:	50
Endurance at 50 kts (hours):	39
Range at 50 kts (miles):	1,950
Engines (2):	Pratt Whitney R-1340-16, 400 horsepower at 1,800 rpm, 3 blade propellers, 10.5 feet diameter

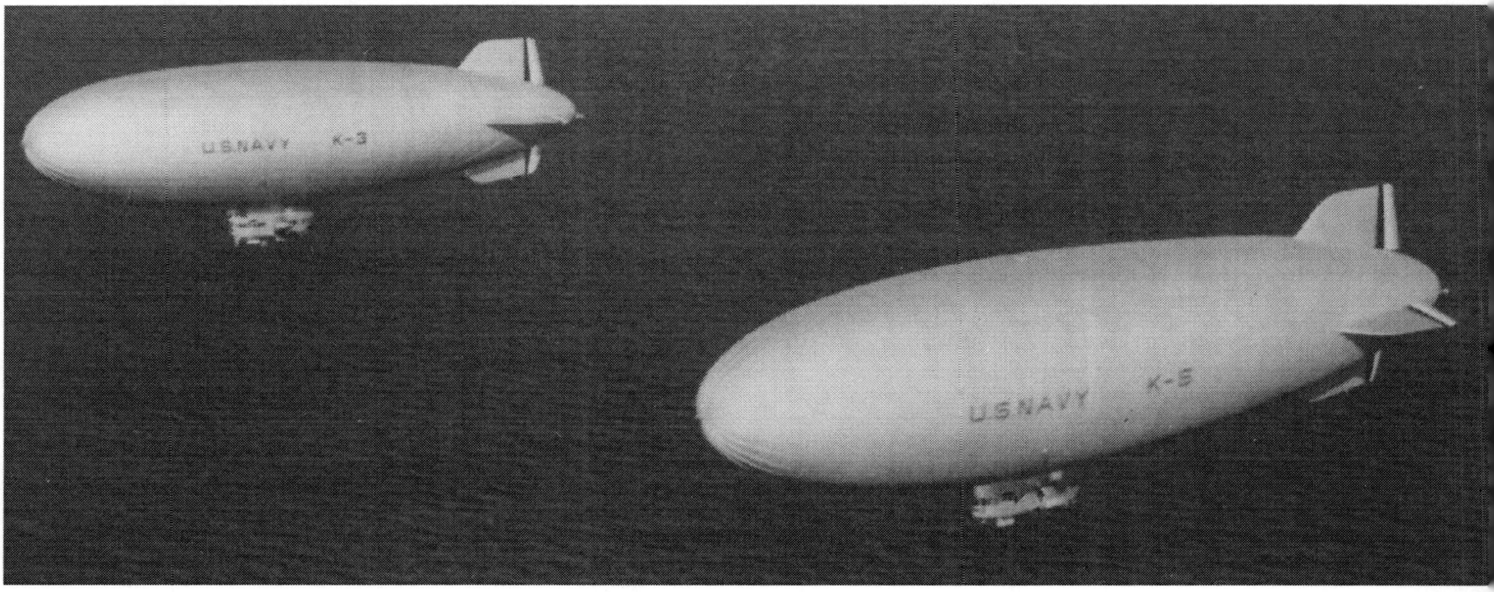

K-3, K-4, K-5 and K-6 Airships

K-3, K-4, K-5 and K-6 were procured on Navy contract 78121 dated 25 September 1940 (some records state October) and included not only these airships but also L-2, L-3, K-7 and K-8. This contract was based on the success of K-2 and the convoy escort and patrol needs apparent with the activity of German submarines by that time in World War II. This was the largest contract issued for non-rigid airships since World War I and until US entry into the WWII on 07 December 1941. The general design for K-3 through K-8 was the same as K-2, with a change in engine type. Only slight other modifications kept cost to approximately $325,000 per airship. K-3, K-4, K-5 and K-6 were the last airships delivered to the Navy prior to 1942. As a result of the Germans massing U-boats off the US east coast early in 1942, these few airships carried out the great majority of the antisubmarine attacks in 1942.

K-3 - Serial 7025, Goodyear envelope D-162 (416,000 cubic feet), control surfaces F-108 and control car C-59. First flight made at Wingfoot Lake 10 September 1941 with Goodyear's Jack Boettner as chief pilot, Karl Fickes, manager of airship operations, H. Webster Crum, chief engineer, and CDR C.V.S. Knox, resident Navy inspector at Akron and others aboard. Paul W. Litchfield, chairman of the board of Goodyear, also made a flight on K-3. Flight tests were conducted at Wingfoot Lake and on 17 September, K-3 was flown to Lakehurst with Karl Fickes as pilot, Web Crum, co-pilot, Harry Haines, engineer, John Meier, flight engineer, CDR Knox and Duane De Vaney, Navy radioman. K-3 departed Wingfoot Lake at 2:50 PM and arrived at Lakehurst at 8:15 PM, the 500 mile trip made in 5 hours, 25 minutes at an average speed of 78 miles per hour.

(Controversial, from VADM Rosendahl) K-3 attacked an oil slick with black object, 22 December 41. K-3 was then assigned to the newly formed Airship Patrol Squadron ZP-12 activated 02 January 1942. While on patrol with LTs L.P. Furculow and Cecil Bolam as pilots on 15 January, K-3 searched for a suspected German U-boat. K-3 spotted the sunken Norwegian freighter *Noress* near Nantucket Lightship. Four survivors on a raft were located. K-3 remained in the area providing temporary rations until the men were picked up by the Coast Guard Cutter *Argo*.[14] This was the first of many rescues by airship during the war. (The German submarine that sunk the *Noress* was the U-123; it had torpedoed eight ships totaling 100,000 tons from 12 through 22 January.) On 17 January, with LT Walter Keen Jr., pilot, a contact was made with MAD (Magnetic Anomaly Detector) gear aboard. The object was tracked and then lost due to problems experienced with the early MAD unit. On convoy duty 18 January, K-3 made another MAD contact, located a U-boat that surfaced and then crash-dived. The U-boat was trailed and attacked without success when the depth bomb failed to explode. Two bombs were dropped on a second contact the same day near Ambrose Lightship near New York harbor, one another dud, with no evidence of damage from the second bomb.[15] K-3 also took over a submarine sighting made by K-5 on 22 January and continued the search. On 15 March, K-3 with ZP-12 Commanding Officer CDR Raymond F. Tyler, pilot, flew to a reported location of gunfire near Ocean City, Maryland, and an oil slick was found. Bombs were dropped on a MAD contact; bubbles, bits of wood and debris surfaced. On 19 March, with LTJG Saxe Gantz, pilot, K-3 investigated reported submarine contact by Cape Henlopen signal station. An Eagle boat had made its location and attempted to mark it for K-3, which attacked with depth charges that failed to detonate, possibly due to shallow water. While on escort duty 24 April, K-3 was ordered to an area near Seaside Heights, New Jersey where a sound contact had been made by a trawler. A bubble buoy dropped by the K-2 was located and strong MAD contacts were made, however the contact proved to be a sunken ship. On 08 May 1942 a lifeboat was sighted with 10 survivors and rescue made with assistance from surface ships. K-3 was the first airship to land at the new Naval Air Station, Weeksville near Elizabeth City, North Carolina, on 06 May 1942, on loan to ZP-14 until their airships arrived.

---

[14] During this same period, in addition to U-123, the U-66 sank 4 ships totaling 50,000 tons, U-130 sank 3 tankers and a freighter totaling 30,748 tons and U-103 and U-106 had a combined total of 60,000 tons. From January to June 1942, the Germans sank 397 merchant ships and naval vessels in U.S. coastal waters and killed 5,000 seamen. In comparison, U.S. losses at Pearl Harbor were four battleships sunk, 2,403 dead and 1,178 wounded.

[15] In the early part of the war, airship search devices and armament were major problems and were not really resolved until 1944.

Next with ZP-11 at Naval Air Station, South Weymouth, Massachusetts on 03 June, K-3 made the first operational patrol. On 09 June K-3 sighted a torpedo that had hit a freighter in a convoy, searched for the U-boat without success and stayed with the freighter until it could be towed to Nova Scotia. K-3 had been in the air for 15 hours. (Controversial) On 9 June 1942, the K-3 (W.R. Peeler, command pilot) was approaching a convoy, Peeler states "We were searching NE towards Halifax when I saw a torpedo plume over the horizon 25 miles distant...full throttles...K-3 made a MAD search, had three contacts within range of [torpedoed freighter] *Kronprinsen*, dropped one bomb ... I have often wondered how close we were and if he knew we had located him." U-432 (Heinz-Otto Schultze) log recorded 1312 Hr. 9 June 42: "In periscope airship came into sight which shortly afterwards passed right overhead and forced us to dive deep." Peeler was transferred to ZP-33.

Then with ZP-14, K-3 (Possibly 10th Fleet #1010): Alfred Cope, Command pilot, attacked a MAD contact, 3 July 1942. *Tenth Fleet* author Farago "The [U-215] had vanished unrecorded and unclaimed by anyone on our side…the German roster gives July 3 as the date of its demise and "off the American coast" as the last location heard from."(Controversial) With ZP-14, Peter "Ace" Culbertson states: "According to my log book, I was command pilot.... of K-3 again on July 17th... I spotted the conning tower and then the whole sub. We passed over throwing smoke floats and turned around." Eastern Sea Frontier, Northern Group War Diary: "On 17 July [42] ...an airship sighted.... a submarine...at 300 foot altitude the airship dropped three bombs... The submarine was clearly visible as the charges dropped. One bomb dropped at either end and one directly in the center. The bombings resulted in an immediate increase in oil and new sources of air or light oil or gasoline right over the center of the raider." Culbertson continues: "One slipped off the conning tower and exploded causing oil to splatter to the surface. The smoke flares ignited the oil creating a 150 foot fire." Photos were taken. VADM C. E. Rosendahl notes a trawler reported a sound contact; airplanes and surface units then attacked. N.G. Diary concludes: "The submarine was probably fatally damaged." (Note: *Blimps & U-Boats* listed this incident as bombing a wreck, but no known summary contains an "object attacked not a sub" rating on 17/18 July.) Culbertson was transferred to ZP-31. On 29/30 July 1942, severe storms were encountered while K-3 was on routine patrol. Radio communications were lost and loose gear in the control car, including a fully loaded Browning Automatic Rifle, punched out the Plexiglas nose. With rain pouring in the face of the pilot (ENS Lynch) and the rudderman (Aviation Cadet F.G. Burger), a landing was finally made at Lakehurst after fifteen hours in the air. On the 11th of September 1942 K-3 got MAD contact, CG-409 arrived and dropped DCs, MAD contact moved, K-3 bombed, British trawler #29 DC'ed, oil and sewage came up. K-3, back with ZP-12, was used in the 1943 Training Film MN 1539A, K-Ship Operations. It is believed to have stayed at NASL for the duration.

Lockheed Martin Collection/University of Akron Archives

K-4 - Serial 7026, Goodyear envelope D-163 (416,000 cubic feet), control surfaces F-109 and control car C-60, erected and first flown at Wingfoot Lake 09 October 1941. K-4 was delivered to Lakehurst following a flight of 6 hours on 16 October by Karl Fickes (pilot), Web Crum and

Russell Crosier (co-pilots). After 02 January 1942, K-4 was assigned to ZP-12, making the first operational flight 03 January 1942, escorting a 13-ship convoy off the New Jersey coast. (Controversial) On 22 January 1942 K-4, responding to call of twin sub sighting by K-3, encountered “a suspicious, unidentifiable fishing smack…” whose two decks contained “some sixteen metal drums commonly used for carrying fuel oil.” K-4 joined K-3, planes and destroyers, in attacking oil slicks at the site of K-3’s twin sighting. Attacked a submerged target on 30 January, and again on 10 February, with K-6. On 01 March 1942 two depth bombs were dropped on a suspicious oil slick. On 11 April, K-4 located a life raft with seven survivors from a ship that had been torpedoed 2 weeks earlier. K-4 remained with the life raft until rescue was made by a Coast Guard ship. On 21 April, a periscope was spotted but contact was not made due to a faulty MAD unit, K-5 was notified for support and K-4 returned to Lakehurst.

K-4, her number blotted out for wartime, covers the rescue of sailors from the torpedoed SS *Persephone*. US Navy photo via the Navy Lakehurst Historical Society.

(Controversial, but verified by sub log:) The submarine U-593, after firing four torpedoes unsuccessfully at 1505 on 25 May 1942, later spotted the SS *Persephone*, which U-boat commander Kelbling logged as a “single 6,000 ton tanker” though it was actually part of a convoy line of ships with K-4 four miles ahead. U-593 fired two torpedoes then turned tail to make off at high speed. Using his periscope to check for pursuit after having felt the torpedo detonations, he made note of a "luftshiff.” It was the K-4, racing to the stricken but not sunk *Persephone*. K-4 stood by until the crew of the *Persephone* was rescued. K-4 made an attack on or about 1 May in conjunction with another airship, another attack on 25 May, and another the first week in June. On 10 July with ZP-11, K-4 provided all-night convoy coverage using the ASG radar that had then become available.

Lockheed Martin Collection/University of Akron Archives

K-5 - Serial 7027, Goodyear envelope D-164 (416,000 cubic feet), control surfaces F-110 and control car C-61 with delivery to Lakehurst 13 November 1941, the last airship to be delivered before the attack on Pearl Harbor. Assigned to ZP-12, the first operational patrol was made 03 January 1942 escorting a 13-ship convoy off the New Jersey coast. On routine anti-submarine patrol (ASW) 22 January with LT Charles Becker, two U-boats were observed surfacing and then crash-diving. K-5 raced to the scene and dropped three depth bombs from an altitude of approximately 600 feet. No wreckage appeared, and the remaining depth bomb was dropped on some suspicious bubbles. An Army bomber had been notified and the plane dropped additional bombs with no apparent effect. Two attacks against submerged targets were made in February. On 01 March, with LT Frank Trotter, pilot, an Eagle boat that reported a U-boat contact was assisted. Two depth bombs dropped. On 15 March K-5, with LTJG Saxe Gantz, pilot, bombed stationary MAD contact, two duds, followed up by USCG *Icarus*, evaluated as a wreck. On 17 March K-5, with the submarine S-20, tested a new radio sonobuoy. It was found that the sonobuoy could detect a submarine three miles away and that its radio transmission was received by airships at a five-mile range. On 18 March K-5, LT D. L. Cordiner, pilot, noted a disturbance in the wake of a large tanker, attacked MAD contact but two bombs were duds. The airship signaled another approaching tanker to change course, and it left the area. Continuing to track and attack along an oil slick, K-5 released its remaining two bombs, those too were duds. On 17 April with LTJG R. Jackson, pilot, K-5 located a lifeboat with 27 survivors. On 21 April, when notified of a suspected contact by the K-4, K-5 dropped depth bombs that produced air bubbles. The search then continued with airplanes and Coast Guard ships; K-5 was relieved by K-3 and returned to Lakehurst. K-5 made one attack (likely) on June 19, 1942, with K-7. K-5 was loaned to forming squadron ZP-14 in Weeksville. K-5 was later assigned to training duties at Lakehurst. On 16 May 1944, while making practice take-offs and landings, K-5 struck the upper ledge of Hangar No. One at Lakehurst and deflated on hangars no. 2 and 3. Loss of lives included LT Jordan W. Kilpatrick, LTJGs Frank B. Keller, William C. Dunn, John W. Hulm and Cain Smith, R.A. Luther AMRC2c, P.C. Bailey AMM2c, R.G. Wheaton S1c-V-6 and L.W. Hajduk ART1c. William Austin Humphrey, AMM3c was seriously injured but recovered and returned to duty. This was the greatest single loss of airship personnel to that time in World War II.

K-6 - Serial 7028, Goodyear envelope D-165 (416,000 cubic feet), control surfaces F-111 and control car C-62, delivered to Lakehurst 21 December 1941, the first airship to be delivered after the American entry into the war. (The media no longer issued bulletins on deliveries due to wartime censorship.) K-6 served with ZP-12. On 16 January, with LT Douglas Cordiner, pilot, K-6 attacked a surfaced U-boat. 11 March 1942, command pilot George Lee (Controversial, from Rosendahl manuscript, which states 12 March, but he verified from the German side): 1317 hr, the U-94 surfaced directly south of the K-6... approaching astern the blimp surprised the lookouts... sub crash dived but was not fully submerged when K-6 dropped two depth bombs which exploded near the boat. U-94 went to the bottom where damage report showed its port electric motor stopped, blocked stern planes and echo depth gauge out of order. Lacking MAD, K-6 lost visual; U-94 slipped away to deeper water for repairs. (Damage U-94 sustained on 12 March seems roughly similar to that inflicted on SS 212 *Gato* by TC-13 on the West Coast that month.) U-boat was able to make temporary repairs and return to base, its Captain was awarded a medal. K-6 attacked two more submerged targets in March. K-6 was then assigned to South Weymouth and involved in radar experiments with MIT's Radiation Laboratory. K-6 was deflated at the mast during a severe thunderstorm, with a ground crew casualty.

Lockheed Martin Collection/University of Akron Archives

General specifications	K-3 through K-6 (also K-7 and K-8):
Volume (cubic feet):	416,000
Ballonets (2, cubic feet):	114,000
Overall length (feet):	248.5
Maximum diameter:	57.85
Overall width:	62.5
Static lift (pounds):	25,800
Dynamic lift:	2,000
Service load (pounds):	5,000 (greater than K-2)
Speed, maximum (knots):	62.5
Speed, cruising:	50
Endurance at 50 kts (hours):	29 (less than K-2)
Range at 50 knots (miles):	1,250 (less than K-2)
Engines (2):	Curtiss-Wright R-975-28, 424 horsepower at 2,200 rpm, 3 blade propellers, arc of 9 feet

The early K-ships, K-3, -4, -5, -6, -7 and -8 had Wright engines with two-blade constant-speed propellers. They proved to be very noisy. Later K-ships had Pratt & Whitney engines with 12 foot, 3-blade, fixed-pitch propellers.

The early K-type airships were retro-fitted with the forward machine gun mount. Flying without cowlings in this view, the envelope reinforcements in line with the propeller blades are visible. Yet to be added are the radar dome and external depth bombs. US Navy photo.

Non-Rigid airships, Italian semi-rigid O-1 and Metalclad ZMC-2 on hand July 1917 through 1942 (includes airships not inflated)

1917 (06 April)	1	1931	3
1918 (11 NOV)	15	1932	4
1920	16	1933	3
1921	16	1934	2
1922	10	1935	2
1923	(unknown) *	1936	4
1924	1+	1937	4
1925	1	1938	5
1926	1	1939	8
1927	1	1940	6
1928	2	1941	7
1929	2	1942	16
1930	3		

This table is based on Navy records; however, there is some conflict with other information.
* Other records indicate B-3 was in service to February 1925, B-8 to April 1924, B-15 to September 1924 with J-1 entering service in February 1923 and operating at H
+ Assuming a date of June 1924, B-3, B-15 and J-1 would have been in service.

Lighter-Than-Air Equipment Serial Numbers 1917 through 1942 (Original 1914 designations were "D" for airships, "B" for balloons and "K" for kites.)

Number	Source	Item
A-?	Connecticut	Airship DN-1
94	Goodyear	Kite balloon BC-2
95	Goodyear	Kite balloon BC-3
151	Goodyear	Kite balloon BC-4
160	Goodyear	Kite balloon
161	Goodyear	Kite balloon

Note on airships: Goodrich and Goodyear built envelopes only and assembled airships. Connecticut assembled completed airships with U.S. Rubber envelopes. Envelopes carried an "E" number and serial numbers represented the control car. The "B", "C" and "D" numbers represented a complete airship. Goodyear used "D" for envelopes, "F" for control surfaces and "C" for control cars.

235	Goodyear	Airship B-1
236	Goodyear	Airship B-2
237	Goodyear	Airship B-3
238	Goodyear	Airship B-4
239	Goodyear	Airship B-5
240	Goodyear	Airship B-6
241	Goodyear	Airship B-7
242	Goodyear	Airship B-8
243	Goodyear	Airship B-9
244	Goodrich	Airship B-10
245	Goodrich	Airship B-11
246	Goodrich	Airship B-12
247	Goodrich	Airship B-13
248	Goodrich	Airship B-14
249	Connecticut	Airship B-15
250	Connecticut	Airship B-16
251	Connecticut	Free balloon
276-287	Goodyear	Kite balloon (12)
372	Goodyear	Kite balloon
373	Goodyear	Kite balloon
700	Goodyear	Kite balloon

701	Goodrich	Kite balloon
702- 726	Goodyear	Kite Balloon(25)
727- 751	Goodrich	Kite Balloon (25)
763	Great Britain	Kite Balloon (Caquot M Type)
764	Great Britain	Kite Balloon (Caquot M Type)
816	France	Kite Balloon (Caquot P Type)
817	France	Kite Balloon (Caquot P Type)
998	Goodrich	Kite Balloon
1029	Great Britain	Airship O-SS (actually British SS Zero)
1030	Great Britain	Airship O-SS 9actually British SS Zero) cancelled
2208-2214	Goodyear	Free balloon (7)
2215	Connecticut	Free balloon
2216	Connecticut	Free balloon
2665-2844	Goodyear	Kite balloon (records indicate 180 type R and 10 Caquot, serial numbers indicate a total of 180)
2845-2929	Goodyear	Kite balloon (85), cancelled
2930-3020	Goodrich	Kite balloon (records indicate 81 type R and 10 Caquot, serial numbers indicate a total of 91
3021-3204	Goodrich	Kite balloon (184), cancelled
3383	Goodrich	"Gastite Kite" balloon
4109	Goodyear	Airship E-1
4118	Goodyear	Airship C-1
4119	Goodrich	Airship C-2
4120	Goodyear	Airship C-3
4121	Goodrich	Airship C-6
4122	Goodyear	Airship C-4
4123	Goodyear	Airship C-5
4124	Goodrich	Airship C-9
4125	Goodrich	Airship C-10
4126	Goodyear	Airship C-7
4127	Goodyear	Airship C-8
4348	Goodyear	Airship F-1
4450	Goodyear	Airship D-1
4451	Goodrich	Airship D-2 (Revised to Goodyear)
4452	Goodyear	Airship D-3
4453	Goodyear	Airship D-4 (Revised to Goodrich)
4454	Goodrich	Airship D-5

Note: Goodyear actually erected D-1, D-2 and D-3 and Goodrich D-4 and D-5. The system was revised to reflect actual erection or delivery date.

4455-4469	Goodyear (10)	Airship D-type (cancelled)
	Goodrich (5)	Airship D-type (cancelled)
5020	Goodyear	Kite balloon, reduced type R Caquot
5021	Goodyear	Kite balloon, reduced type R Caquot
5022	Goodrich	Kite balloon, reduced type R Caquot
5023	Goodrich	Kite balloon, reduced type R Caquot
5025-5028	Goodyear	Kite balloon, Caquot type P (4)
5029	Goodyear	Kite balloon, experimental
5040	Great Britain	Kite balloon, Caquot type M
5241	Italy	Kite balloon, Avorio Prassone (AP)
5242	Italy	Kite balloon, Avorio Prassone (AP)
5257	Goodyear	Airship B-20
5463	Goodyear	Kite balloon
5464	Goodyear	Updated control car for airship B-17
5465	Goodyear	Updated control car for airship B-18
5466	Goodyear	Airship control car for assumed B-20
5467	Goodyear	Updated control car for airship B-19
5468	Goodyear	Airship (revised B-20?)
5472	France	Airship Astra-Torres AT-1
5473-5482	Great Britain	Kite balloon (10)
5563	Great Britain	Airship SSZ-23
5580	Great Britain	Airship NS-1 (actually NS-11)
5587	Italy	Airship 0-1 (Semi-rigid)
5592	France	Airship Vedette-Zodiac VZ-7

5593	France	Airship Vedette-Zodiac VZ-13
5594-5605	Connecticut	Free balloon (12)
5753-5755	Connecticut	Kite balloon, type AP (3)
5860-5866	Goodyear	Free balloon (7)
5972	Goodyear	Airship D-6
5973	Goodyear	Airship H-1 Towing Airship
6074-6076	Connecticut	Free balloon (3)
6103-6110	Goodyear	Kite Balloon, type F (8) (6109 assigned to Lakehurst to 1923)
6111	Goodyear	Airship J-1
6112	Goodyear	Airship J-2 (not completed)
6445	NAF	Racing balloon (Naval Aircraft Factory)
6527	NAF	Free balloon
6698-6700	Goodyear	Free balloon (3)
7381	Army	Kite balloon, type R
7382	Army	Airship J-3, Army TC-type
7386-7389	Goodyear	Free balloon (4)
7490-7392	Goodyear	Kite balloon (3)
8277-8281	Meadowcroft	Free balloon (5)
8282	Aircraft Dev.	Airship ZMC-2
8476	Goodyear	Free balloon
8608	Goodyear	Kite balloon, type C-3
8609	Goodyear	Kite balloon, type C-3
8610-8612	Goodyear	Free balloon (3)
8924-8927	Goodyear	Free balloon (4)
9344	Air Cruisers	Kite balloon
9345	Air Cruisers	Kite balloon
9992	Air Cruisers	Kite balloon
9999	Goodyear	Airship G-1

Serial numbers revised to begin with 100,000 and "A-" discontinued.

1210	Goodyear	Airship L-1
1211	Goodyear	Airship K-2
1471	Goodyear	Free balloon
1472	Goodyear	Free balloon
1473	Goodyear	Free balloon
7025	Goodyear	Airship K-3
7026	Goodyear	Airship K-4
7027	Goodyear	Airship K-5
7028	Goodyear	Airship K-6
7029	Goodyear	Airship L-2
7030	Goodyear	Airship L-3

There are also references to Connecticut Aircraft Kite balloons AX-1 and AX-2, contract C-49259, aerological research kite balloons, with AX-1 received at Pensacola 05 October 1920 and stricken circa July 1923 (salvage for coverings, painting, clothes, etc.) There are no details on AX-2. Airships Inc. also produced aerological balloons AX-3 and AX-4 (contract 5652) with AX-3 at Lakehurst 31 July 1928 and AX-4 burned completely circa 04 April 1929 and stricken 30 April. It is possible that AX-3 and AX-4 could be shown as the Meadowcroft 5277 through 5281 series or serial numbers 9344 and 9345 shown as Air Cruisers. No references are made to K-1, TC-13 and TC-14 in the Navy serial number records.

PART V: Pressure Airships During World War II
1942 Through 1945

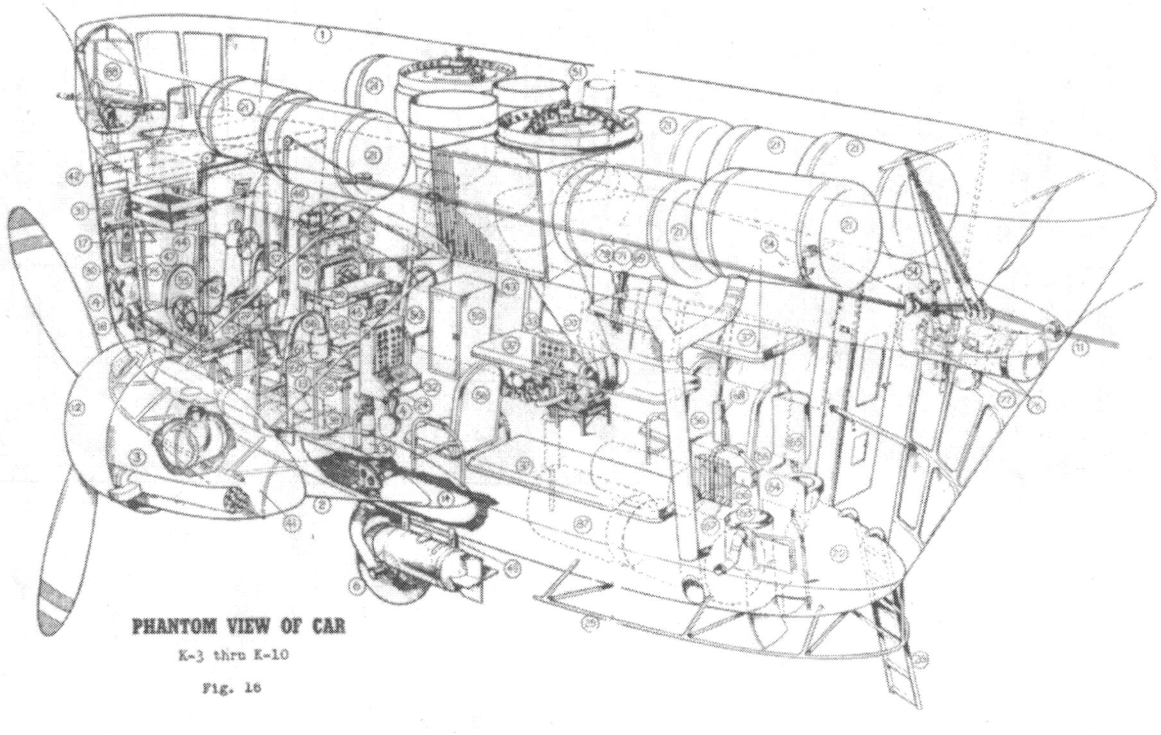

PHANTOM VIEW OF CAR
K-3 thru K-10
Fig. 16

The largest quantity of airships produced during World War II were the K-type patrol airships. The original pre-war contract (Navy 78121) was for K-3 thru K-6 and L-2 and L-3, with an option for two more airships (K-7 and K-8). The option on K-7 and K-8 was accepted in June 1941. These two airships were delivered after the Pearl Harbor attack. This original order was supplemented by an additional order for 21 airships in October 1941, then to an authorized 48 and finally to a total of 200 on 16 June 1942. Contract 78121 included K-3 through K-50 and contract NOs-257 (originally NXs(a) 10086) included K-51 through K-135. K-9 through K-13 were 416,000 cubic feet in volume. K-14 through K-50 were 425,000 cubic feet in volume with eventual volume reaching 456,000 cubic feet. The airship control cars were initially fabricated and assembled at the former Goodyear-Zeppelin Airdock (Harold W. [Web] Crum, manager) and were erected and test flown at Wingfoot Lake, except where noted. Sub-contracts were let to two local bus manufacturers (Twin Coach at Kent, Ohio, and Flxible at Loudenville, Ohio) for control cars, outriggers and control surfaces (primarily for the L and G-type airships) and some envelopes were sub-contracted to the Dunlop Company in Buffalo, New York. Forty-one K, L and G-type airships were erected at Moffett Field. These airships were originally planned for erection at the Goodyear facility at Litchfield Park, Arizona, but, due to lack of hangar space, were transferred to Moffett Field and erected in the Navy steel hangar.

At peak production, 2,500 Goodyear employees were assigned to airship construction at Akron. The Wingfoot Lake force attained 300 employees (Karl Fickes, manager) and many experienced personnel were transferred to Moffett Field (with Henry [Hank] H. Nettling, manager) for airship erection while others were diverted to airship bases (150 men were assigned to Richmond, Florida). Top production of K-type airships was in July 1944 when 11 airships were delivered (3 L-type airships were also delivered this month). Goodyear also provided approximately thirteen test and delivery pilots (Jim Bode, Chris Christie, Russ Crosier, Web Crum, Irv Eastin, Karl Fickes, Ed Hamlin, Bill Knight, Walt Kominic, Walt Massic, Dean

Mealy, Jack Porosky and Sam Sheppard) for the completed airships with delivery to the acceptance center at Lakehurst. Crum became manager of the control car manufacturing and assembly at the Airdock, Fickes became manager at Wingfoot Lake and Sheppard was assigned to the airship bases. Nineteen former Goodyear airship pilots served with the Navy (Joe Amrein, John Blair, Jack Boettner, Pres Dixon, Larry Furculow, Ollie Hess, Rolland "Hobie" Hobensack, Karl Lange, Fred Lueders, Jim Maloney, Jack Purkiss, John Rieker, Art Sewell, Verner Smith, Clarence Stacey, Len Stillwell, Frank Trotter, Bill Vinson and Cliff Zimmerman. Bob Wilson was also a member of the Naval Reserve but it is uncertain if he served with airships during World War II. Although Fickes, Crum and Al Rodgers held Naval Reserve commissions they were held at Akron (Rodgers, envelope superintendent) for production responsibilities. Other Goodyear pilots served in engineering, production or as airship field engineers at the various bases. No serious accidents were recorded by Goodyear during the entire delivery program.

The airships comprised three major assemblies: the envelopes, which were identified by Goodyear with a "D" number and were primarily manufactured in the balloon rooms of the main Akron Goodyear plant, which occupied three floors (and later at Litchfield Park, Arizona); the control car, which was identified by a "C" number and manufactured initially at the former Goodyear-Zeppelin Airdock; and the control surfaces, which were identified by an "F" number and consisted of the upper, port, starboard and lower fins with moveable rudders and elevators and were manufactured in the Goodyear gymnasium in Akron. The control car remained as the principal identification of an airship. In addition to the original envelope shown for each airship, spare envelopes were also furnished. Lakehurst and Moffett Field were the receiving points for all airships. Some confusion exists between the airship serial numbers shown in UNITED STATES NAVAL AVIATION 1910-1970 and other records. Only 122 serial numbers are shown for K-type airships in that volume but 135 K-type airships were erected. No reason is apparent for this discrepancy. The serial numbers shown are based on the best available information. Goodyear envelope, control car and control surfaces are the original numbers as furnished to the Navy. (Airships shown as deflated does not usually indicate a total loss as replacement envelopes were available and the airship was soon back in service. The airships were easily repaired; only major control car damage would delete an airship.)

K-7 -Serial 01729, Goodyear envelope D-170 (416,000 cubic feet), control car C-65 and control surfaces F-114, delivered to Lakehurst 29 April 1942, the first airship delivered after the Pearl Harbor attack. K-7 was the first car featuring a split forward suspension mount that allowed the mounting of the .50 caliber machine gun turret topside forward (right). This was made possible by moving the forward fuel tanks aft. K-7 was in patrol service in June. On the 11th ZP-12's K-7 under D. L. Cordiner joined in a joint air and surface attack on an oil slick, which produced more oil but no wreckage. On the 1st of August 1942 K-7 directed PYC-37 to deal with a loose floating Army mine. Later assigned to training at NASL, collided with ZP-12's K-64 in poor visibility off Barnegat Inlet, New Jersey on 16 October 1943. K-7 returned to base. However K-64 caught fire and was lost, with only one survivor.

K-8 - Serial 01730, Goodyear envelope D-171 (416,000 cubic feet), control car C-66 and control surfaces G-115, delivered to Lakehurst 17 May 1942; assigned to Weeksville. On 01 June 1942, K-8 investigated wreckage and located two floating bodies nearby. K-8 located six surviving crewmen of a U-boat sunk by an Army bomber on 07 July 1942. The survivors had been in the water for 18 hours; K-8 dropped supplies and marked their position for pick-up by Coast Guard plane. 8 AUG 42 ZP-14's K-8 found an oil slick and developed MAD contacts over it. Surface craft arrived and depth-charged the contact, which brought more oil to the surface but no other results. On the 22nd of August 1942 W. H. Keen and the K-8 crew dropped two bombs on an oil slick that had not set off the MAD needle. K-8 summoned surface craft to destroy a floating mine it spotted on the 23rd of December 1942. 2nd of March 1943 ZP-12's K-8 under LT W. F. Lineberger worked a MAD contact with surface units, including the PC 554 which is listed as making "mousetrap attacks" without visible results.

The K-7 at Wingfoot Lake. During the summer of 1942, the airship's ID numbers were blotted out and their red, white and blue control surfaces were painted over. Note the less than full complement of windows around the new gun. Radar not yet added, K-7 is also flying the national ensign from the stern, later deleted. Lockheed Martin Collection/University of Akron Archives.

Immediately after Pearl Harbor was attacked, Goodyear employees reportedly decided to switch back to the quieter Pratt & Whitney R-1340 engines. K-9 was the first car built with the necessary changes, so the older K-ships were not completely compatible with later K-types.

K-9 - Serial 04359, Goodyear envelope D-173, control car C-67, control surfaces F-117, delivered to Lakehurst 29 June 1942, assigned to ZP-14 at Weeksville, North Carolina. K-9 located survivors of the *Moldanger* on 15 July 1942. It lowered provisions and notified surface craft for rescue. On 16 AUG 43 ZP-14's K-9 established multiple MAD contacts and attacked with four bombs, bringing oil and bubbles to the surface. 16 AUG 43 ZP-14's K-9 dropped 4 bombs on MAD signal – evaluated as a wreck. K-9 suffered a hard landing 7 July 1944, was then repaired. With ZP-11 on 18 April 1944, K-9 effected the rescue of three Navy fliers after a collision of two planes off Nantucket Island. When it was clear surface craft would not reach the life rafts in time, K-9 dropped its bowlines and carefully towed the life rafts for more than nine hours. It is believed K-9 was the airship flown from South Weymouth to Sydney, Nova Scotia, on 16/17 September 1944. It landed after a seventeen-hour flight, was refueled and proceeded to Argentia, Newfoundland. Total flight time was thirty-one hours. Due to foul weather it was kept at the mast for one week and then flown back to South Weymouth. On 30 September 1944, it was flown to Yarmouth, Nova Scotia, and landed to an inexperienced Royal Canadian Air Force handling party without a U.S. Navy officer present. When it appeared a man was entangled in the long handling lines, power was applied to one engine. Off-wind and insufficient speed, it was unable to clear the mast. It struck the mast and the envelope deflated.

K-10 - Serial 04360, Goodyear envelope D-174, control car C-68, control surfaces F-118, delivered to Lakehurst 12 July 1942; assigned to ZP-14 at Weeksville, North Carolina. On 15 November 1942, K-10 located a four-masted schooner flying a distress signal and summoned the Coast Guard. On 03 December, K-10 located the unescorted British merchantman *Boltonhall* and signaled a course change to prevent it hitting a mine, then escorted the ship through the minefield. In August, it depth-bombed a MAD contact, now thought to be a wreck. On 10 February 1943, K-10 located the wreckage of a Navy OS2U-3 plane in dense swamp near Moyock, North Carolina. It lead a search party to the scene after dark by flying over forest roads and flashing signals by blinker. On 16 FEB 43 ZP-15 got its second airship, the K-10, on loan from ZP-14. Its crew found the remains of a crashed B-24 on the 28th. Life jackets and a raft were located, but no survivors were ever found. On the 5th of July 1943 K-10 sighted what appeared to be an underwater explosion, and making for the scene, found discolored water but no magnetic contacts. All that was found for the day's strange events was an empty life boat. On 16 May 1944, K-10 notified Key West, Florida of an "uncontrollable fire" in the hold of a cargo ship. A fireboat was dispatched to the scene. On 01 June, it directed the Coast Guard to the aid of a small craft out of fuel. K-10 was used for experiments in water recovery in late 1945/early 1946 (right, Goodyear photo) it was equipped with bow planes for experimental flight at Wingfoot Lake. Assigned to Glynco in 1953, K-10 assisted in the search for two persons lost in the bay near Brunswick, Georgia, directed a Coast Guard crash boat to a downed Air Force C-47, investigated a report of a parachute sighting by an Eastern Airlines pilot near Savannah, Georgia (it was a pilot-less drone plane from Hunter Air Force Base) and then searched for a body near Harris Neck, Georgia, at the request of state police. This was all on the same day.

K-11 - Serial 04361, Goodyear envelope D-175, control car C-69, control surfaces F-119, delivered to Lakehurst 05 August 1942. 17 SEP 42 K-11 reported for duty at ZP-11, the first production airship actually assigned, not loaned, to the Massachusetts squadron. On 02 November 1942, K-11 located a disabled trawler and directed another trawler to assist. On 08 December, it searched for and located USCG vessel 3032, dropping rations and standing by until tow arrived. On the 2nd of November 1942 the K-11 located the disabled trawler *Inca* and directed a tow. 23 DEC 42 K-11 was sent out and found a stranded Coast Guard ship. K-11 then summoned more CG to help, dropping rations while they waited. Its envelope deflated after hitting trees and a barn in a storm 31 July 1943, it was rebuilt and in service at South Weymouth July to November 1944. Purchased as surplus by Goodyear in 1946, not erected. The control car was revised to ZP2K/ZP3K type and resold to the Navy in the early 1950's.

K-12 - Serial 04362, Goodyear envelope D-176, control car C-70, control surfaces F-120, delivered to Lakehurst 22 August 1942. On the 1st of September 1942 K-12 attacked a MAD signature near a convoy, but could not regain the contact. On 13 SEP 42, as K-12 was escorting a convoy from the Ambrose Lightship, Walter Aymond in K-12 got a moving MAD contact, dropped 3 bombs, surface craft also bombed, no evidence of damage. On 17 SEP 42 LT F. S. Rixey in K-12 got a MAD signature while escorting a convoy. Marking it then bombing it, surface craft also attacked. The ZP-12 history details, "The K-12 pilot was at this time informed that what appeared to be a periscope had been sighted immediately after the first bomb had been dropped by the airship. This appeared about 75 feet behind the point of the second contact. Three members of the crew saw the object which was black, about three inches in diameter, and projected about one foot or one foot and a half above the surface." It was later decided a sub might have gotten away while the MAD stuck on a wreck. With ZP-14 on 22 December, K-12 located the lost Coast Guard ship 3070 that had once been located by CG 462 only to be lost again. K-12 stood by until aid arrived. K-12 was the first airship to be docked in the timber hangar at South Weymouth, Massachusetts, on 31 October 1943. On 06 December 1943, K-12 located four survivors who were rescued by surface craft. On the 8th, K-12 located two survivors of a plane crash.

K-13 - Serial 04363, Goodyear envelope D-178 (last of the 416,000 cubic feet envelopes), control car C-71, control surfaces F-121 and F-123. On a Goodyear test flight from Wingfoot Lake and over Lake Erie (Jack Boettner, pilot) K-13 lost altitude due a faulty helium valve. 55,000 cubic feet of helium escaped; K-13 reached shore by skillful flying at only 200 feet altitude, where the superheat allowed a return to Wingfoot Lake. Delivered to Lakehurst 11 September 1942; based at Weeksville in July 1943. On the 26th of January 1943 two mines floating away from a Cape Hatteras minefield were spotted by K-13, which oversaw their recovery. On 18 MAR 43 ZP-14's K-13 established a MAD contact and a CG cutter depth charged it, but there was no further result. K-13 attacked a MAD contact on 7 JUL 43 without visible results. On 18 July, it bombed another MAD contact. K-13 exhausted its fuel, made an emergency landing and was deflated near Charleston, South Carolina, on 8 November 1943, after 19.5 hours in the air flying through at-sea storms. It was rebuilt. In service in April 1944, with ZP-15 at Glynco, Georgia, K-13 made a patrol when all heavier-than-air craft were grounded. Rebuilt and flown to Richmond, Florida (date unknown) in 13.5 hours (average speed of 125 miles per hour, LCDR Andrews, pilot), later assigned to ZP-14 at Weeksville, North Carolina. Transferred to ZP-32 where on 28 June 1945 searched for and located runaway pontoons on the shoreline near San Gregorio. On 4 October 1945, K-13 searched for and located a lost fishing boat, summoning a Coast Guard vessel for tow. ZP-32's last rescue was on the 4th of October 45 when K-13 located a fishing boat run aground north of Pigeon Point and stood by until a CG vessel took it in tow. K-13 was revised to ZP2K/ZSG-2 type.

K-14 - Serial 04364, Goodyear envelope D-180 (425,000 cubic feet volume), control car C-72, control surfaces F- 122, delivered to Lakehurst 11 September 1942; first airship to dock in the new steel hangar at South Weymouth, Massachusetts. The following April a locking key failed in the steering linkage, drifted until temporary repairs could be made in flight. On 12 JUL 43 the K-14 attacked a contact, incident rated 'I.'

On 2 July 1944, a fishing boat reported a submarine sighting off Bar Harbor, Maine, at 1045 hrs Queen. K-14 was dispatched to investigate and began a MAD search at 2115. APC-94 crew recorded feeling two depth charge concussions about 2130, fifteen minutes after K-14 arrived on the scene. Three fishing vessels and an onshore CG watchman also reported gunfire, flashes and detonations at that time. At 0855 on 3 July, APC-94 encountered a ½ mile long heavy oil slick and stayed on course to find K-14 in the water. Eastern Sea Frontier - Northern Group Reports: "There have been numerous reports of heavy explosions and gunfire and machine gun fire at or about the time the K-14 crashed which may have been responsible for the crash." 5 July salvage diver reported... "a lot of .50 caliber shells all strewn around..." 7 July... "No offhand explanation could be given for the failure to find two known depth charges in the after racks and no accounting was given for the dead fish in the area..." Board of Inquiry's Finding of Facts: "...the arming wires were still attached to the bomb racks, indicating that the bombs left their racks armed... examination of the bag showed there were about 40 feet of the after section missing. Numerous small holes were found..."

K-14 photo, taken from Army crash boat, has hand-written caption on the back "...was shot down by U-boat." Photo courtesy Edward Michaud.

(Controversial) ZP-11 pilot Lou Prost stated: "The skipper, LCDR C.A. Bolam... informed us that we should not blame [pilot at controls] Ernie [Sharp] for the crash but he could not tell us any more... Ernie Sharp was transferred out of the squadron immediately." Board of Inquiry report findings: K-14 was assigned a low-level (below 200 feet) special MAD search off Bar Harbor, Maine, early morning of 3 July 44. Command pilot ENS William McDonnell was attempting to adjust his radar picture from "sea return" when K-14 struck the water. The Court of Inquiry determined the loss of K-14 was due to "pilot error," a common reason presented when no other cause can be established for an accident or incident. The board refused to hear shore-based witnesses who reported tracer fire, nor boat based witnesses who reported concussions, a large fish kill and oil slick. Neither would they admit the salvage diver's report of many 50 caliber shell casings in the car. Neither would they admit alternate K-14 pilot LT Grant Southward's findings. During Southward's supervision of the bag recovery, the party found numerous holes in the envelope seeming to enter aft of the car and exiting topside amidships.

A NAVY MAVERICK COMES OF AGE, Alex W. Moffat, CDR, USN (Ret) Bantam Books, 1977: "But it was obvious that the court wanted no record of any sub attack in those waters. At the hearing they admitted no evidence except that obtained from interrogating the survivors. It would not even accept in evidence the written statement of the technicians that they found many bullet holes in the fabric... When the bag was spread out on the field they were able to determine that the bullets entered the bag aft of the car and exited at the top amidships." McDonnell, who was not actually at the controls, was blamed, and was not credited for saving the lives of at least two of the crew. The Board of Inquiry minority opinion, noting the fact the depth bombs were dropped armed, refused to rule out enemy action. McDonnell's only public comment in 50 years was "The Navy had good reason for doing what it did." There were many that did not agree with the Court of Inquiry and reliable sources stated it was directed by higher authority to ignore any reference to it being shot down by a U-boat. VADM Rosendahl relates U-boat crews claimed having shot down blimps, (note *plural*) so K-14's attacker might have made it back to France. Survivors of the U-233, sunk by the USS *Card* ASW group on 5 July coming into the Halifax area, were told the group was looking for an *outbound* submarine. The circumstances of the loss of the K-14 are likely to remain a mystery since no published account places a U-boat in that area at that time. The six crewmen lost were LT Charles W. Kluber, ARM2c John B. Powles, AMM2c John V. Oldar, AR2c Edward J. Drzewiecki, ARM3c William H. Munro and AEM3c Walter O. Ozeski. Activist's efforts continue to award them the Purple Heart.

K-15 - Serial 04365, Goodyear envelope D-179, control car C-73, control surfaces F-123 and F-124, delivered to Lakehurst 21 September 1942. 29 MAY 43 K-15 spotted a slick and did get a MAD contact, as well as a radar blip some four miles away. The airship was unable to locate the source. 01 JAN 44 ZP-12 made the inaugural flight of their new torpedo recovery service with K-15 under ENS D. Wallstein. 05 MAR 43 K-15 searched for and located a missing vessel, escorting it back to convoy. In service at South Weymouth June to December 1944.

K-16 - Serial 04366, Goodyear envelope D-181, control car C-74, control surfaces F-123, F-124 and F-125, delivered to Lakehurst 25 September 1942. First airship to use hangar No.1 at Richmond, Florida, reassigned to ZP-51 for Caribbean operations, LTJG Hummers, pilot. On the 3rd of April 1943 K-16 reported down to Trinidad to become ZP-51's second airship. On 26 April 43 K-16 worked a MAD contact with no results. While on routine ASW patrol on 15 AUG 43 the K-16, under LTJG Francis D. Verdery, spotted a small disabled fishing boat. Lowering an emergency Red Cross kit, the crew determined the boat contained three missing Army soldiers. Following a little Army-Navy liaison by radio, boats arrived to pick them up. Returned to Lakehurst and On 26 APR 45 the K-16, LTJG S. Liss, command pilot, was ordered off barrier patrol to investigate a snorkel sighting, and dropped sono-bouys. On 06 May 1945 (with K-58) was assigned a special MAD patrol in search of a U-boat believed in the area east of Long Island, New York in the area where the SS *Black Point* had been torpedoed 12 hours earlier. The destroyer USS *Ericsson* directed the airships to an area where several surface ships had made attacks on the U-boat, strong MAD contacts were made and the area marked with dye markers. K-16 informed the *Ericsson* that the target was stationary and the USS *Atherton* (DE-169) made a depth charge attack. For 20 minutes four more attacks were made, the target was again located by K-16 and another attack made by the *Ericsson.* K-16 sighted patches of oil and air bubbles coming to the surface and then dropped a sono-buoy and heard rhythmic pounding on a metal surface, K-16 made a running attack at 150 feet and dropped four "rocket bombs" ('hedgehogs' without propellant) which exploded within 3 seconds after entering the water and bringing debris to the surface. K-

58 then made MAD passes and another bombing run, debris that floated to the surface was recovered that included a German officer cap, equipment, two submarine recovery breathing lungs, one Captain's life raft, five other floats and a piece of chart table. U-853 had been sunk, possibly the last German U-boat sunk in American waters before the war ended. Transferred to ZP-32 where on 25 June 1945 it conducted an inspection flight of landing facilities at Stockton, California.

K-17 - Serial 04367, Goodyear envelope D-182, control car C-75, control surfaces F-125 and F-126, delivered to Lakehurst 29 September 1942. With ZP-14 on 17 January 1943, K-17 located a lost Coast Guard ship. Assigned to Richmond and flown into Biscayne Bay during delivery, temporarily abandoned. Reclaimed and flown out of water by LCDR Alfred L. Cope. On 16 FEB 43 the K-17, first American airship to operate in another hemisphere, arrived in Trinidad and was on patrol over the 'upper bauxite lane' the next morning. 02 Mar 43 an air attack was made on a suspected submarine off Trinidad. "...a light blue oil slick accompanied by bubbles was located by the airship about 12 miles south of the position of a night attack made twelve hours before... a slow moving contact was registered on the graph..." After working the contact with smoke flares, K-17 dropped 3 depth bombs and noted "...the flow of oil appeared to increase." ZP-51's skipper wrote, "It is believed that the bombing of the enemy submarine by Pilot Cormier inflicted damage upon the submarine which caused this new oil slick to appear." K-17 returned to Trinadad and re-armed. Committee voting 'E' on that attack noted "Large amount of oil and plotting room opinion regarding sub reporting attack and therefore probable damage." At 0955Z ZP-51's ENS J. F. Bishop, ENS B. F. Burgess, ENS W.C. Baird, six enlisted crewmen (with an Army Lt. A.C. Hartman along as an observer) took off in K-17 and about 1200Z found a two to three mile long oil slick at that approximate location. K-17 dropped a marker buoy at the apparent origin's end. MAD was off line until 1504Z at which time it registered contact that appeared to be moving slowly. Three Mark 44-1 depth bombs with Mark 24 fuses set for 50 feet were dropped, but one took 20 seconds to explode. Oil appeared to increase, and K-17 worked the contact until returning to base at 2200Z. ZP-51's skipper, G.D. Zurmuehlen, then took ENS Baird and a fresh crew in the re-armed K-17 back to the scene. He found no reason to make another attack, as it appeared the object was not moving and was below 300 feet in depth. He wrote a few days later that in his opinion "no attack should have been made by the airship under those circumstances," but notes that Bishop's malfunctioning depth charge might have lucked out. "It is possible that the explosion of this depth charge resulted in the final destruction of the submarine if the submerged object was that type of craft." VP-53 flying boat pilot J. E. Dryden sank U-156 on 8 MAR 42. On 16 APR 43 the ASW Unit in Boston noted the later action and wrote, " Accordingly, the opinion expressed that no damage was done is changed to an opinion that [the earlier blimp] attack resulted in possible slight damage to the submarine." (Since no U-156 survivors were ever found, there is no way to know if the K-17's attack played a role in U-156 not diving 3 + days later.) K-17 reported a drifting freighter and directed surface craft to the location on 05 September 1943. Later based at Houma and nick named "Dopey". With ZP-21 04 MAY 44 the K-17's routine patrol noticed a tanker heading for a KN convoy but was unable to get it to change course using the Grimes light. Finally, training the K-17's spotlight on the errant ship, the surface escort was alerted to come over and order the ship to change course, preventing a collision. 18 APR 44 K-17 vectored a fire boat to the scene of a cargo vessel burning out of control. K-17 was on an assignment for BuOrd on 8 SEP 44 when it came upon an open boat adrift, summoning a salvage team.

K-18 - Serial 04368, Goodyear envelope D-183, control car C-76, control surfaces F-126 and F-129, delivered to Lakehurst 08 October 1942. Ferried from Lakehurst, it was the first airship to land at Richmond, Florida on 14 October 1942. 02 DEC 42 ZP-21's K-18 got its first MAD signature, but it was judged faulty equipment. 10 DEC 42 K-18, assigned a convoy escort, was also ordered to search for survivors of a Navy plane crash. With ZP-21 on 06 April 1943, K-18 located two survivors on a life raft from a crashed Army plane, they dropped food and summoned surface craft. On 04 May it assisted in the rescue of three lifeboats containing an estimated twenty-five survivors. K-18 also assigned to ZP-14 at Weeksville, North Carolina. K-18 served with ZP-15 in 1945. On the 3rd of January 1945 K-18 located a fishing boat in distress and stood by so the CG could home in. Transferred from ZP-15 to Hedron One, NASL, April, 1945.

K-19 - Serial 04369, Goodyear envelope D-184, control car C-77, control surfaces F-127; delivered to Lakehurst 19 October 1942, transferred to Richmond. In January 1943 K-19 flew to San Juan, Puerto Rico, first airship to make that flight. In March it became the first airship to fly to Santa Fe, Isle of Pines, Cuba. 14 MAR 43 K-19 depth-bombed a MAD contact later evaluated as faulty MAD. K-19 located a wrecked B-25 on April 20th 1943 but only the parachute of the survivor. In service at Richmond with ZP-21 on 29 July 1943, K-19 assisted in the rescue of two survivors from the crash of a Navy plane at sea. ZP-21's K-19 crew flying on August 3rd 1943 were sure they'd spotted a surfacing submarine, which quickly dived, but they made no attack and the incident was rated 'doubtful.'

On 06 August, it directed search parties to a plane that had crashed in the Everglades. On 09 January 1944, K-19 located fishermen in a rowboat adrift in the Gulf Stream, summoning surface craft. On 05 April, K-19 assisted in a rescue by arranging a rendezvous between a tug and a disabled fishing boat. Serving in Brazil, it reported blips indicating U-boat in the area. On 29 July it suffered a dual engine failure; free ballooning, the crew jettisoned equipment and landed safely. Revised to ZP2K-19 and based at Lakehurst in 1951, appeared at rowing races on Severn River in 1951 advertising Armed Forces Week. Served at NARTU, Santa Ana, 1955.

K-20 - Serial 04370, Goodyear envelope D-185, control car C-78, control surfaces F-128 and 129, shipped to Lakehurst 19 October and ferried to Moffett Field from Lakehurst via Charleston, South Carolina; Jackson, Mississippi; El Paso, Texas and Litchfield Park, Arizona (with a temporary stop at El Centro, California) arriving 31 October 1942 with LCDR E. J. Sullivan and LT F.J. Tobin as pilots. K-20 was the first delivery of a production model K-type to the west coast. With ZP-31 on 20 March 1943, K-20 sighted a burning yacht and guided a destroyer to pick up two survivors. On 22 April with K-21, assisted planes and surface vessels in the search for three flyers on a life raft, one was located and rescued. 26 MAR 43 K-21 searched for and found a wrecked P-38 but the pilot's body was never located. 21 and 22 APR 43 K-21 searched for a TBF lost following launch from the USS *Block Island,* but found only a mattress. K-20 relieved K-21 at the site of a suspected submarine near Oceanside, California 01 June 1943. 07 AUG 43 the K-20, while investigating a suspicious object, was inadvertently flown into the water and three crewmen were ejected. Without any electrical system, pilot F. W. Kelly managed to get the K-20 back to Santa Ana and a nearby DD picked up the dog-paddling crewmen. On 14 March 1944 with K-99, it was ordered to the aid of a pilot adrift in a life raft and stood by until the pilot was rescued by a crash boat. On 27 MAR 45 ZP-31's K-20 escorting the new battleship *Iowa* noticed an airplane trying to attract attention. Following its lead, K-20 came upon a lone man in a life raft, then summoned a destroyer to pick him up. Revised to ZP2K/ZSG-2 type.

Note: Most K-type airships were delivered to Moffett Field by rail; only K-20, K-21 and K-22 were ferried to Moffett Field during the war. The first K-ship to be assembled at Moffett Field, the K-23. was delivered to the squadron 19 December 1942. Airships were later transferred across country. On 25 November 1944, 11 K-ships were ferried from the east coast to the west coast with the transfer completed by 14 December.

K-21 - Serial 04371, Goodyear envelope D-186, control car C-79, control surfaces F-126, F-128 and F-129, delivered to Lakehurst 31 October 1942 and ferried to Moffett Field, arriving on 08 November. With ZP-31 on 22 April 1943 with K-20, assisted planes and surface craft in the search for three survivors in a life raft. Next day K-20 discovered and warned a ship in danger off Catalina Island, preventing a certain stranding.

K-21 flight deck following 1944 modifications. US Navy photo courtesy Richard Barkley.

Attacked possible submarine (Anderson, pilot) 01 June 1943, 23 miles from Oceanside, California, after sighting an oil slick and following a MAD contact, dropped bronze bombs (to disperse the oil slick) and released two depth bombs. One did not explode. A fresh oil slick appeared and no further MAD contact was made; relieved by K-20. On 01 July it sighted a fishing boat in distress and directed surface craft to the scene. On 17 September K-21 searched for and located a missing Marine Corps plane and stood by until the survivor was taken aboard a seaplane.

The K-21 was modified under a grant from BuAer of some $40,000 to Blimp Hedron Three, Moffett Field, California, and which was obtained in early 1944 as a weight reduction program developed and proposed by LCDR Richard L. Barkley, CO Hedron Three and ENS Richard D. DeLauer, Engineering Officer, Hedron Three. These modifications included a servo-booster yoke control system which allowed one pilot to easily fly and handle all internal power, fuel and radio systems as was common in multi-engined heavier-than-air craft. Also incorporated in the design were the first automatic tensioning devices for the long airship control cables, patterned after the tensioning devices used on throttle cables in the Boeing B-29. An autopilot and the formation stick from the B-29 were added. Reversible propellers were included for ease in ground handling. The changes resulted in a total of 1200 lbs. being removed and made available for fuel or additional armament. The work was largely completed in late April 1944. LCDR W. W. Bemis was the first pilot on the initial flight. K-21 also tested a trim tab design by former Goodyear man V. J. Rubino, then in uniform. In early 1945 BuAer authorized the modification of 44 additional K-type airships to the K-21 configuration. All work was stopped on 5 May 1945, VE-Day. In 1950, K-21 was tested with bow elevators, oversize valves and ballonet capacity to provide better control at slow speeds while towing sonar sounding devices, with this experimental change was able to climb almost vertically at a rate of 3,000 feet per minute. On 8 November 1944, K-21 made the first in a series of torpedo recovery flights in Monterey Bay for torpedo plane squadrons training in the area. Results were very satisfactory. Revised to ZP2K/ZSG-2 type, deflated in landing accident at Glynco, Georgia June 1956.

K-22 - Serial 04372, Goodyear envelope D-187 (records state "wrecked," replaced by D-202), control car C-80, control surfaces F-130 and F-132, delivered to Lakehurst 04 November 1942. First K-type flown to Santa Ana, CA on 11 November 1942. K-22 was accepted by ZP-32 at Moffett Field on 20 November. K-22 located an Army P-38 down at sea on 22 November, then stood by until the pilot was rescued. K-22 was deflated by falling glass from the airship dock at Moffett Field 21 January 1943, rebuilt. Struck a hilltop near Hollister, California, 23 January 1943, it was rebuilt. It was again deflated when grounded in fog near Sargent, California, and settled into Chitenden Pass on 13 April 1943. Command pilot R. M. McBride was injured, as were all the crewmembers. A total loss, the K-22 had flown for 828.2 hours. A partial skeletal framework that could be from the K-22 car (the collection includes that number off the skin) was located in a corner of Hangar No. 1 at Moffett Field. The tubular structure is in two pieces and consideration has been given to possibly placing it on display.

K-23 - Serial 04373, Goodyear envelope D-188, control car C-81, control surfaces F-131, delivered to Moffett Field 15 December 1942, becoming the first K-type airship to be erected at Moffett Field. K-23 was accepted by ZP-32 on 19 December 1942. On 4 January 1943 K-23 became the first K-type of ZP-32 to operate from a remote base, Watsonville, California. On 21 January 1943, K-23 was torn from the mast by a 60-knot gale when the mooring disc and nose battens failed in high winds at Watsonville. There were two injuries: ENS R. M. McBride, and AMM1/c A. A. Schreiber. K-23 was purposely deflated; the control car had been badly bashed and was beyond economical repair. It had flown only 289.1 hours.

K-24 - Serial 04374, Goodyear envelope D-189, control car C-82, control surfaces F-132 and F-136, delivered to Lakehurst, 18 November 1942. Based at Guantanamo; MAD contact reported to surface ships on 3 March 1943 which attacked with no apparent results. With ZP-51 on 07 August it dropped a kit to the stranded crew of the K-68 on Blanquilla Island off the coast of Venezuela. K-24 then provisioned the K-68 salvage party, LTJG Verdery, pilot. On 28 January 1944, K-24 saved two merchant ships from collision. On a 07 February patrol, it assisted surface craft in the rescue of a F6F plane crash survivor. 27 JAN 44 ZP-21's K-24 was routinely escorting convoy GK-784 when a radar contact approached the convoy sixteen miles from port. Investigating, it was found to be a straggler tanker, and the K-24 returned to station. The late tanker was on a collision course with the last ship in line and only quick action by the K-24's signalman allowed them to miss each other by fifty feet. Grounded and deflated near Isle of Pines, Cuba, 17 July 1944, rebuilt. K-24 located a ship making only five knots in the direction of Key West, standing by until surface craft arrived. Flown (LCDR. J.A. Priory, pilot) to eastern Pennsylvania and Delaware areas for Navy Day 26 October 1946. Revised to ZP2K, then as ZP3K-24, was deflated when it struck a cliff on landing at Guantanamo Bay, Cuba, 08 September 1953, apparently a total loss.

K-25 - Serial 04375, Goodyear envelope D-190, control car C-83, control surfaces F-133, delivered to Moffett Field, 31 December 1942; nicknamed "Patient Pat". On 30 January 1944 K-25 located and escorted a lost surface ship off the Farallons, escorting her into port. In service with ZP-11, (Controversial) in flight on 25 August 1944, mentioned in the action but proved not to be involved with suspected U-boat sunk off Chatham, Massachusetts. Still with ZP-11 on 23 October, assisted K-27 in the rescue of plane crash survivors. Transferred back to California, on 3 April 1945 K-25 searched for and located a tug that had lost its cargo barge and directed the USCG *Shawnee* to the scene. K-25 hit power lines 1900 feet north of the Moffett Field runway and its gasoline burned the airship to its framework on 21 April 1945. There was no loss of life.

K-26 - Serial 04376, Goodyear envelope D-191, control car C-84, control surfaces F-154, delivered to Lakehurst, 23 March 1943. K-26 was dispatched to the area of a crashed Navy TBF, located the pilot's body and directed a surface craft to its recovery. ZP-12's K-26 was pulled off torpedo duty to find for a crashed airplane on 4 MAR 44. The airship crew marked the pilot's body for surface craft. Aloft on the 27th of May K-26 under LT M. Manolkin came upon a floating body clad in a German uniform, wearing a US Navy like lifebelt. A surface craft was summoned and the squadron history states the body was found to be one Carl Ludwig Johnke (or Jahnke). 5 JUN 44 ZP-12's K-26 under LT H. Manulkin spotted a floating body and directed nearby British corvette J-332 to it. The body also turned out to be clad in a German uniform. K-26 broke away from its mast and deflated at Watsonville, California, 28 December 1944.

K-27 - Serial 04377, Goodyear envelope D-192, control car C-85, control surfaces F-135, delivered to Moffett Field, 12 January 1943, nicknamed "Dirty Duck." Returning from a ZP-32 patrol on 27 May, K-27 discovered Navy lighter YF-577 adrift in the San Francisco Channel and stood by until it was taken into tow. On 4 FEB 45 K-27 searched for a crashed PV northwest of Point Reyes, California, but found no more than bits of debris and human bodies. 10 MAR 45 the K-27 help locate and stood by two airplane survivors in a raft. A line hook failed during undocking at Moffett Field and K-27 deflated after striking the dock on 24 April 1945.

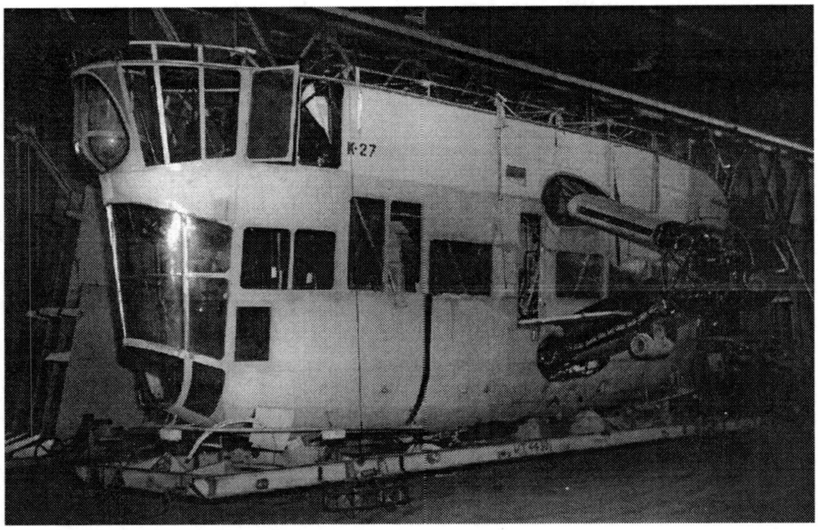

K-27 prepared for overland transportation, note shipping cradle. Lou Prost photo.

The post-war history of the K-27 remains unclear. It was apparently purchased as surplus in 1946 by Bruce McCarty of the San Francisco area for advertising purposes. It was re-erected at Moffett Field and sold to Douglas Leigh after the advertising venture did not seem cost effective. It was apparently assigned registration NC-67095 and then NC-27A. It was flown from Moffett Field to Santa Ana and then cross-country to El Paso, Waco and Dallas, Texas. It was damaged at Love Field, Dallas, repaired and then flown to Glynco and Weeksville where it was damaged by high winds while on the mast. It was then flown to Lakehurst and repaired. The subsequent history is unknown.

K-28 - Serial 04378, Goodyear envelope D-201, control car C-86, control surfaces F-134, delivered to Lakehurst 10 December 1942; assigned to ZP-14 at Weeksville. Later assigned to ZP-24, on 3 June 1944 K-28 was dispatched to the scene of a Navy F4F land crash. It located the plane in ten minutes and directed the ambulance by radio. Following ZP-14's transfer to the Med and ZP-24's moving to Weeksville, K-28 was selected to be the subject of a photo booklet entitled "An Operational Flight" made by ZP-24 officers and men. (This is the best overall daily account of a typical airship's day in WWII.) Later with Airship Utility Squadron ZJ-1, probably at Key West, Florida. Purchased by Goodyear 31 July 1946 and named *Puritan,* registered as NX-21A/NC-21A/NC-10A, and used as a commercial advertising airship. It was the largest airship to be operated by the Goodyear fleet.

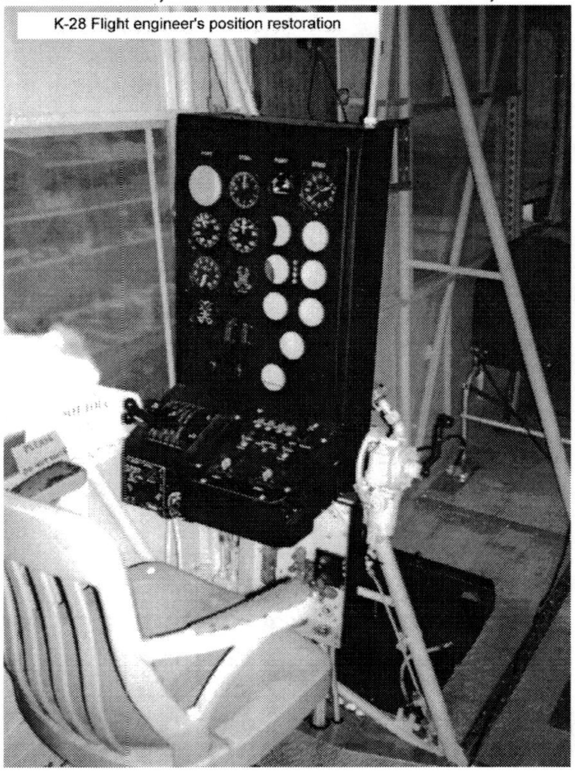

K-28 Flight engineer's position restoration

K-28's mechanic's station undergoing restoration. NEAM photo.

Re-erected at Wingfoot Lake (new envelope D-237, control car revised for Trans-Lux running copy type night sign), first Goodyear flight 27 March 1947, toured eastern and Midwestern states. Dismantled 20 April

1948 due to excessive operating costs and stored at Wingfoot Lake until donated to the Connecticut Aeronautical Historical Association Museum (now the New England Air Museum) at Bradley Field, Windsor Locks, Connecticut in August 1980. It is available for viewing while under rebuild, with the goal of restoring this single remaining K-ship to WWII trim.

K-29 - Serial 04379, Goodyear envelope D-196, control car C-87, control surfaces F-137, delivered to Lakehurst 26 January 1943. Assigned to ZP-31, on 19 July, K-29 located a survivor of a beached plane near Laguna Beach, California. While being maneuvered on the ground by a handling party, K-29's tail pendant struck high tension lines near Lompoc, California 13 August 1943. Four crewmen were electrocuted via the ship's continuity and their touching ground; the airship was not damaged. K-29 landed aboard aircraft carrier USS *Altamaha* (CVE-18) off San Diego (based at Santa Ana, California) 4 February 1944, the first successful landing of an American non-rigid airship on an aircraft carrier, recorded with color motion picture film. 7 JAN 44 ZP-31's K-29 located a crashed F4U and stood by until the pilot's body was recovered. On the 8th of February 1944 a quick coupling was used to refuel the K-29, additional ballast and a passenger were loaded, and a rolling takeoff some 2100 pounds heavy was assisted by increasing the USS *Altamama's* speed. In May it located three men in a raft from a crashed Navy TBF, then notified and directed surface craft to the rescue. On 17 July it located and marked a crashed Navy F6F, whose pilot was then rescued by flying ambulance. K-29 was in service at Santa Ana in December 1944. Purchased by Goodyear as surplus in 1946, not erected. Control car revised to ZP2K/ZP3K type and resold to the Navy in the early 1950's.

K-30 - Serial 30152, Goodyear envelope D-197, control car C-88, control surfaces F-130, F-132 and F-136, delivered to Lakehurst 13 January 1943 (with K-32). K-30 was deflated in trees after engine failure at Richmond, Florida 17 July 1943. Rebuilt, with ZP-21 on 8 December, it directed a crash boat to a downed plane at sea, resulting in an estimated two people being rescued. K-30's disappearing radar blip on the 5th of September 1944 was ZP-21's last of the year.

K-31 - Serial 30153, Goodyear envelope D-198, control car C-89, control surfaces F-139, delivered to Moffett Field 03 February 1943. K-31 flew up the coast with USS *Macon* rigger William Clarke aboard to become the first airship to land at the new Tillamook, Oregon Naval Air Station on 15 Feburary 1943 and commenced the first ZP-33 patrol one month later. K-31 was the first to dock in hangar "B" on 18 August 1943. Assigned to ZP-33, then K-31 broke away from its mast and deflated at Watsonville, California, 27 March 1943; there were no injuries to the crew.

K-32 - Serial 30154, Goodyear envelope D-199, control car C-90, control surfaces F-138, delivered to Lakehurst 13 January 1943 (with K-30). On the 5th of April 1943 ZP-21's Detachment 1, out of Guantanamo, Cuba, K-32 "worked MAD contact and judged sub was moving 070 degrees at 3 knots. Dropped two DCs from 400 feet, set for 50 feet but did not explode until 100 feet, no results." In service at Richmond, K-32 departed on patrol with the K-74, but toward Palm Beach, missing the famous combat on 19 July 1943. K-32 found K-74's pilot LT Nelson Grills, then sighted a periscope from a possible U-boat on 22 July. With ZP-51 on 06 July 1944, with K-108, it assisted in the rescue of an estimated five Navy PBM crash survivors. 15 JUL 44 LTJG Richard D. Harold was aloft in K-32 when they were ordered to search for a crashed PBM. Locating a raft with the three injured survivors, K-32 tried lowering supplies, then got a radar fixed location and reported same before retiring. K-32 had three crewmen spot a periscope's wake on the night of 22 July 43. The MAD would not balance due to an excessive noise level. On 02 October 1944, K-32 lowered emergency rations to a small boat with a mine sweeping crew marooned on a sand bar in the Gulf of Paria, Trinidad, BWI, and summoned surface craft for the rescue.

K-33 - Serial 30155, Goodyear envelope D-200, control car C-91, control surfaces F-141, delivered to Moffett Field 12 March 1943. (Controversial) It is reported that on 17 June 1943, K-33 was dispatched from Tillamook to the mouth of the Columbia River following a report of a sinking of a merchant ship by submarine. In contact with three surface ships, a MAD contact was made on a submerged submarine. The first MAD contact was confirmed by sonar on a surface patrol craft. The suspected submarine was tracked and two depth bombs dropped. The bombs produced an oil slick and the remaining two depth bombs were dropped with no visible results. (A sinking was never confirmed and published Japanese records state no submarines were in the area at the time. The story is also denied by several officers that served at Tillamook at the time and were in a position to know if the incident occurred. However a local salvage diver has located a long cylindrical object in the target area.) K-33 suddenly had both engines cut out on 03 OCT 43 but, thanks to quick action by command pilot LTJG T. H. Ralston dumping bombs and tanks, damage by water impact was manageable. K-33 was in service at Santa Ana December 1944. ZP-31's K-33 spotted a quickly disappearing object on January13th 1945. Attacking with three depth bombs, the object failed to yield a MAD signature. On the 19th of March 1945 K-33 was vectrored to an F6F crash site and stood over its survivor until the CG picked him up.Revised to ZP2K/ZSG-2 type, torn away from mast and deflated during a twister at Key West, Florida, on 28 September 1953.

K-34 - Serial 30156, Goodyear envelope D-193, control car C-92, control surfaces F-140, delivered to Lakehurst 22 January 1943; first airship to land at the new Glynco, Georgia, Naval Air Station, 13 February 1943. K-34 was the first airship to land at Charleston, South Carolina, in March. On the 26th of March 43 K-34 attacked a MAD contact with three depth bombs, later judged to be a wreck. Escorting SS *Albert Gallatin* off Savannah, Georgia, on 28 August 1943, K-34 was alerted by a MAD contact. The German submarine U-107, commanded by CaptLt. Volker von Shimmilmacker, launched a torpedo attack that missed the merchantman but alerted the blimp to its track. K-34 pursued the torpedo tracks, dropping depth charges and radioing for support.

K-34. US Navy photo courtesy CAPT Henry Eppes.

U-107 escaped, recording the depth charges having fallen very close. (This is possibly the only WWII incidence of a U-boat having seen a blimp escort and still pursuing an attack.)

Operating from Naval Air Station, Charleston, November 20, ground crewman (H.F. Mras) became caught in the drag rope and, in attempt to rescue the man, K-34 went down a seaplane ramp into the water. The pilot LT Lawrence J. Mack jumped from a window, saved the man. K-34 was pulled ashore and masted. Mack was awarded the Navy and Marine Corps Medal. Following Lakehurst overhaul, assigned ZP-11. (Controversial) 5 November 44 assigned to escort troopship USS *Wakefield* (AP-21), command pilot ENS Livingston. K-34 scanned for subs in the path, saw the ship safely into Boston, and was then ordered to return immediately. Airship entered a storm front and was tossed in currents, lost buoyancy and impacted the water. Crew members stated icing was never evident, and that the crash was most probably due to extreme up and down wind currents that caused a tear in the envelope. (No airships were reported lost to icing.) They also stated they were certain the airship would not have been lost if it they had not been ordered into the storm, and the final-hour rescue of those that survived the cold was a random chance their flare pistol was seen by the passing ship, since there had been no answer to their distress call. ENS Voss and crewman Spalding were lost. Eight rescued by the USS *Kline* (DE-687) included relief pilot Don Venton and rigger Tom Johnson.

K-35 - Serial 30157, Goodyear envelope D-214, control car C-93, control surfaces F-143, delivered to Moffett Field 22 April 1943, nicknamed "Hawkshaw." With ZP-32 on 29 December it searched for a crashed Navy F6F, finding it on 30 December some 11 miles north of Watsonville. On 25 February 1944 K-35 located and reported wreckage of a Navy plane 10 miles off Point Ano Nuevo. In March 1944, K-35 assisted a crash boat in locating an F6F plane forced down on the beach at Rio del Mar, California. On 04 May while escorting USS *Indianapolis*, K-35 assisted in spotting and recovery of two men washed overboard by high seas, then searched for an additional 2.5 hours for other personnel believed lost. On 19 October, K-35 received a blinker message from landing craft LCS-35 requesting aid for an ill man; K-35 relayed the message and assistance was sent. On 24 October K-35 spotted for gunnery practice of the SS *James Lick* and SS *Jose M. Moreles*, such work first of its kind and successful. On 12 June 1945 it escorted the LCT-163 to port after the vessel's compass failed.

K-36 - Serial 30158, Goodyear envelope D-203, control car C-94, control surfaces F-142, delivered to Lakehurst 02 February 1943, assigned to ZP-14 at Weeksville. That month it was forced to land at Norfolk, its fuel exhausted. On the 5th of July 1943 ZP-14's K-36 got a radar contact but it disappeared and could not be re-established. K-36 landed in sea upon landing approach at Weeksville 08 July 1943. Rebuilt, assigned to Brazil and on 08 January 1944 (LT Cecil London, command pilot) searched life boats from the German blockade runner *Brugenland* that had been scuttled after attack by the USS *Omaha*. Flying out of Fernando de Noronha, K-36 located three life boats and stayed with the boats until the survivors were rescued by the USS *Marblehead*; K-36 had been in the air for 22 hours, 20 minutes and credited (with K-98) for the rescue of 73 survivors. Grounded and deflated in trees in fog near Ilha do Cabo Frio 17 January 1944.

K-36. US Navy photo.

K-37 - Serial 30159, Goodyear envelope D-204, control car C-95, control surfaces F-144, delivered to Lakehurst 05 February 1943, assigned ZP-15 at Glynco. With LT H. W. Gasque, command pilot, K-37 was ferried, with two other ships, cross country. Departing 02 December 1944, K-37 made stops at Houma, Hitchcock, Abilene and El Paso Texas, through the Guadalupe Pass to Davis-Monathan Air Base, Arizona, and Santa Ana. Later attached to ZP-33 at Tillamook, K-37 struck the mast and deflated at auxiliary air station at Shelton, Washington, on 11 June 1945.

K-38 - Serial 30160, Goodyear envelope D-205, control car C-96, control surfaces F-145, delivered to Lakehurst 12 February 1943. Transferred, K-38 deflated at mast at Watsonville, California, on 28 December 1944. Rebuilt, On 1 JUN 45 word came two TMBs were overdue returning to their carrier and ZP-12's K-38 was dispatched to search. K-38 was flown (LT. W.J. Moore, pilot) for Navy Day celebration at Lakehurst, 26 October 1946. Revised to ZP2K/ZSG-2.

K-39 - Serial 30161, Goodyear envelope D-206, control car C-97, control surfaces F-147, delivered to Moffett Field 12 February 1943. On the 9th of May 1943 the K-39 arrived at Tillamook to put ZP-33 back in two-airship strength. K-39 broke away from the handling party during high winds and rolled, damaging both propellers. The crew pulled the rip cord and K-39 settled in trees at Quillayute, Washington on 04 January 1944. There were no injuries to crew.

K-40 - Serial 30162, Goodyear envelope D-207, control car C-98, control surfaces F-146, delivered to Lakehurst 10 February 1943; based at Houma and dubbed "Marauder." Radar detected a surfaced U-boat that apparently crash-dived on 14 May 1943, Coast Guard evaluation as possible U-boat. Attached to ZP-15, on 16 July 1944, with K-102, K-40 assisted in a rendezvous between destroyer and tanker to transfer an ill seaman. On 22 October K-40 located eight survivors of a tanker lost in a hurricane. K-40 was in service at Santa Ana in December 1944. ZP-31's K-40, while escorting the USS *Pensacola,* on the 22nd of July 1945 had the happy task of dropping a life raft to a pilot who had survived the crash of his SC-1. Revised to ZP2K-40 and served at Lakehurst in 1951 and at Oakland, California, with Reserve Squadron ZP-871 in June 1956. Revised to ZP3K-40, it was rigged with a topside microphone for acoustic tests to determine the effect of fixed and rotary wing aircraft's flybys on the hull. The airship's engines were shut down and the vehicle was free-ballooned. Said to have been sacrificed during the atomic tests.

K-41 - Serial 30163, Goodyear envelope D-208, control car C-99, control surfaces F-148, delivered to Lakehurst 22 February 1943. On 08 Jan 44 K-41 broke its nosepiece and got away from her ZP-15 handlers, resulting in an emergency landing and their adding additional lines for 200 men to finally get the ship docked. On the 14th of May 1944 the K-41, escorting a tanker, was asked to locate a convoy straggler lost for some time. LT H. W. Gasque, CAC #4 Commander, and crew located the disabled vessel flying the distress signal and arranged for a tow, earning a "Well Done" from the Commander, ESF.On 12 March 1945, participated in a search for a downed PB4Y and two SB2C's downed from Jacksonville, Ensign Farr, command pilot. With ZP-15 Detachment One, K-41 received a blinker message from the freighter *William A Dobson* 15 MAR 45 concerning a death aboard, summoned Coast Guard cutter to remove the body. K-41 conducted visual and radar observation of Army "robot bombing" experiments off Eglin Field, 16 April 1945, G. E Russel, command pilot. K-41 assisted in calibration of Jacksonville's Coast Guard RDF station, J. A. Tebben, command pilot.

Still cameras were carried, but most photos taken during missions remain unpublished. Anti-Submarine Warfare, much of it conducted after dark, makes for poor photographic records. USN / Jim Plummer.

K-42 - Serial 30164, Goodyear envelope D-209, control car C-100, control surfaces F-149, delivered to Lakehurst 01 March 1943. With ZP-12 on 29 March K-42 sighted smoke and located a tanker that had broken in two, assisted surface craft in the rescue of some 15 persons. 1 AUG 43 ZP-11's K-42 rudderman ENS W. J. McDonnell spotted oil slick, got weak MAD, dropped 2 DCs. K-37 also depth bombed contact with no result, relieved by K-12.

On 9 August 1943, while on patrol from South Weymouth, K-42 (LT Robert T. Connor, command pilot) sighted an oil slick on the track of Boston-to-Halifax convoys. The MAD gear detected a submerged submarine, which was then tracked for over two hours. Oil and air bubbles were also evident. The track was bracketed with two 350 pound depth bombs. Diesel oil rose to the surface moving against the current and wind, indicating damage to the U-boat.

With no air or surface support available, and with low fuel and darkness approaching, K-42 returned to base. ZP-15's ENS John P. Hely, escorting a freighter with the K-42 on 28 October, got a strong MAD contact in 300 fathom water, making signature from a wreck unlikely. The marker's short life and excessive drift did not allow the crew to assess the submarine's position when a small radar return was noted. Before it could be chased down, PLE was reached. K-42 made it back to Charleston after 18.9 hours in the air. ZP-14's K-42 found a TBF wreck on the 8th of December 1943 without survivors but wound up helping the ground search party by lowering provisions. With ZP-24 on 16 October 1944 K-42 effected a rendezvous between a Navy tug and the disabled Army tanker *Primus*. With ZP-14 at Weeksville, on 28 November 1944 it searched for and located a downed Navy SB2C plane on Ship Shoal Island, NC. K-42 landed on the beach and picked up the pilot. K-42 was at Santa Ana in December 1944. Revised to ZP2K/ZSG-2 type, attached to Reserve Airship Squadron ZP-651 in 1949. Based at Naval Air Station, Akron (Municipal Airport) with hangar facilities at Wingfoot Lake. Revised to ZP3K/ZSG-3 type, returned to active service at Naval Air Station, Glynco, Georgia. With ZP-1, on 05 March 1957 returned from a training mission when a fuel system problem was discovered. The landing caused the main gear to collapse because it was improperly locked, leading to fuel leaking from the slip tanks. One prop touched the ground and power was cut, but the fuel caught fire as the car skidded. The crew abandoned ship with four minor injuries. ZP3K-42 ballooned into two parked masts and was destroyed.

<u>K-43</u> - Serial 30165, Goodyear envelope D-210, control car C- 101, control surfaces F-151, delivered to Moffett Field 08 May 1943. 5 MAY 43 K-44 had no less than three radar contacts that disappeared each time they were approached. With ZP-31 on 09 August, K-43 marked the spot of wreckage using aerology balloons attached to 50 feet of small line, permitting a search party to easily locate the scene. 09 October 1943 saw ZP-31 making its first docking, as K-43 was backed into brand new Hangar One. On the 28th of March 1944 K-44 under LT Douglas C. Adie patrolled the Nicholas Channel opposite Cuba's Cay Sal Bank. They spotted a wrecked boat and two survivors clinging to the Cayo Megano Light. After several attempts finally got them lowered food, the K-44 summoned surface rescue. On 15 September 1944 it searched for and located survivors of a plane crash at sea, then stood-by until a PBY took the survivors aboard. K-43 struck an unlit water well drilling rig derrick and deflated near Santa Ana, California, on 07 October 1944, during a night landing. K-43 was rebuilt. Poem written on K-43 entitled "The Saga of King Four Three". In service at Santa Ana in December 1944. On the 17th of February 1945 the K-43 was escorting the USS *St Louis* when the cruiser's seaplane capsized as it tried to land. K-43 dropped its life raft to the lucky pilot. Assigned to Lakehurst, revised to ZP2K-43, it was damaged and deliberately deflated during high winds 11 March 1952. Crew was LT E.O. Smith, LT. F. Peterson, LTJG John F. Schneider, Jr., CAPT T.E. Willoughby, AL1 R.H. Webb, AD2 W.A. Steell, AD3 C.B. Pogue, AM1 H.A. Showers and AN A.C. Greenwood. Revised to ZP3K/ZSG-3 type. With NARTU Lakehurst in 1956, on ferry flight to Glynco on 11 June, damaged landing wheel when thought to be landing light. The last wartime K-type airship to fly, retired in a ceremony at Lakehurst 19 March 1959 with VADM C.E. Rosendahl (USN, Ret.), CAPT J.R. Van Evera (Commanding Officer at Lakehurst) and CAPT M.H. Eppes (Commanding Officer, Fleet Airship Wing One) aboard.

K-44 - Serial 30166, Goodyear envelope D-211, control car C-102, control surfaces F-150, delivered to Lakehurst 08 March 1943. With ZP-21 on 28 March, K-44 located two shipwrecked men marooned on the Cayo Megan Lighthouse near the Cuban coast. On 21 September, K-44 was attempting a message drop to a two-masted schooner. The car struck the mast, breaking its top two feet off, damaging the car and seriously injuring the bombardier. Landed safely at Guantanamo, K-44 was temporarily repaired and flown back to Richmond. With ZP-15 on 16 April 45, sustained a 15.9 hour ASW patrol, C. E. Napier, command pilot, and on 18 April, an 11 hour ASW patrol, M. D. Griep, command pilot. Transferred back to NAS Richmond 28 May 45.

K-45 - Serial 30167, Goodyear envelope D-223, control car C-103, control surfaces F-152, delivered to Lakehurst 09 March 1943. On 26 April 1943, K-45 attacked a shallow water MAD contact with three Mk 17 bombs, also photographed disturbed water with sand streaks. U-boat tower became visible aft of the blimp, radar contact established. Disarmed, K-45 circled and observed oil slicked debris. Surface ships arrived seven hours later and continued search, two oil slicks, oily waste and pieces of wood appeared. Four bombs were dropped on a MAD contact two nights later. On 26 APR 43 ZP-15's K-45 on patrol worked a MAD contact and after an hour dropped three Mk 17 bombs on strongest contact; two were duds. At Glynco, suffered hard landing on 26 February 1945. Repaired, K-45 conducted visual and radar observation of Army “robot bombing” experiments off Eglin Field, April 1945. On 11 April 1945, K-45 stood by the disabled Mexican tanker *Presidente Madero* and directed boats to the tanker, and later proceeded to Brunswick for repairs. K-45 transferred to Blimpron One, Lakehurst, 22 April 1945. Purchased as surplus by Goodyear in 1946, not erected. Control car revised to ZP2K/ZP3K type and resold to the Navy in the early 1950's.

K-46 - Serial 30168, Goodyear envelope D-213, control car C-104, control surfaces F-153, delivered to Lakehurst 12 March 1943. With ZP-21 o 03 April, K-46 located wreckage and fifteen survivors of the torpedoed SS *Gulf State*; K-46 summoned surface craft and dropped a life raft. On 28 April K-46 scraped some trees; the crew used their shirts to stuff in the holes and slow the leaks. On 19 September it located a disabled freighter and directed surface rescue. Later that month K-46 led a submarine chaser into Miami harbor after its compass had failed. On the 3rd of July 1944 ZP-21’s K-46 was vectored to make a MAD search where the USCG *Pandora* had an earlier sound contact. In spite of lookouts reporting visual contact with a tear-shaped object, no attack was made. On the 6th K-46 had a series of MAD contacts and surface support was called out, but nothing was found. Located an abandoned ship in 1944. K-46 struck dock and deflated while undocking at Santa Ana, California 26 May 1945, rebuilt. Revised to ZP2K/ZSG-2 type, it broke away from the mast and deflated in Nevada 18 April 1957 during the atomic tests.

K-47 - Serial 30169, Goodyear envelope D-319, control car C- 105, control surfaces F-155, delivered to Moffett Field 19 May 1943 and erected, nicknamed "Early Eta." The first ZP-32 airship to operate from the auxiliary base at Eureka, California, 22 MAY 43. On July 1st 1943 SecNav Fran Knox and his party were welcomed aboard the K-47 by ZP-32 skipper R. E. Bly. Operating from Alameda, the party made an inspection of the Bay area’s Naval establishments. (Controversial): It is reported K-47 initiated an attack on an alleged Japanese submarine near Trinidad Head (near Eureka, California) in mid-late 1943, Peter "Ace" Culbertson, command pilot. A contact was reported on MAD gear by radioman Simon Beattie, and the Commander, Western Sea Frontier, was contacted; no American submarines were in the area. K-47 proceeded to drop depth bombs and was later joined by the Coast Guard Cutter *Shawnee* that also dropped depth charges. Relieved by K-55, which also dropped charges, K-47 returned to Eureka, was refueled and returned. Local witnesses remember a "combat" day of many explosions and metallic object(s) register on magnetic detector gear in these same off-shore waters. On 29 December K-47 discovered a fisherman’s body on the beach and directed a search party to the scene. On 07 June K-47 made MAD runs off Point Pinos to find two sunken amphibious tanks 600 yards off shore. At Santa Ana in December 1944 where it also carried an "X" designation. 17 FEB 45 the K-47 got to exercise its machine gun, sinking a barrel found adrift near its charge, Task Group 14.4.On the 5th of August 1945 K-47 made ZP-31's last wartime drop delivery - radar parts and secret orders to the USS *Miami.* K-47 served at Lakehurst with Naval Air Reserve Training Unit from approximately 1947 through 1951.

K-47 on the tripod mast at Eureka, California, in 1943. Simon Beattie photo, with ZP-32 shipmates who crewed the K-47.

Revised to ZP2K. Served with ZX-11 in 1955 and 1956, as a ZP3K type, retired in 1956 and sold after it was declared surplus. Stored in an open field (along with six other airship cars). Sold again. K-47's car (with parts cannibalized from K-88) was carefully reconstructed with Naval Airship Association volunteers to provide a representative ZP3K-type airship car for display in the National Museum of Naval Aviation at Pensacola, Florida. The first public viewing was 19 September 1991 at the Museum, during the Naval Airship Association Reunion. Suspended from the overhead, the ZP3K-47 is a permanent display at the NMNA.

K-47 at Eureka. Note single engine blower and duct mounted on the handrail adjacent to the sandbag ballast. The duty man on pressure watch could add air to ballonets by starting the blower. Simon Beattie photo

K-48 - Serial 30170, Goodyear envelope D-216, control car C-106, control surfaces F-156, delivered to Lakehurst 29 March 1943. Arrived for operations in Guantanamo on 29 April. The K-48 on 28 JAN 44 overflew USS *Blue Gill* and a couple of boats escorting her through friendly waters, but the senior escort was having trouble linking up with them. K-48 found the sub-chaser about eight miles away and blinkered range and bearing information. With ZP-41 on 06 July 1944, it landed Army personnel to investigate plane wreckage near Tutoya, Brazil. Replacement envelope Goodyear D-386 was in service for over one year under the adverse conditions of the tropics.

K-49 - Serial 30171, Goodyear envelope D-215, control car C-107, control surfaces F-157, delivered to Lakehurst 20 April 1943 (with K-50). On 26 May it got a MAD contact and surface craft bombed the target. Transferred to Weeksville, North Carolina, with ZP-14, K-49 located a missing tug and lighter around Pamlico Sound, North Carolina. It reported the position and stood by for surface craft. K-49 deflated in the steel dock during overhaul 29 April 1944.

K-50 - Serial 30172, Goodyear envelope D-245, control car C-108, control surfaces F-158, delivered to Lakehurst 20 April 1943 (with K-49). 20 August 1943 another airplane had crashed north of Jacksonville; ZP-15's K-50 found the wreckage, but there were no survivors. On 12 October 1943, K-50 struck the hangar while undocking at Glynco and was deflated. It was repaired and returned to service.

Note: The final order for the World War II K-type airships was contract NOs-257 (was NXs(a) 10086). This order covered K-5 through K-135 and all were with envelopes of 425,000 cubic feet, although eight envelopes of 456,000 cubic feet were provided on contract NOa(s)-869, fifteen additional on contract N288a (15939) and thirty on contract N288s (17654). These envelopes were designed to accept the standard K-type control car.

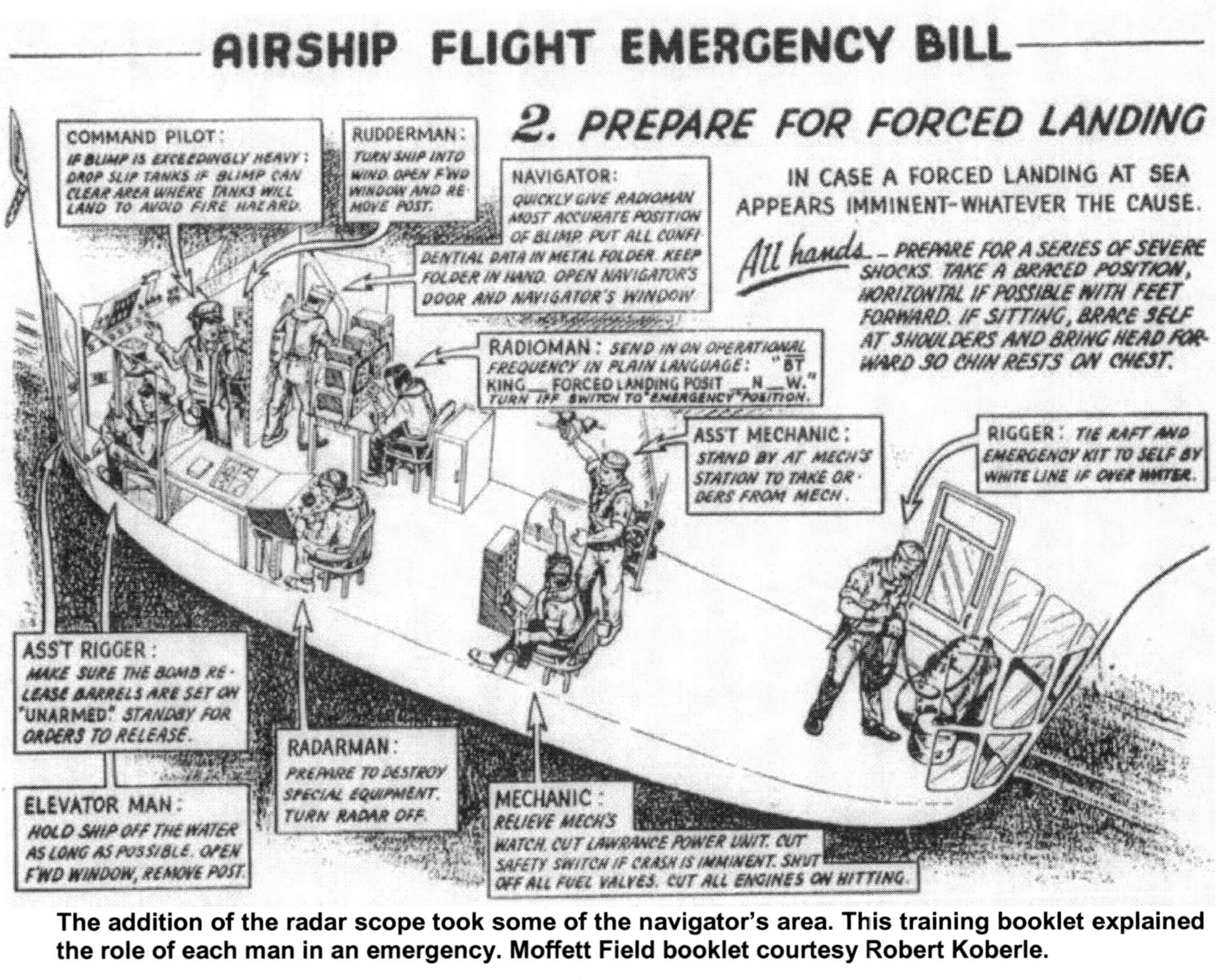

The addition of the radar scope took some of the navigator's area. This training booklet explained the role of each man in an emergency. Moffett Field booklet courtesy Robert Koberle.

K-51 - Serial 30173, Goodyear envelope D-221, control car C-110, control surfaces F-162, delivered to Moffett Field 29 May 1943. 31 MAY 43 marked the arrival of ZP-33's third ship, the K-51. 03 OCT 43. K-51 reported seeing a possible submarine periscope off Alsea Bay, Oregon, in position 44-24 North, 124-46 West. One depth charge was dropped with oil bubbles reported after attack. At 1300T, an object resembling a conning tower was sighted. Two depth charges were dropped with negative results. Letter "Anti-submarine operations of 2-3 October 1943, Report of," containing statements of K-51 crew York, Bailey, Johasson and Steinberg. Accounts relate working an oil slick until an object sighted, attacked with .50 cal gun, later one bomb, and later .50 cal gun was observed to make direct hits. With ZP-22 on 21 December 1943, K-51 reported a critically ill man aboard a merchant ship. On 3 May 1945, a fire started due to gasoline fumes from auxiliary power unit in control car, fumes exploded and K-51 burned near Santa Ana, California, 03 May 1945, with eight lives lost. There were two survivors.

K-52 - Serial 30174, Goodyear envelope D-222, control car C-111, control surfaces F-163 and F-164, delivered to Lakehurst 22 April 1943. With ZP-15 on 06 June an engine cowling was lost puncturing the envelope in two places while approximately 50 miles from base. ENS Louis P. Reeder successfully piloted the K-52 to base and was awarded the Air Medal for his actions. On 02 July, K-52 searched for and located fifty survivors in lifeboats. An Op-16-B-5 report states "US Navy blimp K-52 had sighted the survivors between 0930 and 1000 GMT, 2 July, and signaled that a rescue ship was on its way. The blimp and later a PBY Navy plane stayed with the survivors until they were rescued... At 1402 GMT, the day of the attack, all survivors were rescued by the SC-1049..." On the 29th of September 1943 ZP-15's K-52 got a MAD contact and dropped its full stick of bombs, but nothing else was seen. With ZP-41 K-52 departed Sao Luiz, Brazil, for NAS Glynco on January 18, 1946, the last U.S. airship to leave the South American area. While masted at Key West K-52 briefly became 'Navy One' as US President Harry S. Truman climbed aboard for inspection.

K-53 - Serial 30175, Goodyear envelope D-212, control car C-112, control surfaces F-163 and F-164, delivered to Lakehurst 24 April 1943. With ZP-21 on 28 May, K-53 located a Pan American Airways plane forced down on the water. K-53 made a radar contact with an object six miles away on 18 June 1943, then pursued. From one mile away contact disappeared, but it was identified as a probable U-boat. K-53 did not attack, but probably forced the U-boat to submerge and prevented an attack on the convoy the sub was tracking by the full moon. Reported disappearing radar blips while on patrol 20 December 1943. K-53 was also in service at Houma, where it was nicknamed "Acey Ducey," and in Brazil. K-53 was deflated in the sea off Jamaica 07 July 1944, one crewman lost, balance of crew rescued 09 July.

K-54 - Serial 30176, Dunlop envelope D-269, Goodyear control car C-113, control surfaces F-165, delivered to Lakehurst 02 May 1943; based at Houma, Louisiana, and nicknamed "Jean La Fitte" for the old pirate. Typical "J" type flight of 7.5 hours on 26 January, 1944 with ZP-22 C.O. LCDR Harris, pilot. Transferred from Hedron Two, Richmond, to ZP-15, arriving 29 April 45, and back to Richmond on 28 May. 25th of April K-54 was ferrying from San Julian to Richmond when it was ordered to search for a missing B-29. One survivor was found amid the extensive floating debris, and his rescue was directed.

K-55 - Serial 30177, Goodyear envelope D-225, control car C-114, control surfaces F-166, delivered to Moffett Field 12 June 1943; nicknamed "Royal Flush". With ZP-32, operated from the mast base at Eureka, California. (controversial) Relieved K-47 and dropped depth bombs on suspected Japanese submarine near Trinidad Head. On 06 May 1944 K-55 sighted an oil slick and obtained a MAD signature, but it was judged a shipwreck. On 18 June it assisted rendezvous of British bark *Pamir* and tug ATR-24. 22 NOV 44 the USS *Eldarado* (AGC-11) was escorted by K-55 when the airshipmen spotted a downed plane. The airship stood over the two lucky survivors until rescued by a launch from the ship.

K-55 at Eureka, CA. Simon Beattie photo.

On 22 November while escorting USS *Eldorado*, K-55 observed a plane crash in adjacent waters. It directed a motor launch from the *Eldorado* to the scene, rescuing the pilot and radioman. 15 FEB 45 K-55 searched for a lost F6F but found only a oil slick and green dye marker. K-55 was damaged in a landing short of the mat at Watsonville, 23 June 1945.

K-56 - Serial 30178, Goodyear envelope D-226, control car C-115, control surfaces F-167, delivered to Lakehurst 13 May 1943 (with K-57); based at Houma, Louisiana, and nicknamed "Dominque You." Blown out of the hangar 20 April 1944 when hurricane force winds disengaged the hangar doors. K-56 struck the hangar overhead structure and was blown tail first out of the hangar and crashed outside of the air station, there were no injuries. Control car returned to Wingfoot Lake for rebuild, provided with a new envelope and assigned to Richmond, Florida for moored-out fabric exposure tests.

K-57 - Serial 30179, Goodyear envelope D-227, control car C-116, control surfaces F-168, delivered to Lakehurst 13 May 1943 (with K-56). Reassigned to Houma, Louisiana, nicknamed "Nez Coupe." On 22 August 43 ZP-22's LT A. L. Gillogly and his K-57 crew spotted another crashed Army plane, this time a B-25 down in the swamp. When a summoned crash boat was unable to find what was easily seen from the airship, the K-57 dropped a slick to mark the location of one body. Widening the search, K-57's crew found two more luckless airman's bodies about a mile from the wreck.

March 1944 (George Seibold, pilot) gusty and shifting winds changed a normal landing to a dangerous landing. AMM3 H. E. Putney of the ground crew on the car rail did not let go after the release order was issued and was carried aloft (left). K-57 was skillfully landed, and the ground crewman was removed unharmed. Seibold was given a commendation from the Commander of Fleet Airships Atlantic and a personal letter of congratulations from Rosendahl.

Line handler holding fast to the K-57 rail. US Navy photo courtesy George Seibold.

K-57 was blown out of the Houma hangar when hurricane force winds disengaged the hangar doors. K-57 tore loose from its moorings and was blown out of the hangar sideways. It crashed outside of the air station; there were no injuries.

K-58 - Serial 30180, Goodyear envelope D-228, control car C-117, control surfaces F-169, delivered to Lakehurst 23 May 1943. ZP-12's K-58 under ENS Britton found the wreck of SS *Restor* on the 20th of July, 1943. On the 29th of July 1943 ZP-12's K-58 made an attack on what was later judged to be a wreck. 02 FEB 44 K-58 got MAD contacts over an oil slick, surface vessels investigated and one attacked without visible result. Based at Santa Ana in December, 1944. Reassigned to Lakehurst, on the 13th of November 1944 ZP-12's K-58 searched for and located another barge adrift. K-58 was on a special Eastern Sea Frontier barrier patrol of the N.Y. swept channel (from Ambrose lightship to point Zebra) when a submarine conning tower was seen breaking the surface at 0830 by Cordisco A. M., ARM2c, a member of the crew. The airship was brought about and altitude decreased as it came over the spot. MAD contact was received over the spot and an AK Mk.5 float light was dropped, which failed to light. A one-mile trapping circle was employed, signals received and flares dropped, but no definite pattern showing sub movement appeared. The circle was widened with airships K-77, K-30, K-98, and K-16, and surface units got a sound contacts. Many units made attacks, no evidence of damage to a submarine resulted. On the 29th of April ZP-12's K-16 and K-58 responded to surface craft's sound contact, dropping sono-bouys following a MAD signature. No submarine noises were heard, and the affair was written off as a wreck. On the 8th of May 1944 a message relay was performed by ZP-12's K-58, orders to replace two ill Armed Guardsmen on an inbound merchantman. K-58 participated (with K-16) in the sinking of one of the last U-boats in American waters before the end of the war (see K-16 for more complete narrative). Revised to ZP2K/ZSG-2 type, during a carrier take-off 25 November 1952, the aft handling lines caught on a carrier gun mount causing a 12-foot hole in the stern of the envelope. K-58 settled into the sea; an engine fire was extinguished as it sank. Submarines USS *Bauer* and USS *Sea Poacher* rescued the crew.

K-59 - Serial 30181, Goodyear envelope D-229, control car C- 118, control surfaces F-170, delivered to Moffett Field 23 June 1943. Reportedly the first airship to effect a sea-to-air rescue. While on routine patrol out of Santa Ana and under the command of ENS Lowell E. Buys, rescued Marine pilot Lt Harvey Metcalf when his TBF Avenger lost an engine and went down off the California coast. Metcalf was injured in the crash but his gunner, Sgt. James W Laing, was unhurt. Other planes in the Marine flight signaled K-59 and within 5 minutes it was on the scene. Buys flew over the inflated life raft and dropped a first aid kit. About 25 feet above the waves, lowered a parachute harness to Sgt. Laing who adjusted it to the shoulders of Lt Metcalf, who was then hoisted hand over hand until Chief Boatswain's Mate George F. Graffe could swing out the aft door and help Metcalf into the control car. The actual rescue from raft to airship was completed in 20 seconds. Metcalf was given first aid and Laing was rescued by a PBY. An ambulance was waiting at Santa Ana when K-59 arrived and the injured Marine was in a hospital bed within 90 minutes after the crash of his plane. (Actual date of this rescue is uncertain.) 5 APR 45 ZP-31's K-59 was filming routine bombing runs off Pt. Loma when an F4U crashed before them, killing the pilot. Revised to ZP2K-59, it was damaged while docking in Hangar No. 6 at Lakehurst 06 August 1951, repaired. Shipped to west coast 19 September 1951 (by trailer truck to Point Pleasant, New Jersey, by barge to Brooklyn, New York, and by freighter through the Panama Canal) and assigned to Reserve Airship Squadron ZP-951 at Santa Ana in 1952, deactivated in 1959). With NARTU Santa Ana in 1955.

K-60 - Serial 30182, Dunlop envelope D-270, control car C-119, control surfaces F-171, delivered to Lakehurst 23 May 1943; assigned to ZP-23 at Hitchcock, Texas, one of the first airships (with K-62) to be based at Hitchcock. In July K-60 fled a hurricane to Glynco. On the 10th of September 1943 ZP-23's K-60 under LT Janecky helped locate wreckage of two B-17s crashed off Texas. On 04 December K-60 located and covered the aftermath of a collision of a tanker and a cargo ship for ten hours. The next day, with command pilot LT C. H. Janecky, K-60 was a routine patrol and became lost after the 14 hour patrol. K-60 wound up in the state of Mississippi and was directed to a temporary landing for fuel at Columbus. ENS John G. Kennedy was lowered to organize a landing party. Re-fueled with automotive gasoline and flown to Columbus Army Air Field and refueled with aviation gasoline. Flown by LCDR Ayers (ZP-23, commanding officer) became lost again in fog without radio communications and let down in Lake Pontchartrain due to a faulty altimeter. Followed the highway for the airship base at Houma, Louisiana, with lift loss due to tears in the envelope, it landed temporarily at the Lafayette, Louisiana training station. K-60 finally reached Hitchcock after flying a total of 54 hours, 25 minutes and 1,750 miles. K-60 was repaired and was on patrol the next morning. Assigned next to the Panama Sea Frontier K-60 became the first airship (LTJG Gordon Burke, command pilot) to land at Vernam Field, Jamaica. On 10 July 1944 located survivors from the lost K-53 in the sea off Jamaica and dropped rations. Transferred to ZP-32, on the 3rd of

January 1945 K-60 followed up on a report and got MAD contacts, but was unable to localize a submarine. On the 22 FEB 45 the K-60 was escorting the USS *Gilbert Islands* (CVE-107) when the alert crew spotted a floating mine in time for the vessel to divert around it. On 28 February K-60 located a crashed F6F west of Point Pinos, California. The survivor was spotted and surface craft summoned for the rescue. 27 AUG 45 was the last WWII submarine rendezvous arranged when K-60 brought together the *Sargo, Saury,* and *Searaven* with their Coast Guard escort *Ariadne.* Purchased as surplus by Goodyear in 1946, not erected, control car revised to ZP2K/ZP3K type and resold to the Navy in the early 1950's. (This was the airship mistakenly identified as the K-135.)

K-61 - Serial 30183, Goodyear envelope D-231, control car C-120, control surfaces F-172, delivered to Lakehurst 28 May 1943. With ZP-12 on 05 June, K-61 searched for and located the tug *Point Loma*, reported her position, requested a tow, then assisted the tow in locating the tug. An estimated three people were rescued. On 03 JUL 43 ZP-12's K-61 under ENS W. R. Bricker followed up on several good MAD contacts asking surface vessels to listen in, but heavy fog rolled in, shutting down the operation. On 05 July K-61 located another disabled tug, and an estimated three more people were rescued. On the 5th of May 1944 ZP-12 supplied the K-61 to form the nucleus of a combined task force training exercise, with airplanes homing in on the blimp to attack the target marker it dropped. On 20 July 44 K-61 under ENS E. Cusworth sighted tug ATR-8 and was requested to locate one of her tows which was missing; K-61 located it and directed the tug to it. On the 26th of August 1944 K-61 had a radar blip at 15 miles, but when it turned to intercept, the blip disappeared when the airship was three miles away. On 31 October 1944, K-61 sighted and reported the position of Coast Guard ship 3091, which had engine trouble. It stood by the ship until a tow arrived. ZP-12's K-61 was ordered to fly out to the tug *Humrick* and deliver orders to change its destination on 20 OCT 44.

Escort duty made for long flying hours. ZP-24 photo.

K-61 struck the dock door and deflated while undocking at South Weymouth, Massachusetts, 14 December 1944; it was rebuilt. Revised to ZP2K/ZSG-2 type, it made several training landings on aircraft carriers while based at Weeksville between 1949 and 1951. Deflated in a landing accident at Lakehurst 22 January 1956.

K-62 - Serial 30184, Dunlop envelope D-271, control car C-121, control surfaces F-173, delivered to Lakehurst 29 May 1943; first airship to land at Hitchcock, Texas Naval Air Station on 19 June 1943. Evacuated to Glynco to avoid a hurricane in July. K-62 on 20 August 1943 located a B-24 Liberator reported crashed the afternoon before, presumably off Corpus Christi, Texas. No survivors were ever found. With ZP-23, K-62 sighted and assisted in the recovery of bodies and debris from a Navy PBY crash on 17 November 1943. Based at Houma, K-62 was blown out of the hangar when hurricane force winds disengaged the hangar doors (with K-56 and K-57). K-62 was on a mooring mast and was unmasted, kited, struck the floor of the hangar breaking the landing gear, the anchoring lines parted, the tail rose and struck the hangar overhead structure, swung about, struck a mast and bounced at the northwest hangar entrance. The slip tanks then caught fire (probably from a spark caused by the control car dragging on the rails embedded in the floor or the concrete floor itself). One burning slip tank fell at the hangar door and then K-62 was blown out of the hangar onto the field where it was destroyed by fire.

K-63 - Serial 30185, Goodyear envelope D-233, control car C-122, control surfaces F-174, delivered to Moffett Field 29 June 1943, nicknamed "Margie." On 2 August with ZP-32 skipper LCDR R. E. Bly, K-63 flew a congressional committee of ten senators and representatives on an inspection tour of the Bay area. On 8 March 1944 it reported a menace to navigation a huge redwood tree 20 miles at sea, and on 27 March K-63 sighted a house on fire at Trinadad Head. K-63 notified Arcata's Fire Department and guided fire units to the scene in time to avert a possible forest fire. On 15 July 1944 it searched south of Pegion Point for two crashed airplanes, locating an oil slick and directing Coast Guard to the scene. On 16 August the K-63 observed and marked the location of a crashed Navy F6F from the aircraft carrier USS *Takanis Bay* and stood by until surface craft effected a rescue in rough seas. On 21 August K-63 assisted in a search for 8 escaped prisoners of war near King City, California, and on 29 August attempted to tow plane pontoons floating in the water. On 08 September K-63 carried members of the San Francisco Bay Area Chamber of Commerce on a tour. On 22 SEP 44 ZP-32's K-63 found a crashed airplane in Half Moon Bay and stood by until the pilot's body was recovered by USS *Foote.* Revised to ZP2K-63, it served with the Airship Training Center at Lakehurst in 1951. Deflated during a routine undocking from hangar No. 6 due to wind change direction on 17 December 1951, repaired. It flew VADM John Dale Price, then Chief of Air Training, to New York City and environs for familiarity with airships 10 June 1952, provided escort (with ZP2K-67) for SS *United States* southeast of Ambrose Light and escorted into New York harbor on 23 June 1952.

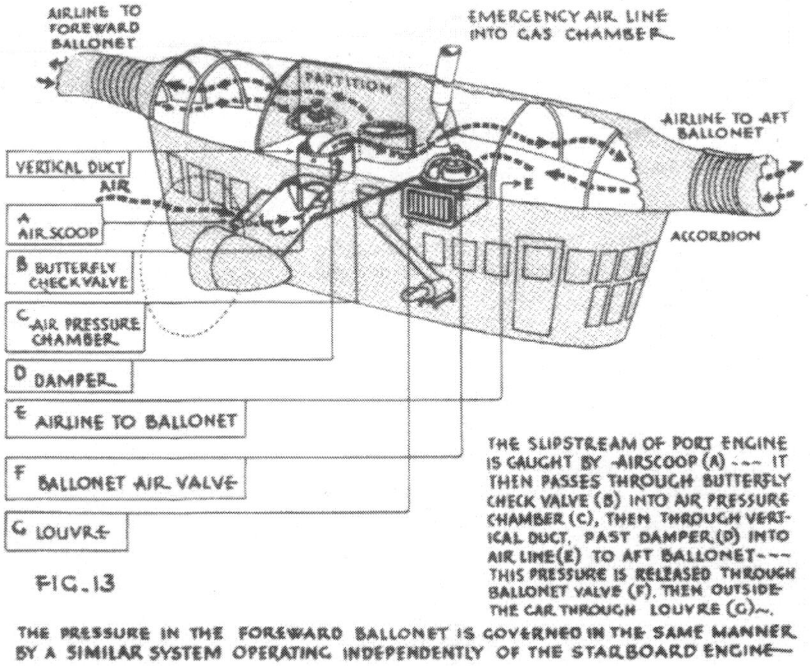

FIG. 13

Moffett Field training manual explains the operation of the forced air system to pump air into the ballonets to maintain proper pressure in the helium filled envelope. To prevent loss of control when there is a large helium loss, the emergency air-line can be opened to pump air into the deflating bag. Courtesy Robert Koberle.

K-64 - Serial 30186, Goodyear envelope D-240, control car C-123, control surfaces F-175, delivered to Lakehurst 05 June 1943; assigned to ZP-12. Lost in mid-air collision with K-7 near Barnegat Inlet, New Jersey 16 October 1943. Caught fire, most of crew killed, one survivor.

K-65 - Serial 30187, Goodyear envelope D-224, control car C-124, control surfaces F-176, delivered to Lakehurst 08 June 1943. 21 JUL 43 K-65 got a MAD contact rated 'doubtful.' With LT James W. Punderson as senior pilot carried medical aid and doctor CAPT Paul D. Huber from Lakehurst to a stricken merchant marine sailor aboard the SS *Alexander W. Doniphan*; a "Well Done" was received by the crew. In the Caribbean on 21 September 1943, K-65, LCDR Louis M. Ayers, command pilot, located two members of a missing British A-30 Baltimore bomber that had crashed on Andros Island in the Bahamas. Ayers landed on the one wheel and the survivors climbed aboard and were taken to Main Field, Nassau. Ayers was awarded the Air Medal, the first of many one-wheel rescue landings. On the 5th of June 1944 ZP-21's K-65 got yet another "doubtful" radar contact, and a disappearing radar blip on the 28th of July 1944. The last days of August 1944 found ZP-23's Mandinga detachment moving over to the Pacific side, at Chorrera, with K-65 first to mast.

K-66 - Serial 30188, Goodyear envelope D-230, control car C-125, control surfaces F-177, delivered to Lakehurst 10 June 1943; upper control surface (fin) brace wire failed and punctured the envelope. The crew was rescued by an American submarine; a tow was attempted but K-66 went down in the sea off Glynco, Georgia, on 11 October 1943.

K-67 - Serial 30189, Goodyear envelope D-237, control car C-126, control surfaces F-177, delivered to Moffett Field 08 July 1943. With ZP-31, K-67 located a fisherman at sea who was wanted by his draft board. Messages to the effect were wrapped around oranges and dropped to his boat. On 12 May 1944, with K-59, K-67 was ordered to search for survivors of a crashed Navy F6F and a PBY sent to rescue them off San Nicholas Island, California. Survivors were located by the K-59; K-67 commanded by ENS John Road spotted an F6F pilot in the water and dropped a raft. Five were rescued and one body was recovered. Command Pilot ENS John Hoag, USNR, flew K-67 to within 20 feet of the water to drop a life raft to the F6F pilot who appeared to be face down, swimming weakly. The raft dropped within 15 feet of the man in the water, then inflated automatically. Aviation Rigger's Mate 1/c J. A. Sosnowski volunteered and was lowered from an altitude of ten feet, but a large swell knocked him away from the raft. K-67 towed Sosnowski to the PBY now drifting close to F6F pilot. A line was thrown to Sosnowski and he was safely hauled aboard the PBY; when it drifted further the F6F pilot was reached and found to be dead. The USS *McFarland* arrived on the scene about 30 minutes later, launched a boat and all the men were taken aboard. The swamped PBY was destroyed by gunfire. K-67 was in service at Santa Ana in December 1944, and also carried an "X" designation. 21st of April 1945 found ZP-31's K-67 again visiting Mexico and taking senior Mexican Army officers on observation flights.

NAS Richmond riggers. US Navy photo.

Revised to ZP2K-67 and served with the Airship Training Center at Lakehurst in 1951, provided escort (with ZP2K-63) for SS *United States* from Ambrose Light to New York harbor 23 June 1952. Envelope damaged beyond economical repair after striking hangar door at Lakehurst 28 October 1952. Rebuilt with new envelope and flown from Lakehurst to California, experienced turbulent flying conditions over the mountains between El Paso, Texas and Litchfield Park,

Arizona and believed to have caused breaks in a portion of the catenary, envelope deflated and stored 27 May 1955.

K-68 - Serial 30190, Goodyear envelope D-232, control car C-127, control surfaces F-179, delivered to Lakehurst 15 June 1943 (with K-69). Transferred to Houma, LA and deflated in dock when struck by K-46 during undocking operations, rebuilt, transferred to ZP-51. T. Savas's "Silent Hunters: German U-Boat Commanders Of WWII" and G. Kelshall's "The U-Boat War In The Caribbean" both credit K-68's very long loiter time orbiting the retreating U-615 as pivotal in replacement airplanes relocating the sub after it shot down two airplanes. K-68's action was on 6 August 1943 with Wallace Wydeen as command pilot. Ordnanceman William Voda stated he clipped all three belts of 50 cal. ammo together prepared to go in, but airship was ordered to circle, pinpointing the sub for sinking. Fuel consumed, K-68 barely made the island of Blanquilla, British West Indies where the crew secured it to trees. Contrary winds necessitated ripping the bag, and owing to an incorrect location report, no rescuers appeared. Following a nine-day ordeal and final rescue, most of the crew was transferred, some to ZP-14; (Wallace Wydeen remained with ZP-51, later lost with K-94.) Rebuilt, 9 OCT 44 the Houma detachment sent the K-68 to investigate a report of a torpedoed ship that was sinking, but nothing was found. On the 27th of November 1944 the K-68 assisted the disabled Sub Chaser #1292. later revised to ZP2K/ZSG-2 type. Used in 1946 filming of Training Film MN-4370A, Blimp Air-Sea Rescue.

Recovery of the K-68, showing how local lumber was used to fashion an engine hoist. Former Goodyear man John B. Rieker was OinC of the salvage operation. A "jeeper bug" was employed

to carry the disassembled car's stern and push it, balanced with rocks, on its wheel to the beach for loading on a net tender. Goodyear/ Akron Historical Center photo via Larry Karadin.

K-69 - Serial 30191, Goodyear envelope D-234, control car C- 128, control surfaces F-180, delivered to Lakehurst 15 June 1943 (with K-68). K-69 was deflated 13 August 1943 when its starboard stabilizer struck the structure of the steel hangar at South Weymouth. Rebuilt in the timber hangar at South Weymouth, first airship to be undocked from this hangar. K-69 was in service at Weeksville from July 1942 to May 1944, and South Weymouth from June to November 1944. K-69 was revised to ZP2K/ZSG-2 type.

K-70 - Serial 30192, Goodyear envelope D-235, control car C-129, control surfaces F-181, delivered to Lakehurst 19 June 1943. With ZP-21 in 28 March 1944, K-70 stood by a disabled ship for more than eight hours until damage was repaired and the ship could proceed. On the 1st of October 1944 ZP-21's K-70 dropped a note on the deck of an unresponsive freighter at the request of the commander of GSF.

K-71 - Serial 30193, Goodyear envelope D-241, control car C-130, control surfaces F-182, delivered to Moffett Field 15 July 1943. With ZP-14 in October, it located a portion of a crashed FM-1 plane at sea by sighting its oil slick. K-71 was grounded and deflated near Long Beach, Washington, after fuel was exhausted 20 November 1943, then rebuilt. On the 3rd of August 1943 ZP-33's K-71 searched and located a crashed B-17 nearly inaccessible on Cape Lookout, directing rescuers to its lone survivor. At Tillamook the K-71 was coaxed into Hangar 'B' for the station's first docking on 18 AUG 43. 3 OCT 43 K-71 attacked a MAD contact which yielded oil, but it was later determined to be a wreck. On 30 August 1944, it searched for and located two men in a life raft from an Army crash boat. On 09 November, it operated off Cape Arago, Oregon, to assist in the rescue of a Navy pilot that had crashed at sea. K-71 was revised to ZP2K/ZSG-2 type.

K-72 - Serial 30194, Goodyear envelope D-236, control car C-131, control surfaces F-183, delivered to Lakehurst 24 June 1943; in service at Weeksville July 1943. Served with ZP-51. With ZP-14 on 05 December 1943, with K-82, located 12 survivors from the sunken Cuban freighter *Libertad* off the North Carolina coast and summoned surface help. On the 2nd of May 1944 ZP-14's K-72 was escorting a convoy when the MAD gave a signature. A surface vessel responded to their call and attacked, but there was no visible result On 31 October 1944 K-72 investigated a reported downed Navy PBM; K-72 located the plane and effected a rendezvous with surface craft. (Controversial) 18 April 1945 K-72 crew, including James Hughes, pilot and CBM G. W. Roberts, stated that working with Coast Guard cutter [USS *Annapolis*] K-72 located and tracked sub with sono-buoys, ordered cutter back four miles and to shut down engines. K-72 crew dropped their MK 24 homing torpedo code named 'Fido.' Explosion registered on headset followed by no more sub noises. During debriefing torpedo expert told crew he was certain they had struck the submarine. During 1968 search for USS *Scorpion* a U-boat hulk was found in that area, about 75 miles off Norfolk, Virginia. U-boat records list U-857 as Missing In Action, no explanation, off the American coast in April 1945. (U-boat net now lists K-72 as U-857's possible fate.) Revised to ZP2K/ZSG-2 type, in service at Lakehurst with Naval Reserve in 1952/1954. Envelope painted with Wings of Gold and "Be A Naval Aviation Cadet" recruiting paint scheme. Featured in newsreel about Naval Reserve flights showing New York harbor, "K-72" visible on lower fin.

K-73 - Serial 30195, Goodyear envelope D-243, control car C-132, control surfaces F-184, delivered to Lakehurst 03 July 1943; in service at Weeksville in July 1943 and Santa Ana in December 1944. With ZP-14 on 12 September 1943, it sighted the merchant ship *Benjamin Franklin* around; K-73 stood by for 9 ½ hours until recalled to base. On 17 September 1944 it located and reported a fishing boat in distress. 1 FEB 45 K-73 delivered a packet of secret operations orders to USS *Birmingham* (CL-62). K-73's crew was commended for the perfect drop on the deck in spite of the high winds and 200 foot ceiling. A TBM crashed in view of K-73 off Pt. Loma, 5 APR 45, but there were no survivors to rescue. Purchased as surplus by Goodyear in 1946, not erected, control car revised to ZP2K/ZP3K type and resold to the Navy in the early 1950's.

K-74 - Serial 30196, Goodyear envelope D-238, control car C-133, control surfaces F-185, flown to Akron for a special employees ceremony on Navy Day 1943. Dedicated by LT (later CAPT) Joy Hancock of the WAVES (herself twice widowed by the fledgling rigid airship program) at Akron (left). Delivered to Lakehurst 02 July 1943, K-74 was assigned to ZP-21 at Richmond, Florida. K-74 departed 18 July 1943 for patrol of the Florida Straits off the southern tip of Florida. With no submarine activity reported in the patrol area, a radar contact was made just before midnight and K-74 headed for the area. The German submarine U-134, with CaptLt. Hans-Gunther Brosin in command, was spotted on the surface. The submarine had already survived an airplane attack; doctrine required that an airship locating an enemy submarine was to remain upwind and guide planes and surface ships to attack. The K-74 crew elected to begin an attack up moon at 250 feet, trying to cross at an angle of 30 degrees to bracket the U-134 broadside with depth bombs. U-134 turned and opened fire, the turret (with the .50 caliber machine gun) was hit but fired at U-134 until the sub passed under the airship and did not present a target.

As K-74 pressed the attack, the main gun of U-134 opened fire. Two depth bomb (set for 50 feet and could not be reset in the air) levers were pulled, but nothing was seen to happen. U-134 continued to fire until K-74 was damaged by hits on the control car, the starboard engine and the envelope. K-74 settled into the water tail first and all hands abandoned the control car. Bearing in mind the two depth charges that were suspected of hanging on the bomb racks, the K-74 commander (LT Nelson G. Grills) swam back to the control car and removed all classified material. The remaining crew, wearing life jackets, were still close enough to the K-74 to ascertain the U-134 apparently pulled part of the wreckage aboard and took photographs.

The night battle of K-74 vs. U-134, depicted by Cortney Skinner.

U-134 radioed a message "Attacked at night by Navy airship with bombs and cannon." The depth bombs had likely went off underwater and caused some damage; the 50 cal machine gun was probably responsible for more injury to U-134, reported by radio as main ballast and quick-diving tank damage. During the night Grills and the rest of the crew failed to locate each other. One crewman, AM2/c Isadore Stessel, was lost in the water, probably to a shark attack.

K-74 stayed afloat until 08:15 on the morning of 19 July. The majority of the crew were located in the morning by an amphibian search plane with the commander of ZP-21 aboard, but it could not land due to the heavy seas. Rescue was made by the destroyer USS *Dahlgren*. LT Grills was swimming toward the Florida Keys some 40 miles away when he was spotted by the aft lookout of the K-33. Grills was rescued at 19:30 by the submarine chaser SC-657, having made six miles in his swim.

The U-134 may have chosen to abandon its mission of marauding in the Caribbean. The U-boat was attacked by airplanes but escaped during a thunderstorm, was attacked by a hunter-killer group and fought them off with its guns for 55 minutes to limp back to the Bay of Biscay. After the photographs that were taken of the K-74 wreckage had been transferred to another submarine, U-134 was finally sunk by the British. There were no survivors.

Controversy regarding the incident after the loss of K-74 continued within the anti-submarine warfare circle on whether Grills should be court-martialed or commended; neither occurred. Grills became gunnery officer with Fleet Airships Atlantic to develop improved tactics and ordnance. US radio intelligence decoded the U-134 message but originally mistranslated it as "Attacked at night by Navy flying boat..." Unlike all others, the combat was not kept classified, but does not appear in the NAS Richmond history. After intensive examination of British decrips of German U-boat transmissions by Gordon Vaeth, it was discovered that K-74 had actually damaged the U-boat's ballast tanks during the attack; Americans had first mistranslated the message as "flying boat." Admiral Rosendahl described the attack "as an engagement unparalleled in naval history" and stated it proved the airship is capable of attacking submarines. When the record became evident, a commendation from the Secretary of the Navy was presented by VADM C.E. Rosendahl (Ret.) to LCDR John Jan, navigator of K-74, at a ceremony at Lakehurst 17 February 1961 The citation read as follows:

"For heroic achievement on the night of 18-19 July 1943 while serving as Navigator of the United States Navy Airship K-74 during an attack against a surfaced enemy submarine in the Straits of Florida. When the enemy submarine opened fire with 20 MM guns, Jan participated in a low-altitude, machine-gun and depth-bomb attack by his craft, which inflicted damage upon the submarine and caused that vessel to disappear. While the K-74 was severely damaged and losing altitude rapidly, he aided in conducting a skillful landing in the sea without injury to any of the crew. Jan's courage, skill, and devotion to duty in the face of hostile gunfire were in keeping with the highest tradition of the United States Naval Service."

LCDR Nelson G. Grills, the K-74 commander, was finally awarded the Distinguished Flying Cross in 1961. Isadore Stessel's Purple Heart medal was not delivered to his family until members of the Naval Airship Association, led by YNC Anthony Atwood, USNR, arranged for a presentation on Armed Forces Day, 1997.

<u>K-75</u> - (Last series of K-type airships, K-75 through K-135), Serial 33467, Dunlop envelope D-273, control car C-154 (note gap in control car numbers from C-134 through C- 153 which were assigned to G and L-type airships), control surfaces F-206, delivered to Moffett Field 29 July 1943; nicknamed "Lady Luck". With ZP-32 on 3 April 1944 K-75 aided PC boats to rendezvous with American submarines. On 31 May it participated in salvage operations of the SS *Henry Bergh*, around the Farallon Islands, California, by assisting surface craft in the rescue of more than 1300 passengers, receiving a 'well done' from the Commander, WSF. K-75 under LTJG F. S. Lynn reported on phases of the rescue operations and photographed the scene. On August 18th it was directed to search for a crashed Army P-38; it located the pilot in a life jacket swimming to shore, and directed a crash boat to his rescue. On 19 August searched for a TBM wreck, then stood by while four crash boats worked salvage. On 5 January 1945 K-75 continued ZP-32's good relations with local fishermen by reporting a large sardine school in sector 11; then on 24 January it summoned PC-799 to assist two fishing boats in distress. On 15 January K-75 dropped target balloons and stood by for gunnery exercises of the SS *Sarazen*. K-75 conducted first series of special flights in the San Francisco Bay area for representatives of the United Nations Conference beginning on 01 May 1945.

K-76 - Serial 33468, Goodyear envelope D-239, control car C-155, control surfaces F-207, delivered to Lakehurst 13 July 1943. Assigned to ZP-14 at Weeksville July 1943 to May 1944. With ZP-14 on 18 December 1943, K-76 searched for a lost PBM, located it, and assisted in the rescue of four crew members. K-76 also served with ZP-12 and flew more than 5,000 hours on patrol and convoy escort missions. 22 MAR 44 K-76 arrived on scene of CG-112 mousetrap attack, developed moving MAD contact, surface craft summoned, attacks made, K-76 dropped 3 DCs, no results. K-76 was used in the filming of the movie "This Man's Navy" with Wallace Beery, Tom Drake, Jan Clayton, Jimmie Gleason and others.On the 6th of September 1944 ZP-12's K-76 under ENS J.J.F. Louglin was pulled off patrol and vectored to a suspected plane crash site, locating an empty raft but no other signs of life. 6 OCT 44 ZP-12's K-76 was sent to search for a crashed airplane but only located an empty life raft. On 7 JUN 45 the K-76 out of Fisher's Island was enlisted to help recruiting for the submarine service. The week of the 21st of July 1945, the K-76 took MIT lab personnel aloft to test how a small balloon released by a downed pilot might aide in its location. ZP-12 was represented by K-76 as the U-858 surrendered on May 14th, 1945. Purchased for $10,000 by the Douglas Leigh Sky Advertising Company in February 1946 at Lakehurst. K-76 is believed to have been registered as NC-67095 (later N27A). It advertised "Tydol Flying A" gasoline in 1947 (with an "A" and night sign wings that flapped) and Flamingo Orange Juice in 1950 (with a flamingo that flapped its wings on the night sign). The registration was cancelled 06 June 1951. Former Navy pilots that flew the airship included James M. Punderson, Jr., chief pilot, Augustus S. Lynch and Edgar L. McCartney. The Tydol ship was blown off the mast while at South Weymouth on 18 September 1948, a total loss.

K-77 - Serial 33469, Goodyear envelope D-242, control car C-156, control surfaces F-208 and F-216, delivered to Lakehurst 13 July 1943; assigned to ZP-23 at Hitchcock, Texas, and evacuated to Glynco to avoid a July hurricane. K-77 flew through four hours of severe thunderstorms on 06 November 1943, and was used to locate the lost K-60 on 06 December 1943. On 21 JAN 44 San Benito, Texas, became ZP-23's Advanced Operating Base as K-77 diverted there following a patrol. Next day K-77 performed another patrol and returned to Hitchcock. With ZP-51 on 07 November 1944, K-77 located a disabled crash boat and stood by until surface craft arrived. 11 FEB 45 K-77 followed up on a surface vessel's attack and established numerous MAD contacts moving within a large oil slick. Marking them with floats for the surface craft, K-77's crew noted the contact's approximate depth and decided it was pointless to drop their own 25-foot set depth charges. Revised to ZP2K-77 and served with the Airship Training Center at Lakehurst in 1951, deflated during dust storms in Nevada 15 June 1957 being readied for the atomic bomb tests.

K-78 - Serial 33470, Goodyear envelope D-244, control car C-157, control surfaces F-209, delivered to Lakehurst 14 July 1943. With ZP-12 on 19 September 1943, K-78 sighted two small lifeboats and directed the Coast Guard to the position. Eight people were rescued. On 22 October, K-78 was ordered to the area of a two ship collision, searching the area and directing three amphibious planes to find three life rafts. 20 people were rescued. K-78 landed in trees and was deflated near Lakehurst on 07 November 1943, but was rebuilt. 23 JUL 44 LT Silas L. McHenry and his K-78 crew searched for survivors from a three-airplane crash site. The C-47s had left only some white boards with stripes. No other wreckage – or survivors, from any of the three – was ever found. With ZP-15 and sister ship K-41, it searched for a crashed Navy F4U on 21 October 1944. The pilot's body was found and surface craft directed for the recovery.

K-78 searched for a sunken airplane off Pautuxent River NAS on 18 March 1947, LT J. W. Vaughn, pilot. K-78 tested a winged MAD sensor designated as "dual towed birds." K-78 was revised to ZP2K/ZSG-2 type.

K-79 - Serial 33471, Goodyear envelope D-342, control car C-158, control surfaces F-131 and F-210, delivered to Moffett Field 14 August 1943. With ZP-33 on 30 April 1944, K-79 searched for and located a crashed Royal Canadian Air Force Ventura on Vancouver Island, British Columbia. On 28 August 1944, K-79 searched for and located three men from crashed airplanes about 90 miles west of Cape Alava, Washington. It then assisted the Russian ship *Maximum Gorki* in their recovery. On the 2nd of June 1944 the Commander Northwestern Sector WSF CAPT C. B. Kerrick checked out ZP-33 and took a flight with skipper Bill Peeler on the K-79. K-79 was active in experimental land and sea rescue operations in September, 1944. The first test was to hover over a designated spot on the landing mat at Tillamook and lower a life raft. The second test was made at sea and included hoisting, by hand winch, a life raft with one man to the control car. The third test consisted of a suspended life raft over land and the 'survivor' jumping into the raft. On 16 SEP 45 the K-79 assisted the CG in finding the lost fishing boat *King Salmon*. Revised to ZP2K/ZSG-2 type. Revised to ZP3K/ZSG-3 type, at Glynco on 18 July 1955, damaged in a hard landing. Three days later during a ferry flight to Lakehurst for repairs, the emergency landing wheel had been installed incorrectly and the car was further damaged during the landing complicated by thermals.

K-80 - Serial 33472, Dunlop envelope D-272, control car C-159, control surfaces F-211, delivered to Lakehurst 23 July 1943. K-80 was in service at Weeksville. On the 20th of July 1943 ZP-12's K-80 assisted a disabled merchantman. 04 DEC 43 K-80 dropped three charges on an oil slick that appeared to be moving, but since one hung on the rack and another was a dud there was no visible evidence of submarine damage. The airship was deflated a couple weeks later when undocking, taking it out of service for more than a month. On the 3rd of April 1944 K-80 had a disappearing radar contact. December 04 dropped three bombs on an oil slick. At Glynco in 1944. A rescue demonstration was staged for crowds celebrating Navy Day on 27 October 1945, with K-80 hoisted a man from a crash boat in Willoughby Bay, Norfolk. K-80 was at Lakehurst in 1947. From March, 1950, to February, 1951, it participated in carrier operations with the USS *Mindoro*, USS *Siboney* and USS *Sicily*. On 26 June 1950 (John A. Fahey, command pilot) it demonstrated an airship carrier landing to the Commander-in Chief, Atlantic Fleet, and Commander, Air Atlantic. Aboard the ship for the landing were Flag Officers RADM Robert Hickey, Commander, Fleet Air Wings, Atlantic and COM Herbert Graves. RADM Hickey acted as the rudderman for the return landing. A "well done" was issued by the Commander-in-Chief, Atlantic Fleet, for the excellent carrier landing demonstration. K-80 was revised to the ZP2K/ZSG-2 type. Revised to ZP3K/ZSG-3 type, car painted Navy blue for experimental flights from Key West, Florida, serving with ZX-11. (See "ZP3K/ZSG-3 Airships.")

K-81 - Serial 33473, Dunlop envelope D-274, control car C-160, control surfaces F-212, delivered to Lakehurst 27 July 1943. K-81 made a night radar contact where a U-boat was known to be in the area on 16 August 1943 (also listed as 26/8) and was evaluated as a 'possible.' Due to strong winds at Weeksville, North Carolina on 29 September 1943, was unable to return and landed at Camp Davis, North Carolina (original site of the Army Barrage

Balloon Training Center) with only 31 gallons of fuel remaining. Flown to Naval Air Station, Charleston, South Carolina, the crew was relieved by a fresh crew from ZP-15. Returned to Glynco and remained there until 01 October, flying to Weeksville on 02 October. With ZP-14, on 07 January 1944, K-81 located 21 bodies after the collision of USS *St. Augustine* with a tanker off Cape May, New Jersey. 11 Jan 44 K-81 attacked a MAD contact later evaluated as a wreck. On the 3rd of May ZP-14's K-81's crew attacked a 'sound contact' with bombs. A slight amount of oil was noted. Transferred to Lakehurst with ZP-12, on 05 December K-81 searched for and located the target ship *James Longstreet* adrift from its moorings; it stood by and effected a rendezvous with surface craft. K-81 was deflated after striking the doors while undocking at Lakehurst 22 December 1943; it was rebuilt. On 20 August a combination of errors led to a botched landing and the deflation of the K-81. There were no injuries or fire. Revised to ZP2K/ZSG-2 type, ZP2K-80 deflated while on a local training flight from Lakehurst 19 December 1950. Again rebuilt, it tore away from its mast and deflated during a twister at Key West, Florida, on 28 September 1953.

<u>K-82</u> - Serial 33474, Goodyear envelope D-341, control car C-161, control surfaces F-213, delivered to Lakehurst 30 July 1943. Made possible contact with U-boat while on night patrol in 1944, original contact made from seven miles away, proceeded to location and contact from five miles, area was searched for three hours before resuming patrol. K-82 was assigned to ZP-14 at Weeksville in November 1944. On 05 December 1944, with K-72, located ten survivors and summoned surface craft. On 20 January 1945, the K-82 aided the merchant ship SS *Proctor* in distress. ZP-11's K-82 was also present at the last attack off the American coast. Purchased for $10,000 by the Douglas Leigh Sky Advertising Company at Lakehurst in February 1946, registered NX-94800 (later N28A), used for advertising with registration cancelled 06 June 1951. K-82 was Revised to ZP2K/ZSG-2 type.

<u>K-83</u> - Serial 33475, Dunlop envelope D-275, control car C-162, control surfaces F-214, delivered to Moffett Field 27 August 1943; assigned to ZP-33 at Tillamook. June 1944 K-83 was searching for survivors of a B-25 crash when struck a mountain and deflated near Nanaimo, Vancouver Island, British Columbia, 05 June 1944, without injuries to its crew. A mule team haulded the wrecked car from the woods, while other parts remained on site.

<u>K-84</u> - Serial 33476, Goodyear envelope D-340, control car C-163, control surfaces F-215, delivered to Lakehurst 06 August 1943. K-84 departed Lakehurst 10 September 1943 via Glynco, Georgia; Richmond, Florida; Guantanamo Bay, Cuba; San Juan, Puerto Rico arriving at Edinburgh Field, Trinidad, where it was retained for duty from 14 to 23 September. K-84 flew on to Paramaribo, Dutch Guiana. With LT "Hobie" Hobensack and LT Loy Dixon, pilots, K-84 became the first non-rigid airship to cross the Equator on 26 September, then on to Amapa and Igarape Assu, Brazil before landing at Fortaleza, Brazil, on 27 September 1943. K-84 Made first operational patrol of the South Atlantic 28 September; operational at Fortaleza, Brazil on 08 November 1943 and reported radar blips of a suspected U-boat on 14 October 1943. First Navy airship to use the Santa Cruz hangar. Returned to Richmond. K-84 transferred from ZP-21 to ZP-15, arriving 22 April 1945, and back to Richmond for the airship pool on 9 May 45.

<u>K-85</u> - Serial 33477, Goodyear envelope D-343, control car C-164, control surfaces F-208 and F-216, delivered to Lakehurst 15 August 1943. Assigned to ZP-21 on 14 August 1944, K-85 sighted a disabled cabin cruiser near shore and summoned a nearby Coast Guard ship. It was in service with ZP-33 at Santa Ana in December 1944. On 7 JUL 45 ZP-33's K-85 made a practice landing on the USS *Puget Sound*. (CVE-113) on 07 July 45 (left, US Navy /J.

Cook). Revised to ZP2K-85 at Lakehurst, beginning on 16 September 1951, it operated from a portable stick mast at Quonset Point, Rhode Island Naval Air Station for five weeks, making twenty-nine flights. Revised to ZP3K/ZSG-3 type. Attached to NARTU Lakehurst, on a ferry flight from Glynco in adverse weather, it suffered a structural failure, loss of pressure and controllability; it settled into Pamlico Bay North Carolina 15 August 1957. A fishing vessel rescued the crew. A possible cause for the accident was offered as the thunderstorm having thrown the ART-13 trailing wire antenna into the starboard prop, which slashed the envelope.

K-86 - Serial 33478, Goodyear envelope D-339, control car C-165, control surfaces F-217, delivered to Lakehurst 19 August 1943. K-86 was photographed with "experimental scatter bombs" (p.104), the ASW ordnance also known as "rocket bombs" although the rocket propellant was removed. Transferred to ZP-32, K-86 assisted AVR-7 and 8 to rendezvous with a crashed PBY-5A. On 28 AUG 44 the K-86 on night patrol received a vessel's blinker message requesting the ship's owners to obtain certain repair parts for their next port of call. K-86 was revised to ZP2K/ZSG-2 type and on 10 July 1952, it was forced down at sea, damaging both propellers. The submarine USS *Sea Poacher* successfully towed the ZP2K-86 back to shallow water off Boca Chica, Florida (left). An AVR took over and towed the airship to the vicinity of NAS Key West.

K-87 - Serial 33479, Goodyear envelope D-338, control car C-166, control surfaces F-218, delivered to Moffett Field 21 September 1943; assigned to ZP-32 at Moffett Field. 4 MAR 44 the K-87 helped a PC boat find the friendly submarine it was supposed to escort off California. 15 OCT 44 an airplane crash into a residential area of Coquille, Oregon had to be photographed from the K-87 owing to the dangerously low ceiling. On 29 and 30 October K-87 searched in vain for a downed Navy S03C plane. With ZP-33 at Tillamook 22 FEB 45 K-87 arrived at the scene of a double airplane crash and stood over survivors for surface rescue, but then searched in vain for four victims that were never found. On 2 April 1945, while assigned to ZP-33 at Tillamook, a Japanese type 93 buoy mine was spotted four miles from the entrance to Gray's Harbor near Hoquiam, Washington. A Coast Guard ship was notified which attempted, unsuccessfully, to sink the mine by gunfire. After the Coast Guard ship left the area, K-87 fired its .50 caliber machine gun at the mine. This too was unsuccessful. K-119 arrived on the scene and fire from its machine gun finally hit the mine causing it to explode. On 24 April 1945 demonstrated air-sea rescue of LTJG Bruce Kelly in Tillamook Bay (LTJG George Woerfel, pilot), rescue observed by Royal Canadian Air Force pilots from Vancouver, British Columbia. One of the last two K-types to operate at Tillamook, Oregon, transferred to Moffett Field on 23 October 1945. Revised to ZP2K/ZSG-2 type, envelope painted with Wings of Gold and "Be A Naval Aviation Cadet" recruiting paint scheme, "K-87" visible on lower fin.

K-88 - Serial 33480, Dunlop envelope D-276, control car C-167, control surfaces F-219 and F-231, delivered to Lakehurst 20 August 1943; assigned to ZP-41 and operational at Fortaleza, Brazil, on 08 November 1943, nick-named "88 Keyes," featured on nose art. On 21 August 1944 (LCDR John J. McLendon, command pilot) lowered Navy doctor LT Bryan St. J. Moynahan to the seaplane tender USS *Lapwing* to tend an injured seaman. K-88 suffered an accidental deflation. On 03 February 1945, with pilot LTJG Rapstine, K-88 searched for two missing F6F planes and located wreckage in the Florida Everglades. Out of Weeksville on 16 October 1945 K-88 stood by the survivors of a crashed SB2C. K-88 served at Glynco 1946-47. Revised to ZP2K/ZSG-2 type, and suffered a hard landing with damage to car and props on 20 NOV 51. Later revised to a ZP3K/ZSG-3 type. The control car was sold to a surplus dealer and stored in a field near Lakehurst. Cannibalized to provide parts for a representative K-type control car for display in the National Museum of Naval Aviation at Pensacola, Florida, K-47. Cannibalized remains shipped from Pensacola February 1991 to the United Kingdom for rebuild by No. 4 School of Technical Training at RAF St. Athans in South Wales for eventual display at the Airship Museum to be possibly located in Cardington, Bedfordshire, England.

K-89 - Serial 33481, Dunlop envelope D-277, control car C-168, control surfaces F-220, delivered to Lakehurst 28 August 1943. On 01 October 1943 with ZP-11, located four life rafts with fifteen survivors from the sunken Coast Guard cutter *Wilcox*. On 05 October it aided in the rescue of a survivor from the crash of a Navy SOC plane. On June 9th 1944 ZP-12's K-89 under ENS C. Amy spotted a body clad in aviation flying uniform, but could not get a surface craft to recover it. The same ship and the K-37 tried to relocate it the next day but found only a life jacket. On 22 SEP 44 ZP-12's K-89 found a number of empty life rafts and a lifeboat but no survivors. On 11 September 1944 it sighted the tanker *Appomattox* disabled with engine trouble; surface craft were notified. Also serving at Weeksville, K-89 was flown to Lakehurst in April 1945 where it was modified for a trans- Atlantic crossing. Returned to Weeksville, K-89 departed 28 April as a replacement airship for ZP-14. Together with K-114, it flew on a southern route for Port Lyautey (now Kenitra, Morroco) via Bermuda (a 10 hour flight) and Lagens, Azores (the longest leg of the flight, 1,881 miles, flown in 29.5 hours), arriving at Port Lyautey 01 May 1945. K-89 responded on the 17th of July 1945 when the Liberty ship *John H. Hammond* struck a mine. Deflated 23 August 1945 at Pisa, Italy when the airship overrode the mooring mast, planned to be re-inflated at Cuers, but was not re-inflated when ZP-14 was ordered deactivated 15 November 1945.

K-90 - Serial 33482, Goodyear envelope D-345, control car C-169, control surfaces F-221. In test flight, engine oil caught fire, cutting fuel to engine and using fixed and portable extinguishers failed to stop the fire. Russell W. Crosier's actions saved the ship, and he received the Goodyear medal. Other crewmembers commended. K-90 was delivered to Lakehurst 18 September 1943, then assigned to Brazil. On 04/05 February 1944 it rescued survivors (with K-114) of a downed A-30 airplane. While on routine patrol 07 February 1944 entered a rain squall, later experienced failure of both engines and landed in some trees with no loss of life. K-90 was salvaged, crew supplied with provisions by K-114, and local laborers employed.

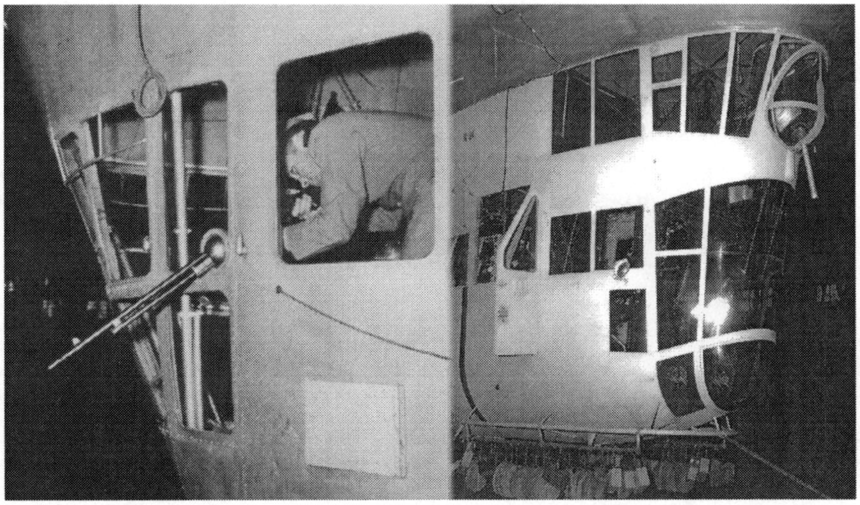

K-91 explored the mounting of a Browning Automatic Rifle, aft, to supplement the standard 50 cal machine gun forward. Hepburn Walker, Jr. (K-91 crew chief) and NARA (via Eric Brothers) photos.

K-91 - Serial 33483, Goodyear envelope D-358, control car C-170, control surfaces F-222, delivered to Lakehurst by truck, probably September 1943, and car mounted in a cradle for various test purposes. Erected by the Navy at Lakehurst. Tested BAR mount in ball socket aft. 8 through 20 May 1944 tests of "Fido" homing torpedo, LT James Punderson, Command Pilot, Hepburn Walker, Jr. crew captain. VADM Rosendahl on board for several of these flights, using the obsolete USN submarine O-1 as a "target." During one test the unarmed torpedo struck the submarine with sufficient force to cause an increase in leaks. Flown to South Weymouth 18 December 1944, with crew of LCDR Winston (pilot), LTJG Ashe (co-pilot), Oden Chaney and a radioman, flight was 10.7 hours. K-91 was grounded in a snowstorm on 19 December. Flown 20 December for 7.1 hours and returned in a snowstorm, grounded due to snow on 21 and 22 December. Returned to Lakehurst 23 December after accumulating ice and snow over New York and New Jersey. Used for experiments with "scatter bombs" (contact fuse bombs) provided to Lakehurst for use against submarines in March 1945. Original pilot was to be LT Harry Titus, later replaced by LT James Punderson; RADM Rosendahl aboard as observer. Contact bombs were released but struck each other before hitting the water, the explosion jarring the ship and hurling VADM Rosendahl to the deck. K-91 returned to base with 246 holes in the control car and envelope. K-91 was then refitted with the new 456,000 cu ft envelope. Revised to ZP2K/ZSG-2 type.

<u>K-92</u> - Serial 33484, Goodyear envelope D-347, control car C-171, control surfaces F-223 and F-232, delivered to Lakehurst 08 September 1943. Assigned to ZP-12 on 22 October 1943 it sighted a circling and flashing SOS and located two life rafts during the night. K-92 dropped flares and led an escort ship from a convoy to recover an estimated two survivors. The next day, K-92 aided survivors of a crashed plane. On July 19th K-92 spotted a free floating mine and a surface craft was summoned to sink it. On 28 October, K-92 was instrumental in locating a Navy ship YP448 in heavy seas. Notifying base and requesting surface craft, K-92 stood by until Coast Guard ship 833313 and the tug *Martin* arrived and took YP 488 in tow. ZP-15 was tasked to find some lost barges and K-92 reported their position on the 19th of March 1944. When surface craft failed to locate them in the undesirable weather, K-102 braved the conditions found them again the next day allowing the tows to catch up. On 6 October 1945 ZP-12's K-92 was inadvertently dunked trying a rescue, chopping its ballast bag to recover. Purchased inflated for $10,000 in February 1946 at Lakehurst by Douglas Leigh and used for advertising Ford Motor Company with the logo "Ford's Out Front" on the starboard side of the bag, the Ford logo on the port. Registered as NX-94800, this registration was cancelled 14 October 1955. Though records do not indicate Goodyear repurchasing K-92, it was revised to ZP3K/ZSG-3 type and likely sold back to the Navy. On 15 June 1957 "Airship BuNo 92" was moored at Yucca Lake, Nevada, when 'dust devils' tore it from the mast with two men aboard. Ascending, the engines were started and the ship brought down in partial control allowing the men to jump clear. The ship drifted for miles until a ground party caught up in trucks to pull the ripcord.

<u>K-93</u> - Serial 33485, Goodyear envelope D-359, control car C-172, control surfaces F-224, delivered to Lakehurst 10 September 1943; assigned to ZP-42 in Brazil. 12 JUL 43 ZP-51's K-93 under ENS Sidney Verier spotted a periscope. The navigator set recorded their position as 19-56N, 73-19W. Half an hour flying MAD traps to got a signal some four miles away, but tracking showed the contact was moving at about two knots. HTA and surface support was called in but never arrived; no attack was made, so no action report was filed. Ordered returned to Richmond, March 1945 and then to Weeksville, North Carolina for deployment to England as part of Fleet Air Wing Seven (war ended before airships could be deployed). On 14 March K-93 was damaged when a filler block loosened from a hurricane fell from Hangar #2's timber roof and punctured the envelope. Emergency patches were applied and helium pumped back in to save a complete deflation. 21 AUG 45 the K-93 located a crashed FM-2. *Kite Balloons to Airships...* states K-93 made the last flight of ZP-21 on 5 November 1945. The ZP-21 ships had been stored at Richmond, the fire/hurricane occurred 15 September 1945 and other records show it destroyed on this date. Yet on 23 May 1950, K-93 demonstrated airship carrier landings aboard the USS *Mindoro* and in-flight refueling to the Chief of Naval Operations who was aboard. Records also show K-93 advertised for Naval Reserve in 1946 while based at Lakehurst, flown to Akron with CDR Verner L. Smith as pilot.

With the new radar sets classified, there are few photos of the radar scope in place across from the radioman. Simon Beattie photo.

<u>K-94</u> - Serial 33486, Goodyear envelope D-349, control car C- 173, control surfaces F-225, delivered to Lakehurst 23 September 1943. K-94 mysteriously burned and was lost off Puerto Rico with the loss of all eight crewmen 30 October 1943. ZNATEC Message of 15 Aug 47 signed by T.G.W. Settle "Blimp Casualty Statistics, War Period 1942-1945" lists loss of K-94 as "burned and sank (B-25 similarly lost same place few hours later)" and cause as "unknown (possible enemy action)." Gasoline fires destroyed 11 other K-ships but there are no other cases of fire spreading to another aircraft in flight hours later. The cause was never determined; it may have been from gunfire from a German U-boat discovered surfaced (as in the case of the K-74), or more probably, the result of a gasoline problem. Some airship veterans, including alternate K-94 command pilot Julian Parrish, feel certain the airship was fired upon by a submarine and the single B-25 sent out as a result was also lost to the submarine. Published records do not show a U-boat in the area at the time.

<u>K-95</u> - Serial 33487, Dunlop envelope D-278, control car C-174, control surfaces F-226, delivered to Moffett Field 20 October 1943; assigned to ZP-31 at Santa Ana, California and involved in two rescues, one at sea and in the desert. 13 MAY 44 Marine Corps ace Capt. F. B. Baldwin survived his airplane crash. K-95 was ordered to the area and hailed him by megaphone. The crew rigged a special harness and lowered it to Baldwin, who was hauled aboard, bedded down and fed a hot meal. (Goodyear company publicists noted the pilot was wearing a Goodyear-made vest, got into a Goodyear-made raft, and was rescued by a Goodyear-made airship.) The next rescue was of two downed Navy pilots in the middle of the desert area near Holtville, California. The pilots had been on a routine training flight 02 July 1944 from the Sand Hills Aerial Gunnery Range firing at towed targets when one of the pilots was forced to parachute due to engine failure and seriously injured. A second pilot then parachuted to assist. A rescue party was organized, but due to the extreme heat all but two were forced to return to Holtville. Santa Ana was contacted and a request made for a rescue attempt by airship. LT Peter I. Culbertson (known as "Ace" for his exploits) had just returned from routine patrol and landed the K-95 and was given the assignment to rescue the downed pilots. Through heat and turbulent winds in the mountain passes, K-95 made it to the area of the downed pilots that had now been joined by two rescuers from Holtville.

It was determined the only way to provide assistance was to make a controlled crash landing, the starboard engine was killed and the port engine switched off as the control car plowed into the sand. K-95 was severely damaged with two propellers bent, the landing wheel knocked off and lines loosened, the final blow was that it was too late to rescue the seriously injured pilot who had died. K-95 was lightened as much as possible, the two members of the rescue party, the second parachuted pilot and the deceased pilot taken aboard. Despite the damages, K-95 managed to take-off with Culbertson running along under the control car and pushing up for lift and then hoisting himself on board. An Army airfield was reached in spite of severely bent port propeller. (Note moderate damage to starboard prop above.) Two bladed props from Army airplanes were borrowed and K-95 returned to Santa Ana to land without a wheel. For this rescue, Culbertson was awarded the Distinguished Flying Cross on 14 October 1944 by RADM Rosendahl. The citation read as follows:

"For extraordinary achievement while participating in aerial flight as command pilot of the airship K-95 on 02 July 1944, when engaged in a rescue mission involving the saving of lives of aviation personnel who were marooned in the desert near Holtville, California. Voluntarily and in the face of great danger, he crash-landed his airship among the sand dunes and effected the rescue of three physically exhausted men and the removal of the body of another. Through his superior skill and airmanship he undoubtedly saved the lives of these three men and returned safely to an emergency base with his damaged airship. He then made ingenious temporary repairs to his airship and flew back to his home base. His conduct throughout was in keeping with the highest traditions of the naval service. C.W. Nimitz, Admiral, USN."

With ZP-32 on 19 October 1944, K-95 sighted a forest fire near Pigeon Point, California, and dropped messages to the lookout station, standing by until fire equipment arrived. On 25 November it sighted a fire east of Point Ano Nueve, again dropping messages to the fire lookout who dispatched fire equipment to the scene. On 25 October it conducted the first in a series of radar calibration flights for Army radar stations along the coast, the Army reporting this method proved excellent. On 15 November K-95 conducted the first in a series of VHF tests for Pacific fleet submarines, that day with the USS *Tautog* (SS-199), and the following day USS *Pompom* (SS-199). On 10 February 1945, it searched for and located a crashed F6F north of Dumbarton Bridge, marking the location for surface craft. On 23 March K-95 searched for and located the distressed SS *Mission San Miguel* and effected a tow by the ATA-192. On 27 June sighted a plane crash four miles north of San Mateo Bridge, then directed surface craft to rescue the survivor.

K-96- Serial 33488, Goodyear envelope D-348, control car C-175, control surfaces F-227, delivered to Lakehurst 24 September 1943; assigned to Richmond, Florida. On 24 January 1944, attached to ZP-51, K-96 aided in salvage operations of a crashed B-24 in the Brazilian jungle. With ZP-21 in August, K-96 operated from Guantanamo, Cuba, with at least six 12-hour flights. K-96 was destroyed in the NAS Richmond hurricane and fire of 15 September 1945.

K-97- Serial 33489, Goodyear envelope D-344, control car C-176, control surfaces F-230, delivered to Moffett Field 30 October 1943. With ZP-31 on 25 August 1944, K-97 sighted a small craft abandoned and adrift in high seas; K-97 identified it as the small tug *Man-o-War*. Notifying base, K-97 stood by until a Coast Guard crash boat arrived, then illuminated the tug so it could be taken into tow. K-97 was later assigned to ZP-33 and was one of the last K-ships at Tillamook. Revised to ZP2K/ZSG-2 type.

K-98 - Serial 33490, Dunlop envelope D-279, control car C-177, control surfaces F-228, delivered to Lakehurst 06 October 1943; assigned to Brazil with ZP-42. 13 DEC 43 the first ZP-42 operational flight was made by K-98 out of Maceio. Commanded by ENS Eugene Pace, located a life boat while escorting convoy PT-19, 26 Germans and 8 Italians were rescued, credited with rescuing 106 survivors (with K-36). On 08 February, it searched with K-110 for survivors of an Army B-24, which had crashed in the Brazilian jungle. In July 1945 K-98 located a downed A-26 on a Brazillian beach, made a landing, and recovered the crew. Revised to ZP2K/ZSG-2 type. During ASW exercizes with ZP-2 on 12 JUL 1951 ZP2K-98 suffered thrust reverer failure leading to port engine failure. First pilot ENS Tom Culbert and crew were commended for their actions which saved the ship.

K-99 - Serial 33491, Goodyear envelope D-346, control car C-178, control surfaces F-234, delivered to Moffett Field 09 November 1943; assigned to ZP-31. On 14 March 1944 with K-20, was ordered to aid in the rescue of a pilot adrift in a life raft. They located the life raft and stood by until the pilot could be taken aboard a crash boat. On 04 July, K-99 coordinated the rescue of an injured man aboard the tanker SS *Tejon* at sea. K-99 was in service at Santa Ana in December 1944, also carried an "X" designation. 8 NOV 44 ZP-31's K-99 got a MAD signature five miles out to sea. Two hours later a surface craft arrived, got a sound contact and depth charged it. K-47 and K-67 were vectored to the scene and later K-115 relieved all, but the contact was later evaluated as a non-submarine, possibly a geologic formation. K-99 distributed war bond leaflets flying over Los Angeles on 14 May 45. On the 21st K-99 searched in vain for the pilot of an F4U crash off Sunset Beach, CA. 10 MAR 45 the K-99 carried the Test Conductor to control a large ASW exercise. Assigned to ZP-1 at Moffett Field, it carried three civilians on a sea lion photographic mission on 13 July 1947 at the request of the California Division of Fish and Game. K-99 was inadvertently flown into the water, washing one pilot out the smashed window. The crew successfully abandoned ship and were rescued in about thirty minutes. K-99 free-ballooned some three hours and finally came to rest in trees between two hills 16 miles north of Arcata, California. Salvage team removed a least some of the major assemblies.

K-100 - Serial 33492, Goodyear envelope D-316, control car C-179, control surfaces F-229, delivered to Lakehurst 12 October 1943. K-100 operated as part of ZP-51 at Paramaribo, Dutch Guiana on 06 November 1943. Later assigned to ZP-42 in Brazil, it was named "Lovely Ilona" in honor of Ilona Massey, who had entertained the troops. The actress visited the squadron and signed her ship (photo). On 21 AUG 44 ZP-51's K-100 was sent out to look for another lost airplane, a C-87, and spotted two parachutes in the trees. In spite of K-100 finding a clearing and discharging LTJG Jack Armstrong and CAP Richard Nye to search on foot, no trace of the airplane men was ever found. Ordered to be returned to Richmond, Florida, 10 JAN 45 K-100, while looking for a crashed B-29, prevented a freighter from running into shallow water. In the last contact for ZP-21, on 22 JAN 45, the K-100 had a clear and strong radar blip that disappeared before the blimp could arrive. A surface vessel got a sound contact about the same time and area but no records indicate a U-boat was in the area. Selected for deployment to England with ZP-42 (war ended in Europe before airships could be deployed). Revised to ZP2K/ZSG-2 type. Later revised to ZP3K/ZSG-3 type, with ZP-2 at Glynco, was extensively damaged when it struck trees following takeoff on 14 Feburary 1956.

K-101 - Serial 33493, Goodyear envelope D-360, control car C-180, control surfaces F-219 and F-231, delivered to Lakehurst 20 October 1943. ZP-12's K-101 under ENS D. Wallstein was busy late in December, first standing by a disabled freighter on the 26th and then under ENS C. Greim on the 30th running off all shipping so the Army could test its big coastal guns off Navesink Light. Firing over the horizon, K-101 reported on the shells' impacts. The fog of 11 APR 44 prevented one vessel from joining its convoy in New York's swept channel. K-101 located the ship on radar and giuded it in without actually seeing it. With ZP-12 on 14 May 1944,

K-101 directed a straggler by radar, its convoy in zero-zero visibility. K-101 was assigned to ZP-14 and flown from South Weymouth to Craw Field, Port Lyautey, French Morocco (now Kenitra, Morocco), arriving 01 July 1944. Due to carelessness during some blasting operations at Port Lyautey on 14 September, two 3-pound rocks were hurled through the envelope. K-101 was repaired. It conducted minesweeping operations in northern Italy (LT John F. Keefe, pilot). Based at Pisa, Italy, patrolling the Ligurian Gulf, K-101 flew to Rome's Littorio Field for mine sweeping. It was dubbed "Minnie the Miner" (left, Walt Chimil photo). On March 3rd 1945 the K-101 was able to locate the sunken USS *Swerve* at Anzio using MAD, then plot the minefield the vessel had fallen victim to. First week in March 1945 K-101 worked with Task Group 81.12 to clear ninety-seven contact mines from Cagliari. On May 4th the K-101 set up shop in Pisa, Italy, to begin demining operations in Genoa Bay. Escorted the surface fleet that carried President Roosevelt and Prime Minister Winston Churchill to the Yalta Conference with Premier Joseph Stalin in February 1945.

<u>K-102</u> - Serial 33494, Dunlop envelope D-280, control car C-181, control surfaces F-223 and F-232, delivered to Lakehurst 24 October 1943. On the 2nd of February 1944 ZP-15's K-102 located a still-floating B-18, but in spite of a combined search no trace of the crew was ever found. On 20 March 1944, K-102 relocated three barges separated from a tug that were originally located by K-92 the previous day. It requested assistance from surface ships. On 16 July with the K-40 it assisted in the rendezvous between a destroyer and a tanker to transfer an ill seaman. K-102 was destroyed by gasoline fire in the dock during refueling when proven procedures were not followed at Glynco, Georgia, on 04 August 1944. There were no injuries or damage to the timber hangar.

<u>K-103</u> - Serial 33495, Dunlop envelope D-282, control car C- 182, control surfaces F-238, delivered to Moffett Field 18 November 1943; served at Tillamook, Oregon. On the 13th of March 1944 ZP-32's K-103 located an airplane wreck and directed the CG to recover the bodies. Third week of April 1944 K-103 pulled a 1,017 mile mission lasting almost 24 hours escorting the battleship *Mississippi*. 25 OCT 44. the K-103 returned to Tillamook after a long patrol but found the station fogged in. The K-103 loitered until a partial clearing allowed a landing, completing ZP-33's longest mission to date, more than 28 hours. On the 29th of December 1944 ZP-33's K-103 had to locate the SS *Dolly Madison,* and when it did so the vessel asked a change of destination be relayed by the airship. K-103 deflated over Tillamook Bay on 18 March 1945 without injuries. Portions of the airship were recovered.

<u>K-104</u> - Serial 33496, Goodyear envelope D-350, control car C-183, control surfaces F-233, delivered to Lakehurst 30 October 1943. 23 NOV 43 the K-104 was escorting a convoy through the Providence Channel and got a strong radar contact, rated 'doubtful.' With ZP-21 on 28 March 1944, K-104 located a tanker with damaged engines and directed surface craft for tow. On the 19th of July 1944 K-104 searched for a lost P-39 out of Naples, Florida. On the way they spotted a downed C.A.P. Stinson and verified the pilots were okay before proceeding to the target area. An airplane had sighted the P-39 wreck, and K-104 stood over it until a crash boat could be directed by megaphone. On 3 Oct 44 the K-104 answered ComGulfSeaFron's request to find a disabled Army tug and barge, then stood by it until surface rescue located them. K-104 was destroyed by the hurricane and fire at Richmond, Florida, 15 September 1945.

K-105 - Serial 33497, Goodyear envelope D-303, control car C-184, control surfaces F-242, delivered to Moffett Field 27 November 1943. While assigned to ZP-32 on 01 July 1944 K-105 searched San Francisco Bay for bodies from a crashed airplane and on 08 July conducted a MAD search by the Farallons following up a sound contact by a surface craft. On 01 December K-105 located and reported a lost tow and directed surface craft to the rescue. On 16 January 1945, K-105 located Union Oil tanker *Paul M. Gregg* ablaze, directing crash boats to the scene. The airship spotted and marked the position of a man overboard who was then rescued. K-105 became a total loss as it struck a Weeksville hangar door on 06 January 1950.

K-106 was one of the airships that enjoyed the use of the ex-Zeppelin hangar at Santa Cruz. Ladders and equipment built to service the *Hindenburg* helped in the K-ship erection process. Hal Neuman photo.

K-106 - Serial 33498, Goodyear envelope D-308, control car C-185, control surfaces F-235 and F-251, delivered to Lakehurst 30 October 1943. Assigned to ZP-41, K-106 evacuated personnel and equipment of a downed Army C-47 near Amapa, Brazil, 23 December 1944. On 11 February 1944 with K-114, it made landings in the Brazilian jungle to rescue ten flyers from three Army B-25s that had crashed. Crewmen of the K-106 disembarked and acted as a landing party. The downed pilots were picked up and delivered to Amapa. The ship was then returned and picked up more crew members until all were returned to Amapa. On 15 February, K-106 returned to the site to recover ordnance, the radio and other salvageable equipment. On the 21st of August 1944 ZP-41's K-106 located a downed PBY, but in this case command ordered the airship pick up and bring in an officer who possessed some vital, though unspecified, information. An estimated three people were rescued. On the 12th of March 1944 LT Vernon E. Teig, crew and K-106 set up ZP-42's Detachment Six at the *Hindenburg's* old ar at Santa Cruz. Based at Correra, Panama, on 21 March 1945, it located a crashed Army P-39 pilot in the Gulf of Panama. Command pilot Harry Titus oversaw the survivor board a native canoe and then transfer to an Army crash boat. K-106 was destroyed by the hurricane and fire at Richmond, Florida, 15 September 1945.

K-107 - Serial 33499, Goodyear envelope D-351, control car C-186, control surfaces F-236 and F-246, shipped to Moffett Field 08 December 1943. K-107 rescued downed pilot LTJG Gordon W. Dooley when he crashed off the California coast 23 October 1944. Dropping a life raft on first approach and then a long line, K-107 hovered and then pulled him aloft when directly under K-107. The event was covered by San Francisco newspapers. On 18 November K-107 assisted PC-799 in effecting the rendezvous of USS *Bonefish* (SS-223) when adverse weather made it impossible without the airship. K-107 rendered torpedo recovery for three destroyers on 05 and 09 May 1945. It conducted a special air-sea rescue demonstration at NAS Alameda on 26 August 1945. K-107's envelope was punctured on doors of Hangar No. 1 at Moffett Field in 1947 and not salvaged, as it was judged not worth repair costs at that time.

One crewman doubled as cook, a hot meal helping to humanize the long, loud and often boring night flights. US Navy photo via Jim Plummer.

K-108 - Serial 33500, Dunlop envelope D-283, control car C-187, control surfaces F-237, delivered to Lakehurst 20 November 1943. Attached to ZP-21 K-108 received an SOS from the British ship *Enak* on 07 December. It located the ship, notified base and a tug was sent to the rescue of an estimated ten people. On 26 December K-108 reported radar blips from a suspected U-boat. On 23 March 1944, with ZP-51, K-108 discovered the British merchant ship *Palmyra*, flying the US ensign upside down, drifting out of control in the Gulf of Paria near Trinadad, BWI. "Need tow" was painted on the deck. K-108 led a British patrol boat to the scene and *Palmyra* was taken in tow. Approximately 10 people were rescued. 15 JUL 44 K-108 was dispatched with LTJG Clyde A. Lineberger, who reached the scene reported by K-32 after dark. Illuminating the raft with searchlight and summoning surface craft by blinker light, K-108 then answered the crash boat's question as to the course for home. On 16 July 1944, with K-32, the K-108 assisted in the rescue of a Navy PBM's crash survivors. On the 4th of April ZP-41's K-108 located a downed Brazillian C-45 and effected a rescue by replenishing the plane and crew.

K-109 - Serial 33501, Goodyear envelope D-305, control car C-188, control surfaces F-236 and F-248, delivered to Lakehurst 17 November 1943; assigned to ZP-14 and flown from South Weymouth to Port Lyautey, French Morocco. Arrived 15 June 1944. (Controversial) On 4 July 44 convoy escort; at 1700 made MAD contact running about 300' depth east to west, parallel to the convoy. Smoke floats determined direction, dropped two depth charges. Two escort destroyers joined the search as the 100- ship convoy deployed from a heading of 270 degrees to 240 degrees. Escort Commander radioed 'job well done' - one possible U-boat kill. 5 OCT 44 the K-104 recorded its last MAD contact, which was rated false. Flown from Cuers (France) to Sidi Ahmed Field, Bizerte (LCDR F.S. Rixey, pilot) arriving at the old Italian airship base 03 November for mine sweeping operations in the Tunisian War Channel. Sweep for mines completed in 14 days, two mines were found and sunk. Joined American and British minesweepers off the southern coast of Sardinia 21 November operating from Elmas Field, Cagliari where 268 mines were located. K-109 escorted President Roosevelt from the Crimea after the Yalta Conference. Due to increased submarine activity assigned to daylight convoy patrol in March 1945 (with K-112), also based at Littorio Field at Rome, Italy. Destroyed at Port Lyautey, French Morocco 26 March 1945 when the mast was overturned during a violent wind; it was torn from the mast and caught fire.

K-110 - Serial 33502, Goodyear envelope D-313, control car C-189, control surfaces F-239, delivered to Lakehurst 24 November 1943, assigned to ZP-42. On 08 and 17 February 1944, with the K-98, searched for survivors of a crashed Army B-24 in the Brazilian jungle. On the 3rd of March 1944 ZP-42's K-110 delivered fuel to a beached PBY 180 miles southeast of Fortelaza. On 22 March 1944, K-110 located a Brazilian training plane forced down near Santa Cruz, Brazil. On 21 through 25 July with K-125, it assisted in the search for survivors of a crashed Navy PBM. Reassigned to ZP-41, on 08 December 1944, K-110 searched for and located a Navy PBY off the coast of Brazil, lowering gasoline and other supplies to the crash rescue boat sent to the scene. Approximately eight people were rescued.

K-111 - Serial 33503, Dunlop envelope D-281, control car C-190, control surfaces F-239 and F-250, delivered to Moffett Field 17 December 1943; in August 1944 (LCDR F.N. Klein, Jr., pilot in charge) demonstrated the feasibility of refueling and replenishing from an aircraft carrier. During a 72.5 hour mission the crew was relieved every 12 hours, and for one thirty-two minute period remained on the deck of the escort carrier USS *Makasser Strait*. On 17 October 1944 and while on patrol from Del Mar, flew into the heights of Santa Catalina Island in dense fog, the gasoline and four depth charges exploded and six of the nine aboard were lost. These were LTJG Wallis H. Marriage, LTJG Thomas R. Smith, ENS Edward T. Groskie and crewmen Preston L. Girard, Gordon F. Kaiser and Tactical Unit Instructor LT Thomas H.Ralston. Survivors included AMM 3/c Ernest H. Jarke, AP 1/c James R. Baker, ARM 1/c Robert N. Cravens and AM 2/c Bertie L. Samuels.

K-112 -Serial 33504, Goodyear envelope D-315, control car C-191, control surfaces F-240, delivered to Lakehurst 07 December 1943; assigned to ZP-14 at Weeksville. K-112 conducted anti-submarine training flights from Key West. K-112 was flown from South Weymouth to Port Lyautey, French Morocco, arrived 01 July 1944, completing the shortest flight from the US to Africa, 52.1 hours. First US airship to land in Europe, K-112 made two landings at Gibraltar, 18 July and again on 21 July, to test the emergency base established on "the Rock." (Above, left: Gibraltar was never an operating base; a mobile mast was set-up for emergency landings for airships on MAD operations). Assigned to the Eighth Fleet Escort Sweeper Group for mine sweeping operations, flown to Cuers-Pierrefeu Aerodrome after the liberation of Toulon. Flew from Port Lyautey (with a fueling stop at Oran) landed at Cuers 17 September, made first mine sweeping operation in the Gulfs of Juan and Napoule 18 (or 20) September. Logged approximately 70 hours on mine operations by end of September and flew two special night missions of approximately 15 hours each on 23 and 24 September to establish a Magnetic Airborne Detector barrier across the entrance to Toulon harbor. Photographic missions were also flown. On the 24th of September 1944 the K-112 flew MAD patrol all night to intercept suspected German one-man submarines, the single mention made of an airship trying to detect mini-subs during the entire war. On the 13th of October 1944 K-112 carried two French officers for the first joint minesweeping effort. On the 12th of November 1944 the mine-spotting K-112 was asked to look for a missing P-39, and turned up another unreported crashed airplane instead – the original P-39 had made it to another airfield. Due to the success of K-112, K-109 was also assigned to Cuers, with K-123 flown back to Port Lyautey for overhaul in December. January 30th 1945 found Cuers-based K-112 flying down to Port Vendres to operate with sweepers, then flying back – 150 miles each way – to the base. It provided escort for President Roosevelt to the Yalta Conference in February 1945. Due to increased submarine activity, K-112 was assigned to daylight convoy patrol in March 1945. K-112 made the last anti-submarine patrol of the war; it was flown 06 June 1945 during which a fifty-five ship convoy was escorted.

K-113 - Serial 33505, Goodyear envelope D-289, control car C-215, control surfaces F-297, F-442, F-443, F-446, F-448 and F-450, control car C-192 destroyed by fire while in transit by rail to Moffett Field and replaced by control car 215 (originally designated for K-139 which was not erected), delivered to Lakehurst 06 April 1944 (with K-135, the last K-ship delivered). As a result the K-113 was the smallest K-number ship with aft-opening "clamshell" doors replacing the side-opeing door on the starboard aft. With ZP-15 on 12 March 1945, participated in a search for downed PB4Y and two SB2C's downed from Jacksonville, LTJG Donnovan, command pilot. 15 March rendezvoused a destroyer and tanker to arrange evacuation of sick gunner. Sustained a 12.1-hour ZP-15 ASW patrol on 17 April 1945, J. A. Teben, command pilot. Became part of ZP-21, Detachment 11, when ZP-21 assumed NAS Glynco duties, 30 May 45. Some sources state revised to ZP2K-113, served with the Airship Training Center at Lakehurst in 1951. On 26 February, the landing gear failed while landing. There were no crew injuries.

K-114 - Serial 33506, Dunlop envelope D-291, control car C-193, control surfaces F-241, delivered to Lakehurst 02 December 1943; assigned to ZP-41 in Brazil. 30 DEC 43 K-114 opened operations at the ZP-41 detachment at Amapa, making a total of five airships for

the squadron. K-114 assisted in the rescue of a downed C-47 in February 1944, then assisted in the rescue of survivors from a downed Canadian A-30 airplane 04/05 February 1944. With command pilot LT James Davis, it made two landings in a jungle clearing and rescued Flight Officers Doherty and Clarke. Dropped provisions to the downed K-90 on 10 February. The next day it located a downed B-25 bomber, then landed and picked up the two downed pilots. On the 5th of March 1944 K-114 recovered survivors of a B-24's forced landing some 22 miles from Bolam.
On 05 March K-114 landed and evacuated five survivors of an Army B-24 airplane crash in Brazil. Transferred to Weeksville and then to Lakehurst in April 1945, K-114 was modified for a trans-Atlantic flight (with K-89). K-114 departed Weeksville 28 April using the southern route via Bermuda and Lagens, Azores, on the 29/30th, 29.6 hr. leg, LT Quale, pilot. Arrived Africa 01 May 1945. Maintained operations from Cuers as the last airship in ZP-14 service; deflated and crated for shipping 15 December when ZP-14 was ordered deactivated 15 November 1945.

ZP-14 airships were equipped with the new twin-head MAD sensors, installed via rope ladder while at the mast. Other squadrons received the upgrade; additional gear is seen above the radarman in this view of the K-28 interior. ZP-24 photo.

K-115 - Serial 33507, Goodyear envelope D-304, control car C-194, control surfaces F-252 and F-284, delivered to Moffett Field 30 December 1943. On 14 FEB 44 ZP-31's K-115 was about a mile from a CVE when the crew noticed a launching TBF wasn't going to stay airborne. Pilot P. I. "Ace" Culbertson made for the impact site and ran aft to drop the blimp's life raft. It landed on the TBM's wing tip, the plane's pilot ran across the wing and jumped inside, and the airplane sank from the British aircraft carrier HMS *Nabob*. On 03 September, it sighted and reported Army tug *Blue Fin* aground on Santa Rosa Island, California. K-115 dropped a survival kit to the men on the beach and stood by until Army surface craft arrived. On the 23rd of August 1944 K-115 was landed at the Mexican Army Airfield Ensanada. Several officers were taken aloft for observations flights. On 13 SEP 44 ZP-31's K-115 crew got to use their machine gun to shoot up and sink a large boiler floating adrift, fouling the shipping lane. K-115 assisted in the rescue of a plane that had crashed off Oceanside, California, on 07 December 1944. K-115 worked as plane guard for USS *Ranger* (CV-4) and was on the scene of the SB2C crash the morning of 5 FEB 45 only to have the pilot go down with the plane. Only hours later the exact same thing happened in spite of K-115 arriving in 30 seconds.10 MAR 45 K-115 carried photographers and special observers for a large ASW exercise.

K-116 - Serial 33508, Dunlop envelope D-292, control car C-195, control surfaces F-243, delivered to Lakehurst 17 December 1943 (with K-117). With ZP-42 on 15 May 1944 K-116 sighted a lifeboat full of survivors from a sunken British merchant ship. Emergency rations were dropped and surface craft were directed to the scene to take them aboard. On 08 November 1944, K-116 landed at the scene of a crashed A-35 plane that went down in Brazil, assisting in the rescue of an estimated two people. On 15 NOV 44 ZP-42's K-116 found a stranded Army pilot who'd crashed north of Caravellas. On 15 November, K-116 searched for a second missing A-35 plane, which it located on a beach. An estimated two survivors were rescued. K-116 was flown from Panama to Jamaica on 27 October 1945 and to Richmond on 28 October. It is reported to have been the last airship returned from Central and South America. Revised to ZP2K/ZSG-2 type. As ZP2K-116 it suffered a hard landing, crumpling the car bow.

K-117 - Serial 33509, Goodyear envelope D-309, control car C-196, control surfaces F-244 and F-251, delivered to Lakehurst 17 December 1943 (with K-116). On the 21st of September 1944 ZP-42's K-117 was employed to find a Cruserio do Sul airplane that had crashed near Bahia. It directed a search party to the location and relayed information from the rescue party to base. K-117 was destroyed by the hurricane and fire at Richmond, Florida 15 September 1945.

K-118 - Serial 33510, Goodyear envelope D-310, control car C-197, control surfaces F-245 and F-249, delivered to Lakehurst 30 December 1943. Assigned to ZP-41 in Brazil, K-118, during the transfer flight on 23 January 1944, sighted and reported a downed Army B-25 medium bomber. It located two survivors of the crash in the Brazilian jungle. On 24 February, K-118 received a light signal from the SS *Hillsboro Inlet* that she had collided with the Cuban freighter *Mimina*. K-118 summoned surface craft for the rescue of an estimated 20 people. On 04 April it assisted in the salvage of an Army B-25 that had crashed in Brazil. K-118 located a crashed Army A-36 Vultee *Vengeance* thirty miles north of Amapa, Brazil, on 16 July. LTJG C. A. Coulter, pilot, landed on soft tidal flat sand to evacuate two survivors and equipment before high tide claimed the wreck. Crewmen acted as handling party while downed Army fliers load their gear aboard the airship. Lack of motion cooling rapidly heated the envelope. (Above, photo by Henry L. Durnan, K-118 crewman, via Walter Swistak.) 18 JUL 44 K-118 ferried workers to the jungle crash site of an Army A-35 for salvage. On 11 JUL 45 the K-118 was assigned as an air-sea rescue ship and was put to work the next day on a P-51 crash. Spotting the oil slick, the airship directed an Army crash boat to recover the plane and pilot's body on the bottom. With ZP-15, K-118 practiced air-sea rescue operations July through November 1945, during which on 21 September, it located a crashed Navy SB2C along the Georgia coastline. On the 27th it found a crashed PV, and on the 29th yet another. A demonstration of rescue from the water was made for an audience that attended the 1945 Navy Day celebration at Charleston, South Carolina. This mission was flown with only one pilot after the co-pilot had been accidentally sprayed with gasoline while refueling at Charleston prior to the flight. The man rescued from the water was landed at the Charleston Naval Air Station and the co-pilot picked up and returned to Weeksville with the airship. K-118 was revised to ZP2K/ZSG-2 type.

K-119 - Serial 33511, Goodyear envelope D-306, control car C-198, control surfaces F-222 (these same surfaces were given for K-91 which were revised to F-222A), delivered to Moffett Field 07 January 1944. On the 10th of October 1944 ZP-32's K-119 touched down on the USS *Yorktown* to pick up some ComFairSeattle training observers and returned them to base. 2 APR 45 K-119 was able to detonate the mine found by K-87, later identified as a Japanese type 93 model 1. Returned to east coast, served at Richmond. Revised to ZP2K-type. On 07 November 1952 ZP2K-119 was lost when a broken piece of Plexiglas window hit the propeller and then pierced the envelope, command pilot George R Keiser. The 11 survivors were rescued by the submarine USS *Sea Dog*.

K-120 as rescue airship at NAS Banana River, NARA photo courtesy Eric Brothers.

K-120 - Serial 33512, Goodyear envelope D-307, control car C-199, control surfaces F-247, delivered to Lakehurst 10 January 1944. K-120 is believed to be the first production "clamshell-door" equipped K-ship. The single side door was eliminated and two swing-open doors were added at the aft end of the car, equipped with a fold-down egress ladder. K-120 made anti-submarine training flights from Key West in 1944. Flown to Santa Ana (LCD Charles Koehn, command pilot) with stops at Weeksville, Glynco, New Orleans, Dallas and El Paso, and Litchfield Park, Arizona. K-120 was modified as a prototype sea-rescue airship and operated from NAS Banana River, Florida (Now Patrick AFB) in September, 1945 (above). Large block letters below "U S Navy" spelled RESCUE on the envelope. Revised to ZP2K, then ZP3K type. ZP3K-120 assigned to Reserve Squadron ZP-871 (deactivated 31 December 1958) at Oakland, California and stricken due to the envelope condition that could no longer pass standards.

K-121 - Serial 33513, Dunlop envelope D-287, control car C-200, control surfaces F-246, F-253 and F-288, delivered to Moffett Field 20 January 1944. On 14 June 1944 with ZP-32, K-121 searched for and located a coastal launch with five men aboard; it remained on the scene until the Coast Guard rescued them. On 02 July, with K-55, it searched for and located YMS-140 and SC-546 47 miles south of the Farallons; the vessels were given their true position and headed to join their group. On 09 August K-121 witnessed the rescue of one man from a crashed Navy plane, guided the crash boat to the rescue of a second survivor and, on return to base, requested medical assistance be made available on the crash boat's arrival. On 12 August an estimated four people were rescued when K-121 sighted a fishing boat in distress. K-121 contacted surface craft by dropping a message; poor visibility made blinker contact useless. On 26 September K-121 located the missing tug YTL-425, beached at Cape Mendocino. On 08 March 1945, K-121 received a blinker message from the SS *Thomas A. Hendricks* and relayed the message enabling a Coast Guard cutter to arrive and remove a sick man for hospitalization ashore. Two days later it located two survivors of a plane crash in a raft and directed an Army crash boat to their rescue. On 27 March K-121 searched for and located the SS *Pennsylvania* and arranged for the USS *Fox* (AG-85) to remove an appendicitis victim. K-121 was revised to the ZP2K/ZSG-2 type.

K-122 - Serial 33514, Dunlop envelope D-285. control car C-201, control surfaces F-248 and F-290, delivered to Lakehurst 11 January 1944; assigned with ZP-14 at Weeksville and then the Caribbean. With ZP-23 on 11 July 1944 survivors from a torpedoed tanker were located; LTJG W.J. Boehrs, command pilot, ordered ENS Lewis dropped off to form a landing party. The most in need of medical care were taken aboard and the balance later rescued by surface ships directed to the location. K-122 also made a flight of 15.1 hours in November 1944 with John Sciambra as pilot. K-122 arrived to assume new ZP-23 duties at Mandinga, Panama, on 17 APR 44. 25 November 44 found K-122 performing ZP-23's last escort flight. On the 6th of April 1945 Max Zabst, pilot, and the K-122 got a MAD contact and marked it for surface craft to attack. One of the followup attacks appeared to hit something, and K-122 recovered what appeared to be some large chunks of cork. On 3 APR 45 K-122 got a MAD signature with the chart showing the closest wreck a mile away.

Clamshell doors open after landing in Argentia, the K-123 crew was (keeling, from left) LTJG R.L. Kersey, ENS D.D. Crowder, ENS L.P. Lylenda, ENS J.C. Kane. (Standing, from left) ACRM C.J. Dempsey, ARM2 R.A. Baney, AMM2 W.H. Rediker, BM1 E.D. Kinsley, and AMM3 F. B. Schuler.

K-123[16] - Dunlop envelope D-286, control car C-202, control surfaces F-249, F-251 and F-253, delivered to Lakehurst 22 January 1944. K-123 was the first ship delivered with aft-opening "clamshell" style doors in the car's aft, replacing the side opening door. 5 MAR 44 ZP-12's K-123 located a disabled fishing boat. K-123 was flown to South Weymouth in May 1944 and modified for the trans-Atlantic flight. CDR Emmett J. Sullivan, pilot and ZP-14 commanding officer, K-123 departed 28 May 1944 (with K-130) for Port Lyautey, French Morocco, via Argentia, Newfoundland (arrived 29 May and departed 30 May). It arrived at Lajes Field, Terciera Island, Azores, on 31 May, and then to Port Lyautey, arriving 01 June 1944. K-123 made the first flight in Africa 03 June, and first operational flight over the Straits of Gibraltar on 06 June. Accidentally deflated at the mast 15 January 1945 at Port Lyautey, French Morocco

[16] Note: For some unknown reason no serial numbers were issued for K-123 through K-135.

when a French officer (some reports say he was an impostor) driving a jeep snagged the rip cord extender on the windshield causing both rip panels to be pulled. K-123's car was shipped to Cures for the first French-based airship erection of the war. Goodyear sent two technicians in March to direct the reconstruction, but the gear they needed did not arrive until July. Re-erected Cuers. Assigned to Malta when damaged again on 10 October 1945, replaced by K-134 and repaired at Cuers. Final deflation at Cuers 10 December after ZP-14 was ordered deactivated on 15 November 1945.

Upon arrival in French Morocco the first thing out of K-123's clamshell doors was mail for the squadron. ZP-14 photo.

<u>K-124</u> - Dunlop envelope D-293, control car C-203, control surfaces F-390, F-251, F-253 and F-390, delivered to Lakehurst 23 January 1944; transferred to the Caribbean with ZP-51. On 10 JUN 44 the K-124 obtained a MAD contact and an oil sample taken indicated diesel oil. Target was stationary and was assessed by ComCaribSeaFron as possible submarine. The next day K-124 obtained 12 consecutive contacts within ¼ mile of contact the previous day. Surface craft dropped depth charges and brought up oil slick. MAD contacts were lost following depth charging. During a routine patrol on 13 June K-124 sighted a sailboat with six occupants all clad in striped prison uniforms. Emergency rations were dropped, base notified and a surface craft was dispatched to pick the men up. On 8 July 1944, a flight to demonstrate the airship's features and capabilities was made for President Vargas of Brazil and a party of five other officials. It assisted an Army launch adrift without engine power on 11 July 1944. K-124 towed it for approximately seven miles until a surface ship completed the tow, saving seven men from possible internment in neutral Venezuela. Struck the mast and deflated at Guantanamo Bay, Cuba 10 August 1944, (a logbook shows 2nd), rebuilt. Flying out of Weeksville, made first in-flight re-fueling of a K-type airship on 11 January 1950 from USS *Mindoro,* John A. Fahey, pilot. K-124 made first night carrier landing (probably the only night landing) aboard USS *Mindoro* 06 February 1950. It made five landings and tie-downs with John A. Fahey, pilot, and George Stadler, co-pilot. Revised to ZP3K/ZSG-3 type, it was later assigned to Naval Reserve Squadron ZP-651 at Akron and took part in maneuvers at Guantanamo Bay, Cuba, December 1956.

<u>K-125</u> - Dunlop envelope D-294, control car C-204, control surfaces F-235, F-249, F-252, F-253 and F-287, delivered to Lakehurst 02 February 1944. K-125 was flown to Brazil and served on night scouting missions. On the 8th of July 1944 ZP-42's CO CDR Charles Werts flew the K-125 to Lago de Marambia so as to observe a Brazilian ASW exercise. Among the observers aboard was President Getulio Vargas, who watched the live fire demonstration from the bombardier's seat as the Brazilian flag flew from the ship. Returned to Lakehurst, K-125 was then transferred to Santa Ana. On 27 AUG 45, the 30th anniversary of Naval Aviation, ZP-12 sent K-125 to carry a Boston broadcaster to record a message for later broadcast. Revised to ZP2K-125, it was assigned to Reserve Airship Squadron ZP-951 in 1952 (ZP-951 deactivated in 1959).

<u>K-126</u> - Goodyear envelope D-312, control car C-205, control surfaces F-252, F-285 and F-289, delivered to Lakehurst 08 February 1944. K-126 was assigned to ZP-42 in Brazil, then was ordered returned to Richmond 29 March 1945, and then to Weeksville for deployment to England with Fleet Air Wing Seven. The war ended in Europe before airships could be deployed. Transferred from NASL Hedron One to ZP-15 on 03 April. K-126 conducted visual and radar observation of Army "robot bombing" experiments off Eglin Field, April 1945. Sustained a 16.3 hour ASW patrol on 17 April, H. W. Gasque, command pilot. Transferred to

Blimpron One, NASL, 26 April 45. K-126 was destroyed in the hurricane and fire at Richmond, Florida 15 September 1945.

K-127 - Dunlop envelope D-284, control car C-206, control surfaces F-285, F-287, F-288 and F-290, delivered to Lakehurst 16 February 1944; assigned to ZP-42 in Brazil. K-127 struck mast at Igarape-Assu, Brazil 27 July 1944, and was rebuilt. Ordered returned to Richmond 29 March 1945 and then to Weeksville, North Carolina for deployment to England with Fleet Air Wing Seven. The war in Europe ended before airships could be deployed. With ZP-15, assisted in calibration of Charleston's Coast Guard RDF station, R. L. Stawbridge, command pilot, 12 April 1945. On 15 April sustained a 20.6 hour ASW mission. Survived a port engine fire 15 April, M. D. Griep, command pilot, returned to Glynco on one engine after 20 hours. CAC #501 was credited with coolly following the fire bill, extinguishing the fire and ending the emergency. Transferred to Hedron One, Detachment 24, Weeksville, 19 April 1945. K-127 departed South Weymouth at 0702 5 JUL 45 and began patrol; at 1205 word came of a midair collision of to fighters some 10 miles to the north. K-127 arrived on scene and found no survivors amid the burning wreckage. A week later the scene was repeated with the same airship over a land crash. K-127 was sent to operate out of a mast base in Eglin Field (and later Apapachicola) and hover in the Gulf to photograph Buzz Bomb flights' terminations. Revised to ZP2K/ZSG-2 type, then ZP3K/ZSG-3 type. As ZP3K-127 carried lower fin designator ZT-3. In 1955, attached to NZTU, NAF Glynco, GA, carried envelope wording "Fly Navy." Used to demostrate hurricane fallback in 1955, masted at Lovell Field, Chattanooga TN, with Naval Reservists, Tom Cuthbert, command pilot.

K-128 - Dunlop envelope D-295, control car C-207, control surfaces F-286 and F-288, delivered to Lakehurst 19 February 1944. With ZP-12 on 22-26 July K-128 searched for survivors of the Brazilian escort ship *Camaqua*, which had capsized. On return to base 23 JUL 44, K-128 was directed to the scene of a Navy Air Transport Service plane crash. K-128 assisted the rescue party in locating wreckage and delivered supplies to the salvage and rescue groups. K-128 was equipped with a special radar and conducted tests for he Bu of Ord first week in July 1945. K-128 was destroyed by the NAS Richmond hurricane and fire 15 Sep 1945.

K-129 - Dunlop envelope D-296, control car C-208, control surfaces F-253, F-287, F-289 and F-291, delivered to Lakehurst 21 February 1944; assigned to ZP-23. On 17 October K-129 relieved a Navy PBM airplane at the scene of a plane crash in the Caribbean. It also arranged a rendezvous between surface craft and the crashed plane. On the 9th of December 1944 the K-129 flew the 15th Naval District Commandant and staff on a topography tour when it was realized an airplanes' stall speed was still too fast for an airborne study. 27 MAR 45 the K-129 used her MAD to find and mark a submerged F7F in Sebastian Inlet. K-129 was destroyed by the hurricane and fire at Richmond, 15 September 1945.

K-130 - Dunlop envelope D-298, control car C-209, control surfaces F-289, F-291 and F-292, delivered to Lakehurst 24 February 1944. On 14 APR 44 ZP-12's K-130 sighted an unusual type of buoy thought to be an enemy radar decoy or listening instrument, and it is known now the U-550 was in the area. Assigned to ZP-14, K-130 was flown to South Weymouth for modification for the trans-Atlantic flight. Departing with K-123 on 28 May 1944 for Port Lyautey, French Morocco, it arrived 01 June 1944 - the first airship to land there. Altitude during the flight from the Azores to Africa averaged 500 feet, fuel consumption had been 30 gallons per hour, overall flight time from South Weymouth had been 58 hours at an average ground speed of approximately 54 knots. On the 19th of June 1944 the K-130 was flying the inky blackness of night on the Straits of Gibraltar when she received a urgent message to withdraw as enemy aircraft were approaching. Following the doctrine to turn for the open sea, darken ship and fly at very low altitude, the K-130 accidentally hit the water, losing its radar hat and radio altimeter antenna. Repair, it was again damaged on take-off at Port Lyautey when a ridge of soft earth was struck doing considerable damage to the control car, two slip tanks, the radar beehive, the tail wheel and the lower fin. K-130 was repaired again, then finally disassembled on 22 November at Cuers when ZP-14 was ordered deactivated on 15 November 1945.

K-131 - Dunlop envelope D-297, control car C-210, control surfaces F-290, F-292 and F-293, delivered to Lakehurst 24 March 1944 (some accounts give this date as 17 March 1944 which conflicts with the Goodyear record); assigned to Richmond. On the 7th of May 1944 ZP-41's K-131 made several landings to replenish, then rescue the crew of an Army A-20. On the 11th of January 1945 two Brazillian SNJs collided in front of the K-131, which called for help and marked the spot. Rescuers found no survivors. K-131 was lost on 17 February 1945 during a "light" night landing at Fortaleza. K-131 hit high tension lines, puncturing the envelope forward. All the crew escaped except the pilot, who was pinned and repeatedly shocked before being rescued with severe burns and cuts. The gasoline ignited and K-131 burned to a total loss.

K-132 - Dunlop envelope D-299, control car C-211, control surfaces F-291, F-293 and F-294, delivered to Lakehurst 10 March 1944. K-132 was flown to Brazil via San Juan, Puerto Rico, then Trinidad, Dutch Guiana and on to San Luiz, Brazil, 21 March 1944. Goodyear representative Harry H. Haines was aboard on an inspection tour. On 23 April K-132 located a missing boat 100 miles south of Maceio, Brazil. Transferred from ZP-21 to ZP-15, arriving 11 May 1945. K-132 again became part of ZP-21 at Apalachicola when ZP-21 assumed ZP-15 utility duties, performing "robot bomb" (V-1) spotting duties. Destroyed by the hurricane and fire at Richmond, 15 September 1945.

ZP-22 personnel muster to honor their fallen comrades of K-133 at Houma, Louisiana. Note unique doors, which made this shed the largest timber hangar ever constructed. US Navy photo.

K-133 - Dunlop envelope D-300, control car C-212, control surfaces F-293, F-294 and F-295, delivered to Lakehurst 21 March 1944; assigned to ZP-22 at Houma, Louisiana. K-133 was forced down during heavy thunderstorms over the Gulf of Mexico while on patrol 19 April 1944. Only one crewman, ENS William Thewes was rescued, and were nine lost. Recorded as the only airship lost in flight due to weather. (See K-34. Other records state K-133 was the last airship assigned ZP-15 when the squadron was disestablished, 30 May 1945.)

K-134 - Dunlop envelope D-301, control car C-213, control surfaces F-294, F-295 and F-296, delivered to Lakehurst 24 March 1944; assigned to ZP-14 and flown from South Weymouth to Port Lyautey, French Morocco, arrived 15 June 1944. Assigned to Cuers on minesweeping operations (relieved K-112) on 07 December 1944, diverted a French ship from a moored mine;Believed to be the only pressure airship to carry an intercontinental stowaway when, on V-E day, a 13 year old Algerian boy hoping to visit his sister in America hid in the K-134 bomb bay during a refueling stop in Algeria. Command pilot was ENS James Hotham. In March 1945 Cures-based K-134 had begun minesweeping support in the Baie de Sanary, in which seven mines were cut loose and destroyed. On June 10th 1945 K-134 set up shop in Lido, Italy, where it began minespotting just two days later. On July 30th K-134 overflew Yougoslavia's Baker Bay, checking Karaljevicki channel. It later visited the Gulf of Fiume and the Canale Della Panesina to check their known mine fields. Replaced K-123 at Malta in October 1945. Deflated 02 December at Cuers when ZP-14 was ordered deactivated on 15 November 1945.

K-135 - Dunlop envelope D-302, control car C-214, control surfaces F-296, F-297, F-441, F-444, F-445 and F-448, delivered to Lakehurst 06 April 1944. K-135 was the last of the wartime K-type airships to be delivered. It arrived with K-113 and was assigned to ZP-21. In May 1944 the second ZP-23 detachment set up shop with K-135 at Barranquilla, Columbia. On 04 August it searched for and located a sunken landing craft off Miami Beach, Florida, and directed the Coast Guard to the scene where they placed a danger buoy. On 13 August, while enroute to intercept and cover a southbound convoy, K-135 noticed numerous radar blips, indicating another convoy 23 miles away. Observation showed that a collision was imminent. The southbound convoy was informed and both convoys turned to starboard. The convoys were only four miles apart and 45 minutes away from collision. On 21 December, K-135 completed a well coordinated rendezvous between a landing ship and a submarine chaser for the purpose of transferring a critically ill seaman. K-135 was destroyed by the hurricane and fire at NAS Richmond, Florida.

This combat aircrew manned the last Navy K-ship of WWII.

K-136, K-137, K-138 and K-139 were planned. Two envelopes fabricated (D-288 and D-290) and furnished to the Navy as spares. The K-139 control car may have been completed by Goodyear and may have been re-designated K-113 to maintain sequence. (The original K-113 burned on a railroad car.) It is also reported that the control cars for K-136, K-137 and K-138 were delivered to Lakehurst to replace damaged control cars or for parts.

Goodyear analysis of 1948 estimated cost for a single prototype K-type airship of 416,000 cubic feet (based on quantity production) as $318,000, but varying between $261,500 to $333,000, depending on quantity. The 1949 estimate for the post World War II more electronically sophisticated K-type of 456,000 cubic feet was $2,736,000 with envelope cost doubling and control car cost increasing eight fold.

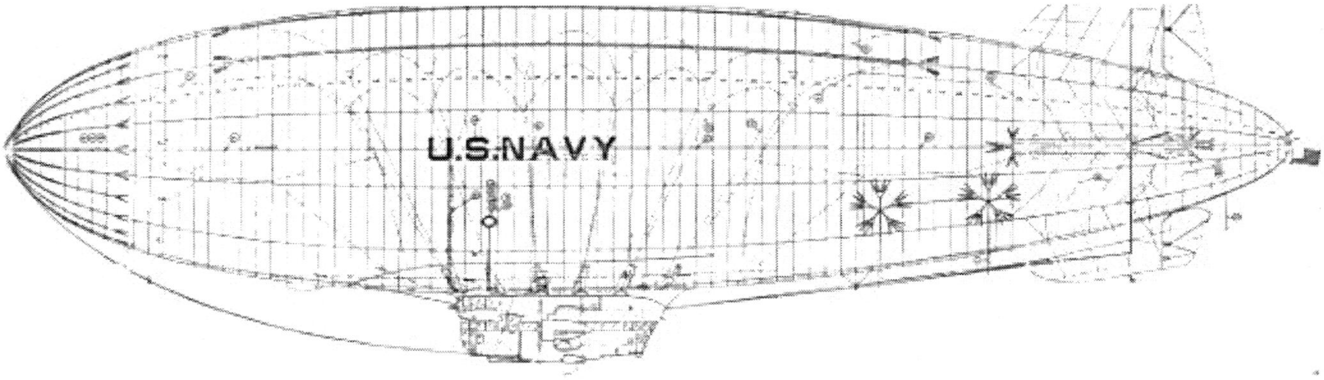

K-type airship general specifications: (K-7 and K-8, same as K-3 thru K-6, see Part IV):

	K-9 to K-13	K-14 to K-135	K modified
Volume(cubic feet)	416,000	425,000	456,000
Ballonets (2) (cubic feet)	111,400	111,400	119,500
Overall length (feet)	248.5	251.7	253.0
Maximum diameter (feet)	57.85	57.85	60.0
Overall width (feet)	62.5	63.5	65.0
Static lift (pounds)	26,325	26,970	27,400
Dynamic lift (pounds)	2,000	2,000	2,500
Service load (pounds)	4,775	5,120	4,100
Speed, maximum (knots)	67.5	67.5	67.5
Speed, cruising (knots)	50.	50.	50
Endurance at cruise (hours)	36.5	38.2	59.0
Range at cruise (nautical miles)	1,850	1,910	1,460
Engines (2)	All models Pratt and Whitney R-1340-N2,425 horsepower at 1,775 rpm, Curtiss variable pitch, 3 bladed propellers, propeller diameter 12.5 feet.		

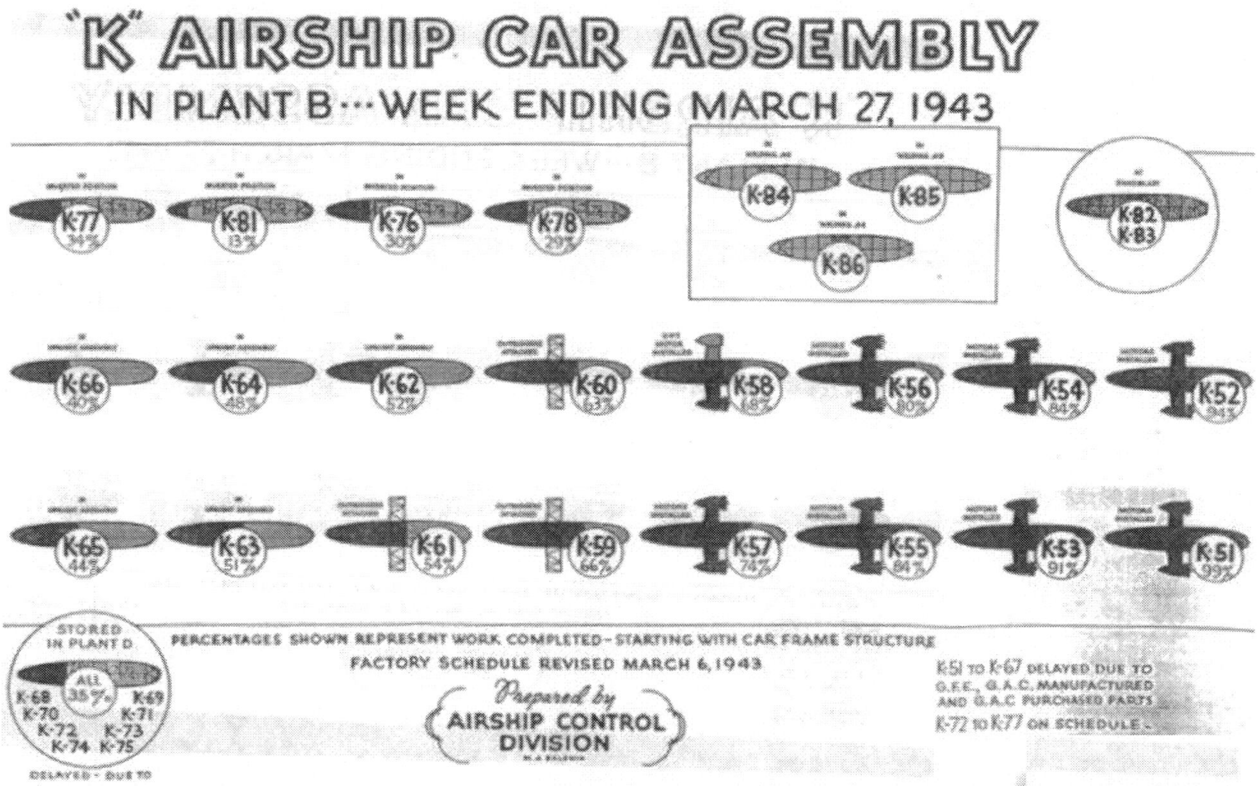

K-type airship delivery by year and month, 1942 thru 1944.

	Lakehurst	Moffett Field	Total
1942			
April	1		1
May	1		1
June	1		1
July	1		1
August		2	2
September	4	1	5
October	2	2	4
November	1	1	2
December	1	2	3
Subtotal	12	8	20
1943			
January	3	2	5
February	5	1	6
March	6	1	7
April	4	1	5
May	7	4	11
June	7	3	10
July	8	3	11
August	5	2	7
September	6	1	7
October	5	3	8
November	3	3	6
December	6	3	9
Subtotal	65	27	92
1944			
January	3	2	5
February	6		6
March	4		4
April	2		2
Subtotal	15	2	17
Total	92	37	129

Note: The highest production month for Goodyear was July 1944 when fourteen airships were produced (11 K-type (8 to Lakehurst and 3 to Moffett Field) and 3 L-type (1 to Lakehurst and 2 to Moffett Field)).

The L-type Airships

The L-type training airship was second in quantity to the K-type produced during World War II. Prior to World War II the Navy inventory included only the L-1, L-2 and L-3 airships, however during the war this total increased to 22. The L-type airship was the Goodyear fleet advertising airship. Immediately after Pearl Harbor, the Navy took over five airships (and three spare envelopes D-217, D-218 and D-219, 123,000 cubic feet) from Goodyear using them for both training and patrol where necessary as they were the only airships available. At least four L-type airships were erected by personnel at Moffett Field, California under purchase order 291-43 dated 10 September 1942 (completed by 20 April 1943) under the supervision of LCDR Joseph Finch. Ten L-type airships were constructed by Goodyear (with sub-contracts for control cars and surfaces to the bus manufacturers Flxible and Twin Coach as previously stated) on contract NOa(s)-151 (was NXs(a) 10076). These airships were L-13 through L-22 delivered during 1943. Exact Navy serial numbers and Goodyear envelope numbers may be questionable.

L-4 - L-4 was the original Goodyear airship Resolute NC-15A based at Los Angeles since 1940. *Resolute* (envelope D-151 in 1940 and control car C-46) made its first flight 28 April 1932 and was christened 29 April by Mrs. W. C. State, wife of the Goodyear plant engineer. After Pearl Harbor, as a private airship, *Resolute* patrolled the Los Angeles harbor with the Navy until transferred at Moffett Field 10 March 1942. The *Resolute* was the first "privateer" to operate as a Navy ship since the War of 1812 and its only armament the pilot's hunting rifle. Pilot-in-charge of the *Resolute* was Arthur T. Sewell, an airship pilot since 1917 with service in the Navy until 1922 and a Lieutenant in the Naval Reserve. Also part of the *Resolute* crew were Rolland H. Hobensack and James C. Maloney, Sr., both of which served as Navy airship pilots during the war. The entire crew of the *Resolute* enlisted with the Navy (above).

L-4 was received by the Navy on 10 March 1942 and served as a training airship at Moffett Field and Lakehurst throughout the war with the control car reacquired by Goodyear 24 January 1946 from surplus airship material stored at Naval Air Station, Tillamook, Oregon. The control car was stored at Wingfoot Lake until scrapped in July 1980.

Note: The L-type airships were purchased from the War Assets Administration after World War II for approximately $5,000.

L-5 - L-5 was the original Goodyear *Enterprise* NC-16A (original envelope D-144, replacement envelope D-155 and envelope D-158 when rebuilt for the Navy, control car C-49) which made its first flight 23 August 1934, was christened 03 September 1934 at Cleveland and based at Hoover Airport, Washington, DC and Teterboro Airport, Bendix, New Jersey. In November 1941 it was returned to Wingfoot Lake for airship pilot training and also used to check the effectiveness of blackout measures in the northern Ohio area. *Enterprise* was deflated 15 January 1942 and shipped to Moffett Field.

Re-erected 25 May 1942 at Moffett Field, L-5 served as a training airship throughout the war with the control car reacquired by Goodyear 24 January 1946. The control car was rebuilt as a spare for Goodyear GZ-20 airships in 1969 with the registration N4A transferred to it 12 May 1970. The control car was used with *Columbia* (IV) N4A which made its first flight 12 July 1975 and was in service to 1986 with a new control car. It is now in storage at Wingfoot Lake.

L-6 - L-6 was the original Goodyear *Reliance* NC-14A which made its first flight 05 November 1931 and was christened 06 November 1931 at Cleveland. The original Goodyear envelope was D-135 (112,000 cubic feet), with D-139 in May 1933, increased envelope volume of 123,000 cubic feet in June 1937 with D-150, D-157 (April 1940) and D-160 in October 1940. The control car is possibly a car built by Great Lakes Aircraft in Cleveland and records state "G.L.A." and no Goodyear control car number is recorded. *Reliance* was in Miami on 07 December 1941, was flown to New Orleans and then possibly flown to Los Angeles in February 1942. *Reliance* became L-6 at Moffett Field 28 February 1942.

Served as a patrol airship based at Wilmington, California in May 1942 with all Goodyear/Navy pilots until K-type patrol airships became available. L-6 served as a training airship at Moffett Field and Lakehurst throughout the war and was apparently deflated and stricken after the war.

L-7 - L-7 was the original Goodyear *Rainbow* NC-9A (registration originally assigned to the 1925 *Pilgrim* which held temporary registration until 19 April 1929) and made its first flight 31 March 1939 and was christened 13 April 1939 by Mrs. H.F. Schippel, president of the Akron Women's Chapter of the National Aeronautic Association. *Rainbow* (envelope D-156, 123,000 cubic feet, control car C-54) was based at the Washington, DC National Airport when the Pearl Harbor attack occurred and was transferred to Wingfoot Lake for airship pilot training in January 1942.

L-7 was taken over by the Navy at Lakehurst 04 March 1942 and served as a training airship. L-7 was deflated when the moorings parted by wash from another airship causing L-7 to strike the dock doors at Lakehurst 12 October 1943 and may have been stricken.

L-8 - L-8 was the original Goodyear *Ranger* NC-10A, envelope D-166 (123,000 cubic feet) and control car C-64. *Ranger* never operated as a Goodyear airship and was shipped to Moffett Field 17 February 1942 with erection completed 22 February and the test flights were made 23 and 25 February. L-8 was delivered to the Navy 26 February and used for ASW patrol, based at Treasure Island in San Francisco Bay. On 11 April L-8 dropped 300 pounds of freight on the deck of the aircraft carrier USS *Hornet* whose flight deck was stuffed with Army bombers, unable to land a plane. The freight was special glass windows for the navigator's compartments of the B-25s that raided Tokyo under Col. Jimmy Doolittle. LCDR John B. Rieker was pilot. (Right, US Navy photo.)

L-8 was deflated under mysterious circumstances on 16 August 1942; the exact details have never been fully explained. Following a weigh-off that revealed morning fog had added condensation weight, the flight mechanic, J. Riley Hill, was given the day off so the full load of gasoline and two depth bombs could be carried. L-8 departed Treasure Island at 0600 on anti-submarine patrol with LTJG Ernest D. Cody and ENS Charles E. Adams. At 07:50 Cody radioed the sighting of an oil slick, five miles east of the Farallon Islands near the entrance to San Francisco harbor, and reported he was about to investigate. This was the last radio message received. About an hour later when no radio contact could be established, two search planes from the Alameda Naval Air Station were dispatched to investigate. They found a ceiling of 500 feet over the area and decided to stay above the clouds. At 10:20 a Pan American Clipper sighted L-8 just breaking through the clouds. At 10:45 L-8 hit the beach near Fort Funston (south of the Presidio of San Francisco) and dislodged one of its bombs near the Lakeside Golf Course. About 30 minutes later L-8 settled at Daly City, California, and no one was on board.

A salvage party from Moffett Field found L-8 in fair condition. The envelope had been deflated, as firemen had slashed the envelope to see if anyone was inside. The control car door was open, but the car was in good condition. The radio was operative, indicating the car had possibly been unmanned as early as 08:05 when Moffett Field last tried to contact L-8. Rubber life jackets were missing and the life raft was in place. The microphone was hanging out of the car door, and an officer's cap was atop the instrument panel. The motors were stopped, although one throttle was open and the other half-open and the ignition switches were still turned on. The propellers were bent, but from all signs they had not been bent while rotating. The classified document portfolio was in order and there was no evidence that the control car had been immersed in the sea. There was no indication of fire even though there was plenty of fuel aboard and the valves to the engine open.

The investigation by CAPT K. L. Lange, executive officer at Moffett Field, presented the following story: After radioing their message L-8 proceeded to the oil slick. Hypothetically, Adams opened the door and leaned out to investigate and slipped. Cody then dropped a life jacket and a smoke bomb. A surface ship entering the harbor observed the airship hovering about 25 feet above the surface and saw the smoke bomb drop, whereupon the captain ordered battle stations and full speed ahead. L-8 then flew over the ship at low altitude and circled it. The crew could hear someone aboard L-8 trying to contact them through a loudspeaker below the control car but could not understand the message. When Cody could not get the ship's attention he must have then returned to the oil slick to rescue Adams himself, donned a life jacket and in the rescue attempt slipped or fallen out. L-8 was then observed to float up into the overcast. The question that remained unanswered is if both pilots were wearing life jackets, and with the area heavily patrolled by surface ships, why were the bodies never located? If they were picked up, who did it? The only plausible answer would be the strong currents in the area. One explanation considered was that they were surprised by an enemy submarine as they investigated the oil slick, however such a surfacing would have been seen with all of the ships in the area and the classified folder remained in the control car. Several other explanations have been heard over the years, but none that could be judged satisfactory. The official report cites carburetor icing as stopping the engines, a common crash cause. The engineman released that morning due to the extra water weight on the bag, J. Riley Hill, has suggested carbon fouling from running lean without periodically enrichening to blow out the carbon. Either way, a distress call may not have been a priority if they had erred either way and attempted to hand-start the engines, very difficult with the airship in flight.

L-8 was reinflated at Moffett Field and served as a training airship. The re-built L-8 was the first airship to land at the new Santa Ana, California Naval Air Station on 19 October 1942. It trained many future airship pilots who were completely unaware of its storied past. The control car was reacquired by Goodyear 02 January 1946. L-8 was stored at Wingfoot Lake until rebuilt as a GZ-20 type for the *America* (N10A) in 1968-1969. Replaced by a new GZ-20A type in 1982, L-8 was placed in storage at Wingfoot Lake, where it remains today.

L-9 through L-12 - These four airships were erected by Moffett Field personnel under the supervision of LCDR Joseph Finch, USNR via Purchase Order 291-43 and with spare envelopes provided by Goodyear. It is known that Goodyear provided envelopes D-194 to Moffett Field in 24 April 1942 and three other spare envelopes (D-127, D-128 and D-129) for the Goodyear fleet airships were taken over by the Navy, May through June 1942. L-9 through L-12 served as training airships at Moffett Field throughout the war. They were apparently never issued Navy serial numbers and very little additional information is known.

L-ship interior. US Navy photo

Of the eleven L-type airships from Moffett Field stored in the airship hangars at Naval Air Station, Tillamook, Oregon after the conclusion of World War II, all were purchased. L-4 thru L-8 were apparently not issued serial numbers.

L-9 was purchased by the Douglas Leigh Sky Advertising Company, was inflated and registered as NC-68265 (later NC31A) and departed Tillamook 28 February 1947. L-9 apparently saw service on the west coast then rebuilt at Lakehurst in August 1948 (Goodyear envelope D-378) and sold to Sky-Ads, Inc. (Robert A. Domin of Turtle Creek, Pennsylvania) and advertised "Fort Pitt" beer. Its registration was cancelled 17 November 1955.

L-10 landed in San Francisco Bay and deflated 18 August 1943. Rebuilt, it was also purchased by Douglas Leigh was inflated and registered as NC-68266 and departed Tillamook for Moffett Field 17 December 1946 and apparently served on the west coast registered as NC-68266.

L-11 was purchased by Howard Hughes, erected and registered as NC-33672 (later N21A), departed Tillamook 09 May 1946. It was used to advertise the movie "The Outlaw" starring Jane Russell. Jim Maloney (Sr.), former Navy and future Goodyear pilot, was the chief pilot. Sold to Douglas Leigh 20 April 1951 and registered as N21A, new envelope and night sign fitted 29 June 1953, advertised Pfeiffer's beer as the *Leader Ship*. One report by Jim Maloney, Sr. states this airship was lost while moored at Midland, Texas, while on a cross-country flight from California to New York for Hughes, and was replaced by another airship. Details, dates, etc. are unknown. If it was lost at Midland, Texas, it may have been re-built.

L-12 was purchased by Douglas Leigh, erected, registered as NC-68225 and departed Tillamook 06 January 1947, advertised Mobilgas as The *Flying Red Horse* based at Santa Ana, deflated and stored at Santa Ana, registration canceled 18 October 1955.

Note: L-13 thru L-22 were provided by Goodyear on Navy contract NOa(s)-151 (was NXs[a] 10076) dated 24 February 1943. Control cars were built by the Flxible Company at Loudonville, Ohio. No serial numbers were located; however, the serial numbers of two L-type airships are shown as 09801 and 09802. No explanation is offered.

L-13 - Goodyear envelope D-246, control car C-134 and control surfaces F-186, delivered to Lakehurst 04 April 1943; based at Weeksville, North Carolina, L-13 was deflated when debris from the roof of the timber hangar fell during a hurricane on 14 September 1944 (28 of 163 planes stored in the hangar were also damaged). Sold to Douglas Leigh in 1952 but never used.

L -14 - Goodyear envelope D-247, control car C-135 and control surfaces F-187, delivered to Moffett Field 10 June 1943. Control car reacquired by Goodyear at Tillamook 24 January 1946 and re-erected with envelope D-247 (123,000 cubic feet) as *Mayflower* (II) N4A (tentative registration NC-5A and NC-15A and temporary NC-10A). This *Mayflower* made its first flight 12 May 1947 and was christened 24 May 1947 by Diana and Carol Bly, daughters of CDR R. E. Bly, resident Naval inspector at Akron. New envelope D-219 was installed in May 1948 and *Mayflower* was dismantled at Wingfoot Lake 04 November 1949. The control car was stored and rebuilt as a Goodyear type GZ-19 in 1958 for *Mayflower* (III) N4A which made its first flight 25 February 1959. This *Mayflower* (III) was retired from service in August 1968 and flown unnamed in tests for the Advanced Research Projects Agency on 22 and 23 March 1969 with a stern propeller for quiet operation ("Silent Joe II") to October 1969 when it was dismantled and stored with the N4A. Registration transferred to the C-49 spare control car (later type GZ-20 *Columbia* N4A) 12 May 1970. L-14 was scrapped in late 1970.

L-15 - Goodyear envelope D-248, control car C-136 and control surfaces F-188, delivered to Lakehurst 28 May 1943. Served at NAS Richmond, Florida.

L-16 - Goodyear envelope D-324, control car C-137 and control surfaces F-189, delivered to Moffett Field 17 July 1943. Control car reacquired by Goodyear 24 January 1946 and used for *Enterprise* (II) (tentative registration NC-6A/NC-16A, temporary NC-8A, permanent NC-

3A/N3A). First flown 09 October 1946 and christened 14 May 1947 at Naval Air Station, Anacostia, Washington, DC by Ms. Ruby Herring, "Miss Naval Air Reserve Training Units." New envelopes (all 123,000 cubic feet) for *Enterprise* were D-268 September 1946, D-468 May 1949 and D-594 June 1954. Last flight was made 25 September 1959 with the control car stored. Rebuilt as a type GZ-20 for *Columbia* (III) N3A which made its first flight 18 August 1969 and was christened 21 October 1969 by the wife of Sam Yorty, then mayor of Los Angeles. The last flight was 29 July 1975. L-16 was dismantled, stored, then scrapped in 1981.

L-17 - Goodyear envelope D-250, control car C-138, control surfaces F-190, delivered to Moffett Field 10 September 1943. Control car reacquired by Goodyear 24 January 1946 and shipped to Los Angeles where it was erected as *Volunteer* (II) NC-2A (previous registrations were NC-17A and NC-18A [tentative] and NC-7A [temporary]). Envelopes were D-251 (September 1946) and D-250 (March 1948). First flight was made 26 September 1946 at Los Angeles with the christening 04 October 1948 by Jan Clayton who starred in the wartime movie "This Man's Navy" with Wallace Beery, Tom Drake, Jimmy Gleason and others. *Volunteer* was deflated at Wingfoot Lake 23 November 1949, the control car stored and then rebuilt as a type GZ-19A for *Columbia* N2A. This *Columbia* (II) made its first flight 23 July 1963 and was christened 19 August 1963 by Miss Jacquelyn Mayer of Sandusky, Ohio, then Miss America. Envelopes (147,300 cubic feet) used with *Columbia* were D-635 (July 1963), D-637 (May 1984) and D-635 (December 1966). *Columbia* was dismantled and stored in December 1969. The N2A registration was transferred to *Europa* and the control car re-built and re-registered for Mayflower N38A (envelope D-639 which was originally built in 1968 as a spare for *Mayflower* [IV] N1A), which made it first flight 17 June 1976. *Mayflower* (IV) was deflated at the mast at Augusta, Georgia 9 August 1978. L-17 was scrapped in 1979.

L-18 - Goodyear envelope D-251, control car C-139 and control surfaces F-191, delivered to Moffett Filed 31 July 1943. Control car re-acquired by Goodyear 24 January 1946 at Tillamook and re-erected as *Ranger* (III) NC-1A/N1A (tentative NC-20A and NC-19A) with envelope D-327 with the first flight 28 MAY 1946 and was christened 26 June 1946. *Ranger* was the first airship to fly in Goodyear service after World War II. 123,000 cubic feet envelopes used by *Ranger* were D-194 (September 1947), D-472 (May 1951), D-474 (November 1952) and D-600 (June 1955). Dismantled 23 May 1949, it was flown again 24 May 1951 and was deflated in high winds at Fort Lauderdale, Florida, 26 January 1958. The control car was stored, then rebuilt as a type GZ-19A for *Mayflower* (V) N1A. This *Mayflower* made its first flight 04 September 1968 (with envelope D-368), made its last flight 14 July 1976, was dismantled and the envelope retained as a spare for *Mayflower* (IV). This *Mayflower*, N38A, was deflated at the mast at Augusta, Georgia 29 August 1978. It apparently was not returned to service, then scrapped.

L-19 - Goodyear envelope D-252, control car C-140 and control surfaces F-192, delivered to Lakehurst 15 July 1943. On a routine training flight 25 November 1944, suffered damage to the landing gear and engine mount during a practice landing and take off. The instructor pilot, LT D.W. Hale, free-ballooned L-19 to a section of pine woods five miles from Lakehurst and successfully landed with no injuries. L-19 was rebuilt by Lakehurst personnel and returned to service. Provided with a Fortisan-Rayon envelope (D-459) by Goodyear in 1947 and retained for experimental purposes until 1951. Purchased by Douglas Leigh in 1952 but not used, sold to the International Sky Advertising Company formed by Charles H. Probst and Kurt Selzer in 1955 and operated in Germany (Goodyear envelope D-459 and U.S. registration N65N) as the hydrogen inflated *Underberg* (German registration D-LAVO), the first airship to operate in Germany since the *Graf Zeppelin II* in August 1939. The instructor pilot was Lou Prost, an ex-US. Navy pilot. Charles Probst had flown 1,700 hours by 1957. A new envelope was provided by Balloonfabrik Augsberg in 1959 and operated as *Guldenring* (cigarettes) in Germany and for Roxy cigarettes in Austria and Holland. Re-named *Schwab* (new German registration D-LAVO [also possibly D-LISA and D-LIBA]), operated ten years and accumulated over 6,000 hours of flight time filled with hydrogen. (Pilot was smoking cigarettes much of the time.)

Hydrogen-inflated ex-L-19 in flight over Germany. Lou Prost photo.

Purchased by Shinzoh Tanaka, erected in Japan with helium from Canada, and named *The Flying Dragon* Japanese registration JA-1001), chief Pilot Roy Belotti, former U.S. Navy airship pilot. First flight in Japan was in September 1962, the first airship to operate there since the Imperial Japanese Navy Italian-built semi-rigid airship No. 8 in 1933. Deflated at the mast 04 April 1969 during a typhoon and not rebuilt. Total length of service - U.S. (helium) Germany, Austria, Holland (hydrogen) and Japan (helium), sixteen years.

L-20 - Goodyear envelope D-253, control car C-141 and control surfaces F-193, delivered to Moffett Field 07 August 1943.

L-21 - Goodyear envelope D-254, control car C-142 and control surfaces F-194, delivered to Moffett Field 23 August 1943.

L-22 - Goodyear envelope D-324, control car C-143 and control surfaces F-195, delivered to Moffett Field 01 September 1943. Purchased by Douglas Leigh and registered as civil no. 9005-H. Advertised Wonder Bread as the *Wonder Ship* and toured most states, destroyed due to strong winds while at the mast near Abilene, Texas, on 25 February 1948. Former Navy airship pilots of the *Wonder Ship* included "Ike" Walton, Walter Bjiere and Charles Probst.

Note: The Douglas Leigh airship registrations were cancelled in 1955 except, for some unknown reason, N21A, the former L-11. This registration remained on the FAA books until 1970 although it had not been active since 1953. The Leigh airships were offered for sale to Goodyear on several occasions in the 1960's with the last inventory (December 1965) including two unidentified L-type airship cars and one envelope (D-324).

The L-22, last L-type built, in civilian attire. Lou Prost photo

L-type airship general specifications (models varied in envelope volume and engine types):

Volume (Cubic feet)	123,000
Ballonet (2) (cubic feet)	29,400
Overall length (feet)	147.5
Maximum diameter (feet)	39.5
Overall height (feet)	54.0
Overall width (feet)	47.5
Static useful lift (pounds)	2,040
Dynamic lift (pounds)	500
Total useful lift (pounds)	2,540
Maximum speed (knots)	53
Cruising speed (knots)	40
Range, cruising speed (nautical miles)	475
Endurance at maximum speed (hours)	5.6
Endurance at cruising speed (hours)	11.9
Engines (2)	Warner, "Super Scarab" R-500-2, 145 hp at 2,050 rpm, direct drive, no gears, flat pitch single blade propellers, arc 8 ft (engines varied)

Facing page, bottom: Mugging for still and newsreel cameras, the Moffett Field primary training L-ships stage a fly-by. It is thought the "109" corresponded to L-9, etc. US Navy photo.

L-Type Airship Delivery by year and month, 1942 and 1943.

	Lakehurst	Moffett Field	Total
1942			
February L-6 (Goodyear *Reliance*) L-8 (Goodyear *Ranger*)		2	2
March L-4 (Goodyear *Resolute*) L-7 (Goodyear *Rainbow*)	 1	 1	2
May L-5 (Goodyear *Enterprise*)	 1		1
1943			
April L-9 through L-12 (Complete by 20 April 1943) L-13	 1	 4	5
May L-15	 1		1
June L-14	 1		1
July L-16, L-18, L-19	 1	 2	3
August L-20, L-21	 2		2
September L-17, L-22		 2	2
Total	4	15	19

The G-Type Advanced Training and Utility Airships

(Designated ZGT after World War II)

In quantity, the G-type airship was the second to last produced during World War II as only seven were provided. The G-type airships were an enlarged version of the Goodyear type GZ-6 *Defender* (NC12A) which made its first flight 20 August 1929. It was purchased by the Navy as an advanced training airship in 1935 as the G-1. It is assumed the G-1 was based on a designation for Goodyear, as the original G-type airship was planned in 1918 as an enlarged patrol airship following the E and F-type airships. This type airship was not built and the Navy jumped to the H and J-types of 1921 for simplification of record. As an advanced training airship, the G-types were in service at Lakehurst and Moffett Field. As a utility airship (due to the more spacious control car) G-type airships were assigned to Airship Utility Squadron (ZJ) One, and served at Fisher's Island, New York, for cooperation with submarines, the Naval Mine Warfare Test Station, Solomons, Maryland, and the Naval Proving Ground at Dahlgren, Virginia. The G-type airships were all Goodyear prime contract with sub-contracts to Twin Coach for control cars and surfaces as previously stated. G-2 through G-8 were built on Navy contract NOa(s) 151 dated 24 December 1942. Navy serial numbers for these airships are unknown.

<u>G-2</u> - Goodyear envelope D-256 (196,700 cubic feet), control car C-144, control surfaces F-196, delivered to Lakehurst 10 September 1943, flown (LTJG Blinkhorn, pilot) for the Navy Day celebration at Lakehurst 26 October 1946, as ZTG-2 operated with the Airship Training Center at Lakehurst in 1951. Used for experiments with Air Surveillance Radar (ASR) at Lakehurst and was the first aircraft to be "talked down" by this equipment.

<u>G-3</u> - Goodyear envelope D-257, control car C-145, control surfaces F-197, delivered to Moffett Field 23 October 1943: reassigned to Lakehurst. Deflated when the handling lines became fouled in the mooring mast 06 January 1945, rebuilt, served with Reserve Squadron ZP-871 at Oakland, California after World War II.

<u>G-4</u> - Goodyear envelope D-258, control car C-146, control surfaces F-198, delivered to Moffett Field 23 October 1943, requested by Federal Bureau of Investigation to assist in locating bodies of a kidnapped bride and her abductor, bodies were located from the air by an FBI agent within

one hour, LTJG H. G. McComas, pilot. Searched for lost child near Ridgeway, New Jersey, on 29 January 1947, LTJG E. M. Gavigan, pilot.

G-5 - Goodyear envelope D-259, control car C-147, control surfaces F-199, delivered to Moffett Field 23 November 1943.

G-6 - Goodyear envelope D-261, control car C-148, control surfaces F-200, delivered to Moffett Field 09 December 1943, shipped from Lakehurst to the west coast 10 July 1951. Re-erected by a civilian crew from Lakehurst at Santa Ana, California in August 1951, rebuilt, first airship since 1947 at Moffett Field 09 January 1956.

G-7 - Goodyear envelope D-260. control car C-149, control surfaces F-201, delivered to Lakehurst 30 December 1943.

G-8 - Goodyear envelope D-262, control car C-150, control surfaces F-202, delivered to Lakehurst 02 February 1944; the last G-type airship delivered. Assigned to Utility Squadron ZJ-1 from 10 February 1944 to 09 June 1945, returned to Lakehurst. Special flight with Pan American Airways officials 19 February 1947, LT G. L. Lane, pilot, deflated and stored until assigned to reserve squadron ZP-951 at Santa Ana in 1951 (ZTG-8). Accidentally deflated in 1954 (fabric deteriorated) and then stricken with the control car and engines salvaged and the envelope sold to a tent maker in Anaheim, California.

General specifications G-2 through G-8:

Volume (cubic feet)	196,700
Ballonets (2) (cubic feet)	49,500
Overall Length (feet)	192.0
Maximum diameter (feet)	45.0
Overall width (feet)	53.5
Overall height (feet)	62.0
Static useful lift (pounds)	2,950
Dynamic lift (pounds)	1,000
Maximum speed (knots)	50.0
Cruising speed (knots)	40.0
Range, cruising speed (nautical miles)	680
Endurance at maximum speed (hours)	6.3
Endurance at cruising speed (hours)	17.0?
Engines (2)	Continental R-270-6. 220 horsepower at 2,075 rpm, two blade, fixed pitch propellers, arc 8 feet, 9 inches. (engines varied)

G-type deliveries 1943 and 1944:

	Lakehurst	Moffett Field	Total
1943			
September (G-2)	1		1
October (G-3, G-4)		2	2
November (G-5)		1	1
December (G-6, G-7)	1	1	2
1944			
February (G-8)	1		1
Totals	3	4	7

An M-type airship (foreground) is compared to a K-type at Lakehurst, 1943. US Navy photo.

The M-type Airships

Reportedly the original concept for the M-type airship began in 1937, when Goodyear-Zeppelin began design work on a large 4-engine non-rigid airship of 800,700 cubic feet. The exercise was to show such an airship could be built for less money than the small rigid airships proposed. Wind tunnel and water model tests were authorized in October 1941 for an airship larger than the K-type, and the Goodyear airship series GZ-5 evolved. The M-type airships were the largest and undoubtedly most efficient non-rigids during World War II. The design was unique: the original airships were to be 625,000 cubic feet volume (with a new three ply rubberized cotton fabric), four ballonets and a long (117 feet in length) articulated control car that consisted of three sections that could flex with the envelope. The control car design was not continued with post-war airships, although many considered it a more efficient design than the shorter two-level control cars. It carried the load over a greater envelope length, kept the catenary loads at almost 90° and minimized the possibility of wrinkles in the envelope. A preliminary contract dated 17 June 1942 was awarded to Goodyear for one prototype (cost $642,600) and six production models. This was later expanded by fifteen for a total of twenty-two, with the contract finalized 11 September 1943. This contract was reduced to a total of four airships that was finalized by contract NOS(a) 146 dated 09 November 1943. No serial numbers were assigned to the M-ships. The envelopes and control cars of the models produced after M-1 were revised with the volume of 725,000 cubic feet. The original M-1 control car was modified to carry a Piper Cub type airplane for stand-off weapons test; it was not practical for pilot transfer from the airship. (The idea originated during the M-type period for a helicopter platform on airships that was studied in the later ZPG period.) Other options studied included a recoilless rifle. The M-types were the first to study a retractable, tricycle landing gear, first to carry a very large radar antenna, and first to act in the AWACS role. They were still flying when the nuclear submarine appeared, and carried equipment to track the sub's heat trail.

The M-type airships were erected at the former Goodyear Zeppelin Airdock at the Akron Municipal Airport (now Fulton Field), the first airships to be erected there since the K-2 of 1938. Although the Wingfoot Lake Hangar was large enough for the M-type, it was too involved with the construction of K-type airships with their immediate need for anti-submarine patrol.

M-1 - Goodyear envelope D-220 (625,000 cubic feet), control car C-109, control surfaces F-161, completed in October 1943 and christened at Akron 27 October (the former Navy Day) by Jean Rosendahl, wife of Admiral Rosendahl. The ceremony was conducted in the landing field near the former Goodyear-Zeppelin Airship Dock with RADM F.D. Wagner, Chief of Naval Operations for Air, as the main speaker. M-1 was delivered to Lakehurst on 29 November where it was assigned to the Naval Airship Training and Experimental Command. Redesignated as XM-1 (experimental) when fitted with a new 675,000 cubic foot envelope at Akron in April 1944, returned to Lakehurst for extended flight tests and to collect information.

XM-1 was flown with an NE-1 Piper Cub airplane on radio control and guidance experiments early in 1944. Several flights were made in March and April 1944 with the Piper Cub ("Glimpy") supported from the forward car section. One airplane (Navy serial #26197), less the landing gear, was acquired on 03 March 1944; a second airplane (Navy serial #26326) arrived on 05 March. On 13 March the manned *Glimpy* was released for return flight at an altitude of approximately 1,000 feet. *Glimpy* flew again on 17 April and 27 April 1944.

XM-1 was flown to South Weymouth and on 20 January 1946 carried three United Nations delegates and six others on a flight over proposed sites for the United Nations headquarters building. On 10 October 1946, XM-1 departed Lakehurst on an extended flight to test endurance and sea-keeping qualities of the M-type and returned to Lakehurst on 14 October after 81.8 hours flight time. On 27 October 1946, XM-1 (CDR H. R Walton, command pilot, with a crew of 13 and a flight surgeon) departed Lakehurst and proceeded south along the coast and then seaward to the Bahamas, to Florida, Cuba, the Gulf of Mexico and returned to land at Glynco, Georgia. This flight of 170.3 hours (over seven days) was made with much of the flight on one engine with the other engine secured and the propeller feathered to achieve the best fuel economy. On 22 September 1948, XM-1 departed Lakehurst (CDR Max E. Cawley, command pilot) on "Operation Attaché," the search for missing Navy aircraft between The Pas, Manitoba (Canada) and Edmonton, Alberta. A non-stop flight was made to Minneapolis, Minnesota, then to The Pas, returning to Lakehurst on 25 September.

M-2 operates with the first tricycle landing gear on a Navy airship. Hepburn Walker, Jr. photo.

M-2 - Goodyear envelope D-352 (647,000 cubic feet), control car C-216, control surfaces F-451, delivered to Lakehurst 22 January 1944; assigned to ZP-21 at Richmond, Florida, on 12 March 1944. Beginning on the 19th of June 1944 and continuing for almost a week, ZP-21 airships - including the new M-2 - searched for survivors of a PV crash off Cape San Antonio, Cuba. Before the week was out the M-2 was working to find survivors from two separate TBFs that crashed on the same day. 20 MAR 45 the M-2 used her MAD to locate a crashed C-54, marking location for divers to reach the wreck. Flown to Santa Ana, California, after the victory in Europe, assigned to ZP-31 and returned to Lakehurst (the first west-to-east ferry flight) on 17 May 1947, LT C.H. Mills, command pilot. Retractable tri-cycle landing gear was tested on M-2 and approved for airships in 1947. On 09 September 1949, a fire in the port engine occurred, fuel to the engine was cut, the CO2 system operated and a normal landing made with the fire extinguished on the ground. On 26 July 1951, the fabric tore along the catenary seam which caused deflation.

M-3 - Goodyear envelope D-353, (647,000 cubic feet), control car C-217, control surfaces F-452, delivered to Lakehurst on 24 February 1944; assigned to Richmond, Florida and while on routine patrol on 03 October 1944 located a disabled tug and barge. In the only reported M-ship contact of the war, ZP-21's squadron history states the M-3 received a strong MAD contact running over an oil slick on 10 JUL 44, then duplicated this several times before seas dissipated the slick. On the 21st of October 1944 the M-3 located the *Rubicon* adrift with no one but a dog on board, and summoned a surface vessel. Present at the surrender of one of the last German U-boats (U-858) in American waters, May 1945. Flown to Santa Ana after V-E Day. Assigned to ZP-31, M-3 returned to Lakehurst in 1947. Equipped with a powerful search radar dome, M-3 was used in preliminary flight tests of a limited Combat Information Center, the first use of an airship as a Distant Early Warning System.

M-3 was used to develop the concept of an airborne combat information center. US Navy photo.

M-4 - Goodyear envelope D-354 (647,000 cubic feet), control car C-218, control surfaces F-453, delivered to Lakehurst on 06 April 1944; assigned to Richmond, Florida, 15 AUG 44 the new M-4 made its first all night patrol. On 16 September 1944 made a flight of 26.8 hours looking for survivors of two surface ships that had been in the path of a hurricane. 8 OCT 44 M-4 suffered the embarrassment of shooting itself with a severely misaligned machine gun, luckily without injury. On 14 November located a grounded freighter and directed aid by surface ships. 17 NOV 44 ZP-21's M-4 under LTJG Byars stood by a sinking freighter, then gathered a summoned tugboat and led it in from 25 miles. On March 2nd 1945 ZP-21's M-4 flew photography for the evaluation of a new radar director designed to work with torpedoes fired from the PT-315. Flown to Santa Ana after V-E Day, it was assigned to ZP-31. M-4 returned to Lakehurst in 1947, then made the first in-flight refueling from the USS *Saipan* on 25 August 1949, with a second refueling on 12 September. In 1955 and 1956, M-4 was used for experiments with a 100-inch airborne radiometer to study the radiant energy from the ocean's surface. A "cover story" was published stating study was to map ocean currents, with the actual purpose of the equipment being the tracing of the heat trail left by nuclear submarines. M-4 operated both over the North Atlantic and the Oriente Deep near Cuba. M-4 made the last flight of an M-ship on 22 September 1956. The M-4 was deflated when the automatic rip panel failed while moored out for tests at Lakehurst on 27 February 1958. Blown off the mast, M-4 deflated in the conservation area of the air station. Wreckage remained there for many years (last known year 1976) before it was removed and junked.

Note: On the flights from Lakehurst to Santa Ana, each M-ship carried its own mooring and tie-down equipment as there were no M-type mooring masts available on the west coast. One of the M-ships was also flown to Moffett Field, California.

Goodyear records indicate the original M-2, M-3 and M-4 were erected with envelopes of 647,000 cubic feet, however at some point in time the envelopes were increased in volume to 725,000 cubic feet as the record also indicates spare envelopes D-355, D-356 and D-357 were fabricated in the same general time frame as the airships. Envelopes D-361 through D-375 (725,000 cubic feet for the additional M-ships were cancelled as were proposed spare envelopes D-402 through D-412. Spare XM type envelopes (725,000 cubic feet) include D-460 and D-461 (neoprene), D-462 and 463 synthetic fabric) and D-548 (3 ply cotton), D-549 (2 ply cotton with D-553 (3 ply cotton) as a spare envelope.

XM-1 upper deck central section during test flight from Akron in 1944. Lockheed Martin Collection / University of Akron Archives.

M-type General Specifications:	M-1	M-2, M-3, M-4
Volume (cubic feet)	625,000*	647,000
Ballonets (4, cubic feet)	193,000	210,000
Overall length (feet)	297	302
Maximum diameter (feet)	66	69.5
Overall height (feet)	89	92.5
Maximum width (feet)	71	74.0
Useful lift, static (pounds)	10,350	13,450
Dynamic lift (pounds)	3,500	3,500
Maximum speed (knots)	69	69
Cruising speed (knots)	50	50
Endurance, maximum speed (hours)*	10.2	14.4
Endurance, cruising speed (hours)**	35.5	50.5
Armament	1-.50 cal. machine gun, 8 depth bombs or 2,400 pounds	
Engines (2)	Pratt and Whitney R-1340-AN-2, 550 horse-power at 2,200 rpm, 3 blade Curtiss electric propellers, arc 12 feet	

*Original configuration, all models later increased to 725,000 cubic feet.
** Still air range was 2,100 miles This range was far exceeded by the XM-1 flight of 170.3 hours in October/September 1947.

Lockheed Martin Collection / University of Akron Archives photos from the XM-1's test flight from Akron in 1944, the catenary-friendly gasoline tank system is seen on the left. On the right is the aft end of the third section, with its clamshell-style doors in their open position.

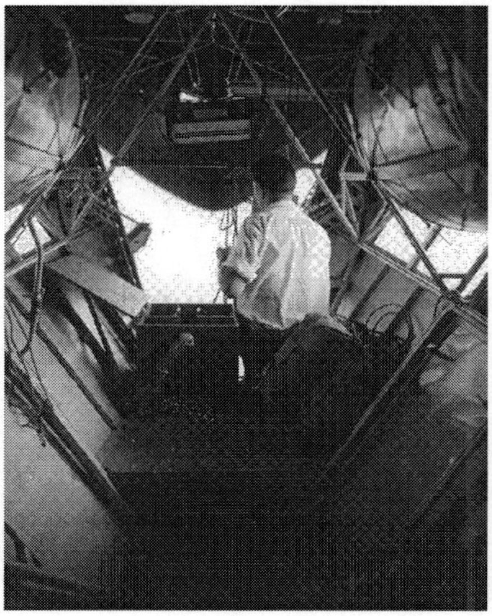

A Goodyear cost analysis of 1948 reports the cost of the single prototype M-1 (625,000 cubic feet) was originally submitted to the Navy as $942,000. This varies from the previously stated $642,000 from other records based on a quantity of 22 airships. The analysis states a 1948 revised cost of $1,355,920. The 1949 estimated cost for an M-type airship was $4,350,000.

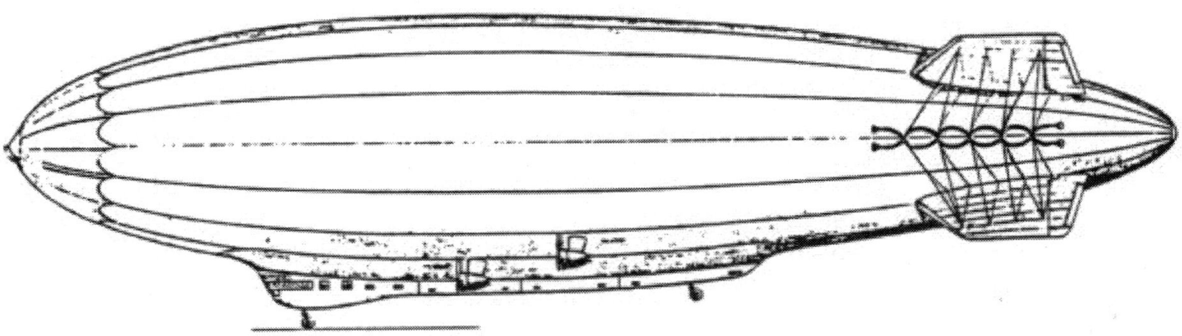

LTAS diagram.

Proposed O-Type

The M-type airship was to remain the largest non-rigid built until 1951. However, an O-type (not to be confused with the Italian-built Navy semi-rigid airship of 1919) had been proposed during World War II. This design was Goodyear project number GZ-8 and a contract for design only was issued 29 May 1943. Two designs of 1,500,000 cubic feet were proposed, primarily the same except one had two engines and the other had four engines. Both were proposed to carry one 5,500 pound airplane, possibly the Curtiss "SC Skyhawk" float plane, or as a drawing suggests, a BT-13 variant. This project, along with some rigid airship proposals, was cancelled.

O-type Proposed Specifications:

Volume (cubic feet)	1,500,000
Ballonets (4, cubic feet)	450,000
Overall length (feet)	396
Maximum diameter (feet)	?
Overall height (feet)	114
Maximum width (feet)	98
Useful lift (pounds)	33,500
Dynamic lift (pounds)	5,500
Maximum speed (knots)	70.5
Cruising speed (knots)	50.0
Endurance at cruising speed (hours)	68
Range at cruising speed (nautical mils)	3,400
Engines (4)	Pratt and Whitney R-1340-AN-2, 580 horsepower at take-off and 450 hp at normal, Curtiss electric propellers

A Memo dated 12 AUG 43 from LTA Design Branch states Contract Noa(s)-771 awarded to Goodyear for a study of a 1,500,000 cu ft non-rigid offers these additional parameters:

Gross Lift (static)	93,000 lb.
Weight empty	57,000 lb.
Useful Load	36,000 lb.
Service Load	11,000 lb.
Fuel load	25,000 lb.
Fuel consumption at 50 knots	370 lb./hr
Airplanes carried	1, class V8

The only non-rigid airships to approach the volume of the O-type were the ZPG-3W types delivered in 1959 and 1960. These airships were 1,516,000 cubic feet in volume and 403 feet in length.

Airships on hand 1942 through June 1945*

Date	TC-type (ex-Army)	K-type	L-type	G-type	M-type	Total
1942						
June	2	8	6			16
December	2	23	8			33
1943						
June	1	63	14			78
December		104	21	4	1	130
1944						
June		119	21	4	4	148
December		113	21	7	4	145
1945						
June		107	21	7	4	139

* This chart is based on Goodyear deliveries to the Navy and does not necessarily agree with the Secretary of Navy Annual Report, Fiscal Year 1945, page A-61, dated 10 January 1946

Airship Units and Headquarters Air Stations 1942 through 1945

<u>Fleet Airship Wing One (formerly Airship Patrol Group One) - Lakehurst, New Jersey</u>

ZP-11 - South Weymouth, Massachusetts
ZP-12 - Lakehurst, New Jersey
ZP-14 - Weeksville, North Carolina (until transferred to Med)
ZP-15 - Glynco, Georgia
ZP-24 - Weeksville, North Carolina (transferred from Two to replace ZP-14)

When ZP-14 was commissioned the *entire squadron* – personnel, facilities, borrowed blimp and equipment – could fit in one picture. By 1945 just the Headquarters Squadron (Hedron) at South Weymouth had this large group of Chief Petty Officers. The maintenance unit's OinC was LTJG Pat Doyle, center; on his right is "Pete" Calande, USS *Akron* engineman. US Navy and Eugene Calande photos.

Fleet Airship Wing Two - Richmond, Florida

ZP-21 - Richmond, Florida (largest squadron)
ZP-22 - Houma, Louisiana
ZP-23 - Hitchcock, Texas (later Vernam Field, Jamaica, BWI)
ZP-24 – Hitchcock, Texas (until transferred to Weeksville to replace ZP-14)

Fleet Airship Wing Three (formerly Airship Patrol Group Three) - Moffett Field, California

ZP-31 - Santa Ana, California
ZP-32 - Moffett Field, California
ZP-33 - Tillamook, Oregon
(and primary airship training 1943 to 1944; L-style trainer, right)

Fleet Airship Wing Four - Recife, Brazil

ZP-41 - Sao Luiz, Brazil
ZP-42 - Maceio, Brazil (to CONUS for transfer to England, V-E day canceled deployment) (utilized ex-German Santa Cruz hangar)

Fleet Airship Wing Five -Trinidad, BWI

ZP-51 - Trinidad, BWI (-52 & -53 canceled)
(First LTA unit to leave North America for overseas duty; utilized former Army hangar re-erected on Trinidad by 80th (Negro) CBs (right, courtesy Carol Marsh, SeeBee Museum)

Naval Airship Training and Experimental Command, Lakehurst, New Jersey

Commander, Fleet Airships Atlantic and Eighth Fleet

ZP-14 (Overseas) - Craw Field, Port Lyautey, French Morocco, organized at Weeksville, North Carolina on 22 May 1944 (secret orders #1-44) to provide MAD surveillance in the Mediterranean Sea and the Straits of Gibraltar. The first personnel sailing aboard the USS *Rehoboth* from Norfolk on 17 May to set up temporary mooring masts. The first airships arrived in Africa on 01 June 1944, and remained after the victory in Europe at the request of the British for mine clearing operations. No enemy submarines passed through the Straits of Gibraltar after airship patrols were started in 1944. Utilized WWI German/French hangar at Cures, pre-WWI Italian hangar at Bizertie. Ordered to be deactivated 15 November 1945, personnel returned to New York aboard the USS *Monticello* with the final deactivation at Lakehurst on 22 January 1946. In recognition of the flights to Africa, CDR E.J. Sullivan was awarded the Bronze Star as the commanding officer of ZP-14, and Air Medals were awarded to LT E.W. Steffen, operations officer and to command pilots LT H.B. Bly, LTJGs J.J. Connery, R.W. Goldstein, R.L. Kersey and E.B. Russell. Letters of Commendation were awarded to the twelve co-pilots and the six navigators. Walt Chimil photo (left).

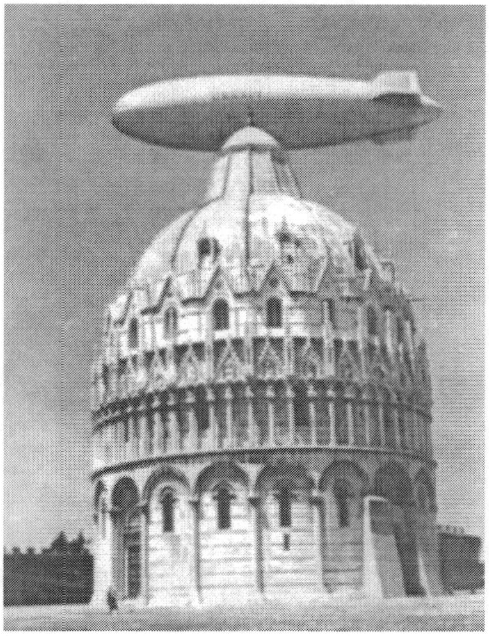

ZJ-1 - Meacham Field, Key West, Florida

Based on the success of ZP-14 in the Mediterranean and Europe, ZP-42 (K-93, K-100, K-126 and K-127) was to be assigned to Fleet Air Wing Seven and deployed to England to combat the new German schnorkel submarine design. CDR H. B. Van Gorder was selected as squadron commander and LCDR Blair as Officer-in-Charge of the Airship Service Group. In April 1945, Cardington, Bedfordshire was determined as the overhaul and maintenance base with the main operating base to be located at Chivener (five miles west of Barnstable in Devon on the Taw River) with St. Eval (six miles northeast of Newquay in Cornwall and near RAF Station Mawgan) as a secondary base Possibly the U.S. Army Air Forces depot base at Burtonwood, near Manchester, was planned as the supply base. A maintenance detachment had been dispatched to England by ship and two flight crews were waiting the arrival of airships in the Azores when the operation was cancelled on 22 May 1945 with the victory in Europe.

Invaluable training was provided by operations with US submarines on both coasts. This is the K-35 crew in training at the mast base established adjacent to Bing Crosby's racetrack at Del Mar, California. Simon Beattie photo.

Highlights of Wartime Airship Service

ZP-12 completed its first 6 months of operation on 02 July 1942 with K-3, K-4, K-5 and K-6 flown 5,393 hours over the six month period for an average of 225 hours per airship per month. 8 airships (K-3 through K-10) were in operation by 02 July and 134 flights (1,747 hours) were made in July. ZP-12 airships were in the air each day of July with all flights over water, no lives were lost and only one casualty sustained (K-6 at South Weymouth).

During World War II (07 December 1941 through 02 September 1945), 29 airships (confirmed and possible) of all types were lost along with 77 airship officers and men and 6 in ground handling accidents (3 officers were also lost in a hydrogen inflated free balloon at Lakehurst in 1943). With the exception of the one loss due to enemy action (K-74), the majority were due to personnel errors (many on the ground) with equipment and design responsible for some losses. The 29 airships lost does not include those rebuilt and returned to service or the 25 (apparently 9 inflated) reported as lost in the hurricane and fire at Richmond on 15 September 1945. As far as could be determined, the following are considered as confirmed losses: K-5, K-6, K-14, K-25, K-34, K-51, K-53, K-62, K-64, K-66, K-74, K-94, K-102, K-109, K-111, K-121, K-131, K-133, L-2, and G-1 (13 lost in patrol related operations [10 in Atlantic and overseas and 3 in the Pacific area], 2 during experimental tests, 2 in training, 2 while hangared and 1 due to enemy action). The possible losses include: K-22, K-26, K-30, K-36, K-37, K-39, K-83, K-90 and K-103 (6 in the Atlantic and overseas and 4 in the Pacific) There are conflicts with this record, particularly with the Goodyear "Summary of Airship Incidents and Accidental Deflations," dated 01 August 1960, which includes several airships known to have been returned to service.

French battleship *Richelieu* seen from an escorting ZP-14 airship. Hal Neuman photo.

Approximately 81,000 ships escorted (70,000 in the Atlantic and 11,000 in the Pacific), 50,000 ships known to be in areas where enemy submarines were operating. Approximately 58,000 operational flights (38,000 in Atlantic areas and 20,000 in the Pacific) of over 545,000 hours (378,000 in the Atlantic and 167,000 in the Pacific) and approximately 280,000 training hours. 87% on-line service at all times, interim overhaul only after 960 flight hours and major overhaul at 3,840 hours. Fleet airships averaged 256.4 flight hours per month. ZP-21 (Richmond) flew every day from 01 November 1943 through 15 May 1945 (965 consecutive days). Airships attacked and participated in the action against the last German submarine destroyed off the Atlantic coast. There were undetermined numbers of search, observation, photography, mine and rescue operations, assistance to people, vessels and navigation equipment. The greatest compliment for the service of the airship as an anti-submarine weapon came from Admiral Karl Doenitz, Hitler's senior U-boat flag officer, who considered airships ("kliene Zeppelins," some Germans called them) operations to be one of the most successful Allied defense systems as they posed a significant danger. The sighting of an airship on patrol or escort, deterred a U-boat attack and caused a change in objective.

Combat Operations not Specific to Named Airships

Wartime literature, obviously subject to security restrictions, nonetheless hinted at success by blimps. Examples: *National Geographic,* July 1943, 'Aboard A Blimp Hunting U-boats,' Mason Sutherland: "... one LTA officer said, 'We have been complimented by the Nazi radio itself on two occasions. While broadcasting excuses for U-boat failures, it has spoken of the airship patrol off our shores." USNI *Proceedings,* October 1943: "... the blimps have been successful in bagging many subs - just how many, the Navy will not yet say."

The Navy *never did* say; there is no official history of USN LTA operations during the war. Semi-official WWII historian RADM Samuel E. Morison ridiculed LTA, and, inaccurately, blamed some specific sinkings on airship inadequacies. In 1986, the Government Printing Office released *Kite Balloons To Airships: The U S Navy's Lighter-Than-Air Experience*, (KBTA) edited by Roy Grossnick. "A detailed history of airship operations during WWII is not possible in this brief narrative, but..." included is a non-specific table that credits blimps with damaging three submarines (the only one detailed is the U-134, damaged by K-74) and lists one blimp-assisted sinking (certainly the U-853, details of K-16 and K-58's involvement in the text).

Controversy over the airships' actual combat record, long scored simply as "blimps-0, U-boats-1" suffers the twin problem of *obliviousness via classification* and the more obvious fact that *those submarines defeated by airships would not have been able to advise HQ as to their fate*. U-boat.Net lists 57 U-boats Missing in Action without explanation; non-European Atlantic MIAs include 2 in '42; 6 in '43; 2 in '44; 1 in '45.

Unable to access Tenth Fleet records, in 1946 VADM Charles Rosendahl dispatched LT Gordon Vaeth on a fact finding mission to England. Though his visit was cut short by illness, Vaeth was able to locate the radio reception from the U-134 and 18 U-boat log entries mentioning "luftshiffe, Zeppelins, Parsevals" etc. (Lost for years, these logs were eventually printed in *The Noon Balloon* many years after Rosendahl's death.) Rosendahl continued this effort and eventually produced *How Soon We Forget: A History Of US Navy Airships In WWII*, a manuscript that accessed 24 U-boat logs showing 45 dates with airship entries; although "...not been included herein many of the reported but unverified airship contacts and attacks on submarines..." The manuscript was not formally published, but was eventually copied and then put on the net by activists of the Navy Lakehurst Historical Society. The work offers so few specifics in log quotes there is little to connect them with a date or action by airship.

Kite Balloons To Airships was compiled more than ten years before the Navy's 10th Fleet records were declassified. Following the 1996 general declassification and subsequent moving of 10th Fleet records to National Archives and Records Administration, members of the Airship Historical Action Team located various formerly secret summaries and reports listing blimp attacks on submarines. This and other research is summarized here and in the individual airship listings.

Interviewed in the 4 August 1942 *Voelkischer Beobachter*, Admiral Karl Doenitz bragged about convoys offering massed targets, his "operating close inshore along the USA" and how airplanes could only harass his boats. Asked if US "dwarf dirigibles" could "rate as particularly effective in defense?" he answered for the German audience, "It cannot be denied that even the 'blimps' have a certain effectiveness, in defense..." From Rosendahl's book, chapter "Enemy Opinion": during interrogation, Field Marshall Herman Goering volunteered that the German Navy was much concerned over blimps. Assuming their mass production and wide deployment "were hampered by high [U.S.] Navy circles" he "spoke particularly of the reconnaissance value of blimps…[German command] was relieved that we failed to do more along airship lines than we did…"

With knowledge of Morison's dismissal of blimps as a supposed *disadvantage* owing to their broadcasting the presence of a convoy, in a 1964 letter to Gordon Vaeth, Doenitz states: "But even if the commander, upon seeing the "blimp," surmised a convoy, that would only be a slight disadvantage to using the "blimp" since it would hinder the U-boat's approach, at the very least severely." Doenitz said: "…the American 'blimps' were very disturbing to German U-boat activity."

"Operation Paukenschlag" chronicler Harry Cooper charges "An oil multi-millionaire set up a chain of supply bases throughout these [Caribbean] regions in 1938, specifically for the purpose of supporting U-boats and a few German blockade runners. Some tankers of America's leading oil companies were fueling U-boats…" Early local refueling capability supports ADM Rosendahl's speculation that K-3's 22 December 1941 attack on an oil slick with black object was actually the first sub bombing of the war, but there is no reference yet found that supports German subs reaching the New York coast before 10 January 1942.

Eastern Sea Frontier, Northern Group War Diary, 1942: "On the 30th of January three airships dropped a total of 12 bombs on an oil slick causing probable damage to a submarine… Five bombs were dropped on February 10 when two airships attacked suspicious oil slicks… results were negative… On March 1, a blimp investigated a moving oil slick...attacked with four bombs. Army and Navy planes and surface craft took part in the attack... the submarine was adjudged as being critically damaged. An attack was made on March 18...the blimp detected a disturbance in the wake of a tanker..." Note in time period: At least two classified summaries state at least two subs were "probably slightly damaged" by blimp attack coordinated with airplanes.

1943 saw the peak of U-boat operations in the Atlantic and airship production was also maximized. Vaeth and Rosendahl both credit airships making nineteen submarine attacks in 1943, but no details are given. Rosendahl relays a U-boat Captain's urgent call to Berlin following a March 1943 attack by blimp whose bombs "did not land too far away." Unaware this was possible, the officer wanted to warn other boats of this seemingly unusual possibility. Another U-boat Captain told Rosendahl of remembering an August 1943 detonation noted without surface units' propeller noises, assumed it a "bomb from a blimp 'released as a routine to scare away U-boats'." ARM1 Al Stahl recalls attacking MAD contact with two depth bombs "along the New Jersey coast ...somewhere around May or June of '43..."

Eastern Sea Frontier – Northern Group War Diary, 1943: "1 August: ZP-11 airship K-37 diverted to assist K-42 sent garbled message '...send bombing planes; K-42 action.' " Both blimps depth bombed contact with no result, relieved by K-12. (Incident matches date with 10th fleet item #4025). Locals are familiar with a wreck in general area and believe an action took place with airplanes in support.

By mid-44, K-ships were being fitted with the Dual Mark VI MAD whose greatly enhanced signal-to-noise ratio and twin installation allowed "The 'Think Box' permitting automatic bomb dropping when a straddle is obtained (equal signals on both heads)..." Rosendahl quotes a mid- July 1944 Mediterranean U-boat War Diary: "It can therefore be assumed that the recently frequently reported zeppelins operating in the Straits of Gibraltar have been placed there to operate against our boats." Tested from K-91 earlier, some LTA units did not receive the homing torpedo "Fido" until late in 1944, others not at all. Some airships were eventually equipped with contact bombs inboard and the homing torpedo outboard.

Hulk of torpedoed U-boat 65 miles off Point Pleasant, New Jersey (ZP-12 patrol area) was unknown to German archives until US diver John Chatterton's artifact recovery during diving and research found it to be U-869, originally "positively certain" to have been lost in combat off Gibraltar(!) In the 24 May 1998 Hunterdon County Edition of the Sunday *Courier-News*, Chatterton says "We learned the official version could be very misleading." No airship crewman has come forward with a report of using a homing torpedo off New Jersey in the February to March 1945 time frame, the estimated time of U-869's loss to a torpedo. Lacking any record of nearby Lakehurst's airship action that is not classified, some have suggested the sub shot itself.

Last WWII combat action in which airships participated was a few days before V-E day. K-16 and K-58 reported having attacked "with rockets" or "rocket bombs." (Pilot Max Zabst explained ordnance used was "hedgehog" contact-fuse rocket-propelled bombs with the propellant removed for mounting on exterior racks and in the bomb bay. Also called "scatter bombs" during 1944 testing on K-91. Bombs could be dropped via intervalometer whose launch timing was crew-adjustable. See K-16.) VADM Rosendahl states ZP-11's K-82 also present at this action.

Several controversial incidents have been reported since this book was first published in 1992. It should be remembered many of these incidents are denied and, in some cases, branded completely untrue. One such incident was reported to have occurred off the coast of Rancho de Oso, Santa Clara, County, California, in 1942. A submarine was spotted by an aircraft warning station and was shelled by a mobile Coast Artillery field piece, with no apparent success. An airship from Moffett Field appeared and dropped depth bombs. An explosion and fire from one of the depth bombs was reported and a statement made that the submarine was destroyed. This airship is unidentified and the story has never been confirmed.

K-25 is said to have been vectored toward an airliner's reported sub sighting in the area of Chatham, Massachusetts, on 25 August 1944, supposedly with LT Joe Fallon, command pilot. (Chatham was site of a WWI blimp base, turned radio listening post in WWII.) Controversy surrounds the 1994 discovery of a large wreck in 60 feet of water off Chatham. K-25 veteran pilots verified no such action took place that date with that airship. US Government spokesmen have alternately denied existence of a U-boat there but later insisted it is a German war grave. German expert Prof. Dr. Juergen Rohwer and Horst Bredow of the U-boat Archiv at Cuxhaven-Altenburuch contend no submarine matching the wreck's description was ever finished. Yet salvage diver Edward Michaud has amassed compelling evidence that the submarine is the supposedly unbuilt U-112. To add to the confusion, another U-boat wreck has been located in the same general area, said to have been attacked in 1943, when Fallon was in ZP-11.

One ZP-51veteran has a memory of an airship wreck draped adjacent to Dutch-style houses on a South American Island. The airship was supposedly damaged in a U-boat fight. Another vet remembers an airship deflated across a Central American rain forest canopy with the crew surviving on collected rainwater before rescue. (No incidents meeting these descriptions have been located in currently available records.)

Mine Hunting & Killing Operations

While all airships were on the lookout for mines, ZP-14 (Airships crossing the Atlantic: K-101, 109, 112, 123, 130, 134) was specifically employed in de-mining operations, even after V-E day. Quotation from: Arnold S. Lott, LCDR, USN, *Most Dangerous Sea*, U.S. Naval Institute, 1959, page 205, US Navy Mine Warfare Operations:

"The Meds' minesweepers also utilized blimps as aerial mine lookouts. In clear waters, mines could be spotted at depths as great as 30 feet. Planes could and did spot mines, but their speed made difficult the task of pinpointing locations. Blimps, being able to stop if necessary, could point out a mine and direct the sweepers to it. During April and May of 1945, while sweepers cleared a 55 mile-long passage along the French coast between Toulon, La Ciotat and Marseilles, blimps K-101 and K-104 searched ahead of those old minesweeping vets, *Auk, Broadbill, Chickadee, Nuthatch, Pheasant* and *Raven*. Minesweepers, used to waiting for explosions to announce the presence of mines, liked having the blimps tell them mines lay ahead. They liked it even better when blimps told them there were no mines ahead.

Blimps had worked with Sweepers earlier on at least two operations. In the Gulf of Tunis, November 1944, Operation *Tromp* consisted of widening the 26-mile-long Tunisian War Channel through several British and one German mine field, and then sweeping another 60-mile channel to the westward. A dozen US sweepers spent a total of 108 ship-days in that operation, lifting only three mines. Some of the same sweepers, with several British craft and the blimp K-109, cleared 22 mines out of the Gulf of Cagliari during November and December. That was Phase Two of Operation *Topiary*.

In Phase One, several months earlier, 130 mines were swept out of the Gulf, where 600 square miles of sea had been mined by the Italians, French, and Germans. In one field where YMSs-17, -164, -250 and 373 cut 40 mines their first time through and 25 the second. Perhaps the busiest minesweeping in the entire Mediterranean took place off La Spezia in February of 1945, where five British ML's (Minelayers) and *Chickadee* cut 21 mines in 18 minutes. In all 385 mines were destroyed in the Gulf, with no minesweeping casualties. The record(s) were partly due to the blimp, which spotted mine lines, drifters and once saved a mine disposal vessel from wandering into a mine field."

Rescue Operations

A large number of airship flying hours were tasked to locate downed airplanes, either on land (left, an Army A-20 on Andros Island on 21 September 1943, crew rescued by K-65 and K-70) or at sea (right, a Navy SO3C and its sole survivor located by K-89). An estimate of 1,000 people having owed their lives to airship rescue would be conservative. These, as well as the more complicated recovery of victims by the airship, have been well documented, yet some have not been included in official Navy summaries.

In late 1944, an unknown airship from Moffett Field was contacted by light signals from a surface ship near Monterey. The ship reported an explosion had occurred aboard a Standard Oil tanker and a man had been lost overboard. The man in the water was located by the airship and, after a fire aboard was under control, was picked up by the tanker. The tanker was then escorted by the airship to port at San Luis Obispo. An airship from Richmond located the wreck of an Army B-29 bomber in 1945.

24 MAY 45 K-93, K-100 and K-127 were assigned to Air/Sea Rescue purposes; their modifications had already started. One ship each was to be assigned South Weymouth, Weeksville and Lakehurst. Early in May 1945 the Cominch and CNO authorized the modification of ZP-21 airships to a new rescue configuration. K-96, K-106, and K-126 were taken inside the hangar to begin removing the gun, adding a searchlight, and removing ASW equipment. K-68, herself rescued from a remote island landing, was used in the 1946 filming of Training Film MN-4370A, Blimp Air-Sea Rescue. *All Hands* magazine featured a story detailing modifications made to the K-65 by NATEC Lakehurst, including a 3000 watt floodlight replacing one slip tank, an additional spotlight replacing the machine gun in its turret, and a new Andover gasoline powered generator to power them. In addition to relocating radar and Loran to be operable by a single radioman, two electric hoists and six lightweight litters were to be installed.

“Robot Bomb” test support

After the Victory in Europe, German V-1 rockets were transferred to the United States. K-45 and then K-127 from Glynco's ZP-15 were temporarily transferred to Eglin Field, Florida, commencing 30 March 45. The field was unsuitable, so the Army Air Force base at Apalachicola was equipped with mast and concrete deadmen. K-126 made the first landing 11 April. Airships were used to observe V-1 rocket launches (“robot bombs”) to target buoys 109 miles out in the Gulf of Mexico. The airships typically hovered in the target's vicinity at 2,000 feet.

Lighter-Than-Air Serial Numbers, Equipment Delivered 1942-1945

Number	Source	Item
03545 through 03548	Lakehurst	Free Balloon (4)
04359 through 04379	Goodyear	ZNPK airships (21, K-9 through K-29)
04421 through 04424	Lakehurst	Free Balloon (4)
09753 through 09764	Lakehurst	Free Balloon (11)
09801 and 09802	Goodyear	ZNN-L (2, L-?, L-?)
30152 through 30196	Goodyear	ZNPK (45, K-30 through K-74)
33467 through 33514	Goodyear	ZNPK (48, K-75 through K-122)
48239 through 48242	Lakehurst	Free Balloon (4)

Note: No serial numbers located for K-123 through K-135 that were in service and the control cars for K-136 through K-139 for K-types not completed.

K-type airship numbers/serial numbers, L-2, L-3 and free balloon contracts to Goodyear (Source: United States Naval Aviation 1910-1970, 1970)

K-3 - 7025	K- 47-30169	K- 93-33485	L-2 -7029
4 - 7026	48-30170	94-33486	3 -7030
5 - 7027	49-30171	95-33487	
6 - 7028	50-30172	96-33488	Free Balloons (4) -
	51-30173	97-33489	03545 through 03548
7 - 01729	52-30174	98-33490	
8 - 01733	53-30175	99-33491	Free Balloons (3) -
	54-30176	100-33492	04421 through 04424
9 - 04359	55-30177	101-33493	

10 - 04360	56-30178	102-33494	Free Balloons (12)
11 - 04361	57-30179	103-33495	09753 through 09764
12 - 04362	58-30180	104-33496	
13 - 04363	59-30181	105-33497	09801 -L- ?
14 - 04364	60-30182	106-33498	09802 -L- ?
K- 15 - 04365	K-61-30183	K-107-33499	
16 - 04366	62-30184	108-33500	Summary
17 - 04367	63-30185	109-33501	
18 - 04368	64-30186	110-33502	K-1 -no serial
19 - 04369	65-30187	111-33503	2 -1211, Cont. 56352
20 - 04370	66-30188	112-33504	
21 - 04371	67-30189	113-33505	3 through 6 -7025
22 - 04372	68-30190	114-33506	through 7028
23 - 04373	69-30191	115-33507	
24 - 04374	70-30192	116-33508	7 and 8 -01729
25 - 04375	71-30193	117-33509	and 01730
26 - 04376	73-30195	119-33511	9 through 29 -04359
28 - 04378	74-30196	120-33512	through 04379
29 - 04379		121-33513	
	75-33467	122-33514	30 through 50 -30152
30 - 30152	76-33468		through 30172
31 - 30153	77-33469	No Record	(All Contr. 78121)
32 - 30154	78-33470		
33 - 30155	79-33471	123	51 through 74 -30173
34 - 30156	80-33472	124	through 30196
35 - 30157	81-33473	125	
36 - 30158	82-33474	126	75 through 122-33467
37 - 30159	83-33475	127	through 33514
38 - 30160	84-33476	128	
39 - 30161	85-33477	129	123 through 135 - no
40 - 30162	86-33478	130	serial number record
41 - 30163	87-33479	131	(All Contr. NOs-257,
42 - 30164	88-33480	132	was NXs(a) 10086)
43 - 30165	89-44381	133	
44 - 30166	90-33482	134	122 total K-ship
45 - 30167	91-33483	135	serial numbers
46 - 30168	92-33484		recorded.

Mine hunting and mine killing operations were conducted from various locations, including the island of Malta shown here, by airships of ZP-14. Malta Historical Museum, via Dorsay Novak.

PART VI: Cold War Airships 1945-1962

Introduction

In June 1945, one hundred thirty nine airships were in inventory. These included thirty K-type with patrol squadrons, thirty-eight in utility and air-sea rescue assignments, seven in training and thirty-two in storage. There were three M-type with patrol squadrons and one in training; two L-type in training and nineteen in storage; four G-type in utility and air-sea rescue, one in training and two in storage. In 1947, the Navy General Board made no further mention of rigid airships, so designations of non-rigid airships became "Z" (formerly they were designated as ZN with rigid airships designated ZR). ZP represented a non-rigid patrol airship; ZS, a scouting (anti-submarine warfare [ASW]) airship; and ZW, a radar warning airship.

In 1946, the decision was made to up-grade the K-type airships then in service. The K-type went through a series of modifications to become the type ZP2K. Later, more extensive modifications created the new type ZP3K (both 527,000 cubic feet). The ZP2K and ZP3K types were later redesignated ZSG-2 and ZSG-3. New envelopes were provided by Goodyear, and some of the control cars altered at Wingfoot Lake. At least 23 cars were modified at Lakehurst from wartime airships. The control cars maintained their original numbers (as an example, K-85 became ZP2K-85, etc.) and the identification appeared on the control car (and in some 3K cases on the lower fin) but not on the envelope. This system makes identification of a particular airship from photographs rather difficult.

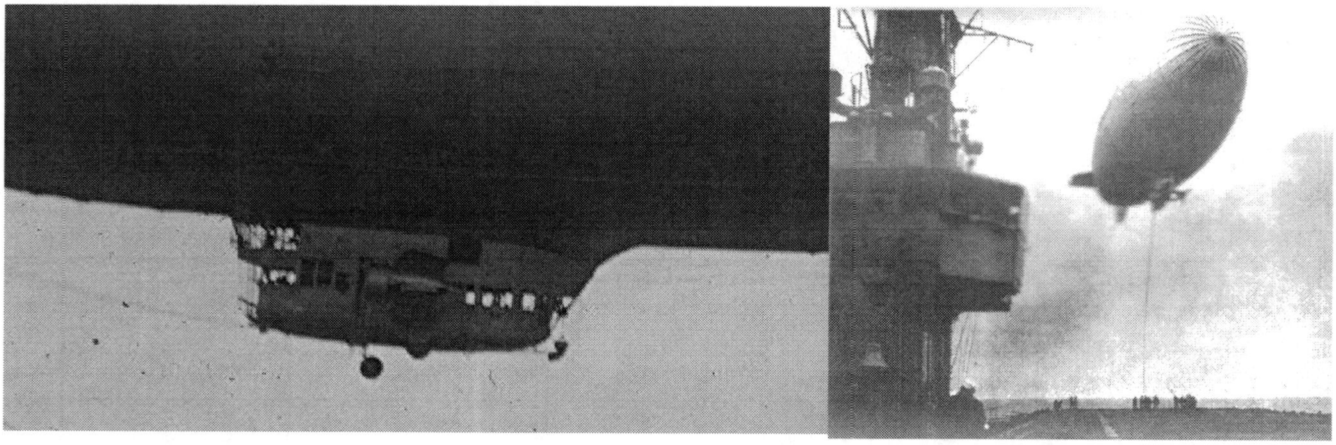

ZP2K at Glynco shows improvements to car's stern including a powerful winch for recoving sea water ballast (with bag seen) and at-sea refueling using the underway methods. Hose method shown at right; bags of fuel were also recovered in flight. (Left: Dan Lindsay; right: USN photo)

The ZP2K (ZSG-2) Airships

The ZP2K (ZSG-2) was designed for general patrol duty, air-sea rescue work, and detection and destruction of enemy submarines. Improvements from the wartime K-type included improved power generation for more electronics, better sonobuoy receivers, radios, radars, and Loran. A power winch, electrically controlled landing gear, reversible propellers, an automatic pilot, and an in-flight refueling system (above, the "hose method") were installed. There were two additional crew stations and revisions to pilot controls. One slip, two main and two drop-able fuel tanks, new interior and exterior bomb racks and other airship accessories were added. Twenty-three K-types were revised to ZP2K at Lakehurst in 1951 and four in 1952. The first ZP2K was delivered 07 August 1951.

The Navy Pilot's Handbook indicates the following K-types were converted to ZP2K-types:
K-13, K-19, K-20, K-21, K-24, K-33, K-38, K-40, K-42, K-43, K-46, K-47, K-58, K-59, K-61, K-63, K-67, K-68, K-69, K-71, K-72, K-77, K-78, K-79, K-80, K-81, K-82, K-85, K-86, K-87, K-88, K-91, K-92, K-93, K-97, K-98, K-100, K-116, K-118, K-119, K- 120, K-121, K-124, K-125 and K-127, a total of 44 airships.

With each modification came more electronics: note third ASW position at the former navigator's table and additional racks mounted electronic assemblies above the 'radio shack.' USN photo

The ZP3K-92, note rare use of K-number on the lower vertical fin. Lou Prost photo

The ZP3K (ZSG-3) Airships

The ZP3K (ZSG-3) type (527,000 cubic feet) was an improvement over the ZP2K (ZSG-2) with all of the ZP2K (ZSG-2) features plus improved landing gear for carrier operations, upgraded electronics, APU and improved operational characteristics. Minor structural revisions to the control car bow, from an outside appearance standpoint, were the removal of the machine gun blister. Aft, the removal of the doors at the stern and extensive reworking of the frame allowed installation of a towing sonar drogue and "bubble" windows. Inside, the flight mechanic's station was eliminated and all engine displays and controls moved to the forward flight deck. The ZP3K (ZSG-2) was mainly intended for carrier-based operations. Thirty of the ZP2K (ZSG-2) types were upgraded to the ZP3K (ZSG-3) with 1 revised at Lakehurst in 1951 and 8 in 1952. The first ZP3K was delivered to Lakehurst on 12 November 1952. The individual ZP2K types converted to the ZP3K are unknown, however the following are known to have been converted: K-24, K-47, K-77, K-79, K-80, K-88, K-92, K-120, K-124, K-127 and possibly K-93 and K-125.

Eighty-Eight envelopes of 527,000 cubic feet were contracted to Goodyear with a total of seventy-one delivered (approximately forty-four complete ZP2K/ZSG-2, ZP3K/ZSG-3 and ZP4K/ZSG-4 airships and spares). Cost for the ZP2K and ZP3K programs was $12,000,000.

ZP3K-80 was given an experimental Navy blue paint shceme during operations at Key West. Extensive stern modifications to accommodate the winch and sonar towing 'fish' are visible aft, and forward the machine gun turret space was used for an ASW position.

In general, the specifications for the ZP2K and ZP3K were as follows:

Volume (cubic feet)	527,000
Ballonets (2) (cubic feet)	121,800
Overall length (feet)	255.58
Maximum diameter (feet)	62.10
Overall width (feet)	65.78
Static lift (useful)(pounds)	6,344
Dynamic lift (pounds)	2,546
Maximum speed (knots)	65
Cruising speed (knots)	50
Range, cruising speed (nautical miles)	2,000
Crew (normal)	8
Crew (extended flight)	11
Armament	8 - Mark 4 or 5 rocket type 65 pound bombs, 2 Mark 54 bombs or 2 ADB depth charges
Engines (2)	R-1340-AN-2 (Pratt and Whitney Wasp, electric propellers, controllable pitch

The ZP3K (ZSG-3) airships remained in service until 1955 when they were deactivated.

A K-type airship mysteriously identified as a "ZSG-1" was moored at the Nevada Proving Grounds, Yucca Flats, Nevada, during two-kilotons atomic bomb tests in June 1957 (and a second airship in August 1957). One K-ship broke away from its handlers during a "dust devil" event and had to be replaced with a reserve airship hastily prepared and flown out from Santa Ana. During a nuke trigger test, an airship was masted 10,000 feet from the blast and was demasted, with no major damage other than the mooring fitting failure. Repairable, it was ordered ripped on the scene. A ZSG-3 airship did take part in nuclear tests known as "Plumbbob" in 1957. The airship contained extensive instrumentation and was exposed to a nuke blast while tethered at altitude. Motion pictures show the blast rippled the envelope; it failed along a circumference in line with the forward part of the car. Separating, the bow departed and the partial hull crashed to the ground, “nose” first. This gave the rather bizarre appearance that the forward hull had been flown into the ground and was buried up to the car. Two of these airships were flown cross-country. One airship that landed at Naval Air Facility, Litchfield Park, Arizona was met by former Goodyear and Navy airship pilot R.H. "Hobie" Hobensack and H.T. Evans, manager of Airship Assembly at the Goodyear Litchfield Park balloon and airship envelope operation. Crew on this flight included R.D. Nye, ADC (AP), chief pilot, LCDR R. Forand, co-pilot, LTJG R.J. Henze, co-pilot, LT J.C. Mitchell, B.G. Underwood, AA (rigger), C.L. Lawson, AD3 (mechanic) and J.L. Simmons SO3 (radioman).

One or more ZP3K airships had their bomb bays modified to accommodate atomic depth charges. An unspecified ZP3K was forced to jettison such an atomic weapon containing a 600 pound TNT detonator but no fissionable material to avoid an accident when both engines failed, there were no injuries. An unspecified ZP3K was modified to carry a “bed spring” radar antenna inside the envelope. The 1960 LTA accident report states an unnamed ZSG-3 attached to NATU Glynco was damaged during a student landing on 18 June 1956.

SCHOOL DAYS FOR MECHANICS—Airship mechanics practice installing emergency landing wheel gear to the ZS3G-124 during the 14 days spent at the Naval Air Station, Guantanamo Bay, Cuba. The Akronites, away from the subfreezing weather, quickly donned Navy shorts to wear under the warm Cuban sun. The emergency landing gear was a World War II development of the Wheel and Brake Division. (Official U. S. Navy Photographs)

LTA Society

The ZP2K and ZP3K were followed by the ZP4K and ZP5K types. The ZP4K (revised to ZSG-4) and ZP5K (revised to ZS2G-1), although they carried the "K" designation, were entirely new airships and were not interchangeable with the earlier K-types or each other. Goodyear continued to designate all envelopes as K-type for the ZP2K (ZSG-2) and the ZP3K (ZSG-3), which were actually K-types and the ZP4K (ZSG-4) and ZP5K (ZS2G-1) which were entirely different from the K-type. This was based on the original airship designations of ZP4K through ZP5K.

ZP4K-type Airships (Redesignated as type ZSG-4)

The ZP4K-types (ZSG-4) resembled the wartime K-types but were an entirely new design (Goodyear type GZ-12). Their creation was based on the successful wartime K-type airships, which were beyond further modification, coupled with the threat of possible submarine activity due to the Korean conflict. They were ordered on Navy contract 51-366c for one type XZSG-4, and contract 51-657 (1951) for fourteen of the type. That latter contract 51-657 was for eight more (total twenty-four), with ten later canceled, making a revised total of fourteen. The cars were skinned with magnesium. The flight deck more closely resembled a modern aircraft, with mirror-image yoke controls for pilots separated by a wide center console. Goodyear apparently sub-contracted electronics work on the ZP4K control cars to Cook Electric. The cars were built at Wingfoot Lake, the airships were erected in the Goodyear Airdock and test flown from the Akron Municipal Airport (now Fulton Field). Fifteen total ZP4K (ZSG-4) airships were delivered, fourteen production models and one experimental type. (Envelope D-528 for a ZSG-4 caught fire while air inflated prior to erection at Akron on 21 January 1955.) In addition to Lakehurst, the ZSG-4 airships also served at Naval Air Station, Weeksville, North Carolina with ZP-1 until mid-1957 when the air station was deactivated. The airships were in service until 1959. Stored, they were scrapped by 01 September 1961. Designations such as ZP4K-1, etc. were no longer carried by the airships and serial numbers were used for identification. The suggested but unapproved code name for the ZP4K /ZSG-4 was *Volunteer*. Cost of the ZP4K/ZSG-4 program was $40,000,000. ZP4K (ZSG-4) (527,000 cubic feet) by Navy Serial Number: [17]

ZP4K (1) (ZSG-4) - Serial 131919, Goodyear order no. 837 and serial 4042, envelope D-520, control car C-225, delivered to Lakehurst 20 June 1954. Following an at-mast storm deflation on 18 March 1956, it is believed to have been rebuilt with one of the first Dacron envelopes built by General Development Corporation of Elkton, Maryland. It made the last flight of a Naval Reserve airship (from Lakehurst) in October 1959. Aboard were CAPT Otto Hugo (shown as pilot but actually a passenger); LTJG Lawrence R. Lanchoney (actual pilot, in left seat); CDR William Talbot (co-pilot and CO of ZP753, right seat); LT D. R. Champion; Chief Petty Officers John Fox and A .J. Lajewski; Petty Officers F. Stout; D. Longbrake and J.F. Hanlon.

[17] There are several date discrepancies in the records of Goodyear delivery dates and the Goodyear 01 August 1960 "accident" letter.

ZP4K (2) (ZSG-4) - Serial 131920, Goodyear order no. 837 and serial 4043, envelope D-521, control car C-226, delivered to Lakehurst 13 September 1954. Attached to NARTU Glynco on 15 March 1958 heavily damaged during a student's landing. Returning to the air, ship remained aloft until winds subsided at sundown; emergency wheel added and ship recovered. Rebuilt, caught fire from the auxiliary power unit in one of the Glynco, Georgia, hangars, 13 October 1958.

ZP4K (3) (ZSG-4) - Serial 131921, Goodyear order no. 837 and serial 4044, envelope D-522, control car C-227, delivered to Lakehurst 14 October 1954. Attached to NAS Glynco on 14 July 1958 car damaged when attempting a landing in gusty conditions.

ZP4K (4) (ZSG-4) - Serial 131922, Goodyear order no. 837 and serial 4045, envelope D-523, control car C-228, delivered to Lakehurst 06 November 1954. The Goodyear accident records indicate 131922 (Goodyear serial no. 4070) was deflated during a landing on 16 December 1953, almost one year prior to delivery to the Navy. The accident was caused when the starboard propeller struck the ground, the control car struck a fence and the rip panel was partially pulled but not enough to cause complete deflation. It is possible this occurred at Akron during flight tests, however the dates are open to question. The original envelope was repaired and placed in storage. (It is believed the correct date for the deflation was 1954 and not 1953.) 131922 was damaged when it over-rode a mast at Weeksville, North Carolina, on 18 October 1955 and partially deflated as a precautionary measure due to the previous damage. The envelope was placed in storage. Rebuilt. With NAS Glynco in 1959, on 10 December during night familiarization training, the forward ballonet ruptured and trim control was lost. The instructor ditched the airship tail first and the envelope was ripped.

ZP4K (5) (ZSG-4) - Serial 131923, Goodyear order no. 837 and serial 4046, envelope D-524, control car C-229, delivered to Lakehurst 01 December 1954. The Goodyear accident report states 131923 was deflated after rubbing against the hangar doors at Lakehurst on 23 September 1954, two months prior to delivery to the Navy. (It is believed 1955 is the correct date for the accident and not 1954.) The envelope was repaired and returned to service. With ZP-4 at Weeksville on 03 October 1955 car damaged when an improper landing was attempted. Car extensively damaged at Elizabeth City 08 April 1957 when pilots did not see a waveoff signal.

ZP4K (6) (ZSG-4) - Serial 131924, Goodyear order no. 837 and serial 4047, envelope D-525, control car C-230, delivered to Lakehurst 17 December 1954. With ZX-11 on 14 November 1955, slightly damaged during a night landing. Deflated by falling hangar debris at Weeksville, NC on 14 January 1957.

ZP4K (7) (ZSG-4) - Serial 131925, Goodyear order no. 837 and serial 4048, envelope D-526, control car C-231, delivered to Lakehurst 19 January 1955. During a student's practice landing 28 April 1958, a thermal drove the airship into the ground at an angle of 10 degrees, extensively damaging the landing gear, radome, props and bottom of the car.

ZP4K (8) (ZSG-4) - Serial 131926, Goodyear order no. 837 and serial 4049, envelope D-527, control car C-232, delivered to Lakehurst 04 February 1955, damaged August 1955 when a skylight from a hangar at an unknown location went through the envelope, envelope repaired, damaged again 04 April 1957, when a contractor working on the hangar roof dropped a hammer through the envelope. The envelope was deflated, repaired and placed in storage.

XZP4K-1 (XZSG-4) - Serial 133639, Goodyear order no. 817 and serial 4041, envelope D-519, control car C-224, delivered to Lakehurst 27 August 1954, was to be fitted with an experimental Dacron envelope built by General Development Corporation of Elkton, Maryland, but actually used a cotton envelope which was retired in November 1956 (an envelope by General Development was accepted by the Navy in late 1955). "639" made first demonstration of in-flight crew change from USS *Tarawa* in 1955 following Project YGAR.

ZP4K (9) (ZSG-4) - Serial 134019, Goodyear order no. 837 and serial 4050, envelope D-529, control car C-233, delivered to Lakehurst 14 March 1955, deflated during a twister at Weeksville, North Carolina on 18 March 1956.

ZP4K (10) (ZSG-4) - Serial 134020, Goodyear order no. 837 and serial 4051, envelope D-530, control car C-234, delivered to Lakehurst 31 March 1955. With ZP-4 in 1956 the airship was conducting ASW sonar towing on 01 March when engine control was lost and the airship impacted the water, tearing off the radar and slip tank as two crewmen entered the water with a life raft. Aloft again, one engine was restarted and the ship returned to base. The two crewmen were recovered by the Coast Guard. With NARTU at Glynco, Georgia 07 February 1959, during a routine landing the port quick-disconnect failed resulting in a 14-inch envelope tear. The ripcord was pulled to prevent further damage. As a result of this accident fittings were replaced and given periodic pull test.

ZSG-4 from ZTG makes a Glynco landing as seen by "mule" operator John Brashears.

ZP4K (11) (ZSG-4) - Serial 134021, Goodyear order no. 837 and serial 4052, envelope D-531, control car C-235, delivered to Lakehurst 29 April 1955.

ZP4K (12) (ZSG-4) - Serial 134022, Goodyear order no. 837 and serial 4053, envelope D-532, control car C-236, delivered to Lakehurst 17 May 1955.

ZP4K (13) (ZSG-4) - Serial 134023, Goodyear order no. 837 and serial 4054, envelope D-533, control car C-237, delivered to Lakehurst 01 June 1955.

ZP4K (14) (ZSG-4) - Serial 134024, Goodyear order no. 837 and serial 4055, envelope D-583, control car C-238, delivered to Lakehurst 14 July 1955. Attached to ZP-4 NAF Weeksville, on 01 December 1955 airship made normal takeoff but reduced power caused it to settle into trees as port engine oversped. Water and gasoline ballast were dropped but the punctured envelope collapsed.

ZP4K (ZSG-4) general specifications:

Volume (cubic feet)	527,000
Ballonets (2) (cubic feet, total)	121,800
Overall length (feet)	266.5
Maximum diameter (feet)	62.1
Overall height (feet, maximum)	83.6
Overall width (feet)	69.4
Cruising speed (knots)	50
Endurance at cruise speed (hours)	59
Crew (pilot, co-pilot, navigator, sonar, radio, ECM, radar and winch operators)	8
Engines (2) Pratt & Whitney R1340-46 radial, air-cooled, 550 bhp at 2200 rpm	

ZP4K (ZSG-4) deliveries:

1954		1955		Totals
June (131919)	1	Jan (131925)	1	
Aug(XZP4K,133639)	1	Feb (131926)	1	
Sep (131920)	1	Mar (134019, 134020)	2	
Oct (131921)	1	Apr (134021)	1	
Nov (131922)	1	May (134022)	1	
Dec(131923,131924)	2	June (134023)	1	
		July (134024)	1	
Sub Total	7	Sub Total	8	15

The ZP5K (ZS2G-1) Airships

The ZP5K (ZS2G-1) was entirely different than any K-type airship. The Goodyear project numbers were GZ-10 for the experimental model XZP5K (XZS2G-1), and GZ-15 for the production models. The original Navy contract 52-985 (1952) was for six airships; this was later reduced to five. The contract number for the XZP5K (XZS2G-1) was 53-0466. Twelve additional types were ordered on contract 55-184 (1955), although the original order was for seven; these car serial numbers were not published. Although at first referred to as "5K," the airship was in no way similar to a WWII or ZP4K type. The most distinctive feature of the ZP5K (ZS2G-1) was the inverted "Y" rear control surfaces or fins. From this model forward, there would be no further cruciform (configuration "+") control surfaces, with the new models either the "Y" or "X" configuration. The longer car's interior forward was dominated by the avionics operator's suite occupying the port side. Aft was a very large sonar-towing winch. The ship was designed for long duration anti-submarine patrol. The suggested code name (not approved) for the ZP5K (ZS2G-1) was *Defender*. Cost of the ZP5K/ZS2G-1 program was $54,000,000.

ZP5K (ZS2G-1) (650,000 cubic feet) By Navy Serial Number

ZP5K (1) (ZS2G-1) - Serial 137486, Goodyear order no. 2455 and serial 4071, envelope D-575, control car C-254, delivered to Lakehurst 26 May 1955.

ZP5K (2) (ZS2G-1) - Serial 137487, Goodyear order no. 2455 and serial 4072, envelope D-576, control car C-255, delivered to Lakehurst 25 July 1955. At Glynco, Georgia, 18 September 1955 (also given as 14 October) during a turbulent landing a propeller blade scraped the envelope causing slight damage. Crew checked landing gear and landed successfully. The envelope was deflated and placed in storage. Rebuilt, with ZP-2 in 1959, proceeded with airship Bu No 146294 on a ferry flight to Lakehurst on 17 February. Due to improper altimeter setting, the airship decended into trees some 43 miles north of Cherry Point, NC. It crashed and burned, killing four and injuring three of the crew.

ZP5K (3) (ZS2G-1) - Serial 137488, Goodyear order no. 2455 and serial 4073, envelope D-577, control car C-256, delivered to Lakehurst 04 October 1955. With ZP-2 in 1956, returning from a training flight on 22 May, thermal turbulence led to a rough landing that damaged the gear and the radome.

ZP5K (4) (ZS2G-1) - Serial 137489, Goodyear order no. 2455 and serial 4074, envelope D-578, control car C-257, delivered to Lakehurst 07 November 1955 and under its command on in July 1958 when its upper fin had been removed for Project LAK-AC7071.2. Returning to flight the cable controls had been reversed causing loss of control. An attempt to dump ballast was unsuccessful when its valve malfunctioned. After several waveoffs a landing collapsed the wheel and the starbord prop struck the ground and carried away. The crew abandoned ship but the airship commander returned to rig a handling line; the ship rose, and he sustained a broken pelvis and elbow in jumping from 20 feet.

ZP5K (5) (ZS2G-1) - Serial 137490, Goodyear order no. 2455 and serial 4075, envelope D-579, control car C-258, delivered to Lakehurst 21 December 1955. With ZP-2 on 26 June 1956 for an ordnance evaluation flight takeoff was attempted with 4452 pound heaviness. The port engine did not develop take-off power due to a failure on the control linkage, and the airship assumed a nose-high attitude in spite of application of forward yoke. The port ruddervator struct the mat and three crewmen disembarked in an attempt to restrict forward movement with the drag lines. Ordnance was jettisoned and the ship became airborne; it was landed on one engine. On 26 July 1956 137490 was thought to have been struck by lightning but was completely destroyed when the envelope caught fire and it quickly spread to the gasoline while moored on the landing mat at Glynco.

XZP5K (XZS2G-1) - Serial 137811, Goodyear order no. 2147, envelope D-574, control car C-253, first flight at Akron 22 July 1954, delivered to Lakehurst 22 April 1955, deflated while landing at Lakehurst 15 August 1955 when a propeller struck the ground and the landing gear collapsed. 137811 drifted with no power and landed in a corn field. To prevent it from striking some wires, the rip panel was pulled and the envelope deflated.

ZP5K (6) (ZS2G-1) - Serial 141564, Goodyear order no. 8055 and serial 4086, envelope D-601, delivered to Lakehurst 28 February 1956.

ZP5K (7) (ZS2G-1) - Serial 141565, Goodyear order no. 8055 and serial 4087, envelope D-602, delivered to Lakehurst 23 May 1956.

ZP5K (8) (ZS2G-1) - Serial 141566, Goodyear order no. 8055 and serial 4088, envelope D-603, delivered to Lakehurst 10 July 1956.

ZP5K (9) (ZS2G-1) - Serial 141567, Goodyear order no. 8055 and serial 4089, envelope D-604, delivered to Lakehurst 04 September 1956. With ZP-2 following an ASW exercise, high winds precluded return to Glynco and the ship was diverted to Bermuda. Adverse weather complicated an at-sea refueling from USS *Leyte*, with only a 50 gallon drum of fuel recovered. After 24 hours of flight the ship reached Bermuda but conditions precluded landing, and the ship refueled. Winds gusting to 42 complicated landing and on the third attempt the yaw lines became fouled in the nose pendant, precluding masting. Inexperianced ground handlers sought to unsnarl the lines when a passing squall caused severe pitch and roll, with port prop hitting the runway. 141567 was ripped to prevent further damage 14 February 1958.

ZP5K (10) (ZS2G-1) - Serial 141568, Goodyear order no. 8055 and serial 4090, envelope D-605, delivered to Lakehurst 24 October 1956.

ZP5K (11) (ZS2G-1) - Serial 141569, Goodyear order no. 8055 and serial 4091, envelope D-606, delivered to Lakehurst 17 December 1956. Reassigned to NAF Elizabeth City, on 21 April 1957 sufered underside damage during a hard landing. Repaired. At Lakehurst on 18 September 1957 when performing routine test flights and touch-and-go landings. A broken wire jammed the control yoke in the down position and the airship struck short of the mat, collapsing the wheel. Further examination led to Service Change No. 71.

Unique stern of ZS2G-1, left. US Navy photo.

ZP5K (12) (ZS2G-1) - Serial 141570, Goodyear order no. 8055 and serial 4092, envelope D-607, delivered to Lakehurst 13 February 1957. With ZP-2 at Glynco in 1958, on 16 September during takeoff for a patrol flight, an improperly manufactured control link failed, throwing the ship into a port orbit. Fuel was dumped and a landing attempted with the orbit, but the wheel struck a stump and carried away, both props hit the ground and 4000 pounds of fuel discharged from the ruptured main fuel cell. The airship free ballooned for an hour while the crew fought to regain control. It settled to the ground some 6 miles north of Darien, Georgia, and the crew abandoned ship. Airship Commander LCDR James Kissick was last to leave jumping with the ripcord. The improperly manufactured seam did not rip and the airship again free ballooned alone until it settled into a marsh near Sapelo, Georgia.

ZP5K (13) (ZS2G-1) - Serial 144239, Goodyear order no. 8055 and serial 4093, envelope D-616, delivered to Lakehurst 23 May 1957.

ZP5K (14) (ZS2G-1) - Serial 144240, Goodyear order no. 8055 and serial 4094, envelope D-617, delivered to Lakehurst 26 July 1957. 144240 became the "Boundary layer control" test ship, equipped with special aerodynamic enhancements. In 1961 144240 was recommended for the installation of two ZPG-3W Wright R-1820-88 Cyclone, 1,275 horsepower engines that could have allowed the ZS2G-1 to attain 100 miles per hour. This was not approved; one of the excuses given by the Navy hierarchy that led to the demise of the airships was that were not capable of attaining a speed of 100 miles per hour. Another plan called for stern propulsion installation, also not approved.

ZP5K (15) (ZS2G-1) - Serial 144241, Goodyear order no. 8055 and serial 4095, envelope D-618, delivered to Lakehurst 30 October 1957.

ZP5K (16) (ZS2G-1) - Serial 146294, Goodyear order no. 8055 and serial 4100, envelope D-623, delivered to Lakehurst 31 March 1958.

ZP5K (17) (ZS2G-1) - Serial 146295, Goodyear order no. 8055 and serial 4101, envelope D-624, with revised electronics, delivered to Lakehurst 24 June 1958. With ZP-2 in 1958, following a training mission on 21 July 1958, pressure could not be maintained. Power could be used to maintain altitude but there was no directional control. Ballast, ordnance and loose gear was jettisoned and a partially controlled landing was effected on the edge of a clearing at Glynco, GA. Cause of accident was improperly manufactured air-to-helium rip sleeve. Envelope repaired and placed in storage.

An unidentified airship of this type suffered dual engine failure during night ASW exercises off Jacksonville, Florida, 05 December 57. Attempts to tow the airship by the USS *H. G. Ellison* (DD-864) were unsuccessful and the crew abandoned ship into the destroyer's whaleboat. LCDR Tom Madagin pulled the ripcord but the panel did not rip properly. Airship had to be sunk with gunfire from the destroyer.

Eighteen total ZP5K (ZS2G-1) airships delivered, seventeen production and one experimental type. In addition to Lakehurst, six ZS2G-1 airships served at Naval Air Station, Weeksville, North Carolina with ZP-4 until mid-1957 when the air station was deactivated and the airships stored. All ZS2G-1s, except one, were placed in storage in the spring of 1959. The ZS2G-1 144240 remained in service until the airship program was terminated in 1961. It was used in 1960 for the initial "flying wind tunnel" tests, which investigated low speed aerodynamics. A large deployable pole carried a small shape model clear of the airship's windstream. "240" was seen in an edited motion picture about the project. "240" was also equipped with special fairings, fin improvements and other enhancements for boundary layer control study. The deflated envelopes of the ZS2G-1 airships were scrapped by September 1961.

Two ZSG-1 airships of ZX-11 serving at Key West, Florida. Note the aft clamshell doors and extended boarding ladder in this Larry Karadin photo.

ZP5K (ZS2G-1) general specifications:

Volume (cubic feet)	670,000
Ballonet, forward (cubic feet)	79,200
Ballonet, aft (cubic feet)	90,300
Overall length (feet)	285
Maximum diameter (feet)	68
Overall height (feet)	96
Overall width (feet)	68
Empty weight (pounds)	29,000
Three fin "Y" configuration:	
Fin area (square feet)	653
Rudder area (square feet)	235
Stabilizer area (2 each, square feet)	653
Elevator area (2 each, square feet)	235
Static (useful) lift (pounds)	41,600
Gross lift (6,000 pounds heavy [pounds])	47,600
Rate of climb (feet per minute)	2,400
Maximum speed (knots)	73
Cruising speed (knots)	50
Ceiling (feet, approximately)	9,000
Fuel capacity (gallons)	2,300
Crew	8 (pilot, co-pilot, command pilot, sonar, navigator, radio-ECM, radar, winch operator)
Engines (2)	Wright R-1300-4, 700 hp, 800 hp at 2,600 rpm take-off, Curtiss 3 blade electric propellers,11'6" diameter.

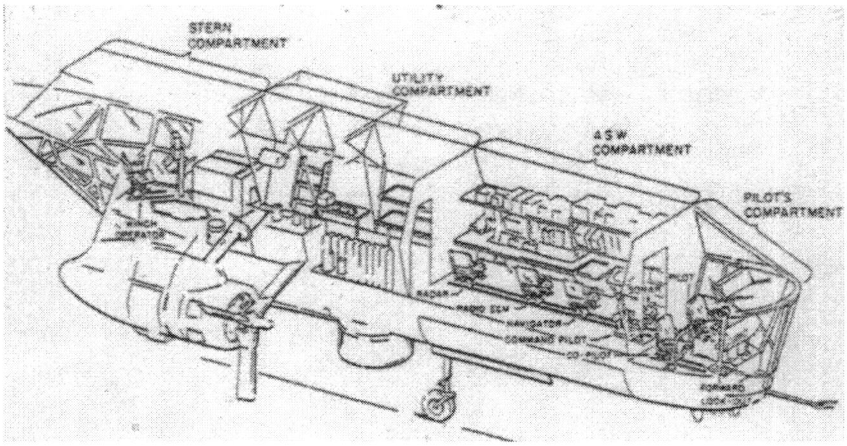

ZP5K general arrangement plan courtsey Ford Ross.

ZP5K (ZS2G-1) deliveries:

1955 (1 each)	1956 (1 each)	1957 (1 each)	1958 (1 each)	Totals
April (XZP5K) (XZS2G-1) (17811)	Feb (141564)	Feb (1415701)	Mar (1462941)	
May(137486)	May (141565)	May (1442391)	June (1462951)	
Jul(137487)	July (141566)	July (1442401)		
Oct(137488)	Sep (141567)	Oct (1442411)		
Nov(137489)	Oct (141568)			
Dec(137490)	Dec (141569)			
Sub Total 6	6	4	2	18

The N-Type (Nan) (ZPN-1/ZPG-1) Airship

The N-type airship was a greatly enlarged, entirely new design that included many innovations. Only one example was built, serving as the prototype of the later ZPG-2 and ZPG-3 series of airships. The concept for the design was to provide a new airship as maneuverable as the rugged and easy to fly K-ship, with the endurance and comfort of the M-ship, but easier to maintain than either. The design ended up a compromise, with the two-deck car the main concern.

The operators desired an articulated car as on the M-ship, with the engines located further aft, allowing low cockpit noise and comfortable sleeping quarters, well removed from the engines. Goodyear also recommended this design but, reportedly, resisted the two-deck car that had originated with Douglas Aircraft. It is reported that since Goodyear would not proceed with a two-deck car design, it was purchased by the Navy from Douglas for the sum of $1.00. The Bureau of Aeronautics then apparently ordered Goodyear to design the airship based on the Douglas proposal. Despite resistance of the pilots, operators, and Goodyear, the Bureau of Aeronautics, naturally, won out.

The ZP2N-1 project number was GZ-11; the car serial number became 4035. The car featured a lower deck for the flight compartment and working areas with the upper deck for sleeping, cooking and messing areas. The engines would be mounted inside of the car where they would be accessible for in-flight repair. (This inside engine compartment design was used for the first time since the USS *Akron,* completed in 1931, and the USS *Macon,* completed in 1933.) The drivetrain was designed for single engine, double propeller operation with one engine driving not only both propellers, but two DC and one AC generators, two inboard gear boxes, two outboard boxes and the winch hydraulic pump. Outriggers with small nacelles accommodated the propeller hub and gear box. Numerous revisions occurred from the original 1947 concept to the completed airship of 1951. ZPN-1 had "X" configuration tail surfaces and wheel/yoke controls similar to an airplane.

The contract for ZPN-1 was NOas 9861, issued 18 May 1948. It was erected in the Goodyear Airdock as were all subsequent Navy airships. Cost of the ZPN-1 program is variously quoted as $3,388,000 to approximately $5,000,000. Goodyear cost data of December, 1948, states $4,871,722 in 1947 and $5,250,000 for subsequent types, approaching the (not adjusted for inflation) depression-era cost of the two rigid airships USS *Akron* and USS *Macon*.

ZPN-1 - Navy serial N-1, Goodyear order no. 9130, mock-up completed in Akron in early 1949. Envelope D-473 (875,000 cubic feet, Fortisan fabric), control car 219, first flight at Akron 18 June 1951. Walter Massic, chief pilot, was awarded the Harmon International Award for Aeronauts at the White House in July 1953. Delivered to Lakehurst 16 June 1952 (CDR M. E. Cawley, chief test pilot and LCDR W.J. Gunther, assistant). Used primarily in research and development work which included towing, from Weeksville. On one occasion ZPN-1 towed a whaler streaming sea anchors, with the boat's engines in full power reverse. The tow force or tension was 6,500 pounds and reached a maximum of 9,500 pounds. During a near hurricane with winds of 70 miles per hour, the tow boat was beached. Since the hangar was full at Weeksville, N-1 moored out at the mast. ZPN-1 returned and towed the whaler off the beach into the water. ZPN-1 was also used from Key West for the testing of mine-sweeping. The conclusion reached was that mine-sweeping by airship was more effective and safer than from surface ships. That envelope was deflated at Lakehurst after a ballonet ruptured 01 July 1953. It was repaired and returned to service and used for a variety of tests and development. ZPN-1 conducted minesweeping tests from Weeksville in the spring and from Lakehurst in the summer of 1956. In 1959, it was involved in high priority experimental missions including radiometer tests over the North Atlantic and the Gulf of Mexico. It went through a major overhaul at Lakehurst in late 1959 with the intention of it becoming a spare ZPG-2 for antisubmarine missions. This proposal was rejected by the Bureau of Aeronautics as it was a prototype airship and not equipped with standard ASW equipment as furnished in the production ZPG-2 airships. It was surveyed circa 1960.

ZPN-1 general specifications:

Volume (cubic feet)	875,000
Ballonets (4) (cubic feet)	220,800
Overall length (feet)	24.41
Maximum diameter (feet)	3.47
Overall height (feet)	99.44
Overall width (feet)	73.47
Static (useful) lift (pounds)	12,470
Dynamic lift (pounds)	4,000
Cruising speed (knots)	40
Radius (nautical miles)	1,360
Range (nautical miles)	3,400
Endurance (hours)	85
Control car: length (feet)	83.0
Width (feet)	11.14
Overall height (feet)	24.2
Weight (gross) (pounds)	36,469
Power plant (2)	Wright R-1300-2, 1 stage supercharger, 800 hp at 2,600 rpm take-off, 700 hp at 2,400 rpm normal, Curtiss electric propellers, arc 18'1"

A ZPG-2 drops a practice bomb. Navy Lakehurst Historical Society photo.

The ZPG-2 Airships

Flights of the ZPN-1 prompted a need for design improvements. These were incorporated into the production models, originally designated ZP2N-1, then later ZPG-2. The major change from the ZPN-1 was an increase in envelope size to accommodate heavier electronics including more sophisticated radar, and armament. The Goodyear project number was GZ-14 and three contracts for the type were issued. These contracts were 51-093 (1951), 52-984 (1952) and 55-169 (1955). Envelopes in each of these contracts differed in some cases using 3-ply envelopes with a lift of 12,800 pounds, 3-ply with a lift of 11,500 pounds, 2-ply with a lift of 13,600 pounds and 2-ply with a lift of 14,700 pounds. The values shown above were routinely exceeded in operations. The ZPG-2 was the most successful postwar Navy airship and its record achievements stand to this day. The code name recommended for the ZPG-2 was *Seafarer*, which was approved. In 1962 the airship designation was revised to SZ-1B.

ZPG-2-types by Navy serial number:

ZPG-2 (1) - Serial 126716, Goodyear order 500 and serial 4036, envelope D-496 (975,000 cubic feet, 3-ply cotton), control car C-220, completed in March 1953. Held for tests at Akron, it was delivered to the Navy on 6 October. Assigned to Chief of Naval Airship Training and Experimental Command (CNATE), many test flights were carried out and it became apparent the ZPG-2 could exceed the endurance promised by Goodyear. Made one flight of 77.1 hours in April 1954. On 17 May departed Lakehurst with a crew of fourteen. With CDR M. H. Eppes in command, 126716 flew to the area of Nova Scotia, south over the Atlantic, Bermuda, Nassau, toward Puerto Rico and the Caribbean and on to Florida.

126716 landed at Key West, Florida on 25 May with an official time of 200.20 unrefueled hours (8.3 days) in the air. CDR Eppes was awarded the Distinguished Flying Cross, presented by Admiral Rosendahl at the Lighter-Than-Air Society Banquet in 14 October 1954, the Lighter-Than-Air Society Achievement Award for 1954, and in 1955 the Harmon International Trophy for Aeronauts. The Air Medal was awarded to the entire crew, which included LCDR R.B. Levitt, LT R. E. Duncan, ALC W. P. Koll, AMC (AP) J. F. Tucker, ALC P. G. Richter, ADAN J. R. Regier, ADC R. N. Hansen, AT2 H. G. Mitchell, AD2 R.C. Hart, AM2 J.A. Reinhart, AN V. J. Hudson and C.R. Porter, Jr. and E.L. Moore of Goodyear. On 18 November 1954, during a 24-hour training flight, an in-flight emergency occurred. A small fuel leak developed and, while attempting to repair it, the fuel tank fitting broke and fuel flooded the bottom of the control car. Since the internal engines were well sealed-off from the interior air of the car, a fire did not occur. On landing, with one engine and no take-off power for a wave-off, the tower reported a fire aboard. The "fire" turned out to be the vaporized fuel streaming from the car.

ZPG-2 (2) - Serial 126717, Goodyear order 500 and serial 4037, envelope D-497 (975,000 cubic feet, Neoprene), control car C-221, first flight at Akron 20 March 1953, delivered to Lakehurst 19 June 1953. 01 February 1960 made first flight of "Operation Whole Gale," Lundi Moore, command pilot; on station 40.8 hours.

ZPG-2 (3) - Serial 126718, Goodyear order 500 and serial 4038, envelope D-498 (975,000 cubic feet), control car C-222. First flight at Akron 19 May 1953 with Goodyear test pilot, Walter Massic. Delivered to Lakehurst 03 November 1953, airship log presented by H.W. Crum, Goodyear Aircraft sales manager to CDR V.E. Tieg at Akron. Crew on flight from Akron to Lakehurst included LT R.E Colopy, command pilot, LT A.E. DeWachter, first pilot, LT D.D. Crowder, second pilot, Bureau of Aeronautics representatives CDR V.E. Tieg and LT R.F. McInnes, C.E. Morton, AL1, E.P. Moccia, AMC, J.A. Caudel, ALC, J.J. Vrboncic, ADC, L.E. Blase, AD1 and E.C. McCullough, AM2. Excessive snow deflated the envelope at South Weymouth, MA 11 April 1958.

ZPG-2 hovers above the oiler USS *Canasted* (AO-99) preparing for a 1958 refueling using the hose method. In this photo by Ted Boyer, the areas of the envelope corresponding to the air ballonets, left unpainted to save weight, are sharply defined on the envelope painted to cut down on helium seepage.

ZPG-2 (4) - Serial 126719, Goodyear order 500 and serial 4039, envelope D-499 (975,000 cubic feet, 20 ply cotton), control car C-223, delivered to Lakehurst 24 January 1954. Used for the training of Marines in airship handling landing procedures and techniques in 1957 (LCDR R. Shannon, command pilot, and Chief Aviation Pilot W. Brewer) at Cherry Point, NC. With ZP-3, involved in a hard landing at McCalla Field, Guantanamo, Cuba on 11 February 1958, resulting in car damage, envelope not deflated. 126719 was overhauled at Lakehurst in June 1958 and assigned to evaluate the use of lighter-than-air craft for support of research in the Arctic. Based at South Weymouth with Naval Air Development Unit (NADU) and nicknamed "Snow Goose." 126719 flew with a crew of fourteen, commanded by CDR H.B. Van Gorder, to Resolute Bay in the Arctic. The crew included LCDRs H. Collins and A. Schou, Canadian observers, scientists and a reporter from the Associated Press. The flight departed South Weymouth 27 July 1958, was weather-postponed at Lakehurst. Second attempt was fouled by hot weather and headwinds, landed at Akron and five crewmen left the airship. 126719 refueled at Lakehead Airport, Ontario, north of Lake Superior. It arrived at Churchill, Manitoba on Hudson Bay 04 August 1958. 126719 reached Air Force Ice Station T-3, 400 miles from the North Pole in the Arctic Ocean, on 09 August, where it dropped a packet of mail to the isolated scientists. Returning, 126719 overflew Resolute Bay, refueled at Churchill and returned to South Weymouth 12 August. 6,200 miles had been covered which included two landings and refuelings on Canadian runways. When asked for a witness for his report on crossing the Arctic Circle, CDR Van Gorder answered "one polar bear." 126719 flew over Glynco, GA on 23 September 1959.

ZPG-2 (5) - Serial 135445, Goodyear order 1792 and serial 4066, envelope D-570 (975,000 cubic feet), control car C-249, delivered to Lakehurst 01 April 1954. With ZX-11 at NAS Key West on 15 Feburary 56, a premature unmasting was followed by a temporary loss of thrust; once airborne, a gearbox oil leak was noticed forcing a decision to return to base. Dropping ballast to land, thrust was again lost and the airship struck the ground drifting to port. Bouncing through high-tension lines and dragging along the ground for 4800 feet, the crew abandoned ship and pulled the rip cord.

Egress via the side hatch was more challenging without the ground equipment ladder designed to reach over the ZPG-2 radome. Larry Rodrigues photo.

ZPG-2 (6) - Serial 135446, Goodyear order 1792 and serial 4067, envelope D-571 (975,000 cubic feet), control car C-250, delivered to Lakehurst 06 July 1954. Participated in "Operation Whole Gale," Casey Sucicki, pilot. In March, 135446 set a record of 63 hours on station during 72.9 hours in the air. Masting at Lakehurst 13 October 1960, 135446 overrode the mast when the port pitch propeller motor failed. Skillful handling of the mast tractor by J.R. Capute prevented damage; Capute was commended. Deflated 09 August 1956 at Lakehurst when the catenary failed.

ZPG-2 (7) - Serial 135447, Goodyear order 1792 and serial 4068, envelope D-572 (975,000 cubic feet), control car C-251, delivered to Lakehurst 22 November 1954. 135447 kited on its mast 21 June 1956, causing internal suspension cables to part which tore holes in the envelope. (The Goodyear "accident report" indicates this envelope number but serial 4067 (135446). Also listed as 1955. It is assumed this is the correct envelope number and the airship is as shown.)

ZPG-2 (8) - Serial 135448, Goodyear order 1792 and serial 4069, envelope D-573 (975,000 cubic feet), control car C-573, delivered to Lakehurst 29 August 1955. Following an ASW training exercize, while attempting a radar approach Lakehurst's instrument conditions 14 May 1959, 13448 collided with the Hangar No. Three and deflated. Crewmen injured were LTJG R.W. Sirch, command pilot, LT R.D. Ecoff, pilot, LT L.R. Harsh, LTJG C.P. Roemer, ENS S.R. McNabb, and AV1C L.J. Cranston, LTJG D.M. Loyd was killed.

ZPG-2 (9) - Serial 141559, Goodyear order 8042 and serial 4081, envelope D-610 (975,000 cubic feet), delivered to Lakehurst 15 March 1956. 141559 was one of two ZPG-2 types to be kept in service following termination of airship operation orders 26 June 1961. It served as the second "flying wind tunnel" airship. The first demonstration was 23 May 1961, with CAPT M.H. Eppes, pilot. 141559 made last flight of a Navy airship, 31 August 1962. This flight departed Lakehurst at 2:00 PM with pilots CDR Robert Shannon, pilot, Lundi Moore, co-pilot, and honorary co-pilots CDRs W.D. Ashe, Max Cawley, Angy James and Gordon Burke, with VADM C.E. Rosendahl, CAPT F.N. Klein, Jr. and CAPT R.F. Schultz (Klein's successor as C.O. at Lakehurst). The last Navy airship flew over the Lakehurst/Tom's River/ Lakewood, NJ area and landed at 3:36 PM. The pressure watch ceased on 24 September. Deflation and disassembly of the Navy's last airship was completed in December, 1962.

ZPG-2 (10) - Serial 141560, Goodyear order 8042 and serial 4082, envelope D-611 (975,000 cubic feet), control car number C-265, delivered to Lakehurst 07 June 1956. Standby airship for "Operation Whole Gale." With ZP-3 on 18 February with Claude Macon, pilot, it was subjected to bad snow and icing conditions with the load so heavy the nose wheel would not go into the lock position. The nose wheel was forced in by the use of a fork truck. Enough snow and ice were lost for take-off and 141560 went on station. The weather was still bad at Lakehurst, and it was diverted to Bermuda after completing the on station requirements. 0n 20 Feburary landing conditions were unacceptable at Bermuda and three inflight refuelings were accomplished awaiting a clearing, at which time the winch failed. Slightly damaged during the following gusty landing that collapsed the already damaged nose gear.

The most famous ZPG-2 of all, the "561". US Navy Photo.

ZPG-2 (11) - Serial 141561, Goodyear order 8042 and serial 4083, envelope D-612, (975,000 cubic feet), control car number unknown. Delivered to Lakehurst 01 October 1956, nicknamed *Snowbird*. Commanded by CDR Jack R. Hunt, it departed South Weymouth, Massachusetts, on 04 March 1957. Hunt's all volunteer crew included CDR Ronald W. Hoel and LCDR Robert S. Bowser (co-pilots), LTs Stanley W. Dunton and Charles J. Eadie (navigators), LT John R. Fitzpatrick and Edgar L. Moore of Goodyear (flight engineers), CPO Lee N. Steffen (crew chief and radar/radioman), PO1 William S. Dehn, Jr. (aerology and photography), PO1 Thomas L. Cox and PO2 James R. Burkett (flight mechanics), PO1 Carl W. Meyer (electrician), PO2 Francis J. Maxymillion (radar/radioman with Chief Steffen), and PO2 George A. Locklear (rigger, doubling with Dehn as cook). CDR Hoel was commanding officer of the Naval Air Development Unit (NADU) at South Weymouth and senior officer aboard. 141561 flew the Atlantic via the Azores, flew past the southern tip of Portugal, then the Canary and Cape Verde Islands. Passing over Africa near Casablanca and Port Lyautey, it flew back across the Atlantic to Puerto Rico and the Caribbean, finally landing at Key West, Florida, on 15 March. "561" had surpassed the record of 200.2 hours of unrefueled flight established by ZPG-2-126716 in 1954 and on the same day (13 March) surpassed the 6,980 mile distance record established by the *Graf Zeppelin* in August 1929. On landing, "561" had flown 264.2 hours (11 days) and a distance of 9,448 miles, after having flown in the area of three continents. No aircraft of any type has ever flown that far or remained aloft for that period of time without refueling, a record that stands to this day. All crewmembers were presented with awards and commendations at Key West by retired ADM William F. Halsey, Jr. on the behalf of President Eisenhower and the Navy. CDR Hunt was awarded the Lighter-Than-Air Society Achievement Award for 1957. He also received the Harmon International Trophy for Aeronauts from President Eisenhower at the White House on 12 November 1957. 141561 participated in "Operation Whole Gale" with Wendell Brewster, pilot. After taking off 22 February with 15,000 pounds of fuel, "561" remained on station 62 hours, 45 minutes. On 26 February it returned to Lakehurst to lower a sailor to visit his seriously ill father.

Serving as a research vehicle for a classified infrared project ("Clinker") that had begun in 1960, it was ferried (03 through 07 January 1961) to the Marine Corps Air Facility, Santa Ana, California, via Laughlin Air Force Base, Del Rio, Texas. It was the largest non-rigid airship to cross the Rockies, and its mast had to be shipped by rail. Renamed *Falcon* and displaying a large number "12" on the car side (above, from *All Hands* magazine) it was the last Navy airship to operate at Santa Ana, California, January through March 1961. The public story was released as "Temperatures of Coast Air & Water being measured," with LCDR William Place as project co-coordinator. Pilots included LTJG P. M. Platt and LTJG W.P. Riordan. "561" departed from Santa Ana 06 March on non-stop flight to Glynco, Georgia. "561" was retained in service (with 141559) after all other airships were ordered retired, 26 June 1961.

The final pressure watch was made 24 September 1962 and on 25 September the storage process started. The control car was later donated to the St. Louis National Museum of Transport, however no action was taken due to the cost of transportation to the location. The control car was stored but not maintained in hangar no. 5 until 1990. Then, little more than a hulk, it was moved outside where it was located in March 1991.

The National Museum of Naval Aviation expressed an interest in preserving and displaying 144561 but the means of transportation to Pensacola was a problem. In March 1992 an Air Force Reserve Transport Squadron based at McGuire Field (Fort Dix), New Jersey was seeking missions for its C-5A weekend training and the result of an investigation revealed that, with some disassembly, the control car could be transported in a C-5A. A somewhat destructive disassembly of the upper deck was necessary. On 31 March the car was moved to McGuire Field on a lowboy trailer and loaded aboard a C-5A. On 04 April the control car arrived at Pensacola where its pieces were piled in an outside location. As of this writing there is little visible means of restoring the now dismembered hulk.

ZPG-2 (12) - Serial 141562, Goodyear order 4084 and serial 4084, envelope D-613 (975,000 cubic feet), delivered to Lakehurst 03 December 1956. Participated in "Operation Whole Gale", CDR Lundi Moore, pilot, and remained on station for 95 hours 29 March 1960. (The original pilot was to be LCDR Ernest Downey; however, he became ill and passed away in the hospital. It was in his memory that this record flight was made.) It was deflated at Lakehurst 16 February 1958 while attempting to remove snow with fire hose spray. ZPG-2-141562 was repaired and returned to service.

ZPG-2 main deck. Larry Rodrigues photo.

ZPG-2s were assigned to "Operation Whole Gale," the last major fleet operation for Navy airships. Atlantic Fleet opinion at the time was that airships could not carry out modern tactics in anti-submarine warfare, while the Airship Wings were convinced they had such capabilities. Taken on as a challenge or dare, the flying was to be performed in the worst possible winter months at Lakehurst, February and March. (In weather terminology, a whole gale is a continuous wind of at least 55 miles per hour.) The units assigned were Lakehurst's ZP-1 and ZP-3, with CAPT F.N. Klein, Jr. as chief coordinator. Six airships were assigned and five crews were assigned with CDRs Ray Dahler and Herman G. Spahr as Command Duty Officers to oversee the operation (24 hours on, 24 hours off). Pilots Claude Macon and Lundi Moore replaced Dahler and Spahr with ZP-1 for flying duty. ZPG-2 airships and combat air crews assigned were 126716, Claude Macon, CAC 301; 126717, Lundi Moore, CAC 302; 135446, Casey Sucicki, CAC 303; 141560, standby airship; 141561, Wendell Brewster, CAC 305; and 141562, Walt Collins, CAC 306. CAC 304 was divided among the other five crews. This provided six pilots in addition to the pilot in charge, and the 14 men in each crew. The basic rules established were:

1. Never launch an airship with less than six pilots aboard. (This was violated on several occasions when five were sent, but only under good weather conditions.)

The ZPG-2's powerful winch was used to lower a and collect seawater for ballast, compensating for weight of fuel burned off in the engines. L Rodrigues photo.

2. Use heavy "Mules" whenever possible to handle the airships on the ground. In bad winds, as many as four heavy DW-20 Mules were used on the tail and two light Mules on the mast to prevent overturning.

3. On return from patrol, the minimum amount of fuel aboard over the base was to be for 10 hours, or 2,000 pounds. (This was broken several times in difficult situations.)

The "On Station" area patrolled was from approximately 150 miles due east of Lakehurst to about 250 miles from SSE of Lakehurst, beginning 25 miles off shore. The mission was to maintain at least one airship over that area 24 hours a day for the entire two months. Submarines could be expected to penetrate the area at any time and the airships were to detect them and maintain sonar contact if possible. Operations began at midnight 01 February 1960. 126716 established a record when it took-off with 15,000 pounds of fuel and remained on station 62 hours, 45 minutes. The results of "Operation Whole Gale" were that the airships were on station 882 hours and 61 heavier-than-air operations had been flown for 92.8% continuous coverage during February. In March, 765 airship hours and 89 heavier-than-air hours were flown. The on-station coverage for the two month period was slightly over 88%, far better than projected. There was no question that airships could operate in any kind of weather.

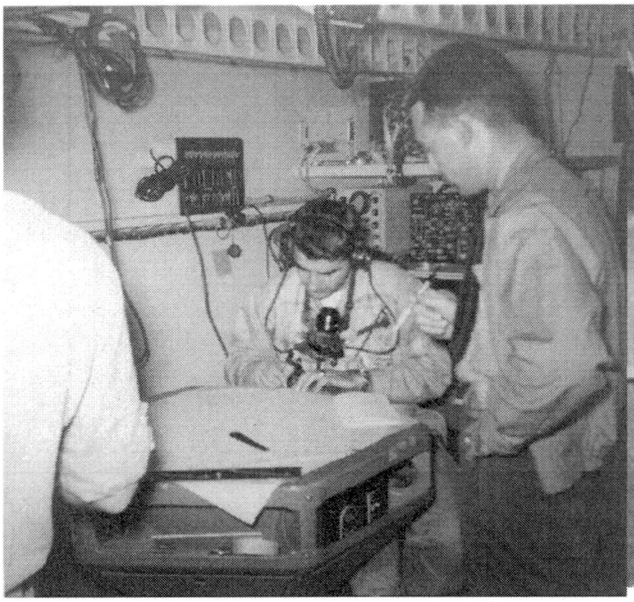

A tour of the Navy's most successful postwar airship is given in these Larry Rodrigues' photos and other photos courtesy Robert Slate.

On 9 July 1960, a ZPG-2 from Lakehurst sighted four people from an overturned motorboat stranded on an island in Barnegat Bay. The Coast Guard was notified and the people rescued.

ZPG-2 and ZPG-2W general specifications:

Volume (cubic feet)	975,000
Ballonets (4) (cubic feet)	247,300
Overall length (feet)	342.65
Maximum diameter (feet)	75.42
Overall height (feet)	94.68
Overall width (feet)	75.42 (same as diameter)
Static (useful) lift (pounds)	5,103 (2W 11,200)
Dynamic lift (pounds)	6,000
Speed, maximum (knots)	68.5
Speed, cruising (knots)	40
Crew (normal)	14
Performance at 40 knots,	full military load, 12,940 pounds of fuel, after a heavy take-off of 6,000 pounds
Range (nautical miles)	2,100
Radius (nautical miles)	840
Endurance (hours)	52.5
Armament:	Optional load of three types of torpedoes, two types of depth charges, no more than two of each (inside control car),
Engines: 2	Wright R-1300-2A. 800 HP at 2,600 rpm at take-off, 700 HP at 2,400 rpm normal. Curtiss 3 bladed electric propellers, 16' 7" diameter.

ZPG-2 deliveries

1953	1954	1955	1956	Totals
Jun (126717)	Jan (126719)	Aug (135448)	Mar (141559)	
Oct (126716)	Apr (135445)		June (141560)	
Nov (126718)	July (135446)		Oct (141561)	
	Nov (135447)		Dec (141562)	
Subtotal 3	4	1	4	12

An advanced auxiliary power unit (APU) is hoisted into place aft. The APU not only provided power for the avionics suite, but also added enough ballast to reduce the number of sandbags needed on the ground. The common APU mounting was to be suspended under the nose landing gear, normally partially folded up to allow the ship to weathervane at the mast. Note direction of main wheels. Larry Rodrigues photo.

ZPG-2 airships in storage after 1 July 1961 included; 126717; 126718; 126719; 135447; 141560 and 141562. 141559 and 141561 were in storage on 1 September 1962. Salvage operations started with all thirteen airships then in storage. Salvage was completed in February 1964.

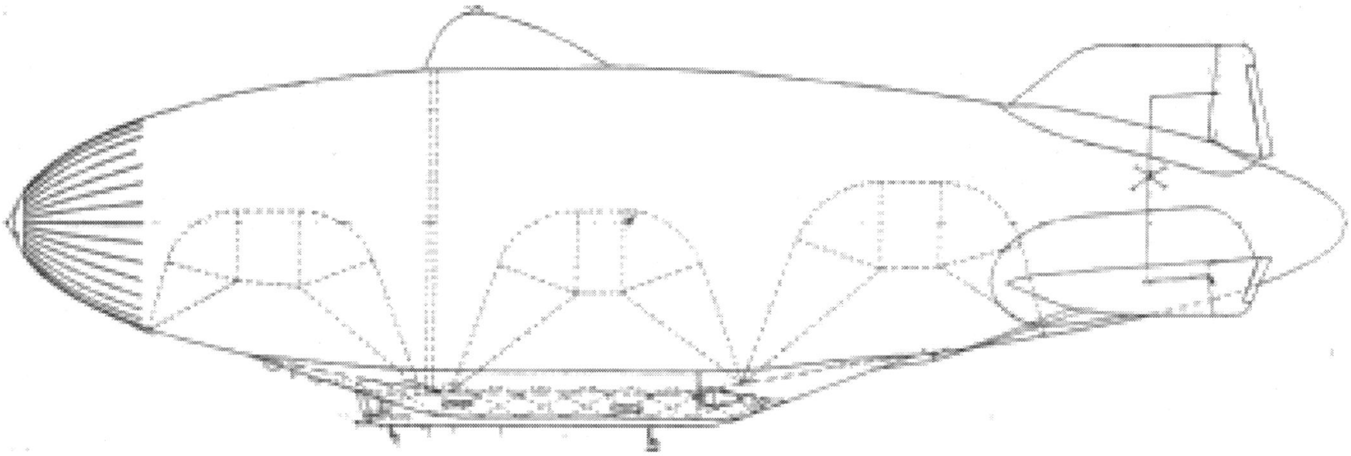

GZ-13 proposal. Goodyear / Jeff Cook.

Outline specification OS-135 was issued 16 April 1954 for a "barrier airship". The Goodyear GZ-16 reached the car mock-up stage and the final selection process with two and four engine versions. The four engine version was preferred by the Navy on grounds of increased safety and fuel economy. This version was to have a 22 man crew with the latest internal and top-mounted radar. Due to the size of 2,800,000 cubic feet, the GZ-16 was comparable in volume to the rigid airship USS *Los Angeles*. Many considered the rigid type superior in this size. Goodyear conducted comparative studies which indicated both of equal merit. The non-rigid was preferred, based on the use of existing technology and the fact that tooling and training to produce a rigid airship would be extremely expensive. The GZ-16 control car was to be of the short, double-deck type that were suitable for rail transport in the event of a deflation away from the main base and preferred by the Navy. Goodyear preferred the longer, single deck control car and their drawings indicate this type of control car. Power plants were to be on the outside of the control car and the control surfaces were to be the inverted "Y" configuration for tail clearance during heavy take-off. The Navy expected the need for an airship of this type to be viable into the late 1960's, when more advanced space borne systems would be available. The non-rigid type was selected, based on lower cost and shorter lead time; however, many in the Navy continued to question the decision. Eventually the GZ-16 was abandoned for greater numbers of the ZPG-2W and ZPG-3W.

General specifications of the proposed Goodyear GZ-16, ZW-1.

Volume (cubic feet):	2,800,000
Ballonets 4, total volume, (cubic feet):	778,700
Fineness ratio:	4.175
Empennage (control surfaces, 3, square feet):	6,855
Propeller type:	Curtiss-Wright, electric, 3 blades
Propeller diameter (feet):	18

The ZPG-2W-type (ZP2N-1W) Airships

The ZPG-2W type was originally designated as ZP2N-1W and was a ZPG-2 (which was an anti-submarine warfare [ASW] airship) specifically modified for airborne early warning (AEW). The Goodyear project number was GZ-14. The general specifications were the same as the ZPG-2. The only exceptions were changes necessary for the AEW electronics. A large radar dome was located on top of the envelope, for height finding, and featured access by vertical sleeve through the helium filled cell. The height finding equipment notified search operators of altitude which was combined with range and bearing data and used to direct defensive aircraft to the targets. A large antenna was located in a radome below the control car. Mock-ups were completed by Goodyear in May 1953. A total of five ZPG-2W types were constructed, the last unit referred to as a ZPG-2W(M) or ZPG-2 1/2. The original procurement was for one unit, but this was increased to two with inclusion on contract 52-984 (1952) for four ZPG-2 types. The second contract for three types was 55-169 (1955). ZPG-2W airships were in service from 1955 to 30 June 1961. Cost of the ZPG-2W program was $23,000,000.

<u>ZPG-2W (1)</u> - Serial 137832, Goodyear order 1792 and serial 4077, envelope D-590 (975,000 cubic feet), control car C-260, first flight at Akron in January 1955, delivered to Lakehurst 26 May 1955. Partially deflated after rubbing against a light in one of the Lakehurst hangars, envelope repaired. Kited while undocking at Lakehurst 08 May 1956 tipping over the mast and deflating the envelope, repaired. On 27 March 1959, 137832 was on stand-by for barrier patrol. It had been undocked in the morning and, by the afternoon, sleet and snow covered the envelope. The winds were too strong to attempt docking so a fly-away crew of four officers and four enlisted men took-off in a very heavy condition (reported as approximately 9,000 pounds). The forward ballonets were adjusted to maintain an even trim, but when take-off was made the ice and snow slid off the bow and the bow rose to an extremely high nose-up position (approximately 30 degrees). The ship wanted to settle tail first and the slip tanks could not be dumped due to the bow high position. There was no visibility in the snow. The ship was in the air for twelve hours with the crew sitting on the backs of their seats. Warmer air to melt the snow on the envelope could not be found and at times the inclination was 45 degrees. It was eventually landed at Cherry Point, North Carolina. A check of the catenary cables found them a little out of limits. Following a mission on 11 March 1960 during a night landing approach the starboard landing gear and low port rudervator collided with a building roof. The ship was landed with no injuries.

ZPG-2W (2) - Serial 139918, Goodyear order 1792 and serial 4078, envelope D-599 (975,000 cubic feet), control car number uncertain, delivered to Lakehurst 21 December 1955. With ZW-1 in 1957, on 14 November it suffered a gearbox failure and proceeded back to Lakehurst on the starboard engine. A landing attempt was partially successful when gusts prevented the starboard mule from connecting, and a waveoff was attempted. Attempting to avoid hitting the hangar, the airship struck a parked mast, gashing the envelope.

ZPG-2W (3) - Serial 141334, Goodyear order 8042 and serial 4079, envelope D-608 (975,000 cubic feet), control car number uncertain, delivered to Lakehurst 30 April 1956.

ZPG-2W (4) - Serial 141335, Goodyear order 8042 and serial 4080, envelope D-609 (975,000 cubic feet), control car number uncertain, delivered to Lakehurst 08 August 1956. At the end of a planned 24 hour mission beginning 3 December 1959, strong headwinds precluded return to Lakehurst, diverted to Bermuda, total flying time 47.6 hours, George Allen, command pilot. Severe gusts drove the nose down, collapsing the nose gear and damaging the radome; a second attempt resulted in more damage before the ship was masted. Records show 141335 was deflated in December 1959 when it brushed against another airship in a Lakehurst hangar during undocking.

ZPG-2W (5) - Serial 141563, Goodyear order 8042 and serial 4085, envelope D-614 (975,000 cubic feet), control car number uncertain, first flight 21 May 1957. It encountered several storms with winds up to 65 miles per hour on a test flight near Akron 19 June 1957, no damage occurred; delivered to Lakehurst 25 October 1957. 141563 was a modified ZPG-2W and is referred to as a ZPG-2W (M) 2 1/2 in Goodyear records. The APS-70 radar antenna used inside the ZPG-2W (M) envelope was a dipole unit which measured forty feet. (The ZPG-3W used a "bed spring" flat configured antenna of forty feet in width.) The lack of a lower car radome gave this airship its unique appearance. It was likely the test bed for the ZPG-3W type that made its first flight in September 1958. 141563 was deflated in a ground handling accident at South Weymouth, Massachusetts 09 January 1959.

Fire hoses were used to cool the envelope, as with "832" at left, to prevent helium loss when summer heat and conditions conspired to reduce pressure height to zero. During Project Lincoln, snow removal tests included the use of a special mast extension (not shown) to blast snow and ice off topside.
Dan Brady photo.

During one test, RADM Charles Lyman stated a ZPG-2W had successfully tracked the Regulus missile by radar. Due to a permeability problem, some older envelopes were painted to improve helium retention. Unpainted trapezoidal sections visible in photographs are the ballonet areas, left unpainted to save unnecessary weight. Since this proved to be satisfactory and saved weight, the practice was continued by the Navy on some replacement envelopes. Goodyear produced five spare ZPG-2W envelopes, D-598, contract 52-984), D-622 (contract 55-169), D-630, D-631 and D-632 (contract N383-58746 and all Dacron). The code name recommended for the ZPG-2W was *Reliance*, which was approved. In 1962 the airship designation was revised to EZ-1B. The ZPG-2W airships were deflated and stored by November 1960 and finally stripped of usable parts and salvaged by February 1964.

The ZPG-3W (EZ-1C) Airships

In June 1954, Goodyear received a letter of intent from the Navy for a contract for the development, design and the construction of a mock-up of the XZWG-1, a non-rigid airship of approximately 2,500,000 cubic feet (Goodyear project GZ-16). Development was performed and the mock-up built when the Navy decided not to complete the design and construction due to economics and a change in requirements. The XZWG-1 was canceled 01 July 1955 and Goodyear received a letter of intent on 21 November 1955 for the ZPG-3W. Detail specifications included the phrase "all-weather" and the primary mission to be "all-weather AEW patrols of long endurance in open ocean areas at an altitude of 5,000 feet. The design ballonet ceiling shall be 10,000 feet." The Goodyear project number was GZ-17. Engineering effort consisted of 1,560,000 man-hours, with 378 engineers assigned at the peak in March 1956. There were 102,000 hours of static tests, 130,000 man-hours for the flight test program, 40,000 man-hours on the engine test stands. The effort produced 120,000 square feet of drawings, 4,800 pages of handbooks, and 26,000 pages of reports.

The ZPG-3W was a totally new design and was specifically designed for airborne early warning (AEW) (the ZPG-2W was adapted from the ZPG-2). The ZPG-3W was equipped with a radar antenna, 40 feet in width, revolving inside the envelope. Four units were constructed on Navy contract 56-383 (1956). They remain the largest non-rigid airships ever built and were last flown in 1960. The code name recommended for the ZPG-3W was *Vigilant*, which was approved. In 1962 the designation was revised type EZ-1C. Cost of the ZPG-3W program was $54,000,000.

ZPG-3W (1) - Serial 144242, Goodyear order 8572 and serial 4096, envelope D-619 (1,465,000 cubic feet), first flown at Akron 21 July 1958. Dean Mealy, Goodyear test pilot, flew with a test crew of 21. The structural flight test airship, it remained at Akron for extensive flight tests. It was delivered to Lakehurst 24 September 1959, by Goodyear test and delivery pilots Walter Bjerre and Russell Crosier and Navy witness pilots LCDRs G.R. Keiser and G.J. Krueger. Tests at Lakehurst were conducted by LCDR R.W. Widdecombe of ZW-1. The first operational barrier flight held on station 49.3 hours, more than double the patrol of the ZPG-2W. With ZW-1 on 25 Feburary 1960 an improperly manufactured gear train gave a down-and-locked indication without the gear being locked. Upon landing the starboard propellor contacted the ground and the ship was waved off. Ballast was dropped, the second attempt damaged the tail, and a third landing was successful. On 06 July 1960, 144242 departed Lakehurst on a routine patrol mission, but with orders to search for a missing yacht. Aboard were LT J.J. Saniuk, command pilot, LT R.E. Leonard, LT O.V. Montgomery, ENS R.H. Pipes, co-pilot, R.H. Clopper, radio operator, LT R.V. Hall, R.C. Kuesel, L.J. Coutu, gunner's mate Ist class, F.M. Furney, aviation structural mechanic, S.B. Thompson, flight mechanic, F.J. Rosley, flight technician, E.B. Turner, Jr., air controller, H.V. Goldbold, air controller, D.L. Saumier, J.G. Culligan, Garrison, Blalock and A. Contreras. (This is not a complete list of the those aboard, lacks three names.) At 2:30 PM an accident occurred which caused deflation off the New Jersey coast near Barnegat Bay with the drowning of 18 of the 21 crewmen aboard. The three survivors were Saumier, Culligan and Contreras. There are many stories connected with this crash that probably helped seal the doom of airships in the Navy.

The reason for the crash seems most likely to have been low envelope pressure, as the airship was witnessed with a sag in the middle several minutes prior to the crash. This indicated the pressure had been allowed to become dangerously low, but low pressure would not by itself cause a tear. The airship apparently buckled, then pitched into the ocean. The impact with the water burst the envelope. After recovery of the wreckage, inspection revealed the rupture did not start in the seam. As is usually the case in such incidents all sorts of other theories were presented from pilot inexperience to improper maintenance. The most logical explanation was presented after extensive investigation by Goodyear. An inexperienced crewman had placed the circuit breakers that controlled air ballonet pressure in an open position while attempting to correct a radar feed pressurization problem. (This was verified in the wreckage of the control car.) The pilot was unaware of this, and he was on automatic control. The loss of pressure was not noticed by the pilot until the nose buckled and the airship pitched down. Also trained in airplanes, the pilot likely instinctively pulled the nose up and gunned the engines. This was the wrong reaction and the nose was forced into the sea.

A trial for $8,000,000 in damages for 11 of the lost crewmen (Saniuk, Leonard, Montgomery, Pipes, Clopper, Coutu, Furney, Thompson, Roseley, Turner and Goldbold) opened in the New York City Federal Court 10 April 1967. The suit was brought against Goodyear Aircraft, builder of the airship; Goodyear Tire and Rubber, builder of the envelope fabric; and the Edwards Company, makers of the warning bell to sound an alarm when the helium pressure fell below a certain limit. The basis of the lawsuit was that the airship had plunged into the ocean following a 135 foot long tear of the envelope. They contended the tear was due to an improperly manufactured seam. The suit against Goodyear and Edwards was dropped on the third day of the trial. The Goodyear analysis was not presented to the court due to the harassing objections by the lawyers opposing Goodyear, the length of time it would have taken for all witnesses to testify, and the fact that Goodyear was already absolved of any negligence. The case was dismissed, then appealed to the Supreme Court on 10 April 1968, and finally denied 14 October 1968. The litigation that started 02 March 1961 was not totally resolved until 08 November 1968.

Not everyone agreed with Goodyear's analysis. An experienced pilot asked what, other than a massive envelope failure could have caused such sudden loss of lift; it would not have been possible to deliberately fly the airship into the water with such a fatal airplane-like impact. One wonders if Navy officials were really interested at this point in time, as the airships were already scrapped and their facilities gutted or reworked to other purposes.

<u>ZPG-3W (2)</u> - Serial 144243, Goodyear order 8572 and serial 4097, envelope D-620 (1,465,000 cubic feet). First flown at Akron 06 September 1958 as the electronics flight test airship; delivered to Lakehurst 19 June 1959. Goodyear pilot-in-charge was Walter Bjerre. Thomas A. Knowles, President of Goodyear Aircraft, presented the log to Lakehurst's commanding officer, CAPT J.R. Van Evera. 144243 flew AT & D experimental flights; 29.3 hours 14-16 August 1959, 38.8 hours 19-22 AUG 59. The longest flight made was 77.5 hours. 144243 was deflated while docking during a wet snow fall on 25 February 1960. Repaired less its upper antenna, '243' made its final flight (South Weymouth to Lakehurst) on 5 May 1960, George Allen, command pilot. Following the deflation of all Navy airships in 1962, the control car of 144243 was stored at Lakehurst in the event of questions regarding the legal proceedings in the 1960 loss of 141242. It was stored until November 1986 when transferred to the Goodyear Airdock for evaluation for

use in study for a prototype surveillance airship. There was discussion of shipping it to the National Museum of Naval Aviation at Pensacola, Florida in 1987. In 1988, CDR C.H. Mills (USNR, Ret.) proposed to the Naval Air Systems Command that the control car be mated to an envelope of 1,750,000 cubic feet, as an interim testbed airship. This request was denied based on bringing the design up to Navy standards and meeting current safety codes. The control car was finally shipped 24/28 April 1989 from Akron to Davis-Mothan Air Force Base, Arizona, for storage pending possible future restoration by the National Air and Space Museum.

ZPG-3W (3) - Serial 144296, Goodyear order 8572 and serial 4102, envelope D-625 (1,465,000 cubic feet), first flown at Akron 21 October 1959, delivered to Lakehurst 17 December 1959. The longest flight made was 58 hours. It made its final flight on 16 June 1960.

ZPG-3W (4) - Serial 144297, Goodyear order 8572 and serial 4103, envelope D-626 (1,465,000 cubic feet), first flown at Akron 01 March 1960. Delivered to Lakehurst 04 April 1960, aboard this flight were Goodyear representatives, Thomas A. Knowles, President, Dr. Karl Arnstein, Chief Engineer, and veteran Navy and Goodyear airship pilot RADM Karl Lange (USNR, Ret.). The longest flight made was 35.5 hours. 144297 made the final flight of a ZPG-3W airship, 22 May 1961.

A ZPG-3W stood radar watch off Washington, D.C. during a forty-hour period when ground radar was down. Spare ZPG-3W envelopes produced by Goodyear were D-621 (cotton); and D-633 and D-634 (both Dacron). ZPG-3W airships were grounded 30 November 1960 after loss of 144242 in July. Only the 144297 flew again. They were all salvaged (except for the control car of 144243) by November 1964.

ZPG-3W. LTAS photo.

ZPG-3W general specifications:

Volume (cubic feet)*	1,465,000
Ballonets (4)(cubic feet)	383,000
Overall Length (feet)	403.4
Maximum diameter (feet)	85.11
Static (useful) lift (pounds)	22,366
Dynamic lift (pounds)	10,500
Maximum Gross Weight (pounds)	93,496
Rate of climb (feet per minute)	2,400
Rate of descent (feet per minute)	1,200
Speed, cruising (knots)	45
Speed, maximum (knots)	82 (94 miles per hour)
Two deck control car length (feet)	83
Crew	25 (Varied)
Endurance, cruising speed (hours)	69 (at 35 knots)
Engines (2, inside)	Wright R-1820-88 Cyclone, 1,275 hp normal, 1,575 hp at takeoff, 3-blade reversible full feathering 18'-0" arc props

* Envelope design volume for the cotton envelope was 1,465,000 cubic feet and was expected to increase to 1,516,000 cubic feet due to stretch or 3.5 %. The demonstrated volumes (based on actual weigh-offs) of the four airships were 1,545,000, 1,542,000 and 1,544,000 cubic feet for the cotton envelopes. The Dacron envelope design volume was 1,490,000 cubic feet based on approximately 1/2 the stretch of the cotton envelope. The demonstrated Dacron envelope volume was 1,509,000.

ZPG-2W and ZPG-3W deliveries

1955	1956	1957	1959	1960	Totals
May (2W-137832)	Apr (2W-141334)	Oc [2 1/2W] - 141563)	June (3W-144243)	Apr (3W-144297)	
Dec (2W-139918)	Aug (2W-141335)		Sep (3W-144242)		
			Dec (3W-144296)		
Subtotals 2	2	1	3	1	9

Airship deliveries 1951 through 1960, exclusive of ZP2K (ZSG-2) and ZP3K (ZSG-3) based on Goodyear records:

	ZSG-4 (ZP4K)	ZS2G-1 (ZP5K)	ZPG-1 (N-1)	ZPG-2 (ZP2N-1)	ZPG-2W (ZPN-2W)	ZPG-3W	Total
1952 June			1				1
1953 June				1			
Oct				1			
Nov				1			
Sub total				3			3
1954 Jan				1			
Apr				1			
June	1						
July				1			
Aug	1						
Sep	1						
Oct	1						
Nov	1			1			
Dec	2						
Sub total	7			4			11
1955 Jan	1						
Feb	1						
Mar	2						
Apr	1	1					
May	1	1			1		
June	1						
July	1	1					
Aug				1			
Oct		1					
Nov		1					
Dec		1			1		
Sub total	8	6		1	2		17
1956 Feb		1					
Mar				1			
Apr					1		
May		1					
June				1			
July		1					
Aug					1		
Sep		1					
Oct		1		1			
Dec		1		1			
Sub total		6		4	2		12
1957 Feb		1					
May		1					
Jul		1					
Oct		1			1		
Sub total		4			1		5
1958 Mar		1					
Jun		1					
Sub total		2					2
1959 Jun						1	
Sep						1	
Dec						1	
Sub totals						3	3
1960 Apr						1	
Sub total						1	1
Totals	15	18	1	12	5	4	55

Airship Inventory, July 1946 through July 1962
(includes airships in storage)

1946 - 93	1949 - 59	1952 - 59	1955 - 61	1958 - 42	1961 - 14
1947 - 66	1950 - 58	1953 - 50	1956 - 51	1959 - 37	1962 - 13
1948 - 56	1951 - 58	1954 - 47	1957 - 54	1960 - 18	

Post World War II Airship Units

Training Command - established 15 May 1943 at Lakehurst, redesignated Training and Experimental Command 06 October 1943, disestablished at Lakehurst in 1953 and transferred to Glynco (ZTG, five airships and two free balloons), reassigned to Lakehurst and disestablished in September 1959.

Fleet Airship Wing 1 - established 20 January 1949 at Lakehurst, transferred to Weeksville in August 1949, transferred back to Lakehurst on 03 September 1957 and disestablished 31 October 1961.

ZP-1 (was ZP-31 established 01 October 1942 at Santa Ana) - established 15 November 1946 at Santa Ana, transferred to Weeksville in 1947 and disestablished 28 June 1957. Redesignated as ZW-1 on 03 January 1961.

ZP-2 (was ZP-12 established 02 January 1942 at Lakehurst) - established 15 November 1946 at Lakehurst, transferred to Glynco in November 1953, transferred back to Lakehurst in September 1959 and disestablished 30 November 1959.

ZP-3 - established 28 Sept. 1950 at Lakehurst and disestablished 31 October 1961.

ZP-4 - established 08 May 1951 at Weeksville and disestablished 28 June 1957.

ZW-1 - established 03 January 1956 (four airships) at Lakehurst, redesignated ZP-1 on 03 January 1961 and disestablished 31 October 1961.

ZX-11 - established 10 May 1950 (four airships) at Key West and disestablished 01 December 1957 with personnel and airships transferred to VX-1 (the first squadron in the Navy to have airships, airplanes and helicopters).

Airship Test and Development - (two airships[18]) 1950 through 1962, Lakehurst.

Naval Air Development (three airships) - 1956 through 1960, South Weymouth.

Naval Air Reserve Units - 1948 through 1958

Lakehurst, Oakland and Akron. (Airship strength of these units varied with the times.)

ZP-51, established 02 June 1947, first reserve squadron, Lakehurst.
ZP-651, established 02 June 1948, second reserve squadron, Naval Air Station, Akron (one airship, housed at Wingfoot Lake).
ZP-751, Lakehurst; ZP-752, Lakehurst; ZP-753, Lakehurst

[18] Airships assigned 30 June 1957

ZP-871, Oakland, California (also one G-type airship, erected at Santa Ana and housed at Moffett Field; USNR photo, right)
ZP-911, Squantum, Massachusetts[19]
ZP-951, Santa Ana, California (five airships at one time)

Airship Serial Numbers Delivered by Goodyear
June 1952 through April 1960

The serial number for ZPN-1 (N-1) was apparently N-1 (1)

126716 through 126719 -	ZPN-1 (ZPG-2) (4)
131919 through 131926 -	ZP4K-1 (ZSG-4) (8)
133639	XZP4K (XSG-4) (1)
134019 through 134034 -	ZSG-4 (ZP4K) (6, last unit produced was 134024, 10 canceled)
135445 through 135448 -	ZP2G-1 (ZPG-2) (4)
137486 through 137491 -	ZS2G-1 (ZP5K-1) (5, apparently 137491 canceled, not shown as completed by Goodyear)
137811	XZS2G-1 (XZP5K-1) (1)
137832	ZPG-2W (1)
139918	ZPG-2W (1)
141334 and 141335	ZPG-2W (2)
141559 through 141562 -	ZPG-2 (4) (141563 was a ZPG-2W)
141563	ZPG-2W (1) (originally shown as a ZPG-2)
141564 through 141570 -	ZS2G-1 (ZP5K-1) (7)
144237 and 14423	ZPG-2 (2, apparently canceled)
144239 through 144241 -	ZS2G-1 (ZP5K-1) (3)
144242 and 14424	ZPG-3W (2) (shown as ZPG-2W)
146294 and 14629	ZS2G-1 (ZP5K-1) (2)
146296 and 14629	ZPG-3W (2)

The basis for the above information is UNITED STATES NAVAL AVIATION, 1910-1970, Appendix VII, Bureau (Serial) Numbers of Naval Aircraft and Goodyear Aircraft Corporation Engineering Project Sheet No. 25, Revision M, November 30, 1956 which lists all airships produced from 1952 through April 1960. As is the case in most of this research information is not only fragmentary, but also conflicting in many cases. A cross-check of information indicates several discrepancies and the Goodyear Engineering Project Sheet has been assumed as the most accurate. For the sake of any future researchers that may attempt to use the serial number appendix to determine airships actually produced during this period, the record will indicate 68 airships and not the actual 55 completed. Discrepancies included in USNA, 1910-1970 include the following:

134025 through 134034,10 - ZSG-4 (ZP4K)-types canceled
137491 included, but not completed by Goodyear
141563 shown as a ZPG-2 when it was actually a ZPG-2W 144237 and 144238 not completed and probably canceled 144242 and 144243 as type ZPG-2W when they were actually type ZPG-3W.

[19] No airships assigned, regularly supported as organized units by Lakehurst.

Decades of Proposals

When Gus Grissom's Mercury capsule was lost in spite of the presence of an entire aircraft carrier group, Admirals Rosendahl and Settle blasted the Navy for not considering that a single airship could have tracked the flight, rescued the astronaut and held the capsule for recovery. As US Navy leadership moved toward a carrier-based fleet, elements not compatible with "flattops" seemed doomed to extinction. In arguments that continue to this day, active duty reformers jousted with retired airshipmen in forums and the press. Within weeks of the last airship flight, the Cuban Missile Crisis demonstrated the US Navy's new lack of long duration aircraft that could actually follow shipping to a distant destination.

One powerful argument made to retire the airships was based on the difficult new mission of defeating nuclear submarines. Unable to "flight the battery" to wear down its submerged adversary, the airship was also hampered by the new subs not showing anything to reflect radar or any exhaust that could be sniffed. When the M-4 and N-1 carried prototype heat sensing gear showing that a nuke boat could be tracked by its heat residue, arguments were made that a faster airplane could search a much larger ocean area in less time. With increased speeds underwater, the subs could turn so swiftly as to outmaneuver a sonar sensing airship, owing to the reaction time, or even outrun by forcing the airship into the wind.

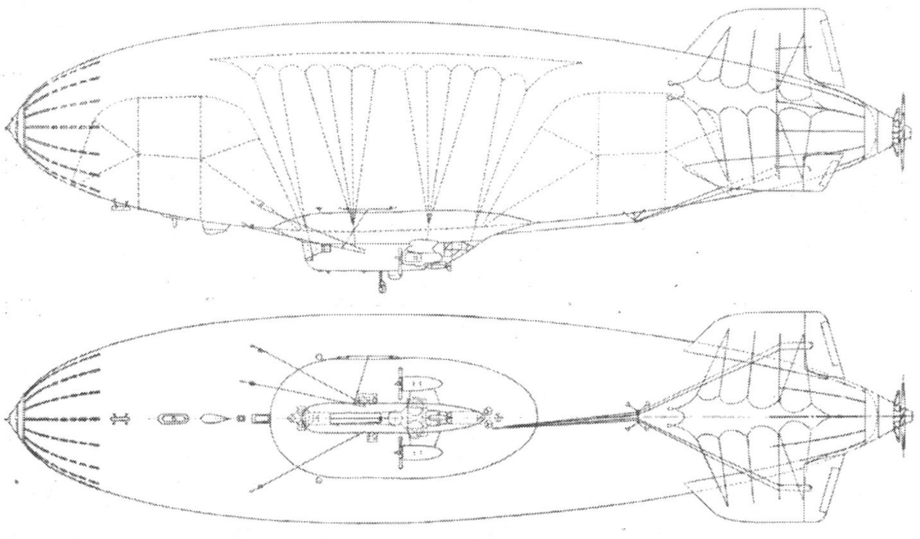

A proposal to equip a 5K with ZPG-3W engines (possibly the "boundary layer" research ship) was shelved. A stern mounted engine, whose prop could have taken advantage of the reduced pressure of the boundary layer, reached the drawing stage (left, via Jeff Cook). Ultimately, the mission to find submarines at sea was no longer dependant on aircraft. The SONUS system, an undersea listening network that was secret at the time, became operational, ironically, with the help of airships that helped calibrate it by radioing back visual confirmation of what the listeners were hearing.

Post World War II Goodyear airship project numbers for U.S. Navy airships constructed and/or proposed:

GZ-9 - N-1 (ZPG-1)
GZ-10 - XZP5K (XZS2G-1) prototype
GZ-11 - ZP2N (ZPG-2)
GZ-12 - XZP4K (ZP4K, XZSG-4/ZSG-4)
GZ-13 - AEW airship (contract NOa [S] 51-211[c])
GZ-14 - ZP2N-1W (ZPG-2W)
GZ-15 - ZP5K (ZS2G-1)
GZ-16 - ZWG-1 (2,800,000 cubic feet, not built) *
GZ-17 - ZPG-3W
GZ-18 - ZPG-3 (not built)

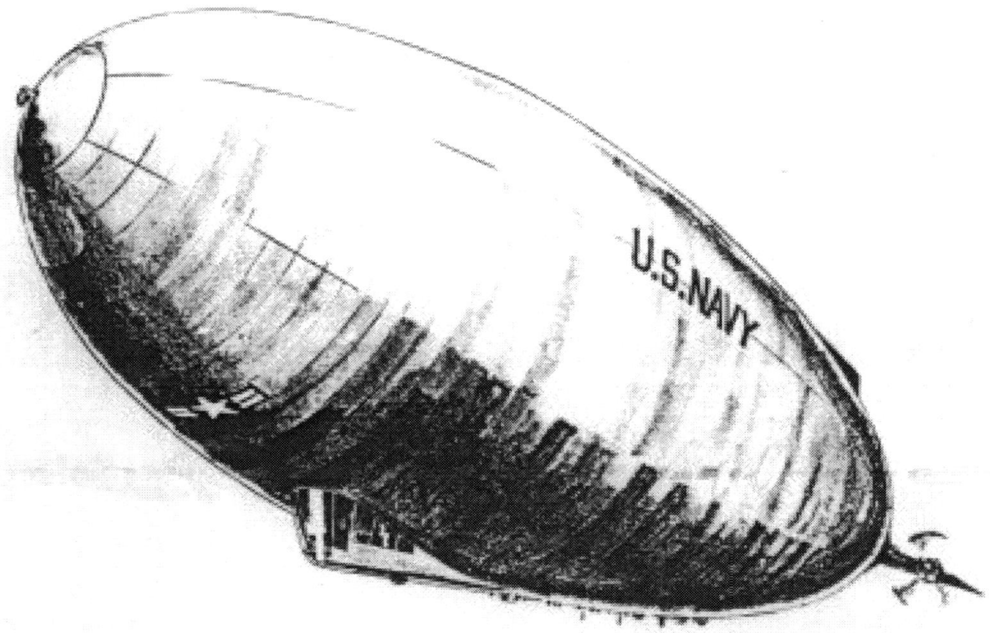

Dominating the later Goodyear concepts was the so-called "hot dog on a roll" designs that would have in part used external suspension. Alternate GZ-13 designs called for fin mounted propulsion (above) and even stern propulsion, borrowed by and later utilized on submarines. Goodyear's "silent Joe" program explored stern propulsion, but the advantages of operating a propeller in the reduced pressure area of the airship's stern is a concept that as of this writing has been tested only in flying models.

Proposed YZE-2A Airship

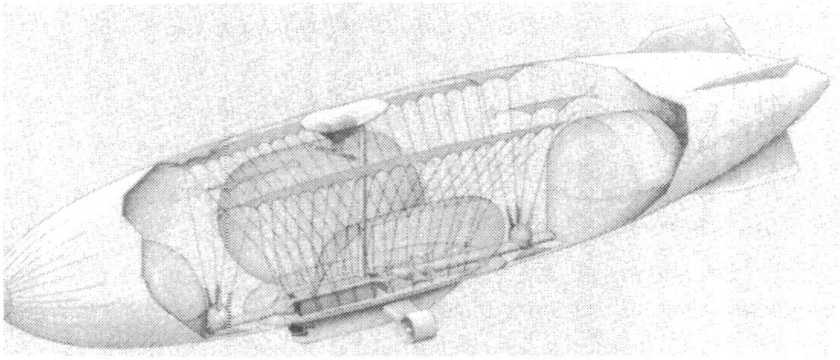

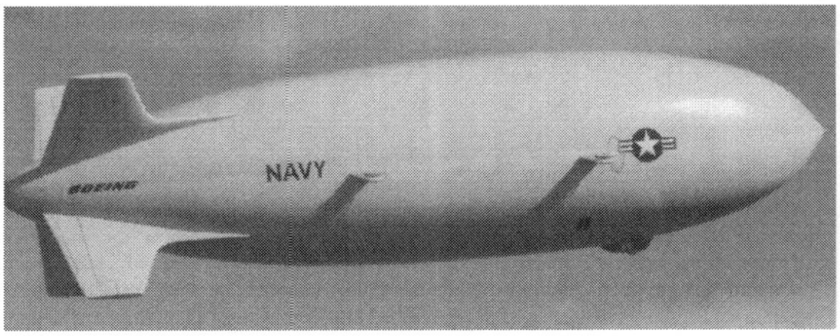

Goodyear Aircraft / Larry Lanchonie **Boeing Military Aircraft**

The Reagan administration reactivated the *Iowa*-class battleships to form Battleship Battle Groups (BBBGs) as a supplement to Carrier Battle Groups. In the absence of AEW for these groups, officers proposed the BBBG Airship to provide early warning of sea-skimming anti-ship missles used effectively during the Falkland Island War and against the USS *Stark* in the Persian Gulf. During the competition Goodyear Aerospace propsed an updated ZPG-3W (above left). Boeing Military Aircraft modeled a single hull rigid airship (above, right).

On June 5, 1987, the joint venture of Westinghouse and the British firm Airship Industries was awarded a $168.9 million contract by Naval Air Systems Command to produce an Operational Development Model (ODM) as part of the Navy Airship Study Program (NASP).

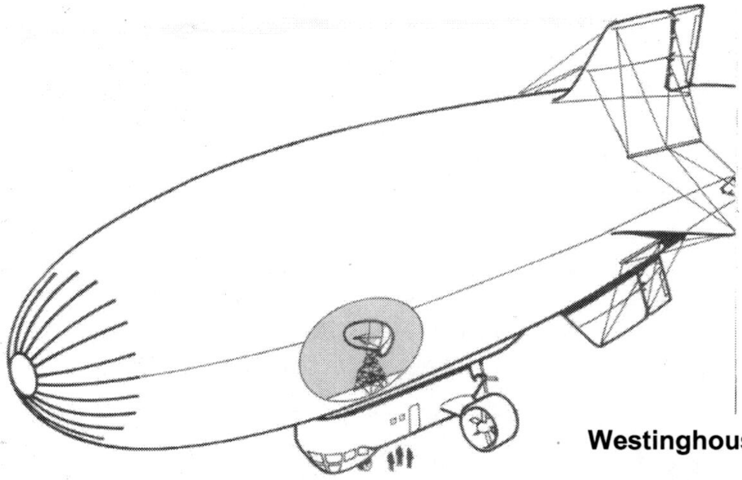

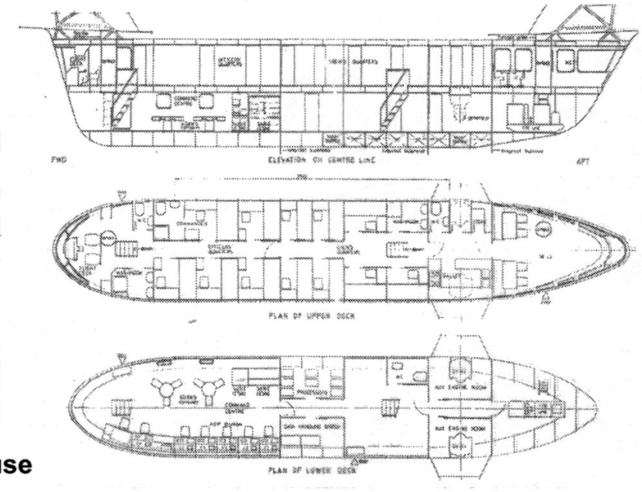

Westinghouse

Plans show an evolution of designs; a number of models and a full-scale mockup of the nearly 20-ft high car were built. Two CRM BR1/2000 modified marine diesel engines were to provide crusie power, while a General Electric CT7-9 was to be the aft-mounted "sprint engine." Funding was not requested for fiscal year 1989 as the Navy withdrew from the program. Airship Industries filed for bankruptcy, and Westinghouse took over the contract for what became the DARPA, then Department of Defese airship program under the Air Defese Initiative (ADI). The company renamed the full-scale ship design the 'Sentinel 5000'.

An existent commercial airship car from a Skyship 600 was equipped with tricycle landing gear, intercooled turbochargers, fly-by-light controls and other modifications. The car was mated to a 354,000 cuft TCOM envelope to create the 'Sentinel 1000' prototype. The 220 foot long airship made its first flight on June 26, 1991, with Carl Daley and Scott Danneker, pilots. Over the next few years the bare envelope was give a 'Westinghouse' logo and eventually the design shown at right.

Global Skyships photo / Gary Burns

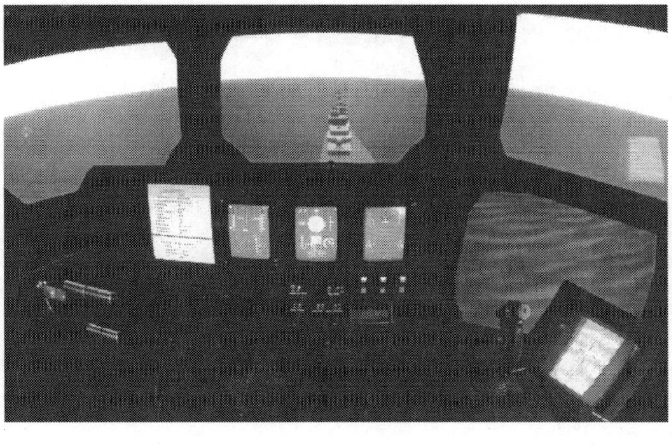

Further budget cuts culminated in a 'stop work' order to be issued May 31, 1992. Work on the full-scale design continued waxed and waned over the years, with design revisions for the full-scale ship reaching model stage. The sophisticated NASA / Ames simulator was configured to simulate the proposed YZE-2A and "flown" through various evolutions, including underway refueling, at-sea replenishment and remanning.

NASA/Ames courtesy Julie Mikula

On June 1, 1992, DARPA awarded a contract to Westinghouse Airship Industries (WAI) for communications relay study work involving flight operations of the Sentinel 1000. Using government furnished communications equipment the airship operated with the USS *Anzio* in a very successful test series. October 26 through 28, 1992, expanded testing to include a shore station, the *Anzio* and the USS *Conolly* relaying UHF voice and Link-11 data in the middle of 72 and 56 NM ranges.

During the next two years the Sentinel 1000 flew various tests under the oversight of Naval Air Warfare Center, Aircraft Division, Warminster, PA (NAWCADWAR). These tests included the installation of a bow thruster and various government-furnished electronic assemblies not originally designed to fit in the airship car.

On August 3rd, 1995, the Weeksville timber hangar burned to the ground. The Sentinel 1000 and most everything concerning ODM / Sentinel 5000 were lost as well. Northrop Grumman purchased most of Westinghouse defense but Westinghouse Airships was sold to the British group London Wall. There were no further developments toward the YZE-2A.

Westinghouse photo

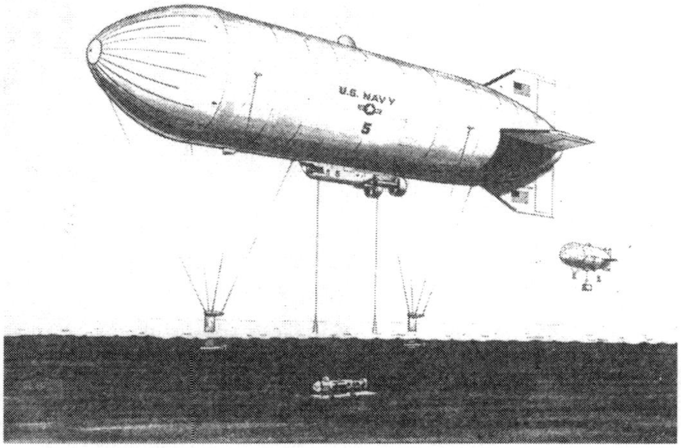

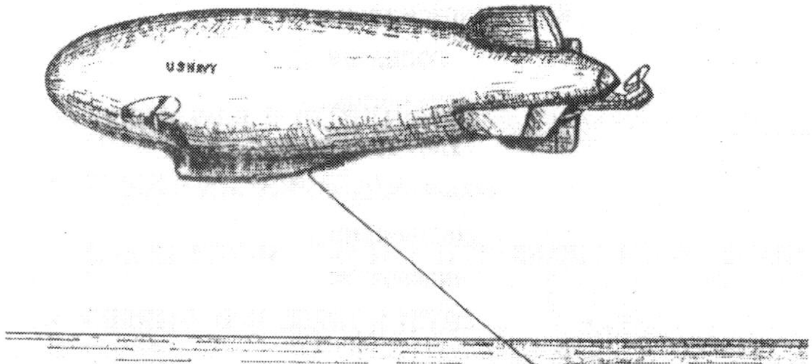

During the later 1990s a number of studies at the Naval Air Development Center (NADC) resulted in several design proposals for modern Navy airships to fulfill a variety of missions. Though discussions continued in various private and public forms, no prototypes were built before several installations were closed and key personnel retired.

U S Navy MZ-3A BuNo #167811 at Lakehurst, May 2007. Rick Zitarosa photos.

The MZ-3A Airship

Following several years of successful tests and demonstrations of airships for various Government missions, Naval Air Systems Command (NAVAIR) chartered an American Blimp Corporation Lightship model A-150 for a series of test/evaluation flights at NAS Patuxent River, MD. Late in 2005 the NAVAIR Special Projects purchased an ABC model A-170. The airship was inflated and erected inside NAES Lakehurst Hangar No. Six in April 2006 by ABC. A crew of 15 Navy Reserve Officers and enlisted personnel were assigned from NAS Willow Grove, PA. Undocked with assistance of members of the Navy Lakehurst Historical Society on 28 APR 06, the first flight of a U.S. Navy airship in 44 years was made May 2 with ABC's Carl Daley as pilot-in-charge, and Navy contract pilot Jim Dexter aboard. In July the Navy, continuing the numerical designation begun more than 40 years earlier, designated the airship MZ-3A, issuing Bu No 167811. Test/Training flights were conducted at Lakehurst from late Fall 2006 thru Spring 2007. Assigned to Squadron VX-20 LTAV Detachment Lakehurst. '

Contract Ground Crew from The Lightship Group service MZ3A #167811 in May 2007. Assigned to Force Aircraft Test Squadron VX-20, airship's call sign was "Waterbug 811."

Following a year of frequent flights without a mishap, the Navy was "very satisfied with the Test/Evaluation period conducted by the LTAV unit at Lakehurst but they have concluded that they do not have mission for the airship." Final flight of the Test Period was May 31, 2007 at NAES Lakehurst. Airship remained inflated and closed out the year 2007 intact under a pressure watch status pending further disposition.

Bibliography & References (by date)

Part I and Part II

Published Sources:

Training Division, U. S. Navy Bureau of Aeronautics, NAVAL AVIATION 1943, U. S. Naval Institute, 1943

Clark Van Vleet, Lee M. Pearson and Adrian O. Van Wyen, UNITED STATES NAVAL AVIATION, 1910-1970, Deputy Chief of Naval Operations (air) and Commander, Naval Air Systems Command, NAVAIR 00-80P-1, Supt. of Documents, Washington, DC. 1970 (aircraft serial numbers and airships in service).

Thom Hook, SKY SHIPS-THE AKRON ERA, Airshow Publishers, Annapolis, MD, 1976 (information on the ZMC-2 and J-3).

Zenon Hansen, THE GOODYEAR AIRSHIPS, Airship International Press, Bloomington, IL 1977.

Roy A. Grossnick, editor, KITE BALLOONS TO AIRSHIPS - THE NAVY'S LIGHTER-THAN-AIR-EXPERIENCE, Deputy Chief of Naval Operations (Air Warfare) and Commander, Air Systems Command, U. S. Government Printing Office, 1986.

Walker C. Morrow, THE METALCLAD AIRSHIPS, privately printed, Grosse Ile, MI, 1987 (includes the original book, WORLD'S FIRST METALCLAD AIRSHIP, published by the Aircraft Development Corporation, circa 1930)

William F. Altfoff, SKY-SHIPS - A HISTORY OF THE AIRSHIP IN THE UNITED STATES NAVY, Orion Books, New York, NY, 1990.

James R. Shock, AMERICAN AIRSHIP BASES AND FACILITIES (includes information accumulated during research), Atlantis Productions, 1996

Adrian O. Van Wyen and the Editors of NAVAL AVIATION NEWS, NAVAL AVIATION IN WORLD WAR I, published by the Chief of Naval Operations, Superintendent of Documents, Washington, DC, 1969.

Patrick Abbott, THE BRITISH AIRSHIP AT WAR, 1914-1918, Terrence Dalton Limited, Lavenham, Suffolk, 1989.

Unpublished Sources:

Richard K. Smith, AN INVENTORY OF U.S. NAVY AIRSHIPS, 1916-1961, privately printed, circa 1964 (a principal source of information).

James R. Shock, U. S. ARMY AIRSHIPS (includes information accumulated during research), forthcoming from Atlantis Productions

Other Documents:

Goodyear Tire and Rubber Company/Aircraft/Aerospace:

"Index of Airships, Record of Goodyear Airship Envelopes, Cars and Control Surfaces, 1911 thru 1940" (retyped 12-22-70 from Goodyear-Zeppelin Corp. Drawing SK-5-2753).

"General Airship Data" (K-L-G-M), circa 1945.

"Envelope Records" (D-1, 1911 thru D-634, 1961).

U. S. Navy:

Various correspondence on the E-1 dated 14, 22 and 24 March, 03, 11, 17 and 23 April 1919 «includes information on the B-15).

"Table Showing Status on Dirigibles", circa May/June 1919 (Zenon Hansen).

"Report on the Crash of the U. S. Navy C-8". circa 1919.

"Synopsis of Work - L/A Construction", memorandum of 13 January 1920 from LTJG F. G. Osgood to Mr. J. H. Torbert (Zenon Hansen).

Copies of telegram, etc., Commander-in-Chief, Pacific Fleet to Navy Department, 28 May 1921 on the use of an airship in the search for the lost fleet tug USS *Conestoga*, letters on same from C. L. Melaney dated 30 June 1989 and replies from M. H. Eppes, G. W. Allen and this researcher May-September 1989.

"War History", Naval Air Station, Lakehurst, NJ, 07 December 1941 thru 15 October 1945.

Research by Don Woodward at Bureau of Aeronautics, date unknown.

A. F. Simpson Historical Research Center, Maxwell Air Force Base, Montgomery, AL:

File K-201-68, Vol. 8, 202298-4A, Goodrich assumes the Curtiss B-type airship contracts.

File 168.6501-40, Jones files, June-December 1920, AIR SERVICE NEWSLETTER, 18 June 1920, B-18 and C-6 to chart Pacific coast.

National Air and Space Museum, Army airship files:

File A 3052000, newspaper article and photographs, C-10 lost on 21 July 1920 while covering the America's Cup Race at Jamaica Bay; photograph of control car at D-6; photograph and article on the flight of the J-1 at Wingfoot Lake and ENS Charles E. Bauch as pilot.

"Airship envelope records, D-2 and D-3", Zenon Hansen and Don Woodward

Research by Zenon Hansen, 1972.

<u>Journals:</u>

AEROSTATION, The Association of Balloon and Airship Constructors (ABAC), Vol. 1, No. 2, 1974, "The Metalclad MC-0.8", by Charles P. Burgess, Design Memorandum dated 28 July 1924. Vol. 14, No. 3, Fall 1991, "The Army-Navy TC-13 and TC-14 Airships", by CDR Charles A. MIlls, USN (Ret.) and Donald E. Woodward

Journal of the American Aviation Historical Society, Vol. 2, No. 2, April-June 1957, "U. S. Navy Aircraft on Hand as of 01 November 1919," see appendix to follow.

U. S. AIR SERVICES (Magazine):

Vol. No. 1, No. 6, July 1919, Crew of the C-5;

March 1924, "C-7 has flown her last".

May 1924, "The Navy's First Airship DN-1", by James F. Boyle

Jerome C. Hunsaker, "The Navy's First Airships", UNITED STATES NAVAL INSTITUTE, PROCEEDINGS, August 1919. (DN-1, B and C-type airships, but no delivery dates for C-type, personal volumes 12 [partial] and 14).

INSIDE THE CONTROL CAR, editor Roy E. Schickedanz, Issue 12, February 1975, "C, D, E, F and H Non-Rigid Airship Data", by Zenon Hansen.

WINGFOOT LIGHTER-THAN-AIR-SOCIETY (now Buoyant Flight), editor Dr. A. Dale Topping, Volume, number and date:

1, No. 3, April 1954, DN-1 history, excerpt from Moffett Field LTA Manual.

5, No. 4, Feb. 1959, "Initial Trip of Goodyear D-2 (envelope number), 1st Navy Coast Patrol Airship, Chicago to Akron, May 29, 1917", by Ralph H. Upson.

8, No. 9, Summer 1961, "The First Airborne Loran". excerpt from "THE RISE OF PSEUDO-NAVIGATION, by John A. Pierce. K-2 as the original test platform.

11, No. 11, Oct. 1964, "C-5 and the Attempted Trans-Atlantic Race", by Hugh Allen.

12, No. 3, Jan. 1965, "An Inventory of Navy Pressure Airships, 1916-1941", by Richard K. Smith. All airships for this period. This account reports a total of 14 French airships. The VZ-3 is shown in this account which varies from the original AN INVENTORY OF U.S. NAVY AIRSHIPS, 1916-1961 by the same author. It is believed that the VZ-type airships carried their original French designations and these were revised by the Navy with VZ-8 revised to VZ-1, VZ-13 to VZ-2 (which is also more or less verified by the research of Zenon Hansen at the National Archives and Bureau of Aeronautics), these were the only Vedette-Zodiac (VZ) type airships received by the Navy and the VZ-3 may be in error. This is certainly understandable with the lack of complete information on French airships acquired by the Navy after World War I.3)
12, No. 5, March 1965, comments on above article by R. K. Smith, principally on the O-1, but also others.
12, No. 7, May 1965, comments by Ralph S. Barnaby (CAPT, USN, Ret.) on the D-6 and O-1.
Vol.16, No. 7, page 8, May, 1969, statements by Zenon Hansen on the serial numbers for the SSZ airships.
Vol.12, No. 7, page 6, May, 1965, comments by Lord Ventry, statements on ZDUS-1, CM-5 control car, T-2 and Capitaine Caussin were same airship.
Vol. 12, No. 7, page 6, May, 1965, comments by Don Woodward, agreement with R.K. Smith (Vol.12, No. 3) on AT-1, AT-13 and the three Zodiac Vedette airships, Capitaine Caussin command transferred at Guipavas, previously operated under French command with mixed French/U.S. Navy crew at Paimbouef, uncertain on AT-17 (under construction at Issy-les-Molineaux in January 1919 and not mentioned by American visiting team as American), AT-18 possibly Escorteur E-5 or E-6 and flown until 1936.
12, No. 8, June 1965, "First There Was the DN-1", by James F. Boyle.
16, No. 1, Nov. 1968, "B-type Deliveries, 1917-1918".
16, No. 3, Jan. 1969, "C-5 Lost and Found".
18, No. 6, Sept.-Oct. 1971, "Baldwin and the Navy B-Class Airship" Donation to the Lighter-Than-Air Society by Stanley Vaughn.
19, No. 2, Jan.-Feb. 1972, comments by Don Woodward on "Baldwin and the Navy B-Class Airship".
20, No. 2, Jan.-Feb. 1973, "To Keep Them Flying", address by M. L. Flickinger, K-2 landing gear, other experiences as a designer and field representative during World War II.
21, No. 3, Mar.-Apr. 1974, ZMC-2 and the David Ossman presentation at the LTA Society meeting in January.
21, No. 6, Sept.-Oct. 1974, "The U. S. Navy K-1 Blimp", by David Hill.
25, No. 6, Sept.-Oct. 19978, "A Short History of the OB-1", by George E. Wright, Jr.; "Untangling H-Ship Puzzles", by A. D. Topping, editor; excellent analysis of articles, statements and comments on Blakemore and Pagon in PRESSURE AIRSHIPS, James F. Boyle, Zenon Hansen, Roy Schickedanz, R. K. Smith, Swanborough and Bowers U. S. NAVY AIRCRAFT SINCE 1911, Hepburn Walker, Jr., George E. Wright Jr., and Don Woodward.
31, No. 3, Mar.-Apr. 1984, "Enemy Off Shore", by Roy Schickedanz (K-3, K-4, K-5, K-6, and U-boat sinkings).
35, No. 5, July-Aug. 1988, "Completed Careers", RADM Scott E. Peck, B-3 and C-5.
38, No. 1 Nov.-Dec. 1990, "Aloft and Adrift in a J-Ship", by J. Gordon Vaeth, "Tex" Settle and the J-3.

<u>Articles:</u>

New York TIMES, 11 March 1915, "Two Dirigibles for Navy -Won't be as large as Zeppelins nor of the rigid type". Dateline 10 March, states two dirigible balloons to be purchased for the Navy and to be used for "practise". Connecticut State Library, Deborah Ducoff-Barone (J. R. Gilbert).

Carl Dientsbach, "The New Navy Dirigible," AIRCRAFT, August 1915 (reprinted from Scientific American). DN-1 reported as designed and being built by Capt. Thomas S. Baldwin, drawing of DN-1 and "method of anchoring naval dirigible." New England Air Museum, Windsor Locks, CT (J. R. Gilbert).

New York TIMES, 21 September 1915, "Navy Balloon Soon Ready - First of Dirigible Fleet Will Undergo Official Tests at Pensacola," Dateline 20 September, DN-1 to be ready for delivery in a few weeks, to be assembled in Boston, "program submitted to Congress will call for a large number of dirigibles and aeroplanes." Connecticut State Library, Deborah Ducoff-Barone (J. R. Gilbert).

New Haven COURIER, 13 March 1917, "Navy Dirigibles to be Built Here - Two 160 foot balloons to be constructed by Connecticut Aircraft Company - part of order for 16 are of non-rigid type and claimed to be more effective than Zeppelins", Navy B-type airships contract for two airships to Connecticut Aircraft $84,000 with delivery in 120 days, 16 airships at a total cost of $649,250, Curtiss Aeroplane Co. 3 airships for $122,250, Goodyear 9 for $360,000 and Goodrich 2 for $93,000, will be able to operate from shore bases and alight on water surface in good weather.

Extensive information on the Connecticut Aircraft Company and DN-1 provided by Harvey H. Lippincott, Director of Museum Development, New England Air Museum, Bradley International Airport, Windsor Locks, CT.

John W. Higgins, "He Invented the Metalclad," POPULAR AVIATION, January 1938. MC-2 and David Schwartz.

John W. Higgins, "Tin Blimp," POPULAR AVIATION, December 1941. This article includes information on the ZMC-1.

Lee M. Pearson, "Naval Aviation in WW II - Wings of Victory," Part III, NAVAL AVIATION NEWS, March-April 1991. Reference to K-5 and sonobuoy experiments.

Cleveland PLAIN DEALER, 01 February 1941, initial flight, photograph and article on L-2.

Cleveland PLAIN DEALER, 04, 10 and 17 September 1941 (K-3), 09 and 16 October 1941 (K-4) and 12 November 1941 (K-5).

Sandusky (Ohio) REGISTER-STAR NEWS, 10 June 194, "13 Missing After Blimps Collide; Rescue Survivor." L-2 and G-1

Detroit NEWS, 22 December 1990, excerpt from OPERATION DRUMBEAT; The Dramatic Story of Germany's First U-Boat Attacks Along the American Coast World War II, by Michael Gannon, Harper and Row, 1990.

Appendix, "Report of the Navy Department of Aircraft on Hands, November 1, 1919, Report of the Secretary of the Navy to Congress, as required by the appropriation bill (Aviation, Navy 1920), United States Naval Aviation," 66th Congress, 2nd Session, House Document No. 452, pages 30 and 31.

JOURNAL of the American Aviation Historical Society, Volume 2, No. 2, April-June 1957, Lighter-Than-Air portion only.

Type of Aircraft	Built	On Contract	Unit Cost ($)*
Free Balloons	10		4,500
Kite Balloons			
Caquot, type R	121		8,000
" " M	17		8,800
Type P	2		6,200
Reduced R	2		6,000
35,000 Cu. Ft.	10		6,000
Misc.	6		6,000
Type AP	3		31,500 (3?)
Dirigibles			
B Class	6		40,000
C Class	4	3	60.000
E-1	1		55,000
F-1	1		50,000
O-1 (Italian)	1		50,000
Zero (British)	1		35,000
Astra Torres (French)	1		80,000
North Sea (British)	1		100,000
ZD-US (British)**	1		100,000
D Class		5	60,000

* Exclusive of radio, ordinance and navigation gear.
** Obvious error, should read French.

AEROSTATION. Vol 3, No. 3, pg. 69 "Canada's Forgotten Phantom Airship Fleet," by A.E. Hill.

THE ZEPPELIN COLLECTOR, Air Log and AFA News, October-December 1984, "Canada's Blimps After WW I," by Barry Countryman.

Additional data on airships in Canada from Kent O'Grady.

Notations by Zenon Hansen to this researcher dated 03 November 1978, on both the N.S.14 (referred to as NS-1) and French airships based on his research at the National Air and Space Museum in 1972.

Personal (1985-1989) research of World War I British non-rigid airships.

Bibliography/References, Part IV, 1942 through 1945 (Sources by date, refer to Part I for previous sources, the following are additional sources)

<u>Published Sources:</u>

Dean, Shafto, TRAIL BLAZING IN THE SKIES, The Goodyear Tire and Rubber Company, Akron, OH, 1943

Allen, Hugh, GOODYEAR AIRCRAFT, A STORY OF MAN AND INDUSTRY, Corday and Gross Co., Cleveland, OH, 1947 (Hugh Allen was the "Dean" of airship writers when employed by Goodyear in the Public Relations Department and wrote THE STORY OF THE AIRSHIP, originally issued in 1925 and released annually until at least 1933, THE HOUSE OF GOODYEAR in 1936, THE STORY OF THE NON-RIGID AIRSHIP in 1943 and (with P.W. Litchfield) WHY? WHY HAS AMERICAN NO RIGID AIRSHIPS in 1945.

Gleason, Spencer, editor, MOFFETT FIELD, FROM LIGHTER-THAN- AIR TO FASTER THAN SOUND, Globe Printing Co., San Jose, CA, circa 1958, statement on G-6 (shown as ZS6-3, should be ZSG-6 or ZTG-6), page 86.

O'Reilly, Maurice, THE GOODYEAR STORY, Benjamin Co., Elmsford, NY, 1983 (contains several inaccurate airship statements).

Journals:

AIRSHIPPING, "A Quarterly Newsletter," editor Roy D. Schickedanz, apparently only Volume One issued, circa 1975.

FOUNDATION, Naval Aviation Museum Foundation, Inc., Volume 2, No. 1, January 1981, "Blimpron 14 - The `Africa Squadron'," by LT J. Gordon Vaeth, USNR (Ret.).

INSIDE THE CONTROL CAR, editor Roy D. Schickedanz, various issues circa 1973 through September 1979 (mainly "Airships in the Mediterranean," issue 20, June 1976, issue 21, Oct.-Nov. 1976, issue 22, Aug. 1977 with excellent comments on page 19 by Emmett J. Sullivan (CAPT, USN, Ret.) on the reporting of deflations and not the more positive aspects, a trap the author would like to have avoided.) Exercise caution in evaluating information in this publication.

THE NOON BALLOON, The Newsletter of the Naval Airship Association, Inc., M.H. Eppes (CAPT, USN, Ret.), editor, various issues.

THE NON-RIGID IN COMBAT, editor Roy D. Schickedanz, Volume 1, Nos. 1 through 4, circa 1968, contains previously printed information from INSIDE THE CONTROL CAR and other publications.

THE POOPY BAG BALLONET, editor and publisher Harry Titus, various issues 1982 through 1989, stories of and about the men that flew the airships.

NAVAL INSTITUTE PROCEEDINGS, August 1979, "Incident in the Florida Straits," by J. Gordon Vaeth, the most complete account of the K-74 and U-134.

BULLETIN of The Wingfoot Lighter-Than-Air Society (now The Lighter-Than-Air Society and BUOYANT FLIGHT), editor Dr. A. Dale Topping (Volume/Number/Page/Date):
14/3/6/Jan. 1967, records of airships and K-74. 16/6/5/Apr. 1969, comments by Hepburn Walker, Jr. on K-113/K-139.
18/2/2/Jan.-Feb. 1971, "Squadron 14 and the Transoceanic Crossing," by Roy D. Schickedanz.
19/2/8/Jan.-Feb. 1972, K-21 bow elevators.
20/1/4/Nov.-Dec. 1972, "A Lesson in Nonrigid Airship Handling" by Roy D. Schickedanz, contains some date discrepancies.
22/4/12/May-June 1975, salvage of the K-68 under John B. Rieker.
23/5/3/July-Aug. 1976, "The M-Ship," by Roy D. Schickedanz.
24/2/7/Jan.-Feb. 1977, excellent comments on the M-type design by Norman J. Mayer.
25/3/12/Mar.-Apr. 1978, "All in a Day's Work," by Roy D. Schickedanz (K-90, K-106, K-114, K-118, may require some checking.
26/4/10/May-June 1979, "South Atlantic Clearing," by Roy D. Schickedanz (K-36,-84 and -98).
27/4/7/May-June 1980, "The Loss of the K-13," by Peter Mayurnik.
28/3/2/Mar.-Apr. 1981, "Cannot Contact Tower," by Roy D. Schickedanz, Part I, Mar.-Apr. 1981, Part II, May-June 1981.

29/1/2/Nov.-Dec. 1981, "The Russians Are Coming," by John A. Fahey (K-124). 30/3/2/Mar.-Apr. 1983 through 33/1/11/Nov.-Dec. 1985, "The Goodyear Airship Pilots," by James R. Shock, Navy service of Goodyear pilots.

<u>Other Documents:</u>

THEY WERE DEPENDABLE: AIRSHIP OPERATION IN WORLD WAR II, Naval Airship Training and Experimental Command, second edition, 1946.

Goodyear Aircraft Corp. inter-office memorandum "Estimated Costs - Single Prototype Airships," 02 December 1948 Cost analyses of K (1937), M (1941) and N (1947) airships, original costs and up-dated costs for 1949 (The Lighter-Than-Air Society.)

Goodyear Aircraft Corp. memorandum PD-19238, by H.T. Cross, "Summary of Airship Incidents and Accidental Deflations," dated 01 August 1960 Navy airship portion based on Naval Airship Training and Experimental Command Summary Report ZNATC-L11-1, serial #975, dated 08 August 1947 (T.G.W. Settle). Covers the periods 08 August 1942 through 15 September 1945 and 06 August 1951 through 06 July 1960 (The Lighter-Than-Air Society.)

"The K-74 Incident," believed written by Roy C. Schickedanz, circa 1979, details of loss and interview with Nelson G. Grills (K-74 equipped with 1921 bombing equipment, as a command pilot had never seen a bomb dropped, etc.).

<u>Naval Air Station Histories:</u>

Lakehurst, NJ - 1919 to 1945, 1921-1944, War History 07 December 1942 to 15 October 1945, appendices 1939 to 1944, supplemental history 01 November 1945 through 31 December 1953.

South Weymouth, MA - History 01 March 1942 to 02 September 1945, administrative history 20 January 1941 to 02 May 45, - History 01 April 1942 to 02 September 1945.

Glynco, GA - History and appendices 25 January 1943 to 02 September 1945, supplemental history 01 September 1945 to 31 December 1952.

Richmond, FL - History 15 September 1942 to 02 September 1945.

Houma, LA - History 06 August 1942 to 21 September 1944.

Hitchcock, TX - History 22 May 1943 to 18 October 1944.

Santa Ana, CA - History 01 October 1942 to 29 September 1945.

Tillamook, OR - History 01 December 1942 to 31 December 1947, also excerpts from the Tillamook County Pioneer Museum some of which conflicts with the official history.

<u>Personal files including the following:</u>

AEROSTATION, The Journal of the Association of Balloon and Airship Constructors, Vol. 6, No. 4, Winter 1979, "Those Phantom Douglas Leigh Airships," by Zenon Hansen.* "Facts About the Tydol Dirigible," Douglas Leigh Sky Advertising Corp., circa 1946.*

JOURNAL, The American Aviation Historical Society, Vol. 4, No.2, Summer 1959, "Barnstorming with a Blimp," by Robert A. LoVece (The Leigh Wonder [Bread] Ship).*

READERS DIGEST, August 1948, "King of the Spectaculars", by C. Lester Walker, states Douglas Leigh purchased 29 surplus airships. (The manager of the Leigh airship organization was Karl L. Lange, former Naval Reserve Captain (later RADM, the highest rank attained by a reserve airship officer) and Goodyear airship pilot Chief engineer and vice president for Leigh was Fred Kerwer. All pilots were Navy World War II veterans with the majority of the personnel also Navy veterans, a ready Naval Reserve source.)

Personal records of Robert A. Baney, former airship radioman with various squadrons at Lakehurst, South Weymouth, Weeksville and Santa Ana. Includes flight records from his log book, station magazine articles, personal experiences, etc.

Bibliography/References, Part V, 1946 through 1962
(Refer to earier Parts for previous sources, the following are additional sources)

<u>Journals:</u>

"Forgotten Giant, Goodyear's GZ-16," AEROSTATION, Vol. 12, No. 1, Spring 1984.

POOPY BAG BALLONET, Harry Titus, editor and publisher, Vol. IV, No.13, Spring, 1985, Vol. IV, No. 2, Summer, 1985, Vol. IV, No.3, Fall, 1985; Excellent accounts of the ZPG-3W- 144242 by the men that were at Lakehurst and involved.

Wingfoot Lighter-Than-Air Society BULLETIN (now The Lighter-Than-Air Society and BUOYANT FLIGHT), Dr. A. Dale Topping, editor; Volume/Number/Page/Date:
6, No. 9, page 6, Summer, 1959, ZPG-3W-144243.
8, No. 1, page 5, November, 1960, U.S. Navy LTA Activities World War II to Present, CAPT F.N. Klein, Jr.
12, No. 2, pages 2 and 3, December, 1964, Operation Whole Gale, by CDR Herman G, Spahr.
14, No. 8, page 7, June, 1967, ZPG-3W 144242 "$8,000,000 Asked in Airship Trial."
14, No. 9, page 7, July-August, 1967, ZPG-3W-144242, "Court Clears Goodyear of Crash Blame."
16, No. 3, page 2, January, 1969, ZPG-3W-144242, "Investigation of the ZPG-3W Accident," comments by S.J. Pipitone.
16, No. 4, page 6, February, 1969, ZPG-3W comments by Robert . Martin of the law firm that prepared Goodyear's case on the ZPG-3W-144242, .
16, No. 6, page 6, April, 1969, comments by Hepburn Walker, Jr. on K-139 burning, unfinished K-type control cars, and ZPG-3W envelope volumes by Don Block.
17, No. 4, page 2, February, 1970, "A Litigation Lawyer's Strategic View of the ZPG-3W Crash Controversy: Seam Failure? Operational Failure? Failure of Proof!" by Robert F. Martin.
17, No. 6, page 6, April, 1970, "The Birth, Growth, and Death of an Airship," by Jack L. Waldman, includes specifications; page 8, CDR Lundi Moore disagreement with statements of CDR Jack Hunt and the Goodyear accident analysis Vol. 17, No.4, page 2).
18, No. 4 page 2, May-June 1971, ZPN-1 stories.
23, No. 6, Page 6, September-October, 1976, "Flight of the Snow Goose," contains map (in Russian) of flight, small article.
24, No. 2, page 8, January-February, 1977, comments on flight of 12719 "Snow Goose" by Roy Schickedanz.
26, No. 3, page 7, March-April, 1979 (comments by H. Walker, Jr. on ZS2G-1 #144240 and maximum speed of ZPG-3W). 26, No. 5, page 12, July-Aug., 1979, Navy airship class names by Zenon Hansen.
34, No.2, page 5, January-February, 1987, CAPT H.B. Van Gorder and the LTA Society Honorary Life Membership and comments on the flight of Snow Goose.
36, No. 1, page 8, November-December, 1988, comments by Hepburn Walker, Jr. on ZPG-3W serial 144243 control car to be shipped by Loral (Goodyear) to Pensacola for he National Naval Air Museum and condition of ZPG-2 serial 141561 control car.
36, No. 5, page 12, "News Log", ZPG-3W serial 144243 shipped to Davis-Monthan AFB.

38, No. 1, page 2, Nov.-Dec., 1990, "Current Airships and Current Needs", by Hepburn Walker, statement on ZP4K (ZSG-4) control cars (probably for interior instrumentation) subcontracted by Goodyear to Cook Electric.

<u>Other Documents:</u>

U.S. Navy Aviation History Unit, "Chronology of Lighter-Than-Air History in the U.S. Navy 1915-1962, " 05 August 1963.
Goodyear Aircraft Memorandum "Estimated Costs - Single Prototype Airships," 02 December 1948.

Bureau of Aeronautics, Pilot's Handbook, Navy Model ZP2K Airships, NAVAER 01-195PAA-501, 01 May 1952.

Goodyear Aircraft Corporation Engineering Project Sheet No. 25, Revision M, November 30, 1956 through April 1960 (all airships delivered during this period).

Goodyear Aircraft Corporation Memorandum PD-19238, by H.T. Cross, "Summary of Airship Incidents and Accidental Deflations" dated 01 August 1960. Navy airship portion based on Naval Airship Training and Experimental Command Summary Report ZNATC-L11-1, serial #975, dated 15 August 1947 (T.G.W. Settle). Covers the periods of 08 August 1942 through 15 September 1945 and 06 August 1951 through 06 July 1960 (Lighter-Than-Air Society).

The *Courier-Post*, Camden, NJ 24 Oct 59, article about last K-ship flight.

The following information is from Goodyear records on 527,000 CF envelopes and is for quantity only and not directly a part of the airship history.

Contract Nos.	Envelope Nos.	Quantity-Remarks
N383S-37735	D-482 thru D-495	14 -Cotton Neoprene
	D-500 thru D-517	18 -Cotton Neoprene
NOa(a)-51-002	D-518	1*-2 ply Fortisan, cancelled
NOa(a)-51-366C	D-519	1-XZP4K-1/XZSG-4-133639
NOa(a)-51-657	D-520 thru D-527	8-131919 thru 131926
	D-528	1*-Destroyed by fire
	D-529 thru D-533	5 -134019 thru 134024
NOa(a)-51-657	D-534 thru D-543	10 -airships ZP4K/ZSG-4 cancelled, 134025 thru 134034
N3839-63051	D-544	1 -cotton to use up cloth
	D-545	1 -purchased for 4K
	546 thru 547	2
	548	1 -3 ply cotton
	549	1 -2 ply cotton
NOa(s)-52-0054	550	1* -Fortisan, experimental 2 ply, cancelled
N383S-66248	554 and 555	2 -3 ply cotton, ZP2K/3/C
	556 thru 569	14 -3 ply cotton, ZP2K/3/C
51-657	581 thru 582	2 -Spares, 2 ply
	583	1 -ZP4K/ZSG-4-134024
	584 thru 587	4* -cancelled

Total 527,000 CF envelopes contracted =	88
Cancelled -	16
lost by fire-	1
Actual quantity delivered =	71

Remains of ZPG-3W Bu Aer #144243 at Davis-Motham AFB. Jeff Cook photos.

Airship Car Salvage for Museum Purposes

In addition to the surviving K-28, ZP3K-47, ZP3K-88, ZPG-2 and ZPG-3W cars mentioned in the text, this much is now known:

When airships were deleted from Lakehurst, Mr. James Johnson purchased a ZPG-2 car and a ZSG-1 ("5K") car. These cars, stored in Mr. Johnson's lumber yard, were vandalized and were eventually scrapped. Mr. Johnson also acquired a new "5K" winch assembly in its crate, said to be superior to the type used in the later ZPG-2s. Following Mr. Johnson's death the winch assembly was donated to the National Museum of Naval Aviation.

A New Jersey salvage yard owner purchased seven airship cars, and their engine nacelles were dismounted for transport. Parts were identified by numbering in pencil, for example, "K-47," even though no WWII original K-types were present. The collection, stored in the open for more than 30 years, included one ZP2K, one ZP4K, and five ZP3Ks. The cars were in a row, with their engine pylons and outriggers standing nearby. The ZP4K car happened to be in the lowest part of the immediate area. When the owner died, the cars were sold. The National Air & Space Museum acquired the only ZP2K, notable by its WWII like appearance including the machine gun. At this writing, it rests upside down under a tarp at the Dulles facility. The National Museum of Naval Aviation is displaying the ZP3K-47 (and parts of the ZPG-2). The "parts car" used for restoring K–47, ZP3K-88, was sent to England.

The only 4K and the three remaining 3Ks were purchased by a Florida collector. However, when they attempted to retrieve the 4K, corrosion had so destroyed the magnesium that the vehicle crumbled trying to pull it from the properties' lowest spot. Various piece parts have since been scattered, and no identification tags were left on the cars. A race to get the parts before smelters collected them was not entirely successful; outriggers and nacelles saved may not be with their original cars. The three remaining 3Ks were taken to Florida, then sold to collector Kermit Weeks. The three, incomplete hulks in extremely bad condition, may be combined into one restoration project at Week's "Fantasy of Flight" museum complex.

Macon took four Sparrowhawks with her to the bottom, but Bu Aer Ser # 9056, following minor reconstruction and later restoration, was donated to the Smithsonian for what became the National Air & Space Museum. It was displayed hanging from its hook until the LTA display section was dismantled. 9056 was then loaned to and displayed in the LTA section National Museum of Naval Aviation in Pensacola, Florida. In 2006 it was returned to NASM. Remaining F9C-2s discovered and explored by Christopher Grech with the Monterey Bay Aquairium and Research Institute robot submarine in 1990 were revisited in September 2006.

About the Author

James R. Shock, in the center of the photo at left, has been a researcher, collector and writer on airship subjects since his high school days. Serving in the US Army during World War II, Shock completed a career with General Motors Corporation as manager of Engineering Facilities. Mr. Shock retired to Ohio, with his wife, Pat. He is seen here with (left) Mr. Eric Brothers, Editor of BUOYANT FLIGHT, who was instrumental in the completeness of this book, and (right) the publisher, R. G. Van Treuren, at the Naval Airship Association Reunion, at Pensacola, Florida, September, 2000.

Other books by James Shock:

AMERICAN AIRSHIP BASES AND FACILITIES
0-9649480-3-6 Atlantis Productions, 1996

THE US ARMY BARRAGE BALLOON PROGRAM
1-57638-052-1 (hardcover)
World War II Historical Society, 1996

US ARMY AIRSHIPS 1908-1942
0-9639743-9-4 Atlantis Productions, 2002